The breast of the earth

A survey of the history,
culture, and literature of
Africa south of the Sahara

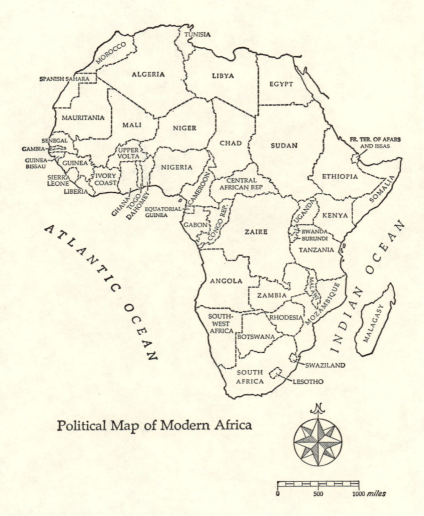

MOROCCO
TUNISIA
SPANISH SAHARA
ALGERIA
LIBYA
EGYPT
MAURITANIA
MALI
NIGER
CHAD
SUDAN
FR. TER. OF AFARS
AND ISSAS
SENEGAL
GAMBIA
GUINEA-
BISSAU
GUINEA
UPPER
VOLTA
NIGERIA
CENTRAL
AFRICAN REP
ETHIOPIA
SIERRA
LEONE
IVORY
COAST
LIBERIA
CAMEROON
SOMALIA
GHANA
TOGO
DAHOMEY
EQUATORIAL
GUINEA
GABON
CONGO REP.
ZAIRE
UGANDA
KENYA
RWANDA
BURUNDI
TANZANIA
ATLANTIC OCEAN
ANGOLA
ZAMBIA
MALAWI
MOZAMBIQUE
INDIAN OCEAN
SOUTH-
WEST
AFRICA
RHODESIA
BOTSWANA
SWAZILAND
SOUTH
AFRICA
LESOTHO
MALAGASY

Political Map of Modern Africa

N

0   500   1000 *miles*

KOFI AWOONOR

The breast
of the earth

A survey of the history,
culture, and literature of
Africa south of the Sahara

ANCHOR PRESS/DOUBLEDAY
GARDEN CITY, NEW YORK
1975

Library of Congress Cataloging in Publication Data

Awoonor, Kofi, 1935–
   The breast of the earth.

   Bibliography
   Includes index.
   1. African literature—History and criticism. 2. Africa—Civilization—History.
I. Title.
PL8010.A9   896
ISBN 0-385-07053-5
Library of Congress Catalog Card Number 72-79371

I wish to express my thanks to the following for granting me permission to quote
from the works of some of the poets I discussed in this book:

To Heinemann Educational Books, for permission to use extracts of poems from
   Selected Poems by Tchicaya U Tam'si.
To Holmes & Meier Publishers, for permission to use extracts from *Zulu Poems*
   by Mazisi Kunene and from *Labyrinths* by Christopher Okigbo.
To Longmans Group Ltd., for permission to use extracts from an anthology of
   West African verse by D. Nwoga.
To Emile Snyder, for permission to use extracts from *Return to My Native Land*
   by Aimé Césaire, published by Présence Africaine, Paris.
To Atheneum Publishers, for permission to use extracts of poems from *Selected
   Poems* by L. S. Senghor, translated by John Reed and Clive Wake.

Dedicated to my mother and father,
the two people who gave me all I have.

Contents

Preface

The essays contained in this volume cover a period of fourteen years of research, teaching, and the creative participation in the theater, movies, television, and the arts in my own country, Ghana, and in Britain and the United States. In the latter country I found opportunity to scrutinize some of my own ideas and expand my intellectual horizons through contact with a number of scholars across many university campuses.

The essays here are by no means definitive or categorical assessments based on what some scholars fondly refer to as objective analyses and unbiased scholarship. They reveal my own preferences, biases, and prejudices as a cultural nationalist, teacher, artist, and above all as an African.

The selection of themes and authors represents a broad spectrum of ideas and sensibilities that I hope fit into the general thematic framework of the book. There are certain subjects which I had to avoid for lack of space, certain areas I barely skirted for lack of firsthand or adequate knowledge. There are some writers I have not included whom many readers would have wished me to discuss. I however hope that these omissions will not detract from the over-all integrity of the book.

This book owes its completion and publication to a number of very good friends and scholars in the field of African studies.

Among those to whom I am particularly grateful is my old friend Dr. Adu Boahen, Professor of History, University of Ghana. My thanks also go to Dr. Emyl Snyder of the University of Indiana, Bloomington; Dr. Bernth Lindfors of the University of Texas, Austin; Dr. Ezekiel Mphahlele, the veteran of all our writers' conferences, who now teaches in Philadelphia; Dr. Thomas Maresca, who provided useful scholarly advice. My thanks also go to the numerous universities across the United States that invited me to give talks and afforded me opportunities to examine some of my own premises and concepts afresh. My thanks also go to my trusted friend and comrade Mr. Victor Ametewee of Cape Coast University, Ghana, who continues to share with me his research interests and to keep me informed of all affairs of the homeland.

The weaknesses of this book are entirely my own. I plead no alibi for the views expressed here. I did not set out to write a controversial book. But I will listen to counterviewpoints and warmly welcome an opportunity to debate some of the issues with any one who so desires.

The study of Africa in the last two decades began with a great deal of promise and hope born within the euphoria of African independence. Before then, Africa was hardly worth the bother of serious scholars except a few "cranky" academics and romantics who trooped into our wilds to unearth curious details about exotic tribes. Africa still occupied a lower level of human existence. These prejudices were strengthened by the myths built around our civilizations which were considered inferior to those of Europe. Because we didn't build St. Paul's Cathedral, Westminster Abbey, or the Eiffel Tower, we were considered the last of nature's creations, half child, half beast, locked in primeval savagery and exotic nobility. Our rivers, mountains, lakes, and people were "discovered" by intrepid travelers who risked our abominable climate to bring us civilization and the salvation of Christ's message. Our cultures and complex mores, our spiritual and temporal concepts and ideals were dismissed as paganistic irrelevancies that stood in the way of the cleansing tide of Christian progress and European enlightenment. It is in the name of these ideals that the "scramble for Africa" occurred and Christian Europe divided the continent among its so-called nations and took possession of our land and resources.

(Islam, of course, had already penetrated the continent from the north and the east and had changed a great many of our indigenous institutions before these European inroads.)

Africa, whether she liked it or not, became involved in the convulsive events of the European world. Two world wars restructured our thinking as we struggled to exist under a new order characterized by exploitation and traumatic dislocation of our traditional institutions.

Marx, Engels, Paine, Rousseau, and many others had already affected the thinking of man by the end of last century. When Africans began to stray into the European's world, they too learned of these ideas. Some of us traveled to Europe and America, read all the books that spoke of liberty, the rights of man, and the equality of all the races. The Second World War put the nail in the coffin of European colonialism. But by then change had overtaken us. Our older institutions had been transformed. Some were being swept aside by the tidal wave of European concepts. Modern politics of the European type had entered our lives. Even though we never participated in it, except as its victims, we were expected to rebuild in the place of our colonial subjugative systems, model democracies based on fair play bipartisan ideals.

But freedom was born in the independence movements that swept across the continent. With it came the need to refashion institutions, create new viable structures. We have had to rediscover ourselves as a people. Cultural self-discovery has become an essential aspect of our new quest for self and race. Pride is part of our dream of self-awareness.

Independence also created new problems for which we have to seek solutions. Our economic structures were no longer the older subsistence and exchange systems. We were part of a global economic order which defined our countries as "developing" and saw us only in terms of the raw materials and markets for finished goods that we can provide. Politics presented new problems in the definition of such concepts as individual liberty, national integrity, and communal responsibility. From 1957 to 1962 the bulk of Africa was decolonized. But questions of economic independence, cultural renaissance, and nationalism continue to demand close attention and energetic appraisal.

Africa's problem today is still the problem of poverty, disease, and illiteracy. Living on one of the richest continents of the world, our per-capita income remains at a paltry ninety dollars per annum. The southern half is still locked in embattled enclaves of racial bigotry and white supremacy regimes. Our mildly progressive governments continue to be victims of concerted interference by the developed world and, at times, subjected to dramatic coups d'état that promise much but are short on delivery. But the continent plods on, seeking, at times very painfully, ways of growth and survival. And in this search, it adapts, adopts, changes, borrows, discards, and continues to build what in essence will be its own true personality.

This book constitutes my personal testament of and salutation to that spirit of Africa that continues through strife, tribulations, and dramatic upheavals to seek her own true self.

Part I

Africa and her external contacts

The history of Africa, as presented by European scholars, has been encumbered with malicious myths. It was even denied that we were a historical people. . . . Such disparaging accounts had been given of African society and culture as to justify slavery, and slavery, posed against these accounts, seemed a positive deliverance of our ancestors.

KWAME NKRUMAH, *Consciencism*

A brief history of precolonial Africa

The history of Africa has been the subject of fierce speculation, debate, and discussion over the past few decades. Africa once loomed in the imaginings of European and other scholars, travelers, romantics, and adventurers as a land of darkness, of mysterious tribes engaged in frightful orgies, of primitive and raw instincts such as cannibalism, of dark sinister practices in voodoo and sorcery, of wide savannas, deep impenetrable jungles, of instant death and breathtaking events, of wild and untamable animals and people. Sad to relate, this image is still fostered by the movie industry and in European and American television. The most persistent mental picture of Africa that a large number of elementary and high school children in America have of Africa is still derived from the Tarzan movies and others of its type. For the mysteries of Africa had long fixed the imagination of explorers and adventurers; its legends of riches and wealth had for long lured the greedy.

Even today, when a new perspective is opened on Africa's history and culture, it continues to suffer from the incubus of misunderstanding and prejudice.

It has been once asked whether Africa had a history. The question revealed not only bigotry but also a very simple-minded type of racist scholarship. History does not exist only in "written" records and books but in such non-documentary sources as oral traditions, the findings of archaeology, of musicology and ethnology. Above all, it is the sum total of a people's way of life, coherently developed in their material and spiritual cultures, in their tools and implements, in their institutions and concepts of God and man, concepts that exist in an order and can be readily interpreted and examined. Any peoples who fashioned tools and institutions of government and organized agriculture cannot be described as lacking in history. And this is true of all surviving civilizations of planet earth.

Africa's history can also, beyond the non-documented sources, be elucidated through the work of Arab and African scholars whose accounts antedate by many centuries the arrival of the modern European in Africa.

This arrival in modern historical times is significant for it has in many ways diverted the path of the continent's history. This event, hitherto interpreted from the standpoint of European scholarship and its attendant ethnocentrism, derived from the eighteenth and nineteenth centuries, must now be examined and evaluated from an aggressively African point of view. The European presence in Africa must be assessed for what exactly it is. Its historical and cultural impact must be qualitatively analyzed.

A close look at the distribution of peoples in Africa today will reveal a great degree of unity in concept and practice among what had hitherto been regarded as vastly different peoples and cultures. The institution of chieftaincy, the divine conception of the role of chiefs, the cult of ancestors, initiation of the various rites of passage from birth to death, the nature and power of kinship groups based on blood, ideas about the Supreme Creator and the role and assignments of minor gods and deities, the metaphysical conception of the world—these are all generally shared in a united culture and origin in the very dim past. Among every African people there are stories of migrations and legends of their movement in vast numbers across great expanses of land over long periods. These waves of migration took place at periods of great intervals and over many centuries. They also would explain the various historical strains and stresses.

The hypothesis that the earliest man had his home in Africa is gaining more and more credence through the work of a number of archaeologists, particularly the Leakey family, whose finds in northern Tanzania of hominids dating back to two to three million years have been hailed as one of the most spectacular additions to human knowledge in our time. Leakey's *Zinjanthropus* is said to be the first man to use tools. Between him and man of the Old Stone Age, a number of important historical, geological, and genetic developments took place, the documentation of which belongs elsewhere.

Archaeologists are still not agreed upon even the approximate details and time of the Neolithic period of Africa. But this period saw great and revolutionary changes in the pattern of human conduct particularly in the Lower Nile where agriculture was practiced over six thousand years ago. Its practitioners have been the first black cultivators in the Nile Valley. The domestication of cereals such as sorghum, millet, and rice marked the first organized agricultural civilization of the continent. It was also accompanied by stock raising, which seemed to have been confined to the eastern section across the Great Rift Valley, particularly in the highlands of East and Central Africa. An important factor which did exert a great influence on the subsequent history of the continent is the dessication of the Sahara. This meant that what was once a large viable tract of land and a great hunting ground steadily shrank. The people who depended on this area for survival had to seek new homes. The watershed period of this important event has been variously put between 2000 and 1000 B.C., the dessication taking over three thousand to four thousand years to be complete.

One significant aftereffect of the appearance of the desert was the human invasion of the rain forests where new crops such as sweet potatoes and bananas became the staples, introduced from the Far East through East Africa.

The beginning of iron culture, variously put at 500 B.C. or a little later, marked an important point in the further development of agriculture and of new political arrangements based on the use of the metal in warfare.

The inhabited regions of the Niger Basin, the Congo Basin, and the East African highlands were the important centers of human civilizations based on settled communities of farmers and cattle grazers.

The introduction of iron also led to great political upheavals that were the result of wars, with the emergence of strong centralized units, political organizations, and politically conscious ruling groups who sought to impose their will on the weaker or less settled groups. This, together with the pressure on arable land stemming from the dessication of the Sahara, could have caused the great migrations that we already spoke about.

So into the Congo Basin, the regions of Angola, and the western savanna came waves of migrants. Beyond the Cameroon mountains and by the river Niger one large group settled. Another wing forged southwards into the great savannas of the south. This coincided with the first thousand years of the Christian era, and evidence as to details of this period remains slim and vague until the emergence of the first West African kingdom of Ghana around A.D. 300. By this time, it can be surmised, Africa's prehistory came to an end. This period was marked by great instability. In the whirling mess, contacts were made, and certain institutional developments in politics and government were already evident.

A great communication line existed between the northern Berber settlements and the Africans below the Sahara. The peoples of Sudan formed the middle link in the great trading caravans that exchanged salt from the Berber mines for the gold of the south. The Niger also provided an important trade route, especially from the east-central parts to the sub-Saharan gold mines and the markets in the region between modern Nigeria in the east and modern Guinea in the west. The opportunity for trade and commerce led to more permanent settlements and terminals for the camel journeys. This resulted in the development of political organizations and centralization of authority over these activities and therefore the emergence of kingdoms and empires. The art of government already possessed by the people and carried from their ancient homes was transferred here.

The history of Africa up to A.D. 1450 seems to be marked by varying degrees of selective growth and contact between trans-Saharan Africa, the Middle East, Europe, Asia, and the Far East. It must be noted that in spite of the coming of Islam in the seventh century A.D., African religious and cultural patterns were well enough formed to constitute the primary base. Islam, we will find, underwent a series of changes and accommodations which were necessary for its own survival.

By the time Europe entered the scene, Islam had made its peace with Africa and had in definite ways become Africanized. It was already serving the purposes of government and politics and provided another world view to the rulers, political aristocracies, and subjects of empires and kingdoms to an extent that Christianity and its concomitant culture could not until the era of African independence. Christianity remained proudly alien, offering salvation to the select few who would desert their homesteads, their fathers, and their mothers.

The kingdoms of Ghana, Mali, Songhai, and Kanem-Bornu were followed by the successive states of Hausa, Oyo, Benin, Denkyira, and others in western Africa. The period from A.D. 300 to 1600 is normally regarded as the African golden age, underscored by a process of independent growth and selective borrowing. These developments of the western part of the continent were repeated in the eastern, central, and southern sections at later dates with the great civilizations of the Congo, Monomotapa, the hybrid culture of Swahili, and in the rise and fall of Shaka's Zulu kingdom and its fiercely proud military tradition that was finally subjugated in 1879 with the defeat of the truly last Zulu king, Cetewayo, by the British.

This quick look at the barest features of Africa's "pre-European" history provides some evidence of continuity, with occasional catastrophic interruptions, in human activity on the continent. The stresses and strains of adaptation, borrowing, and rejection were felt in the long years of contact with external factors which took both peaceful and military forms. A continuum, however, exists in the cultures of the African people. It is this that was the most resilient feature of precolonial Africa. Iron, gold, cotton had become absorbed into the material culture. Centralist organizations were erected around religious ideas. City states had risen and fallen according to the fortunes of their founders. Religion, worship, ritual, art, and a whole way of life had been established which was distinctively African in the pure cultural and geographical sense.

It is this Africa into which Europe came. And that arrival marked the most important turning point in Africa's history and style of life. Modern Africa begins with the era of the European confrontation.

2

Arrival of Europe, indirect rule, assimilation, and Christianity

The most important and in many senses most revolutionary of the contacts sub-Saharan Africa made, including the earlier sporadic ones with the Far East and the more serious links with the northern litoral, was that made with Western Europe. The very first appearance of the white man in black Africa has not been documented. There were early travelers, such as the Greek Ptolemy, who were supposed to have sailed around Africa and produced the first imaginative map of the continent. But these judgments are merely speculative.

The earliest European contact with Africa south of the Sahara must have occurred on the west coast where Portuguese ships once stopped for supplies of food and water on their way to finding a new sea route to the Indies. By the middle of the fifteenth century, according to Portuguese and Spanish sources, the contact was on its way to becoming permanent. Azurara's account *Discovery of Guinea* was completed in 1453. Other chroniclers included Ruy de Pina, who was chief historian to the court of Portugal in 1497; Ca Da Mosto, an Italian in Portuguese service; Duarte Pereira, whose *Esmeraldo de Situ Orbis* gave a vivid description of the western coastline, fantastic stories designed to suit the taste of a sensationally inclined Renaissance Europe, recitals of trading profits, and wondrous speculations on the nature of the African people.

The purpose of this contact was trade in such commodities as pepper, gold, and ivory in exchange for hardware and textiles. The Portuguese were followed by other Europeans, notably the British and the French. The Congo Basin was among the earliest points of contact, along with the trading posts in Elmina, in present-day Ghana, where the Portuguese had built a castle in 1481.

The early contact was said to have been based on mutual respect and profit until the Portuguese decided to pervert the course of this trade and introduce the slave trade. In the sixteenth century Mzenga Nzinga, the Mani Congo, or King of the Congo, had established a confidential relationship with the Portuguese, but when this was undermined, he wrote no fewer than twenty-four letters to the King of Portugal appealing to his good sense and attempting to keep the trade on a constructive basis. He lamented with alarm and disillusionment the introduction of the human trade and his own continuing loss of trust in the overseas visitors. Portuguese missionaries continued to enjoy a degree of acceptance and pursued their work of proselytizing. Nzinga himself became baptized.

The sixteenth century saw the further extension of European contact with Africa, especially when the Dutch, French, and the British entered the picture. The earliest settlements of the Cape of Good Hope area by shipwrecked sailors coincided with the advent of the so-called "chartered companies," the rise of the Dutch and their mercantile and military systems, and the settlement of North America and the West Indies. A large number of factors was responsible for the transatlantic slave trade, the most important being the Industrial Revolution in Europe and the colonization of the New World where cheap labor was needed to grow plantation crops such as cotton and sugar cane.

What in strictly legalistic terms can be referred to as slavery had not been unknown in Africa before the transatlantic trade. Slavery had existed in most parts of the world since historic times. In Africa, where society had no penal institutions such as prisons, it served as a method of controlling and punishing criminals and malcontents and of putting to productive service war captives, hostages, and children of debtors. The personal rights and conditions of slaves under this system were protected by traditional laws and overseen by communal responsibility. Besides, slavery was imposed for a specific period and measured by the nature of the crime, the size of the debt, or the agreement on hostages; it was not a perpetual condition. The "owner" was accountable to the community for the protection and welfare of the slave. It was possible to earn freedom by good behavior or purchase. The slave worked without reward. But in his spare time he could acquire movable property with which to buy his freedom and re-enter society as a man of good standing. Among many groups it worked so well that slaves were known to rise to positions of chiefs, war leaders, and responsible elders. It was a system based on a wider community concept which accepted the essential humanity of the slave and recognized that it was misfortune or fate that led him into such a state. These "rules" prevailed so long as people went into slavery in the next village or, in the most extreme cases, the next land. Confusion and despair arose only when they went into slavery in more distant lands, where their rights as human beings were completely denied. This happened with the spread of Islam, for although the Holy Koran decreed humane treatment, it ignored the right of prisoners of holy wars to decent consideration. Most of the black slaves who arrived in the Mediterranean world encountered conditions that included denial of property rights, perpetual servitude, and at times castration. This type of total slavery appeared in Islamic North Africa and Egypt as early as the eleventh century, when the Arab settlers' control of the Mediterranean and of the Saharan trade routes and the spread of Islam under the Almoravids increased the volume of slave trading. Black slaves were in Turkey providing labor in the building of the Byzantine Empire. The earliest Portuguese explorers could have bought their first slaves from Moslem traders on the coasts of Senegal and Mauritania in the second half of the fifteenth century.

Elmina, the first West African trading post, was built by the Portuguese on the expectations of the gold trade. Fanti chiefs signed treaties with them to supply gold in exchange for cloth, salt, and tools. A few missionaries had visited Benin in the Niger Delta. As stated earlier, contact was made with the kingdom of Nzinga, the Mani Congo.

Nzinga's letters to the King of Portugal, by 1526, began to complain about the "corruption and licentiousness" of the slave raiders who were grabbing his subjects and selling them, thus depopulating his country. He further complained of the kidnapping of noblemen and their sons who were subsequently sold into slavery. Nzinga begged the Portuguese king to send only missionaries who would teach in schools.

The penetration of Benin was recorded by Ruy de Pina, who complained about the "heresies and great idolatries and fetishes which the negroes practice in that land." The Portuguese abandoned Benin when the trade there proved unprofitable and sickness decimated the advance parties.

The wheels of history turned very fast. From a relationship based on mutual profit and esteem, the legitimate African trade with Europe degenerated into the slave trade in which the European buyer, through trickery, bribery, blackmail, and appeal to human greed, persuaded some African chieftains to join. Outright capture of innocent villagers was frequent. In the little village of Vuti, in Anlo-Ewe country, the story is told of how a group of drummers were persuaded to come aboard an English ship to drum for the captain. Those on the shore saw the ship vanish over the horizon. The song "On which shores are they going to land" is still sung today.

Before the Berlin Conference of 1884 the European political map of Africa was a cartographic confusion of indeterminate settlements concentrated in forts, trading posts, and factories. These were overseen by piratical representatives of chartered companies and backed at times by a few drunken troops in ships anchored off shore or quartered in the forts ready to fire their muskets and cannons into the bush at the slightest provocation. The European powers had assumed authority over some tracts of land in the wake of explorers, merchants, and missionaries. As the slave trade had superseded earlier legitimate trade, powerful political administrations were regularly needed to hold territories won, taken formal possession of, "discovered," and "protected" through dubiously worded treaties.

A cursory look at the history of the seventeenth, eighteenth, and early nineteenth centuries will reveal that this was the darkest and most confused period of Africa's relation with Christian Europe. It saw the intensification of European rivalry and of the slave trade which had become a very lucrative business for the big mercantile families of Western Europe and the growing settler-pioneer class of America. This period also was marked by a series of long wars between powers such as Britain, France, Denmark, Portugal, Holland, Prussia, and Sweden. It was also marked by the classic operation of the principle of divide and rule, when Fanti was set against Ashanti, Ewe against Akwamu, Ijaw against Igbo, Yoruba against Fon.

The eighteenth century saw the rapid development of the Industrial Revolution in Europe and the concomitant ruthless prosecution of political and territorial claims in Africa. The Portuguese had settled themselves in forts, castles, and trading stations along the coast of West Africa, Angola, Mozambique in the east, and up the Zambezi River. Britain, Denmark, and France had done the same thing along the Guinea coast, establishing little pockets from which to expand their trade.

The missionaries served essentially as harbingers of European political powers. Where the mission went, the military arm of its country of origin followed to protect the lives of the missionaries. This gunboat diplomacy was to be perfected by later imperialist regimes. The assumption by Europeans of judicial and administrative functions was carried out to protect trade and commerce, which had by now assumed epic proportions, notoriously loaded in favor of one side.

The direct result of this increased interest and intervention was the almost total undermining of existing political institutions which had hitherto governed the African societies. This is dramatized by the confidence and arrogance with which the African Christian converts defied traditional authority and sought the political, judicial, and military protection of the invader in the sure knowledge that it would be extended.

A state of instability now existed owing to the frequency of raids carried out by European pirates, Moslem raiders, and powerful chiefs who were actively encouraged with adequate supplies of arms to lead expeditions against weaker states. Some of the smaller states collapsed through mass exodus and migration and through

depopulation. The ancient kingdoms of Akwamu and Denkyira
in the middle part of what is now Ghana were dismembered by
the invading forces of Ashanti, who carried out wars of expansion
and periodic punitive raids for purposes of politics and trade.

By 1850 the West African slave trade was over. It is hard to
determine whether the abolitionists fought against the trade on
purely humanitarian grounds or because of the changing economic
patterns of the time. Suffice it to say that the abolition movement
did not owe its impetus to purely selfless and altruistic motives.
It was simply a question of "diversify or perish," the motto of all
expanding mercantile systems.

Of course, the first African colonies had long since been established. Portugal's power on the upper west coast had declined in
the seventeenth century and she had shifted her attention to Angola farther south and Mozambique on the east coast. The Dutch
had supplanted her at Elmina in 1637 and forced her to cede all
her bases to the Dutch East India Company, in return for Holland's
renunciation of all claims to Brazil. The British and the Dutch
were joined by the Danes, and in the mid-seventeenth century a
chain of small trading posts and forts built by these two groups
dotted the west coast.

The various European governments granted charters to trading
cartels, thus investing them with a measure of political power and
authority in the areas where they operated. This made the companies accountable to the governments on whose behalf they were
supposed to act. The arrangement implied responsibility, but where
the leaders of trade and of government were the same people, the
theory of accountability was a sham and the periodic scrutiny and
direction to which the companies were supposed to be subjected
negated. It was from these companies that direct European control of the coastal areas of most parts of Africa was later to emerge.

One significant result of the trading operations in the towns of
Africa was urbanization along European lines, which transformed
the traditional structures drastically. The traditional village structure with a few well-ordered compound houses gave way to sprawl-
ing townships in which the local middlemen and entrepreneurs
lived. The core of the older African society was mainly one large
village or town which by tradition had paramountcy because it

was the royal, political, or spiritual center. Smaller villages of fishermen or farmers surrounded this central one. Most of the settlers in the small villages were only temporary sojourners even though the land was theirs. They buried their dead in the central village and returned to it for customary rites, festivals, and political activities such as deliberations, hearings of cases, and trade. With the introduction of European-type townships, the political structure of the old society was inevitably undermined. A new class of Africans arose who had acquired wealth enough to challenge the authority of the chiefs. They even at times founded chiefships and rival stools on which they set themselves up as rulers over slave enclaves. Urbanization, in cases where it was based on existing royal towns, brought into the chiefs' political domain people who owed them no allegiance and over whom they had no effective authority. Some of these African traders became very powerful and even retained private personal armies, like Asamani in the Gold Coast, De Souza in Dahomey, and King Jaja of the Niger Delta in the late nineteenth century. Through alliances with the trading authorities backed by their political mentors overseas and a steady flow of gunpowder, some of these Africans defied the local chiefs and their administrative powers.

The process of urbanization was also accelerated by the missionaries, who had their headquarters in the coastal towns and encouraged European-style architecture which eroded the traditional pattern and its focus on the family compound. The European patterns huddled people together in tighter, more crowded, yet separate surroundings and by its very nature promoted the isolation of individual households which formerly had connections of blood and common usage and custom as their most binding ties.

European colonial expansion took two major forms: treaties of protection signed mainly with coastal chiefs who were mostly the middlemen in trade and provided the basic contact needed by the machinery of economic rule; and direct conquest.

Expeditions in East Africa in the nineteenth century were spearheaded by geographers such as John Speke, Richard Burton, and James Grant, who went from Zanzibar to Lakes Tanganyika and Victoria and the kingdom of Buganda where they came into

contact with expanding Arab commercial power. The work of Sir
Harry Johnston and Lord Lugard led to the establishment of British pre-eminence over most of Central Africa. Through Johnston
a number of treaties were promulgated, most importantly that
which established the British Central Africa protectorate in 1891
through the commercial activities of the African Lakes Company.
One of the protectorate's first actions was to reissue African lands
hitherto held communally by African freeholders and to sell them
to the Europeans at three pence per acre. The local chief, by custom and usage, was not entitled to sell land, for he was basically
the trustee of property held on behalf of the community. Besides,
land represented a spiritual entity which could not be disposed of
through outright sale.

The story differs slightly from place to place. Where the protectorate principle was not enforced, the local governments and
states, already weakened by the slave trade, were overthrown by
superior European artillery and trained local mercenaries.

The protectorate concept, developed in the nineteenth century,
operated in a number of ways. One of the most common was to
persuade the chiefs of the warring intentions of other states and
their need to come under the protection of this or that European
flag. For example, the informal agreement that placed the Gold
Coast under British protection was signed by only a handful of
Fanti chiefs on March 6, 1844. They were, it was quite evident,
persuaded that their safety from the marauding raids of the
Ashanti armies lay only in their acceptance of British political
authority, military protection, and jurisdiction. Before then, as one
of the early governors of the colony observed, some sort of irregular
jurisdiction had grown extending itself far beyond the limits of the
forts and the trading posts by what he characterized as voluntary
submission of the people themselves to British equity. What had
begun as the control of forts held by the British and directed by
the governor in Sierra Leone and for which Britain assumed political responsibility with the founding of the colony, ended in the
bond signed by seven chiefs of the coast, providing a "legal" basis
for British interference far beyond the territories held to that date.
From then on, reasons for punitive and protective wars would be
adduced to support blatant extortionist and aggressive acts against

other groups who did not wish to come under the jurisdiction of the British and who therefore constituted a threat to British power in the area.

The system provided the basis for the introduction of British jurisprudence and legal practice. This had a far-reaching effect. The chief's own authority as president of the court of elders was entirely weakened. The British legal system, based on Roman and English common law and on its own principle of right and wrong, replaced traditional judicial concepts. By the very nature of this new order, the chiefs were forced to abdicate their authority and had handed over power to the representatives of the colonial authority.

The second system of colonial expansion was, of course, by force of arms. Conquered territories formed the bulk of the European imperial domain in Africa. It was the simple case of militarism for purposes of commercial profit and extension of the spheres of influence. The "civilizing mission" was only a stupendous alibi. Ashanti, Benin, Dahomey, Zulu, Matabele are just a few examples of peoples defeated after a series of wars fought on very unequal terms. In these areas, the most visible aim of the colonial government was that of preserving law and order, both through the courts and a rigid system of police and army garrisoning.

Both conquered and protected territories became the areas of overseas European dominion and imperial power, the far-flung outposts of white political authority, lands to be exploited, and peoples to be abused.

Lord Lugard was the father of the principle of "indirect rule," based on the premises of the "white man's burden" and the civilizing role to be played by British merchants and discoverers. It was not enough to "discover" rivers and mountains on whose banks and in whose valleys people had lived for countless generations. A British African empire was the moving dream of the discoverers.

By the time of the establishment of the British colonial administrations, the chiefs had lost most of their power over the coastal areas and over the new urban centers that grew around the trading posts. There was some distant sense of identity and love for pageantry in the British character which was vaguely echoed in the ceremonies and celebrations that surrounded the chief's court. But the British did not grasp the nature of the authority and the judicial system that went hand in hand with African religious and political institutions. Because this authority had long been undermined, the chief was isolated as a figure who was against progress, his office an outmoded institution. People in the protectorates looked to the Crown for law and order and for protection. They also looked to the Christian missions for religious direction. So the chief's functions as judge, war leader, and symbol of the spiritual essence of his people, expressed through the stool, were woefully diminished. What was left for him were some ceremonies which, thanks to the British love of royalty and the fripperies of pomp and pageantry, were vigorously encouraged. Whatever authority remained for him he enjoyed at the pleasure of the Crown's representative.

By the time of the treaties of protection in northern Nigeria with the powerful Fulani emirates of Kano, Katsina, and Sokoto in the latter half of last century, the British recognized a strong and coherent feudal system based on Islam which would be pressed into service as an ally. Here were a people who cared very little for the white man's civilization and had resisted all efforts to Europeanize them much more fiercely than their brothers to the south. Here British authority amounted to very little. Lugard, therefore, hit upon the idea of indirect rule. By it, the chiefs were to exercise their traditional functions as now defined by British jurisprudence and become the medium through which the Crown governed the colonies. They were to be given a portion (the most inconsequential portion) of British power, and, conjoining it with their own, were to act as intermediaries between the British Crown and its subjects. In fact, they were plain lackeys of the Crown. New paramountcies were forged in areas where none had existed. Different groups and peoples were lumped together and placed under a so-called "traditional area" in order to facilitate British administration. It was made clear to the chiefs that they held even their little power under the Queen and at her pleasure. Chiefs, once elected by age-old methods of democratic selection from suitable claimants of royal clans, now had to be approved by the governor, who also had the right to depose them when they acted contrary to British interest. Deposed chiefs were in many cases sent into exile. Prempeh I of the Ashanti was but one example. Lugard saw the administrative machinery of the Fulani rulers as a model for his native administrative system. The difficulty was that the British tried to apply a system of government worked out after a study of a more autocratic African area to the generally democratic areas where a chief was never an absolute ruler but a first among equals, to be installed or destooled if need be according to custom and usage. Where chieftaincy had not existed as a result of history and circumstance, as among the Igbo, the British, with characteristic genius for creating confusion, proceeded to install chiefs for the people. Upstarts and smart alecks, whom the British knew could be used in carrying out their programs in return for certain privileges and compensations, were made chiefs.

Powerfully established chiefs such as the Asantehene in Ghana or the Kabaka of Buganda and their elders, who saw this as a degradation of the institution and opposed it, were swiftly punished. The history of colonial rule was one of long conflict with these rulers.

Indirect rule was bound to fail. The warrant chiefs—those created by the British—were victims of indifference and at times outright mob violence. The protected chiefs were allowed to try petty cases of witchcraft and thievery. Bribery and corruption were rampant. The native authority police force was the laughing stock of the whole population. It was as if the whole program was conceived of with overwhelming cynicism. Urbanization, population mobility, education, and Christianity were factors that worked to further render it ineffective. It was wishful thinking to assume that chiefs whose roles had now shifted to that of Crown agents could command the allegiance and respect of their people. There were even efforts to send the sons of some chiefs to England where they received dubious education among the English aristocracy who found them exotically exciting. These men were supposed to become enlightened native arms of British colonial power.

The French, with the glorious certainty that French culture is God's gift to the world, did not commit what later observers refer to as the "benevolent blunders" of British indirect rule. They proceeded on the assumption that the colonies were part of metropolitan France, and their concept of the civilizing mission was based on a fundamental view of racial superiority which assumed aggressive political and cultural proportions. French culture in its paramount self-confidence was calculated to turn the colonial subjects into French citizens and to wipe out the indigenous culture if need be. The British pattern simply ignored this aspect of the question and thus, almost by accident, left certain features of African culture intact. The French, however, designed and directed their education programs towards the development of French men and women according to the highest ideals of the French Republic. Africans were brought up as Frenchmen in the lycées and finally dispatched to the universities of France. These *assimilés* were encouraged to think of themselves as Frenchmen and to help their new "compatriots" carry out the motherland's programs with ease among their unredeemed kinsmen. This method of direct rule, or assimilation, ensured a more basic cultural dislocation, played down the role of missionaries (whose liberal Christian lack of rigorousness was frowned upon as un-French) in education, and encouraged semisettlement by Frenchmen in any part of their new "motherland," whether in the mountains of Futa Jallon or on the beaches of the Senegal River. It in turn inculcated a strong attitude of dependence on the part of the African population, an attitude which many observers believe not even independence has been able to erode completely. There were always governors and garrisons to carry out France's laws. Besides, members of the new *évolué* class were encouraged to send representatives to the National Assembly in France. During the Nazi occupation of France in the Second World War Charles de Gaulle rallied support for Free France, appealing to the "patriotism" of Africans in West Africa who were ready to die for France. The African soldiers, proceeding on the same principle, later fought in Indochina and Algeria against legitimate anticolonial and freedom fighters.

Assimilation became relaxed only in the mid 1950s with the passing of the *loi cadre,* a law allowing a degree of internal autonomy for the colonies through a local governing council, presided over by the governor, and made up of African ministers.

With all its aggressive cultural imperialism and assumption of political power, assimilation directly dismantled the authority of the chiefs, who were allowed to function, bereft of all power, on the periphery of the French colonial administration.

The Portuguese followed a similar pattern, maintaining a rigid caste of colonial rulers and their allies, the *assimilados,* who were mainly the fruit of illicit liaisons between the conquering masters and local women. This pattern persisted until recently in Portugal's African "provinces" of Angola, Mozambique, and Guinea-Bissau where fierce struggles for independence and guerrilla wars raged until 1974 when internal disorders constrained Portugal to begin to grant independence to the Africans.

By far the most powerful instrument of European cultural contact and change in Africa has been the Christian Church. Even though missionary work began in Africa as a sporadic attempt by parent churches in Europe to extend the gospel to the "unfortunate" heathens, the metropolitan political machinery, as pointed out, became its closest defender, ally, and ultimate beneficiary. It was generally recognized that the conversion of Africans to Christianity undertaken by the missionaries was to the advantage of colonialism. The Berlin Act of 1885, ratifying the partition of Africa by the European powers inserted an article guaranteeing liberty of conscience and freedom for all sects to profess their faith. It further affirmed the churchmen's right to enter, travel over, and live on the African continent.

In fact, from as far back as the fifteenth century, the sacrament of baptism was used as an important excuse for the slave trade. A curse was said to have been placed upon the Negro race supposedly descended from Ham in the Bible, who looked upon his father's nakedness. In 1870 the First Vatican Council received a document from a group of missionaries asking the Pope to release the race from this curse!

The propagation of the Christian faith has always connoted the consolidation of imperial power. The Roman Emperor Justinian encouraged the Christianization of all African chiefs who sought his good will. He even bestowed investitures with robes and honorific titles for chiefs who embraced the Church. Religious propaganda was an essential aspect of imperial expansion, and the colonial powers had long grasped the important truth that it was cheaper in the long run to use the Bible than military power to secure distant dominions.

Azurara, the Portuguese chronicler, described the baptism of a group of Africans in 1444 and stressed the salvation achieved for them under the dispensation of Christ. The basic hypocrisy underlying the concern to save the souls of the pagan Negroes was revealed in Portugal's endeavor to use the Christian Church for imperial and commercial ends as evidenced in her dealing with the sixteenth-century kingdom of the Mani Congo.

The Church basically accepted the slave trade, even though Pius II in the fifteenth century, Paul III in the sixteenth century, Urban VIII in the seventeenth century, and Benedict XIV in the eighteenth century protested against it. These and other protests were ignored by both Catholic and Protestant princes who were the ultimate beneficiaries of the trade.

The assumption that the morals and faith of Christians were superior and infinitely blessed by God provided the unquestioned justification that any means could be used to change the African, who was possessed of savage instincts and was the victim of "degrading fetishism and demonology." The prohibitions and taboos of Christianity were expected to replace paganism.

The nature of Christian theology presented a primary conflict in the minds of Africans. The doctrine of the Trinity was to a large degree antithetical to African religions. God the Father, His Son Jesus, and His brother the Holy Ghost were remote divine personages who seemed to have withdrawn from the world without leaving any religious authority recognizable to Africans. The confusions between the Old Testament and the New were self-evident. The full and complete revelation of God and His divinity could only come through the personality of His Son; it was through Him alone that the Father could be reached. Man could not, apparently, come to Him through knowledge of the universal forces that surrounded Him and bore on Him at every turn. Even St. Paul's statement in his Epistle to the Romans, that whatever is knowable of God is plain to "pagan" nations, including His invisible nature, His everlasting power and Divine Being, was ignored.

For Africans, Christian theology placed God too remote from man in time and space. St. Paul's point in the Epistle to the Romans hits at the heart of the debate between African religious thought, which emphasized the universal self-manifestation of God to all men without exception through the works of His creation and the writing of the law upon the hearts of men, and the Christian faith.

One of the most incomprehensible teachings regarding heaven was the Calvinist doctrine that heaven can be gained only through a simple austere life of self-denial. The idea of heaven as a place where one is rewarded for certain deeds of obedience to God's laws on earth is nonexistent in African religious thought. To Africans, heaven only approximates the good life on earth; it is blessed by the gods, the guarantee of the expected outcome of the proper rites, ceremonies, and sacrifices, and the ensuing prosperity that comes from good harvest, a house full of children, and a good standing in the eyes of the community. In other words, heaven and hell are here with us and are evident in the conduct of our lives according to the wishes of the ancestors and the gods. Man was not born with an original sin; he brings with him his immutable mission that acts as an intervening force between him and the gods.

The Christian Church in Africa refused to accept the legitimacy of the African's religious position. He was accused of being a pagan, a devil worshiper; Satan was said to have employed his agency to erase every vestige of religious impression from the African's mind, leaving him without a single ray to guide him away from the dark and dread futurity. The early missionaries were baffled by the notion of sin as it exists among Africans. The African conceives of wrong as directed essentially against society, the ancestors, and the gods, and as capable of being wiped out by the observance of ritual rites and ceremonies. In essence, the concept means that if one offends the gods, retribution follows, but the offense can be cleansed away not only by the individual offender but also by the whole community to whom a measure of guilt is attached.

But the conflict between the European missionaries and the African world did not lie essentially in the opposing and at times irreconcilable theological positions. It lay in the way in which Christian teaching subverted the solidarity and integrity of the African society. It appealed first to the outcasts, those whom the rigid laws of the group could not tolerate. The teachings of Christ openly preached abandonment of community, clan, and family responsibilities: "Except ye leave your father and mother and follow me, ye cannot enter into the kingdom of heaven," Christ said. The faith insisted upon personal and individual salvation as against the group or communal salvation enshrined in the laws and ways of the land. Furthermore, the missionaries ridiculed African religious practices and at times blatantly, with the support of their converts, provoked open clashes with the priests and diviners. When the Ashanti refused to send their children to school (until 1874), it was because of a deep resentment they built against a religion that presumed that it was superior or had a monopoly of the only true faith. Hardly had it ever happened that one group of African religious leaders went into the land of another group and, accepting the latter's hospitality, proceeded to abuse, ridicule, and ignore the religious mores and beliefs of their hosts. Man, the African affirmed, could never presume to act on behalf of the Divine in the arrogant belief that he understands his total will. So people in Africa never went to war on behalf of gods. The gods themselves knew how best to conduct their struggles for the hearts of men.

The school was the most important instrument of Christian missionary work in Africa. The idea of formal school had been unknown in Africa, except in the special cases of priests and certain devotees in shrines and cult houses who underwent seminarian training in seclusion before returning to the community. A child learned every day the wisdom and trade of his father, and his test scores were based on his ability to accept the authority of the elders, the discipline of the profession (taboos, rites), the responsibility of manhood or womanhood, the tenets of the society, and the laws of the gods and the ancestors.

A child who entered the Christian mission school, however, was expected to cut his ties with the religious and ritualistic structure of his now-"pagan" family. He had to assume a Christian name (meaning a European name like George, Ellen, or Anatole) upon his baptism. Then began his moral instruction in Christian ethics and theology in the form of the catechism, the introduction of rules and regulations that would now govern his home life. He had to avoid the drumming sessions, his household ceremonies, and the public festivals of his ancestors. This weaning-away process was then intensified, exploiting the legitimate aspirations of the child and his parents, who were told that Christian education was their only hope of escape from the torments of hell and from the material degradations of their uncivilized existence. Christian indoctrination was enjoined through the rigid enforcement of church attendance, backed by the lash and the inculcation of the ideas of docility, humility, and unquestioning obedience to authority. The Christ of revolutionary change and opposition to unjust laws was never introduced to the African convert. The only Christ he was made to befriend was the Christ of the other cheek, of absolute obedience to temporal powers, and of an almost moronic refusal to question anything in the sure knowledge that all was ordained by the will of the Father. This was where the frustrations and impotence of the early converts and the first generations of educated Africans arose from. It was these Africans who embraced Christian dogma and life style with a conviction that bordered on fanaticism. Thus the Reverend Ndabaningi Sithole of Zimbabwe (Rhodesia), in his *African Nationalism,* affirmed that the Bible was redeeming the African individual from the power of superstition, witchcraft, and other forces that did not make for progress!

The African, half child, half devil, was the prodigal whose status must be raised by missionary effort. The earliest phase of this effort was naturally aimed at training catechists and teachers who would propagate the gospel. Some of the earliest pupils were slaves whom rich households or royal courts sent to school or slaves directly purchased by the Church, freed, and put to work in the Lord's vineyard. A good number were the social and religious outcasts to whom the Church opened its arms.

Some of the missions actively encouraged the creation of new townships and communities of Christian converts centered around church and school. A typical new township, known as "Salem," was set apart from the main village, its inhabitants encouraged to have nothing to do with the old village. This created an unnatural schism which in many ways eroded the traditional authority and promoted dissension among the people. Those who lived in Salem were taught to look down upon their "pagan" relatives, to adopt European ways of life, and to shun all manner of activity that might indicate a reversal to the barbarous ways of the tribe. The missions encouraged fierce feuds between the converts and the "pagans" in matters of land and water rights. The European legal system was ready to uphold the converts' claims, which were made within the framework of a "civilized" code.

The converts were also encouraged to acquire European material culture (right down to changing their African patronyms to what were considered Christian or European equivalents). The superiority of the European way of life was rigorously inculcated. This led to the growth of an African elite that identified itself with the colonial powers and offered its services in the perpetuation of their regimes. When the anticolonial nationalist movements were born after the Second World War, it was mainly this convert group that was very vocal about the African not being ready to govern himself and insisted upon many more years of colonial tutelage.

The most important church missions in Africa, apart from those of the Roman Catholic Church with its spiritual and material vested interest, were the Scottish Mission (which took over from the Bremen Mission from Germany after 1918), which sent out missionaries like David Livingstone; the Basel Mission; the Wesleyans; the Presbyterians; and the Methodists. These missions vied with each other for conversion grounds and, by their rivalry, sowed conflict among the people. A town that was proselytized by Catholics and Methodists, for example, inevitably became divided along the lines of the conflicting theologies of these two Churches. The schism of the Reformation, it was evident, was transplanted into Africa and served to increase the widening cracks in the fabric of the societies.

Most of the schools discouraged the speaking and use of the African languages by the pupils, even though the missionaries employed pupils to help translate the Bible into these languages. The Basel and Bremen missions provided orthographies for most of the languages and further wrote down rudimentary grammars for them. For it was necessary for the scriptures to be made available in the native tongues to those who were the targets of conversion.

The imitation of Europeans represented the more visible side of the transformation of Africans through the replacement of traditional concepts of social status and self-respect by new ones reflecting education, occupation, and standing in the Christian Church. To the convert Africans the missionaries represented the highest point in good breeding and Christian conduct. The most desirable state was that of the European who was nearest to God and spoke God's language. This situation led to the development of a sense of insecurity and inferiority in Africans, marked by a simple process of the loss of identity and of independence in the most traumatic manner. Most of the time, the Europeans who went into the Lord's vineyard or into the political administration of the colonial powers came from upper or upper middle classes at home, imbued with their own class attitudes and snobberies, often the younger sons of nobility or *nouveaux riches* lured by the romance of Africa. For this group, the bulk of the Africans represented a despicable lower level of creatures, with obnoxious religious and social habits who must not be tolerated around the precincts of decent homes. These attitudes were passed on lock, stock, and barrel to the first generations of educated Africans who also arrogantly and cruelly used the ordinary African in order to continue the European traditions of behavior and outlook. Their descendants, now educated in European primary schools both at home and abroad, still carry on after the manner of their fathers. The earlier generation gave their children European education in the professions: the law, medicine, and the church. It was this group, joined by the sons of a few chiefs, also educated abroad, who believed that they were the natural occupiers of the political seats later to be vacated by the whites.

There was no effort to indigenize the Christian religion. There was no interest in making liturgy and theology African. Christianity maintained its rigid and haughty position as a pure institution resolutely set against corruption, refusing to yield one inch of ground in both dogma and ritual. This superior attitude was designed to keep African religious thought at least at bay and, at best, to discredit it.

It is only recently that Christian theologians have talked about the need for the Church in Africa to speak to God in Africa's own language. The Roman Catholic Church, the most orthodox arm of the Christian faith, finally approved the use of the vernacular instead of Latin in public masses, and in the 1951 encyclical letter, *Evangelii praecones,* proclaimed the need for the Africanization of the church hierarchy and defined new attitudes towards "pagan" religions, citing the need to treat their doctrines with respect and, by so doing, persuade them to free themselves from error and impurity.

It is the breakaway Churches, prophetist movements, and faith-healing tabernacles that are achieving a kind of desirable synthesis of Christian thought and African religious attitudes. In them the joyous drums have taken over from dull hymnal; Christian theological concepts of the eucharist and sacrifice conjoin with the administration of herbs and divination; the evangelical proclamation of salvation now rests firmly within the African's search for harmony with spirits and men to ensure prosperity, success, and longevity here, not in the unknown hereafter. These developments have been roundly denounced by some of the misguided African church leaders, who in their infinite naïveté still cling to theological positions that are, to say the least, unrealistic in a changing sociocultural context. Some openly declared war on these unorthodox groups and in some areas, with the help of African governments, drove them underground or destroyed them.

The preaching of Christian theology in Africa naturally had racial repercussions. Christ was a white man; the saints were white; the missionaries were white. This writer remembers vividly the large pictures of a massively bearded white God with penetrating eyes that hung in the small Catholic chapel in his home town. Continuously the African was told he was cursed in his adherence to the ways of his fathers, and because he was black-skinned, the implications were not lost on him. Christianity, to take root, had to become iconoclastic in most parts of Africa. At the instigation of missionaries, political and military administrators led raids that destroyed shrines, holy places, and religious programs and systems that were drawing a large body of adherents and thus presenting intolerable rivalry to the Church of Christ. The convert was encouraged to desecrate his African holy places and abuse divine leaders.

Christian conversion meant cultural change. The past religious responsibility of the community was replaced by individual responsibility, based on a new religion whose morality was dictated by a distant divine command and whose sole design, it seemed, was to undermine the mores, sanctions, and taboos of traditional law, custom, and usage.

Churchgoing became not an act of devout worship but a social occasion for the display of new clothes and social position. Where religion was once a phenomenon that determined your everyday life, your relationship with your family, elders, clansmen, and the whole community at large, it was now relegated to one day in the week on which you were ostensibly to practice the Christian virtues, leaving the other days to do as much as you wished. Those converts who had more than one wife were asked to select one and dismiss the rest. Refusal led to the denial of the holy sacraments, especially the communion, to the offender. Most of the converts kept their wives, thus forfeiting the holy feast of a little wine and a morsel of bread. ("Christianity is good but there is no feasting in it" is an Ewe proverb.) These converts did this rather than disrupt kinship ties that form one of the basic determinants of polygamy. The Roman Catholic Church was more rigid than other Christian sects in the enforcement of its laws of one wife, even though it was hard put to find theological justification for monogamy as a basic Christian law apart from the marriage at Cana and a few scattered parabolical references to Christ and the Church in terms of a bride and bridegroom in the New Testament.

During the so-called Mau Mau uprising in Kenya, the clergy of the Christian Churches were pressed into willing service by the British political administration in its effort to subjugate the Gikuyus. The Churches themselves, believing that Mau Mau was a reversion to African paganism and barbarism in its oathing methods and advocacy of violence as a legitimate political tool, invoked the New Testament law of "Render unto Caesar those things that are Caesar's." They insisted on the payment by Africans of unjust taxes such as land tax and hut tax to the government and upon an absolute obedience to the harsh and alien temporal power. This was why the Churches came under severe physical attack. The freedom fighters concentrated their anger on missions and the schools, which represented to them pockets of a subversive alien culture and organs of political domination. The Churches' position

on female circumcision, which was one of unalterable opposition, equally drew a great deal of legitimate resentment and popular hatred. Some of those African priests, instigated by their white
mentors, who preached against the Mau Mau from their pulpits,
were said to have been promptly arrested and executed by the freedom fighters. A similar situation developed in Zaire during the
early 1960s when mission posts and nunneries became the first
targets of the Lumumbist Simba nationalist revolt.

Modern Africa begins from this era of Christianity which spearheaded for Africans a new culture and a new conception of the
world. Through this faith, Judeo-Christian material culture was
planted, completing Africa's complex confrontation with Europe.
In southern Africa, Cecil Rhodes's "civilized man" obviously meant
a man educated in English schools, able to read and write English,
attired like an Englishman, and observing the basic customs
and manners of his mentors in his faith, the objects that surrounded him, and the type of house he lived in. This categorized
the *non-évolué*, the unsaved and uneducated African, as uncivilized, primitive, and, at best, a usable chattel for mines and farms.
It is upon the tenets of this exalted ethical position that Ian Smith,
the so-called Prime Minister of Rhodesia, stands today. One of the
obstacles to sharing equal opportunities and votes with the Africans, he once affirmed, was the fact that most of them didn't speak
English!

Alienation, confusion, and uncertainty set in for the educated
African. He was cast in the white man's image, a woeful caricature
of this man, without focus or identity. African education and
Christianity in Africa still serve as the citadels of new-image building. The fundamental erosion of the African's confidence in himself began with the first Christian convert.

Contact with Euro-Christian theology and political ideas has
continued to define Africa's role in contemporary times. Its cities
were mostly built on the lines of European cities, with the exception of those that were allowed to sprawl, with open sewers,
narrow roads, and utter disregard for the barest rudiments of
sanitation. Its schools are modeled on European educational institutions. The application of technology and modern science in
the solution of any of its enormous problems of health, road build-

ing, agriculture, etc., is based on purely European premises. Its architects, doctors, lawyers, and theologians are trained in the European manner and are at no time required to think out the pressing questions of amalgamation, adaptation, and change in the personality of the continent. The new African intellectual was produced to deny the relevance of the African personality and culture to the new, aggressively "progressive" world. African art and music, once aspects of chiefship, religion, and ritual have been relegated to the realm of things that the new African can be legitimately embarrassed by; no viable program of teaching about them exists in African schools. Where they occur, they form part of the so-called extracurricular performances and activities of the school (which the pupils dislike intensely because of the way they are handled), designed to impress Founder's Day visitors. African musicians trained in schools and colleges learn Beethoven and Bach; her artists study Monet, Picasso, and Turner; her elite perform the waltz and foxtrot with agility and finesse.

The total result of all this is the basically wrong assumptions that the African still makes about European institutions. The most dramatic mistakes are still being made in the field of politics and political institutions.

Independence came as a result of post-Second World War agitation and the confrontation between a newly awakened African proletariat and soldiers returning from the Far East and elsewhere where they shed their blood to save the world from Nazi dictatorship. The historical importance of Kwame Nkrumah's work in Ghana cannot be denied. Independence took a giddily short period of five years, from 1957 to 1962, to achieve a strip-down of Europe's colonial empires. In the process, the colonial regimes had been chased out of their power bases, and an African leadership took over.

But most African leaders still believe that the issues of reconstruction facing their countries have a lot to do with the classical European conflict between communism and capitalism, a conflict many assume is largely academic in these days of détentes and new global alliances. Some therefore, at the prodding of their former rulers, began to build what they believed to be democratic institutions, without any recourse to history, social systems or po-

litical developments from precolonial times. Nigeria was the most
striking example of a country that suffered from this deadly political myopia. Where there were attempts to utilize Marxist or leftist
socialist precepts, the leadership was quickly discredited as com-
munistic and dictatorial and ultimately overthrown. Where it was
economically expedient (especially in the former French colonies),
one-party client regimes or one-man governments were enthroned
in order to perpetuate the European exploitation that in some cases
had been only momentarily halted by the independence march.
But in both situations, the alternatives seemed to be defined not
by Africa's own need to reconcile elements of its divergent history,
but by the still-persistent political and economic demands of
Europe. The search for democracy in Africa today becomes a
stupendous alibi for political subservience to empty Western slogans. Revolution and socialist programs degenerate into shouting
matches where new catch phrases are proclaimed to disguise
corruption and political thuggery. Neocolonialism, which some
African scholars naïvely believe was a figment of Nkrumah's imagination, is the real monster of postindependence Africa, manu-
factured in the political enclaves of Europe and America and
wheeled into an African existence by a conspiracy of big business,
international capitalism, and expansionist political systems. It still
terrorizes and holds to ransom the whole of the African continent.
The recent succession of rapid military coups is only a visceral
manifestation of a more deep-seated malaise—the inability of Africa to reconcile herself to herself and to search through the debris
of her history for the pieces with which to build that true self in
her own image.

3

Islamic penetration of Africa

Islam, like Christianity, was an invader's religion. Its spread in Ethiopia followed that of the Christian faith, starting about A.D. 700, when it influenced all of Africa north of the Niger Valley, the Nile headwaters, and the equatorial rain forest. Preached by the Arabian invaders, it quickly took a dominant position, especially on the northern coast. (Resistant Christian enclaves eventually predominated in Ethiopia.)

Mohammed's influence in the Middle East began spreading after his flight from Mecca to Medina in 622. The Holy Koran, compiled after his death and containing his teachings on religion and social and political matters, at once provided directions for the organization and dissemination of the new faith. Islam's first triumph was its swift unification under its law of the scattered nomadic groups of Arabia. From this unity Islam became powerful enough to spread into other lands, in the Fertile Crescent and the northeast, as far west as Algeria and the shores of the Atlantic. Egypt, Spain, and the Pyrenees were under Moslem power by the year 711. The next four hundred years saw the consolidation and growth of Islam as a popular faith. From Libya, Morocco, and Tunisia it was spread across the Sahara through traders, who developed the earliest trans-Saharan caravan routes. When the faith became absorbed by new groups, these in turn ensured its rapid establishment elsewhere. Thus the Almoravids, largely of Tuareg origin, began a series of jihads (holy wars) under their leader Ibn Jasin, attacking and defeating the Ghana Empire in 1076 and introducing Islam into the northern edges of the tropical forest just below the Sahara.

By 1235 Islam had become the official religion of Mali, which covered a wider territory than its predecessor, Ghana, stretching from the Atlantic seacoast to present day northern Nigeria. Its ruler Mansa Musa went on a famous pilgrimage to Mecca in 1323. When Mali was superceded by Songhai, under Askia the Great, a more fierce jihad followed, accompanied by the desire to return Islam to more orthodox ways. By the fifteenth century, during this religious renaissance, the Europeans were in early contact with the African coast. Revolt in the Moslem world north of the Sahara, especially in Morocco with the support of the Castilians and Portuguese, diminished Islamic interest in Africa south of the Sahara.

From 1300 to 1600, the extension of Portuguese influence on the western part of Africa as far down as the Congo Basin meant diversions in the overland trade routes and a major reapportioning of areas for wandering peoples. These last great African migrations must have been a direct result of Moslem harassment and political turmoil all over the continent.

A new burst of life for Islam came in the eighteenth and early nineteenth centuries when the Islamic state of Hausa was conquered by Usman dan Fodio's inspired, fanatic hordes of jihadists. His army of Fulani cattlemen carried out a bloody conquest aimed at wiping out the non-Islamic features of Hausa culture and re-establishing a new political system based on Koranic law and teaching. He established Sokoto as the capital over which he became the first sadauna, or emperor. For each of the districts, he appointed Fulani emirs with whom he ran the empire. It was this system that impressed Lord Lugard so much and led to the concept of indirect rule. Its politics was based on an autocracy deriving from Islamic law, feudalist in scope and maintaining a rigid class system, with serfs and slaves working on farms for their masters. The Fulani masters played an active role at the tail end of the slave trade, raiding the southern states for their human commodity. One of Usman's lieutenants, Ahmadu Lobo, spread Islam as far west as the Senegal River. Samori Toure, who ruled Guinea, and Umar, ruler of Tuculor in the Futa Jallon, are two examples of powerful rulers who emerged in close alliance with Fulani power by the middle part of the nineteenth century. The European penetration and the rise of powerful non-Moslem states in Benin, Dahomey, and Ashanti constituted a check on Fulani power and total hegemony.

East Africa had also been settled by Arab Moslems who were offshoots of the Arab incursion into Egypt. These settlements began as commercial enclaves based in Kilwa. By the middle of the seventeenth century, most of the east coast was taken over by Islam, and cities such as Mombasa, Kilwa, Malindi, and Zanzibar became the most important centers of trade not only with the hinterland but also with Arabia, India, and the Far East. Portugal tried to take over the flourishing centers but to no avail and had to settle for Mozambique in the south since the power of the Sultan of Oman, ruler of the Zenj (Arab settlements in East Africa), was enormous. After a series of sporadic revolts in Mombasa, the sultan moved his headquarters to Zanzibar in 1840.

Meanwhile, the Arab rulers intensified the slave trade; their participation on the east coast brought into the now-fading west coast trade a large flow of slaves, especially across the continent through the Congo (present-day Zaire).

Zanzibar, the headquarters of the Zenj sultanate, became the home of Swahili culture. Its power was paramount until its annexation by the British in 1890.

By the middle of the seventeenth century, then, the Islamic influence in sub-Saharan Africa was well established. The kingdoms of the middle Niger and the western Sudan were centers of learning even though their contact with the wider Moslem world was lessened as a result of the diminishing importance of the caravan trade routes. Islamic education, based on the Koran and taught by the learned imams and sheiks, provided the earliest direction in scholarship. But the politicoreligious structure of Islam was too vast and impractical to hold together. In the face of the resistance of the powerful rising states of the forest belts, the European challenge in trade, and an aggressively competitive Christian religion, the Islamic states began to lose their grip on sub-Saharan Africa.

Swahili civilization, centered in Malindi, Pemba, Mombasa, and Zanzibar, was a distinctive variant of Islamic African culture. Islamic architecture can be seen today in the great mosques of Kano and Mopti and in the general patterns of housing and clothing in all the Moslem areas of Africa. The influence of Islam is also seen in the languages and literatures of Hausa and Swahili, the two large and active linguistic and cultural amalgamations of Islam and indigenous Africa.

Islam's effect was also fundamental. There is still a large traffic of travelers between the Islamic centers of West and East Africa and the spiritual homeland, Mecca, with African rulers, heads of families, and common people undertaking the hadj, or pilgrimage, for renewal of faith with Allah for themselves, their subjects, their households, and of the brotherhood of the Moslem faith.

To a large extent, Islam was able to acclimatize itself in Africa more successfully than Christianity. Its egalitarian nature and its combination of orthodoxy and new ideas—e.g., its allowing local religions to continue their practice, its acceptance of polygyny (thereby maintaining the traditional family and clan structures), and its encouragement to the giving of alms—enabled it to maintain a communalistic system based on public feasts and celebrations not too different from the indigenous system. Its theology was much simpler for the African to grasp than Christianity as it avoided tangled theological quibbles. Above all, its religion was a way of life, a social and political institution, with rituals that brought it closer in form to African religious systems. It produced a strong African elite, completely independent of outside interference in matters of theology and worship, who steered the practice of Islam into a generally harmonious coexistence with older religious institutions. Its message of love, charity, and tolerance was translated into practical everyday terms, for the worship of Allah rests on the three points of love, charity, and fraternity. Its non-racist orientation, seen in the community of worship for both white and black, reveals it as a more progressive faith than Christianity.

Educationally, Islam's influence has been minimal. It lacked the funds and the formalist approach of the Christian missions necessary for it to be able to make any significant impact in this area. Its educational system was limited to the study and digestion of the

Holy Koran. The role of the learned men was to inculcate into the youth the day-to-day adherence to the law and letter of the faith. (It has been said that no one ever graduates from an Islamic school, since, strictly speaking, there can be no end of its demands on the individual adherents in the educational sense.)

Islam's impact on African social structure was enforced through the system of taboos and fasts enjoined by its law and holy men, but its lack of scientific approach made it lose ground to Euro-Christian culture. Moslem culture was neither distinctive nor homogeneous, and it had no clear-cut body of opinions to present a coherent pattern. Moreover, it was tradition bound and presented no challenge to the culturally aggressive Western system. But it was amenable to change, and it was accommodating as far as the traditional religious systems with which it agreed to coexist were concerned.

If the impact—political, social, and economic—of Islam has been minimal, it is because it has lacked an internationally oriented, politically backed power base and a concerted sociocultural program of indoctrination and control. The importance of the Islamic centers across the Sahara diminished through the political conquest of these areas by a succession of other invaders, including Turks and Europeans. The Berber empires and the united Maghrib dominion had been broken up by the middle of the sixteenth century and the important trade in gold had been diverted by the maritime trade. Where Islamic political states survived in sub-Saharan Africa, they were superseded by the European colonial powers who conquered and annexed them in the late nineteenth century. Most of the political conquests in the name of Islam represented inspired zeal without the backing of administrative skill and were, thus, sporadic and short-lived. Successive attempts to purify the faith and return it to its pristine state or insulate it against contamination by indigenous religious systems were, at times, marred by unnecessary fanaticism and bloodshed, which weakened rather than strengthened these efforts. Besides, Islamic missionaries and traders were readily absorbed into the indigenous culture and, in some instances, even if their influence remained obtrusive, this served only to create hybrid cultures such as Hausa and Swahili. Islamic university centers such as Al Azhar in Cairo became moribund and were superseded by Western type institutions. It was only as recently as 1962 that Al Azhar established faculties of medicine, agriculture, engineering, and management to expand beyond its original medieval curricula of Islamic law and religious sciences.

The colonial assault on Africa also took Islamic culture on the continent by storm. The traditional systems fought to keep themselves intact, while Islam struggled to resist Western ways and the corrupting effects of the Christian invader and his materialist outlook. But the military power of European colonialism swept aside the political power of Islam wherever it existed. Islamic religious and cultural features, however, suffered only minimal interference, as is evidenced today in the Sudan and northern Nigeria. At times, colonial rulers warned missionaries away from Moslem cities; this became a factor in the alleged educational backwardness of these areas today. It was to take a long time to work out a compromise between Christian education and Islam so that African children could keep their Moslem faith, since to receive Western type education, it was assumed, one would have to be a Christian.

It has been estimated that a larger number of Africans are now under the influence of Islam than before the establishment of the colonial regimes. This is the case particularly in large urban centers like Kano and Lagos and in the north-central parts of most of the West African nations. With the rapid urbanization of diverse groups, it is only natural that their religious attention would be directed by one of the two large religious systems rather than by the fragmented and locally oriented African religious structures. Besides, these two religions attract people across group boundaries, providing a unifying factor in what is generally an amorphous community. Islam tends to draw its adherents from the large community of common people and migrant workers who have wandered from distant homelands and find a ready support in the brotherhood that the faith provides. Because it lacks a formalist, elitist approach to worship (in this sense it resembles the apostolic or evangelical Christian Churches which also cater to the urban poor) and does not insist upon status, formal attire, or a great social showing, Islam draws to its ranks the very ordinary people hurled together by economic demands into the precarious situation of urban living. Its social laws pertaining to marriage, divorce, property, and responsibility are simple and straightforward, while its theology, after centuries of warring among factions, has settled down into a simple spiritual outlook which concerns itself both with man's survival on earth and his aspirations toward Paradise. Christianity, with its hierarchy of theologies, outlooks, and priests, appeals more to the social climbers and the *evolués*, while Islam's adherents are mainly the lower classes—laborers, farmers, and unskilled workers. The roles of the imams and the Marabouts (hermit saints) still approximate those of the diviners and priests of the indigenous religions. Their contact with their adherents is direct and their help visible.

4

The move for independence

The emergence of Africa into world politics today can be traced back to the close of last century, with the introduction of Western political concepts. However haphazardly pursued, colonialism, in a negative way, prepared Africa for the task of independence. As it planted its political divisions and sociocultural barriers, colonialism threw together peoples with different languages and at different levels of political development. The vertical divisions of the colonial enclaves and holdings weakened horizontal patterns and shattered what in many cases were homogeneous units. Some areas, like Eweland, had their political units splintered and divided among three conquerors. Others, like Yorubaland and Igboland, were hurled into other political arrangements or units, thus destroying the bases of their homogeneity through their expected participation in new and, at times, irksome political alliances.

By the turn of the twentieth century, a few intrepid Africans had begun traveling overseas under their own steam, often spurred on by the great family wealth of merchant princes in places such as Cape Coast, Lagos, Freetown, and Sekondi. The impact of returning Africans such as Edward Blyden, Horton Africanus, and the freed slaves that settled Sierra Leone and Liberia was enormous. Even though a large number of those who returned from the New World were caught in the syndrome of reverse snobbery and total disregard of the native African's political plight, there was a vocal minority of them who were redefining themselves and their countries in ideologically progressive anticolonial terms. These voices were later joined by those of men like John Mensah Sarbah and Casely Hayford of the Gold Coast, Herbert Macaulley and later Nnamdi Azikiwe of Nigeria, Wallace Johnson of Sierra Leone, and a host of others. The work of the American W. E. B. Du Bois, whose earliest active involvement stretched as far back as the Versailles Conference in 1919, where he arranged the first Pan-African Congress, is of overwhelming importance and continued through his later impact on the young African students who gathered in Manchester, England, in 1945. It was at the Manchester conference that the clearest political manifesto was issued attacking the very basis of colonialism and exposing it for the exploitative economic system it was, one designed solely to wrench wealth from Africa and create large markets for the dumping of European goods. In his booklet *Towards Colonial Freedom* written between 1942 and 1945 and privately published in 1946 for the first time, Kwame Nkrumah of the Gold Coast spelled out the political orientation of the new African voice, attacking in virulent terms political subjugation and denial of basic freedoms, the necessary corollaries for the implementation of the colonial economic plan.

The Manchester conference, which met to discuss the question of colonial freedom, included figures such as George Padmore from Trinidad, who later became Nkrumah's African policy architect; Jomo Kenyatta, now President of Kenya; Kwame Nkrumah; and many other African politicians. For the first time, political activists from the New World met with young and restless agitators from Africa to draw up a program for freedom. The conference's charter attacked colonialism in pseudo-Marxist language and exposed the so-called benevolent and civilizing aims of the colonial plan as sheer cant and hypocrisy. It drew attention to the degradation which economic tutelage led to and exposed the humiliation which the African peasants and workers were suffering within a system that claimed its basis in Christian ethics and morality. Coming right after the Second World War, with its dire economic consequences and untold misery, the conference opened the eyes of some of the so-called liberals in Europe who began to think seriously about the alliance between capitalist exploitation and the colonial phenomenon.

It must be remembered that Britain, the world's largest imperialist power, had already been under continuous pressure from the "naked Indian fakir" (Churchill's words) Mahatma Gandhi. With the independence of India in 1947, Britain lost the most glittering jewel in her imperial crown. The strip-down of her colonial empire had begun.

It was not until 1948 that the first major concerted assault was made upon the British African colonial empire beyond a few sporadic and disorganized efforts in the previous two decades or so. This assault took place in the Gold Coast, which until then had been regarded as a model colony. Strikes and boycotts preceded the march of ex-servicemen on the Castle, the seat of government, to present a petition to the British governor asking for the fulfillment of promises made to them for their part in the Second World War. A nervous British police officer opened fire, and the struggle for independence truly began, gathering momentum after years of poor organization. Nkrumah, who had learned a great deal from Gandhi's non-violence movement, adopted a series of positive actions which forced Britain to reconsider the whole question of her African empire. An enlightened governor, Sir Charles Arden-Clarke, was sent out by Whitehall to supervise the period of transition and the transfer of power to the African people on March 6, 1957, thus ending an active British control that had officially lasted for one hundred and thirteen years. Thus was born Ghana, the first black nation south of the Sahara to gain independence from Britain. This event began the whole process of decolonization.

Meanwhile, Nigeria, the largest of Britain's holdings in Africa, was going through a slow transition to self-rule, with such irksome issues as regional autonomy, devolution of powers, and federation on her mind. The basis of that country's recent problems must be traced back to the federal experiment and arrangements of the pre-independence era.

The first independence experiment in Ghana had far-reaching effects on Africa. The All-African People's Conference, held in Accra, December 1958, a legitimate successor of the 1945 Manchester conference, provided within the bosom of a free country, the blueprint of African independence. The continent was not to be the same again.

Between 1958 and 1962, the British colonial empire in Africa came to an end. With the dismantling of the ill-conceived Central African Federation and the so-called Mau Mau revolt, aimed at regaining land for the Africans, East and Central Africa became virtually self-governing with the exception of the territory of Rhodesia, which was held by a white minority. Britain's remaining dependencies, like Gambia and the high commission territories of Swaziland, Lesotho, and Botswana, were granted independence later.

The Belgian Congo, under the nationalist attacks of Patrice Lumumba, who was later martyred by divisive forces in both Léopoldville (now Kinshasa) and Katanga province, achieved independence from Belgium in 1960.

The French colonial empire had suffered from instability under the fortnightly governments of the postwar Fourth Republic. France's military upsets in Indochina, where the colonial forces were pounded into defeat by the guerrilla armies of Ho Chi Minh, had scarcely been adjusted to when the Algerian nationalists took to the mountains. France's dilemma was rooted in a colonial policy that treated overseas colonies as departments of metropolitan France. The *loi cadre* of 1956 introduced a measure of internal autonomy. In 1958 De Gaulle promulgated the Fifth Republic, which created the French Community, extended internal self-rule to France's overseas territories, and brought the African territories under the new constitution. This constitution was decided by the famous *oui-ou-non* referendum which offered two options to the African territories. Only Guinea voted for full independence outside the Community and suffered the consequences of having all French technical assistance withdrawn. By August 1960 the Community's constitution was amended to allow independent African countries to remain members (along the same lines as the British Commonwealth, except in the French system the socioeconomic ties are stronger).

Independence brought an era of euphoria and great hopes to Africa. The dreams of agitators and nationalists were realized when one by one new flags were hoisted in place of colonial flags, and new tunes replaced imperial anthems. In Kinshasa a Congolese participant in the independence celebrations made off with King Baudouin's sword. Nkrumah wept openly and unashamedly at Accra's Old Polo Ground in the balmy night of March 5, 1957. In many countries there were massive jubilations, and many libations were poured and drunk. There was a vague sense of relief among the African people, who were only dimly aware of the nature of the changes in their fortune; everywhere there was talk of Africa's new man: bright-eyed, armed with the righteousness of his cause, ready to take his place in the sun, self-assured, and no longer abused. Aggressively proud, he was to become, once and for all, the master of his own house.

The only colonial enclaves in sub-Saharan Africa left by the mid-1960s were the Portuguese-held territories of Angola, Guinea-Bissau, and Mozambique; the small scattered Spanish-held pockets on the coast of West Africa; the minority-ruled state of Rhodesia, which Britain insists is illegally governed; and the apartheid bastion of South Africa. Britain still claims imperial responsibility for Rhodesia and for the fate of the African majority, while it watches helplessly as the lineaments of racial segregation and white supremacist laws are being extended across the territory from the south.

South Africa, dominated by a Boer majority party of white supremacists and governed by a barbaric code of racial superiority reminiscent of Nazi Germany, has persistently defied the attempts (halfhearted in many cases) of world organizations, such as the United Nations, the International Council of Jurists, and the World Council of Churches, to name only a few, to induce it to return to an enlightened system of government. From the Act of the Union in 1910 to the rise of Daniel Malan and the Nationalist party in 1948, it was clear that the successive colonial governments of Britain were unconcerned about the fate of the majority of Africans. Today, with the apartheid system of the Boers firmly entrenched and the investment of the international business community increasing by leaps and bounds, it is impossible to see a single light at the end of the dark, sinister tunnel of racism and bigotry. The mighty empire of the Zulu has been reduced to a pathetic "tribal" reservation tailored for inferior education and the inculcation of racial inferiority. The vast urban communities of refugee Africans of South Africa are economically at the mercy of vast white combines supported and protected by army, police, and concentration camps. Perhaps of all the detribalized societies on the continent, South Africa represents the most dismal result of the colonial assault and the criminal misuse of power by a foreign invader in our times.

The rise of political organizations such as the African Nationalist Congress and the Pan-Africanist Congress had led to renewed agitation in South Africa which was brutally suppressed. The laws of racial separation—among them the obnoxious Immorality Act (which prohibits sexual intercourse between a black and a white), the Group Areas Act, and the Bantu Education Act—continue to be tightened and maintained by one of the most efficient and repressive police apparatuses in the world today. The more than seventeen million Africans, Coloreds, and Asians continue to be held down by fewer than four million whites while the Western world continues her lucrative business relations with the inheritors of Hitler's political mantle. A good deal of supporting argument will be forthcoming to rationalize the continued alliance, one of them being that South Africa represents a bulwark against international communism, an argument as spurious as it is phony in the context of twentieth-century realities.

The significant fact is that though 90 per cent of Africa is independent, it is clear that this is only a nominal independence. Africa continues to be a large producer of raw materials for the factories of Europe and America and in return is the receiver of finished products from overseas. The prices of some of her raw materials, namely, timber, cocoa, palm produce, and coffee, continue to fall as a result of a manipulatory trade system loaded in favor of the buyers against the sellers. The price of finished products with increased costs in production—capital outlay and labor—soars beyond the means of most African nations and absorbs much of the slim earnings which the raw materials accumulate in order to pay for these goods. In many cases, more than 70 per cent of the national income is spent on them. So in spite of the flags and anthems, African countries have become heavily indebted to the European and

American powers (the "fraternal" countries of Eastern Europe and the U.S.S.R. have also joined in with slogans and fanfare). Sitting on vast resources, the African nations can hardly make ends meet because the economic systems in which they are forced to exist cannot and do not operate in their favor.

Besides this staggering economic disability, the growth of African political processes has been vitiated by unnecessary interference from outside, downright corruption, and blatant abuse and misuse of power. Many of the new leaders, acclaimed and catapulted to great heights by mass popularity, turn into cheap tyrants and petty crooks whose erstwhile virtues as anticolonial combatants are replaced by autocratic tendencies and who openly rifle the national coffers for private purposes. Some, ensnared by the terrifying demands of power, prove vacillatory, weak, and completely under the thumb of foreign financial interests and political bodies, to whom they mortgage their nations' resources in return for a few crumbs. The colonial patterns have thus been neatly replaced generally by neocolonialism, a system of exploitation without responsibility.

The succession of military coups in Africa since 1965 has thrown the contradictions of African independence into bold relief. These coups in themselves are only manifestations of a deep-seated malaise that has afflicted the African body politic, dramatizing in the dash for power the interest of an elitist minority in uniform, armed with the most sophisticated weapons that money can buy. What is not apparent to this soldiery (because of its essentially colonial orientation) is that the money paid for an armored car could provide a small-size clinic for a village of five hundred people and ensure it a steady supply of essential drugs for at least one year. But these coups, as they occur in rapid alternation, continue to bear testimony to Africa's frenetic search for some type of true independence.

Part II

Traditional Africa

When the slave trade and slavery became illegal, the experts on Africa yielded to the new wind of change, and now began to present African culture and society as being so rudimentary and primitive that colonialism was a duty of Christianity and civilization. . . . Our highly sophisticated culture was said to be simple and paralysed by inertia and we had to be encumbered with tutelage.

KWAME NKRUMAH, *Consciencism*

5

Traditional African society and its philosophy

An underlying unity of structure runs through the various patterns of African traditional society. These patterns, as suggested, have all been shaped by a fairly unified historical experience, shared cultural impacts from external sources, and, above all, by a large degree of interaction of one culture with another. Africa's history over the last one thousand and more years is the story of travels and migrations. These important factors had been responsible, with varying degrees of consistency, for a coherence in certain features of African life. It suggests that seemingly isolated peoples in remote mountain areas have had dealings and even affinity with grassland dwellers and vice versa. But the analysis of this hypothesis belongs elsewhere, and I will attempt here only the tracing of some of the patterns in the traditional fabric.

The traditional African society existed and was organized upon certain basic concepts and ideas of the universe and man. Pietistic rather than purely juristic, African society placed man at the center of the universe. The earliest myths of most African peoples are those of the coming of man or of his creation and establish the existence of certain preternatural powers. These powers, invariably identified as the primal force, the Creator God, or the all-powerful, summon out of their indeterminate will or create from their own hand the first parents. Man himself derives his essence from the

Great Ancestor, the Supreme Deity, and the source of life. Man compounds within this essence the totality of a universal consciousness which admits of all things. Life and death exist in an indistinguishable continuum. Man's divinity, however, is in his finite essence, and it is from this that his conduct within the world (spiritual and physical) is determined. Man, therefore, admits of a certain spirituality, a finite physical and religious essence partaking of the Great Ancestor's procreative power, His imminence, His transcendence, and His power to withdraw into the spirit world in order to function as a force for good over the living. It is from this position that Africa accepts the trinity of the dead, the living, and the yet unborn as the eternal cyclic order in which the rites of passage of the living form only an infinitesimal journey or stage. In order for the individual to move into the spiritual abode of the revered Great Ancestor, the necessary rites of passage from birth to death shall have been observed as marking important enlargements or extensions of the original essence which will come into its own after death.

The spirituality of man is the primary reason for the totality of religion in man's life. It is in this spirituality that the trinity mentioned earlier has meaning. The ancestors, those that have gone through the journey, directed by the guiding spirit, join the countless ones that went before. Blood, being the most meaningful force for the living, also unites them to the dead; thus, no family diminishes. The ancestors, by their death, become minor deities in the spiritual hierarchy. They are bound by blood and in constant touch with their descendants. They act as guides and protectors. They are, in what has been mistakenly called "ancestor worship," invoked to give help to their family descendants. In what is essentially an act of communion, an active line of communication is kept open between the living and the dead. The ancestors are respected because they are our predecessors, our elders, and above all they exist in the spiritual state in which they know more than we do since they "can see in the dark." The ceremony of invocation, or libation, brings the dead, the living, and the unborn together in a communion. Like other minor deities, the ancestors can be both praised for achievement and rebuked for failure. Each family, or lineage, remembers its revered ancestors and on important occasions, such as births or funerals, offers prayers and drinks in ritual renewal of this bond.

To speak of the nature of religion in any traditional African society is to attempt to isolate what is the very essence of the society. For the whole society is based on the proper direction of the religious and spiritual obligations of man toward the hierarchical structure in which he takes his own place in all the three stages of his life. Man, in his lonely and at times frightening confrontation with the universal force, seeks harmony and all its attendant good things. The African established, from time immemorial, a spiritual hierarchy which reveals a cunning understanding of natural phenomena and a clever talent for manipulating them toward good for himself and evil for his enemies. Beneath the Creator God is a host of minor deities. By the light of his own logic, the African assigns to the Creator God a certain degree of distance and unapproachability, not because he considers Him unconcerned, but rather because he thinks of Him in his primal ancestral role as the supreme paterfamilias who must not be bothered with the petty details of the universe. He, Himself, appoints lieutenants and assistants who become overseers and guardians of various natural phenomena and faculties. These minor deities are the recipients of sacrifices and messages for the Creator God. He, whom the Ewe calls Mawu, receives no sacrifice Himself; He has neither shrines nor priests.

The intermediaries of the Ewe or *Voduwo* pantheon include Xebieso, or So, the god of thunder who is still actively worshiped today in Eweland; Da, or the snake god; Legba, the household god who oversees domestic harmony and fertility; Gu, the god of iron and all its derivatives; Anyievo, the rainbow god, who is also the rain god; Sakpana, the smallpox god; and a host of other gods whose dwelling places are in hills, rivers, trees, or caves. The Yoruba intermediaries, or *orisha,* include Eshu, the god of fate; Sonponna, the god of smallpox; Shango, the god of thunder; Ogun, the god of fire, hunting, war, and iron; Oshun, the river goddess; Erinle, the god of the forest. A fairly similar deital structure can be found in most traditional African societies.

These minor deities are the Creator God's representatives on earth. They intervene and interfere in the ordering of the spiritual community in which man and the forces of nature are one and interdependent. The institution of these minor deities is an attempt to make sure of the Creator's succor and even to influence it. The minor deities are set up through the priest mediums who function as their spokesmen, oracles, and prophets. Thus, the Creator's power, undefinable and hidden, spreads from the purely religious and spiritual to the social. The minor deities function as consultants to the omniscience of the Creator for order, health, longevity, success, good harvest, rain, avoidance and averting of disaster, and peace among men. They are always associated with a natural phenomenon to which they can be summoned at will. They are sent by the Creator Himself, usually in a flash of lightning. His essence is caught and reposited by the priest and enshrined in any natural object or in a carving. This object, or focus, is not itself sacred; it can be destroyed or renewed at will.

There is assumed to be a close association between the Creator and his subordinates, an association that is extended to man too. Some of these minor deities, like Shango or Ogun of the Yoruba, live in legends as being among man's earliest ancestors. Some derive their powers and attributes from natural phenomena such as Da of the Ewe, whose spiritual derivative is the rainbow, strange and endowed with magical powers, precursor of rain and twined around the earth in an ominous arch. Others, like gods of the sea or the moon, are deemed to possess special munificent powers, which man must actively court for good in order to ensure survival. Thunder, whose god is So among the Ewe, rides a white horse across the skies at certain times of the year and is a deity whose shrines and priests are extremely active even today in Eweland.

Religion and religious practice express the cosmology of the African world. Man's proper function is to exist according to the natural laws of the universe; if there is disaster, then it means that one or more of these laws has been broken and the harmonic chain is shattered. An individual's transgressions bring disaster upon the group. So the group, within whose womb the individual exists through blood and lineage, must as a whole be subjected to the act of cleansing and expiation. Discussing the role of the minor gods among the Akan of West Africa, W. E. Abraham, the Ghanaian philosopher, in his book *The Mind of Africa,* notes:

> Minor gods are artificial means to the bounty of Onyame (Creator God). They are instituted by priests between man and God, with the explanation that they are portions of God's virtue and power sent to men for their speedy comfort through exclusive intervention of the priests who also are their guardians.[1]

It is in the relationship between man and the Creator that art becomes a proper instrument of expression of man's world and a means of measuring his conception of the world beyond the grave. Art, in the puristic sense, is an instrument expressing man's will and wishes to the Creator, an assertion of his own temporality as a *living* being, and, more important, an articulate statement of that spirituality through a cyclic order within his cosmos. Art becomes an extension of the ritualism of the African mind; rites themselves assume serious spiritual importance.

6

Art, music, languages

Any discussion of art—masks, carving, sculpture, etc.—and its function in traditional African society south of the Sahara must be based in a broad philosophical system, which will establish a rational pattern of thought and ideas. This will *explain* somehow the very complex interrelationships and interdependence between *things* (material or matter) and spirits (gods and deities).

Man's essentialist view of himself and his society is the primary reason for the pervasive nature of religion. This essentialism extends to culture and "finds expression in the art, the ethics and morality, the literary and religious traditions and also the social traditions of the people."[1] Objects and things become aspects of this essentialist, or metaphysical, system without necessarily losing their rationalist functions. For example, trees store up medicinal juices in their leaves and roots and are cut down for wood or carving. But there is a tree spirit which partakes of an essentialist entity within the metaphysical order of things. It can be benign or malevolent. Man stands in the center of these opposing faculties and by his sharing of the divine (through the ancestors, deities, etc.), possesses the power to manipulate this spirit for his own benefit. Thus, it is in the relationship between man and the first ancestor, the Creator, that art becomes a proper instrument of man's world and an expression of the world beyond the grave. Thus the carvings that are part of various shrines are instruments of affirming the divine link between man and the Creator (mostly through intervening deities since the Supreme God himself has no shrine or priest). The carvings are the statements of man's homage to the gods; their makers were part of a spirituality, clean and without blemish in the eyes of the gods *during* the period they were engaged in creating such objects. Essentially religious, this art assayed in plastic form to capture the essence of the gods as received through spiritual contact and revelation. The art forms an abstract statement of the divinities' essential powers, never a realistic representation of such deities. For no one deity has one epiphanic form: Sakpana, the Ewe god of smallpox, appears in a thousand different guises, depending upon the spiritual state of his beholder. This religious nature, however, does not deny to art at times a purely secular role in that it also was used as a ready means of speaking about the world around. For we must also remember that this same society is fiercely rationalistic. Ideas that will provide solutions to mundane and, at times, desperate needs for survival are put forward with clarity.

Between secular and religious art there was never a rigid dividing line; the absolutism of religious modes, however, was paramount. W. E. Abraham describes traditional African art as not literary or descriptive but instead as "directly magical, attempting a sort of plastic analogue of onomatopoeia, to evince and evoke feelings. . . . It was a kind of para-ideology in wood, raffia, color and stone."[2] Its statement is one of very complex and incomprehensible forces that hold man in thrall and subject him to their will, make or break him by the presence or absence of a detente between them and him.

African art first struck the attention of the world through the so-called "startling discoveries" made by European art historians, connoisseurs, and explorers in the nineteenth and twentieth centuries. Mary Kingsley, the nineteenth-century English ethnologist, once referred to it as "large grotesque images carved in wood." When it became fashionable in Parisian art circles during the 1920s to rave about these objects, Jean Cocteau's tired remark that the rage for Negro art had become as big a bore as Mallarmé's Japonism was countered by Paul Guillaume's ecstatic reference to African art as the quickening seed of the spiritual twentieth century.[3]

Today the excesses of the 1920s exist only in the work of such a neo-Freudian as Ladislas Segy[4] in his almost atavistic attempt to explain Ashanti fertility carvings as derived from Egypt. Some degree of clear and objective interpretation and analysis of African art is now discernible in the works of such people as Dennis Duerden, Ulli Beier, Frank Willett, William Fagg, etc. Some of these writers are attempting to place African art within its proper ritualistic and religious milieu, to state the unity that exists between art and language through prayer and libation. Art historians are moving away from crude statements depicting African art as samples of "primitive sexuality." The so-called "relationship" between African art and the Cubist movement is interesting only in the sense that it shows that nature of the restless shifts which art theory undergoes at every period, especially within the Western tradition, which tires very quickly of newly acquired sensations. Whatever Cézanne, Vlaminck, Matisse, Picasso, Braque, or Léger took from African art has very little to do with the basic aspirations of this art. Some art critics, Segy included, are trying to deny that the Cubists learned *anything* at all from the Benin and Ife heads or from the Bakongo masks that became the rage of European art circles in the 1920s. The examination of the proper relationship between Cubism and African art, however, belongs to another sphere of comparative studies altogether.

Art is as old as the African peoples. Its function, as stated earlier, was primarily religious, emphasizing the people's need for magic and charm through talismanic objects and amulets and such other carvings that become the media of communication and contact with the spiritual world. It has also served as a medium of veneration, an assertion of the role and function of myths, gods, and ancestors. Religious cults use art forms; there are ancestral masks employed in the renewal of contact with the dead; masks used by secret societies, for example, the Poro of Liberia and Ogboni in Nigeria; masks for initiation as among the Mende; or masks for funeral purposes among the Dogon.

Masks, perhaps the most ubiquitous of the African art forms, having made a more lasting impression on outside observers, do have an immense significance in terms of their varied functions, meanings, modes, or forms from group to group. Their functions being primarily religious, they are the best expression of the African's dependence on symbolic forms and contact for emphasizing the intangible bonds linking man with the spiritual world. Among the Dogon, the dead themselves are said to ascribe masks to the living through dreams. They are the significant links in puberty and initiation rites. They can be described as the approximation of spirits or, more directly, the instruments or objects through which man obtains an instantaneous transfiguration into a spirit form. Baule double masks, Igbo *egwugwu,* or Yoruba *ogungun* masks represent spirits either ancestral or divine. The contemporary African writer Chinua Achebe presents a very vivid dramatization of the ominous authority and power of these ancestral masks among the Igbos in his novel *Things Fall Apart.* When human beings don the masks, they assume the power and voices of spirits. They can only be addressed by their preternatural names and are revered as such. It is an abomination to unmask a spirit. If this happens, the spirit dies and vengeance from the whole spiritual order can be swift and terrible. Masks perform such religious duties as driving away evil spirits, emphasizing within specific rites the concept of rebirth and renewal as in initiation rites, evoking blessings, or striving for unity between the living and the dead. They may assume purely secular roles as in entertainment. The *zagbeto* mask among the Ewe is a good example of this. The mask is at the center of an essentially ritualistic dramaturgy whose scope has not been properly explored owing to the tight secrecy that surrounds its very religious nature. The philosophy of this ritual rests in a complex structure of beliefs and in the sense of religious drama which is unfolded through the gestures, movements, and the dance of the mask. These are enhanced by the combination of colors, the proper use of such materials as raffia, cowries, pieces of cloth, mirrors, horns, etc.

Other art forms range from the terracotta heads identified with Nok culture in the plateau region of northern Nigeria (radiocarbon-dated as about three thousand years old) to the stone figures found in the sacred grove in Ilorin in Yorubaland. The Nok heads have their meaning in ancestral cults and rites and are very simple in form, while the later Ife types are elaborate and highly stylized.

Metal working has always been associated throughout Africa with worship and ritual. The secret of iron was revealed to man by the Great Ancestor through the god Gu (Ewe), or Ogun (Yoruba), who was the first ironworker. An elaborate pattern of iron art work is associated with the Benin, Ife, and Dahomey cultures. In Dahomey, objects depicting birds and animals, symbolic representations of the various wings of the royal clan, ceremonial gongs, and ornamented implements of war and work, such as hoes, spears, and short knives, form an essential part of this iron culture. In Ashanti, renowned oathing swords and other such symbolic instruments of chiefly authority are part of the art. But art work in iron was limited by the scarcity of and the high demand for the metal, mainly because of the religious importance attached to it, especially in the Yoruba, Benin, Fon, and Ewe country where the iron god is also an important medicine or healing god. Workers in iron form guilds linked with other guilds such as hunters or warriors. The elaborate poetry of the *ijala* chants of the Yoruba hunters is linked directly with Ogun who provides the incantations to accompany the celebration of his power.

Copper, silver, and gold have been in use since very early times, especially the latter metal, which drew early European travelers to West Africa, not to mention the trans-Saharan traders from Morocco and other Mediterranean seaports, since the early Middle Ages. Gold and silver are still ornamentally important to traditional royalty of several groups in West Africa. The power and divinity of the Asantehene in Central Ghana is stated in the splendor of his elaborate gold regalia, something which was coveted by a succession of British governors and the cause of many Anglo-Ashanti wars, which lasted till the first decade of this century. Some of the most intricate patterns, mainly of animals and heraldic symbols, are still being wrought by goldsmiths of Ghana, Guinea, and Liberia. Gold is perhaps the one metal in which purely ornamental art works are created. However, its working, like that of all the other metals, is linked to religions. Camara Laye, in his *L'Enfant Noir,* an account of his youth in Guinea, describes in very fascinating terms the mythic and mystical role his father assumed as he prepared to tackle an intricate work in gold.

Bronze and brass were common in Ashanti, where they were used for making the now-famous gold weights, also among the Yoruba of Ife, and in Benin where bronze forms were used by the ruling class and the cult priests of certain deities. Ashanti bronze work was limited almost entirely to the gold weights—small intricate representations of animals that depict legends and proverbs designed for lessons in morals and folk wisdom. The larger bronze works, *kuduo*, served as receptacles for gold dust. They were used as ceremonial vessels and covered with elaborate designs telling some legend or the other. Yoruba, Nupe, and Benin bronze works and notably the famous Ife heads seem almost real. Some represent death masks, at times lifelike representations of important kings, courtiers, and warriors. The large and elaborate sixteenth-century plaques, with pictures of the *oba* or chiefs, at the hunt, of hunters under trees, of deeds of dignitaries and kings, represent some of the only known pieces of landscape representation in traditional Africa, apart from the rock paintings of the so-called "Bushmen" done in red earth, charcoal, or white clay.

The use of bronze and brass spread as far south as the Bakota and Pogwe peoples in the Congo and as far west as modern-day Liberia, where the famous lost-wax method of casting has been extended. The ancient brassworkers' quarters of Benin City in Nigeria today is the most important center of knowledge of brass in West Africa.

Benin art is perhaps the best-known African art tradition outside the continent. This is because of the notorious sack of Benin in 1897 by a British expeditionary force that carried away to Europe art pieces conservatively estimated as numbering 2,400. Based on bronze and brass casting, these were the finest examples of a court art founded on the elaborate ritualism of kingship. This art flourished between the thirteenth and sixteenth centuries with the expansion of the Benin kingdom, passing on to the Ijebu, Igbo, Dahomey, Ewe, and Ashanti lands through conquest and peaceful contact. A series of expansionist wars depleted the coffers of the Benin state and blunted the efforts of the court artists. This led to an almost total artistic darkness for about two centuries until the

British sack of Benin, when the artists fled the city in confusion. It was not until 1915, with the death of the exiled Benin king and the ascension of his son, that the artists or their sons returned and set up shop once more. The sack of Benin indirectly spread the style of its art to Dahomey and elsewhere.

Other art objects are made of ivory and bone. The best of the ivory traditions exists in the Congo among the Warenga and the Bapende, in the Cameroons, in Benin, and in Yorubaland. Congolese tusks have become important additions to travelers' collections. Purely ornamental, they depict elaborate conglomerates of animals and other objects, created for use on ceremonial occasions. Some of these carved tusks are placed in the hollow tops of life-sized bronze heads on either side of ancestral shrines for kings. In Afa (Ewe) or Ifa (Yoruba) divination, small ivory wands are used.

The most widespread material used in African art is wood. It is the most commonplace, sharing with metals a high degree of spirituality. Being part of the dynamic universal force that reposes in all natural objects, the tree has always represented a powerful symbolic element expressive of the life force itself. A carver or sculptor who goes into the forest to cut down a tree must go through a ritual and make an offering to the tree spirit, whose pardon and help he must seek in his venture. An egg is broken against the trunk and the following prayer, with variants from place to place, is offered:

> I am coming to cut you down and carve you, receive this egg and eat, let me be able to cut you and carve you. Do not let iron cut me; do not let me suffer in health.

After the appropriate ceremonies, the tree is cut and brought home and deposited in the carving shrine. In the case of purely religious works, the sculpting is done some distance away from the profane gaze of women and children. Characteristically, African sculpture is hewn out of single pieces of wood. This is to enable the work to keep its integrity and also the wood to keep its grain. Besides, the form of the wood itself may determine the over-all expression in the work. In the carving of deities the god himself is supposed to intervene and impose the form he wishes to take. The result is the artist's unconscious expression of the god, manipulated, directed, and realized by the god himself through the wood. There is no rigid structural principle, but an almost predetermined sense of rhythm and movement. The head, as the seat of knowledge, wisdom, and the spirit, receives prominence in disproportion to other parts. The countenance—the eyes, nose, mouth—is expressive of these spiritual faculties; it is almost always exaggerated. This pronounced aspect of the countenance constitutes a calculated attempt to convey the magical dimensions of the interplay between man and spirits and the secret forces of nature and the universe. The head is normally represented by round forms, juxtaposed with the angular features of the limbs—a style later absorbed by Cubism as one of its basic principles. In the carving of deities there is a certain unconscious abstract effort to create the visible image of the spirit, an incorporeal and formless entity placed beyond time and space and, in the final analysis, beyond man himself, especially in man's living state. It is presumed, therefore, that the mental state in which the artist creates is sacred and pure. What results is the transfiguration and distillation of the essence of this estate, a conceptual realization or imitation of a certain religiously predetermined psychic intent, an ultimate abstraction of the essence. The impulses that go into these creations are both human and spiritual. It is this perfect, or imperfect, co-ordination that results in the artistic or, better still, religious statement.

The objet d'art (a highly inadequate term) made of wood ranges from deities to fertility symbols. Deities themselves are represented by their symbols, their messengers or medium; animals are represented by their totemic symbols. Deital sculptures may be placed in the shrine of the god, used in the proper rites when he is given sacrifices, or they can serve as symbols of the spirit during mask dances. Others, like the fertility figurines—e.g., the *ekuamma* of the Ashanti—serve as spiritual or psychic inducements to comeliness of form or beauty. The twin doll among the Ewe represents the dead brother or sister who remains a companion to the living twin throughout his or her lifetime. Some of the wood carvings, like a good many of the Benin bronze heads, are archival in the sense that they serve both as pictorial records of dead kings and as ancestral masks.

What is important is the spiritual energy of the sculpture. This emerges in the exaggerated and dramatized features that struck Mary Kingsley as grotesque. The artist was the spokesman of the collective outlook of the group, expressing its fears, desires, and aspirations. But, as this writer becomes more and more convinced, the artist in the traditional society is not without a sense of fallibility. In spite of the group authority and will, he often falters and fails; then his work will come to express his own individual agonies or joys. This is very true of the poet in this same societal context. His own overwhelming religious sense of purpose is not always necessarily shared by the whole people in a situation in which gods are made and unmade. The prevalent notion that denies the artist in the so-called "primitive" society of Africa any individuality tends to underrate the very nature of the creative impulse itself. The individual artists are responsible for change, even though change can be forced by external factors upon the whole group. New styles cross frontiers, artists' children emigrate to or marry wives from distant groups. A whole style may be imported with social or political upheavals, as was seen in the spread of Benin art westward in the late nineteenth century. In essence, the artist alone, in a religious sense, becomes the medium through which the god transmits his will. The function of the artist is close to that of the priest. At times he is one and the same person. It is for this reason that most of the time the skill is handed down from father to son and, above all, that a rigid system of apprenticeship is enforced until the young artist branches out on his own.

It is not entirely true to say that all art in Africa has a religious function. Art, like all aspects of life, hinges on man's sacred or ritualistic relationship with the dynamic force. This does not deny decorative art its proper place simply because its primary aspiration is not toward the divine. Pottery, weaving, dyeing, to mention only a few forms, have also been embodiments of some of the aesthetic ideals of African life. On the seagoing canoes of the Ewe or Fanti fishermen are elaborate carvings of fishes, animals, and other things. Calabashes are highly decorated. The famous Ashanti *adinkra* cloth is not only a study in intricate patterns but also a statement in folklore and ontology. Tibor Bodrogi, in his otherwise (photographically) impressive book, states that there is no *l'art pour l'art* in Africa since this is an essential development in only so-called "higher" civilizations. This is as ignorant a remark as it is Eurocentric. In the well-known Ewe performance and drumming style called *adzro*, this writer recalls the numerous *dufozi* (art objects) depicting pageants, love scenes, and scenes of the hunt that went on display in the village square hours before the performance started. Its very name means "town gathers to see." The *zagbeto* masks are children's masks made purposely for the entertainment of children. The carvings on the boats referred to above were simple statements in aesthetics. Purely decorative functions are served by a good deal of what goes into the chief's regalia among the Ashanti. Beads, various types of hairdos, decorated and ornamented shields (never used in battle), costumes for ceremonial dances, decoration on houses, and, at cooking places, ornamental mats and pottery are all samples of objects of high aesthetic appeal.

A great deal of African wood sculpture has not been preserved. This accounts for earlier nineteenth-century European travelers' erroneous assertions that Africa lacked any artistic traditions. In purely religious art, renewal has always been a primary principle rigidly observed. So masks used in an ancestral dance one year may not be used the next. Among the Temne in Sierra Leone, they are thrown away on the outskirts of the village. In several places they are collected and burned or buried. Even objects serving as the mediums for deities may be promptly discarded after the rites and festivals are over. To hang onto them may bring ill health. When the rites are imminent, the priests commission new objects. The renewal principle is at work in most parts of Africa because it falls within the concept of rebirth and the rites of passage, which are in themselves processional advances, with marked out climacterics, made by man on his road to the final spiritual state as a revered ancestor. The "termite theory" of European art historians—that insects destroyed the carvings, thus forcing the African artist to create new ones continually—this writer considers as bogus and trite. Besides, it is not as if African carvers were completely helpless in the face of these ravaging ants. Herbal concoctions exist that are applied to wood used in buildings to prevent termites from eating them; fumigation is another age-old method. The preserva-

tion of art work from termites, if it were desirable, would not have
been an overwhelming burden.

Traditional art still exists today, especially in the largely segmented religious communities, in the shrines of the gods Ogun,
Shango, and medicine deities. A good deal of this art has been
subject to high-pressure European-type commercialism, hence the
emergence of the so-called "airport art" seen in all African capitals.
Founders of art schools, mostly Europeans, have also flushed out
of their natural habitat a large corps of traditional artists and
herded them into the cities where they are taught European art
principles and theories. Some of these art institutes in Africa, especially in schools and teacher-training colleges, have deliberately
ignored traditional art in the main and have gone to Europe for
their models and inspiration. All these factors, coupled with the
slow demise of great courts like those of Benin or Abomey and the
loss of interest by African notables who, in the past, served as
patrons, have all been responsible for the redirection of the art of
Africa.

African art must be evaluated per se according to its own principles, concepts, and preoccupations, as an integral tradition subject to its own laws of change and adaptation. There is a great deal
of sorrow in European and American art circles over the loss of
the old art forms, the commercialization of art in Africa, the death
of court art, and the disappearance of traditional religious institutions which were the greatest inspirers of art in Africa. This is a
vain regret, because Africa, in the very nature of her contact with
Europe and the Middle East and her exposure to the practices of
the European-directed twentieth century is undergoing revolutionary and traumatic changes. In the imminent demise of traditional
gods and shrines, new institutions are being forged, however
haphazardly and painfully. The sociopolitical changes taking place
in Africa are in themselves indicative of the changes in artistic
norms and preoccupations with which we shall deal later.

Music and dance are integral parts of the religiocultural features of the African continent. Music has traditionally been part of
religious rites and ceremonies, funeral and birth rites, and entertainment. The Ewe assemblies called *vu* include religious, war,

medicinal, and lovers' performances. These are not necessarily programmed by orchestral pieces or musical ensembles, though there may be significant moments when specific musical instruments are used. They are marked rather by the rhythm, mood, and tonal quality of each performance. The religious assemblies celebrate aspects of worship in honor of specific gods, such as So, the thunder god, while the medicinal performances celebrate aspects of cure and medicine in specific shrines, such as Dente or Tigare, cure deities. The funeral assemblies feature rites called *agoha* or *akpalu,* which are most popular among the Ewe of the south. Music plays significant roles in the work of various cult and occupational groups such as priests, blacksmiths, fishermen, farmers, and hunters. Above all, music also serves as an instrument of censure. The *halo,* or song of abuse, among the Ewe is a typical example. In politics, social organizations, religion, and all other significant social functions music has a significant place. Songs have been used to record history and to give praise.

Among most African peoples, the importance of song lies in its verbal scope. Rhythm and beat are essential ingredients that determine the dance. The dance becomes the interpretation of the occasion. There are dances for royalty, for commoners, for priests, dances for specific religious and social functions. The Ewe proverb "How the drum beats determines the way you move your feet" emphasizes the importance of the relationship between the dance movement and the rhythm being played by the drum.

The relationship between the word, that is, the verbal form, and music and art cannot be rigidly codified. Music, sculpture, and language exist within the same boundaries of social and religious use. The *wando* mask dance of the Mossi (in Upper Volta and Mali) is accompanied by chants and panegyrics in a secret language. The mask is addressed, implored, and hailed in a series of heraldic expressions. The sculptor's art is verbalized through libations, music, and dance. The mask itself is a study in mobility, and it enhances the spiritual state through the dance. At the initiation rites of the Mende, the dance forms part of the journey into maturity.

While art forms are the visible manifestations of the emotional concerns of their creators and their groups, and the music and

dance the mobile and aural features of highly important social and
religious expressions, the word has the final authority. The sacredness of words is evidenced by the prevalence of secret or cult languages; the words in every song are the only element communicable
to the mind, while the rhythm moves the hearer to movement. The
power and sanctity of the oath underscore the pre-eminence of
the word.

The music–language relationship is clear from the very nature
of oral literature in Africa. In the folktale, which in essence is a
dramatic performance, music plays a major role.

It is estimated that there are about eight hundred major languages in Africa. These are divided into seven broad-based groups.
These are the Niger-Congo, Western Sudanic, Nilotic, Central Saharan, Afro-Asiatic, Khoisan, and Bantu. These classifications,
based on Greenberg's work, run into difficulties now and then
because of new and continuously developing influences on the
languages. Some of them have been influenced by non-African
languages, like Arabic, in which case they are classified Hamito-
Semitic. But the linguistic map of Africa is still a formidable jungle
of conjectures and theoretical postulations, in spite of Greenberg's very valiant efforts.

African languages share certain distinctive features. These common characteristics are the result of contact between peoples during
the period of the great migrations and later contact between settled
communities through bellicose expansion or peaceful trade. Some
phonetic and semantic features are shared, but that should not be
stressed over perhaps the major characteristic of tonality.

Tone, or pitch, occurs in most of the major African languages,
with exception of the Afro-Asiatic group (the Hamito-Semitic languages of North Africa, the Horn of Africa, Ethiopia, and areas
near Lake Chad). Tone serves both grammatical and lexical functions. In Ewe, for example, the word *to* with a rising pitch pattern
means *rhino,* to *boil, mortar, ear,* and *mountain.*

Apart from tone (which is also a common feature of some
Asian and American Indian languages, including Vietnamese and
Hopi), there are certain features that are peculiar to African lan-
guages. A well-known example is the click of certain Bantu lan-

guages of southern Africa, particularly Xhosa. There are also the consonantal clusters of most of the West African languages—*kp* and *gb* of Ewe, Yoruba, and Igbo function phonetically as one sound—and implosive consonantal sounds. The morphological features of African languages reveal a very complex pattern of prefixes for nouns and derivatives of verbs. The word for *patriotism* in Ewe is *dedulolo*, which is a combination of *dedu, homeland*, and *lolo, love*. To *sing* in Ewe is *dzi ha*, singing is *hadzidzi;* note that the last word uses repetition, which is also a feature of the affixation in most African languages. There is also a series of verbal derivatives to express reflexive, passive, and causative moods.

One of the most outstanding features of African languages are the elements called "ideophones." These convey an idea in sound and are used to convey emotion. Sometimes they function as adverbs and, at times, as interjections. Here is an example from Ewe:

Efo tome ne kpāā = He slapped his ear hard.

Notice that the last word, *kpāā,* conveys the sound made by the slap to demonstrate its loudness and intensity. Or in

Evli vadavada = He struggled wildly.

Vadavada is the ideophonic word for the way, or manner, in which he struggled.

The nature of most African languages gives them certain qualities which are exploited very well in the oral literature. Phonic qualities include the ideophones and verbal features such as affixation, an important factor in Zulu oral verse, for example. Important semantic features are the idioms, imagery derived from nature, and figurative use of language to add color and solemnity, especially in praise poems. The tonal quality, which lends musical and rhythmic effect through tonal assonance by way of patterning, becomes very important to the Yoruba *ijala* chant.

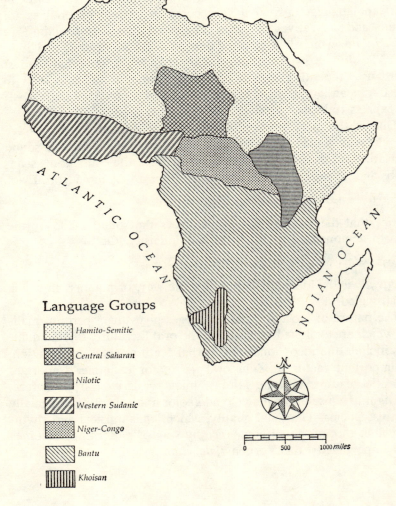

Language Groups

- Hamito-Semitic
- Central Saharan
- Nilotic
- Western Sudanic
- Niger-Congo
- Bantu
- Khoisan

ATLANTIC OCEAN

INDIAN OCEAN

0   500   1000 *miles*

Oral literature: Ritual drama, prose narrative, poetry

In discussing oral literature in Africa, it must be understood that we are discussing a large body of material which can have its total integrity, impact, and realization only within the scope of performance, transmission, and occasion. The performer of oral literature gives body to the material, formulates it, and realizes it, within regulated and specified occasions such as funerals. Transmission means the instruments used. This is the total cultural context of this literature which we can classify broadly as drama, prose narrative, and poetry.

Drama includes masquerades, festivals, ritual performances, and ceremonies pertaining to the secret societies. In this context it will be defined by the elements of presentation—the actors and impersonators, characters, plot, dance, and music. The structure of the African folk tale reveals an intense dramatic form, which lends it to impersonation (of animals) by the storyteller, mime, gesture, and dialogue; but as the folk tale's features are not fully realizable through the use of actors, it remains part of the large corpus of material we might call "prose."

The most significant class of dramatic material is what has been referred to as masquerades—performances of mask dances. This art has been perfected by the Yoruba, Igbo, Ewe, and Fon. The emphasis is on the masks, costume, music, and dancing. The

ritual processional dance is the *raison d'être* of the masquerade.
The Yoruba *agbegijo,* for example, is the mask dance for the Egun,
the gifted community of men trained to communicate with the
dead. The *agbegijo* is pure entertainment, created from caricatures
calculated to draw laughs. It is performed at funerals, marriage
feasts, and annual sacrifices by the worshipers. Ulli Beier refers
also to the *gelede* masquerades, which is performed by women to
placate witches.[1] *Gelede* performance, also of the Yoruba, is typified by a ritual dance that takes place at night, preceded by sacrifices and praise singing. Its drama lies in bringing out into public
the *efe* mask, which is the prelude to afternoon dances designed to
keep the witches in good humor. *Gelede* is more of a carnival than
a theatrical performance, and like *agbegijo* utilizes puppetry as
typified by the *fafa* mask, a dancing raffia mat. *Agbegijo,* Beier
insists, is closer to the theater proper than *gelede.* In another article G. I. Jones[2] stresses the features shared by the mask performances of the Igbo, Ijaw, and Ibibio, including the basic belief in the
supernatural power of the mask. The mask, perhaps the most symbolic of African artistic representations, is the most tangible manifestation of the link between the living and the dead. A visual
representation of the spirit, it is the instrument through which man
achieves a spiritual transfiguration. It is in many instances the
ancestors themselves, returned among the living for the numerous
ceremonies of communion and affirmation. The mask's proper role
exists in the drama of this communion and affirmation. There are
mysteries and rules that bind the man who dons the mask on
festival occasions. The uninitiated hold the mask in great awe,
evidence of its pageantry and dramatic impressiveness. The *mau*
performance is a ghost play and includes a great variety of masks
representing, at times, abstract concepts of beauty and femininity.
Like the *gelede* or the *agbegijo,* the *mau* includes masks which
represent foreigners, Europeans, prostitutes, and other figures of
fun and caricature.

Miming and satire are hallmarks of the masquerade. Stylized
movement, characteristic rhythms, highly trained speech and
voices, and studied gestures create a dramatic link between the
various elements of the masquerade. Emphasis is on music, dance,

and costume over and above linguistic content, except perhaps in songs that accompany the whole performance.

The initiation ceremony and numerous festivals and renewal rites are significant extensions of ritual drama. In these instances, make-believe becomes a reality since the participants (actors) are involved in serious religious matters. These ceremonies cover almost every aspect of life. The Ashanti hunters' funeral for the elephant killed on the hunt is performed long after the real event. The re-enactment of the whole story of the hunt, to the accompaniment of mime and drums, is part of the cleansing and "fortification" ceremony to protect the hunter from possible injuries that can be inflicted by the *sasa* (spirit) of the dead elephant.

> Every stage of the hunt is portrayed, the finding of the fresh spoor, and the stalking of the quarry; the elephant itself (represented . . . by one of the hunters raising his arms up to imitate the tusks), the elephants putting sand on each others backs; the hunter about to fire with his companions lying prone, waiting for the fateful moment; and the cutting up and carrying away of the meat.[3]

There is an element of play in this ritual even though its primary purpose is religious. In this way, actual events become re-enacted and ritualized and commemorated into festivals. The *homowo* festival of the Gã of Ghana re-enacts the story of their arrival in their present home and retells of the early months of a grim famine that beset them until they came upon a field of ripening corn. This ceremony is performed every August; it is marked by thanksgiving, ritual cleansing, reunion of members of families, and masquerade processions throughout the principal streets. The *odwira* festivals of the Akwapim of Ghana are ceremonies of first fruits that come before the main harvest. The *adae* festival of the Ashanti of Ghana is the celebration of the New Year according to the Ashanti calendar; it is marked by ritual cleansing of the sacred stools, renewal of bonds with the ancestors, and making of pledges to those who died during a specific year. What is important about all these festivals is the drama of the religious rites, the chief actors being the priests, the chiefs, the elders, or even the whole community.

African religious belief lends itself to drama. Propitiation, cleansing, sacrifice, thanksgiving, and initiation are all extensions of the African's real life into an area of make-believe, which nevertheless expresses a religious reality for him. Fear of the supernatural and respect for the god's interventionist powers form the basis for the role and function of the priest acting on behalf of the people. History and legend become part of the same dramatic consciousness.

The various celebrations for the Yoruba *orisha* reveal perhaps the most spectacular aspects of the African's concept of gods and their attributes. These attributes express his beliefs and philosophical concepts of the nature of the universe. The rites of the various divinities reveal the dramatic characteristics of the gods (who are part of the ceremonial structure) and their preternatural attributes. The cosmology of the Yoruba is implicit in his social system as well as in his religion. Without storms, Yoruba cosmology establishes, the land cannot have growth, harvest, and hunting. All extremes generate their opposites, and by containing conflict in a state of balance, rather than suppressing it, the generative forces are released.

The principal Yoruba god, the Supreme One, is Oludumare. He sent Obatala, the creator deity, to come down and create the earth. But having developed a terrific thirst on the way, according to one version of the legend, Obatala drank too much palm wine and bungled his work, creating albinos, cripples, hunchbacks, and blind men. For this Obatala, the god of creation and laughter, was imprisoned. There are many variants of this cosmogonic myth.

But the central Yoruba god is Eshu, also known as Elegba, the messenger of the gods. He is the trickster, the mischief-maker who serves as a catalyst, endowed with positive qualities that unify a contradictory and paradoxical world. Eshu has no regard for authority; he fights kings, gods, and men. He leads men to offend other gods so that he can partake of their propitiatory sacrifices. Eshu has been linked with sexuality; his vanity is emphasized by his long hair and his mirror. Eshu festivals are still celebrated among the Yorubas. His literary importance lies not only in his role among the gods and men, but also in his role as archetypal trickster, the principal aspect of the folk tale. Eshu is a wandering, homeless spirit, an *agent provocateur* whose maverick qualities establish his philosophical role as the unifier. Joan Wescott writes of him "All men must acknowledge Eshu, and the first part of all sacrifices to other orisha must be offered to him."[4]

Here are a few of Eshu's praise names:

The anger which prompts retaliation.

The one who is known to all.

The one who is wicked unto death.

The sharer in sacrifice.

He who turns right into wrong and makes the innocent guilty.

If there are no drums, he will dance to the pounding of mortars.[5] His essential nature as one who defies boundaries and prohibitions and his opposition to Ifa (*orisha* of divination) establish him as the principle of chance and uncertainty. At the same time, in his co-operation with Ifa, he helps to promote change. He is a satirist, a seducer, a dweller at crossroads, and the god who supervises money transactions.

The second segment of oral literature is what I will refer to as prose narrative. What distinguishes prose from what I will call poetry is the nature of delivery. Prose narratives do not have the charged ceremoniality of poetry. They are delivered on occasions of renewal of allegiance or at festivals celebrating history, legend, or myth. The folk tale falls within this category, representing the most widely discussed subgroup within the prose segment of African literature.

The folk tale was subjected to the nineteenth-century evolutionists' interpretations of human history put forward by writers like E. B. Tylor and Sir James Frazer. As well as being applied to the supposed unilinear evolution of institutions such as religion or marriage, those theories were applied to the nature and history of literature. "Folklore" became the compendium of beliefs and customs and culture of both early man and his descendants today: the contemporary "primitive" peoples, the modern peasant, the people among whom can still be found the supposed traces of the earlier stages of unilinear human evolution. When similar customs and beliefs are found among the so-called "advanced" peoples, they could be explained as remnants or survivals of the cruder primitive stages of the past. Folklore was, in Frazer's words, "due to the collective action of the multitude and cannot be traced to the individual influence of great men."[6]

This approach naturally plays down the authorship of stories, emphasizing only their collective nature. It also assumes that all folk tales were handed down from father to son, from generation to generation. These assumptions minimized notions of mobility, variation, and the originality of a particular story, of the possibility of expansion, contraction, and variation by the genius of new tellers. The fact that the material adapts itself to contemporary social situations is invariably dismissed or overlooked. The result is that the folk tale has not been examined as literature per se, defining its own intrinsic aesthetics. Rather, the folk tale has served the purposes of anthropology and allied disciplines and not those of literature. Ruth Finnegan, debunking the evolutionist approach to the folk tale, stresses the important factors of verbal flexibility, verbal elaboration, the drama of the delivery itself, and the total aesthetic impact of the tale as a living literary entity. She also places the folk tale within the contemporary setting and not locked into a rigid remote past. She writes:

> In any case, how significant is it if some of the content is old or derivative? Does this tempt us to ignore the literary significance of, say, Shakespeare's *Othello* or Joyce's *Ulysses?* The explaining away in terms of origin of subject matter has really no more justification for oral than for written literature. To suppose otherwise is to assume that in non-literate cultures people accept passively the content in the narratives told them and are not tempted to add or embroider or twist —an assumption which, as will be clear already, there is no evidence to support.[7]

Dr. Finnegan criticizes strongly the so-called "diffusionist school," which pursues a type of speculative deduction by drawing attention to similarities (e.g., in motif) of stories from different regions. Stith Thompson's *Motif-Index of Folk Literature,* she points out, made this approach popular and influenced the works of scholars such as Melville J. and Frances Herskovits and a group of South African folklorists based in Witwatersrand University, including S. M. Mafokeng and S. C. H. Rautenbach. Dr. Finnegan's dismissal of the diffusionist approach, justified on the basis of the performance, local artistry, and inventiveness characterizing each tale, does not entirely invalidate the motif or the purely historicogeneric approach. The Jamaican Ananse, or spider man, obviously Ashanti in origin, and the African ancestry of the Br'er Rabbit of the United States blacks make it difficult to discredit totally this approach.

This writer, however, has come across some corroboration for Dr. Finnegan's unease about certain types of classification, especially the kind that establishes rigid types of folk tale, e.g., very detailed classifications that list "dilemma stories," "astrological tales," etc. Some of these classifications, for example, tend to overlook the fact that in the large majority of the animal stories, men and gods are also present. And so to classify a story on the basis of animal or divine characters presents a basic difficulty. It can be assumed that there is a totemic link between the animals of the folk tale and men. More significantly, the animal heroes are chosen for possessing certain primordial qualities of cunning necessary for survival in an uncertain world. Besides, they partake of a spiritual essence of the universal dynamic force. Above all, the animal hero always shares an aspect of everyman; he is wise, at times greedy, at times generous, he marries, procreates, cheats, attends his relatives' and neighbors' funerals, gets drunk and beats his wife, and dies. He is the everyman of the folk tradition, the archetypal hero who succeeds or fails by his guile or preternatural wisdom or when aided by benevolent spirits and his personal deity. This writer was informed by storytellers in the Ewe tradition that the animal stories are sometimes real events which might have occurred in the lifetime of the people. But in order to avoid embarrassing the participants in the events or their offspring and to keep group solidarity intact, animals became the characters. It is the spider man who once said, "Because I tell stories and never mention people by their names, I have never been a defendant in a court of libel."[8]

Verbal variability is a significant pointer to not only the linguistic differences in the areas in which the story travels, but also the geographicocultural dimensions of the area. The spider man among the Anlo-Ewe, for example, is invariably a fisherman, while among the Ashanti he is a farmer.

As pointed out earlier, the impact of the folk tale lies in its drama and therefore in its performance. Mime, dance, and song are aspects of the telling in which the storyteller takes his audience with him into the very recesses of animals or spirits.

It is generally believed that the folk tale cannot be told in broad daylight. This emphasizes the need to create the necessary atmosphere for the play element to be induced. Besides, nighttime is the time when spirits roam the land and have intercourse with men. The proper atmosphere enables the ghosts and spirits to come close to the circle around the fire and join the human community.

I shall accept W. R. Bascom's[9] three-pronged division of the prose narrative as representing the most intelligent classification available. This divides the subject into folk tale, myth, and legend. My only quarrel with this classification is his apparent refusal to accept historical accounts as narratives per se. The fact that myth and legend may become ingredients of history does not invalidate the historicity of the material contained in that history. After all, much "history" in every culture is essentially a compendium of folk, tribal, or racial myths, inspired guesses, biases, and, at times, blatant fabrications. What emerges as "history" has relevance as literature in that it shares something of the imaginative dimensions of literature proper. The result of an intertribal war varies with the imaginative memory of each tribe. History serves other purposes than that of pure archivism. It is, therefore, untenable to insist on finding a "correct" version of a story, a legend, or a myth. There is an immense flexibility which provides a thousand and one variants of one creation myth. The too-neat classification of material as attempted by Susan Feldman in her *African Myths and Tales*[10] provides a fascinating little book which at the same time presumes a uniformity and simplicity that do not exist.

One of the most frequently recurring themes in the prose narratives is conflict, and the victory of cunning over force dramatizes this conflict. Even the high god himself is outwitted by the trickster-hero (who shares the preternatural unifying force of Eshu-Elegba). The sense of realism and the ironic reflection on life that inform the prose narratives seem to underscore the precariousness of life and emphasize the need for a harmonious relationship between gods and men that will ensure survival. The African mythic system places within the same landscape men and gods, and the spiritual hierarchy is carried over into the social hierarchy. There is no distance between men and god; no god exists in a one-dimensional moral structure. Gods have both a good and bad nature, and man, through the intervention of magic and talismanic influences and herbs, can invoke their innate benevolent essences. There are malevolent forces, however, which exist as an aspect of the primal chaos or conflict. But they are not insuperable. In what men call "life" or "the world," therefore, there are spiritual forces locked in mortal combat.

Thematically, the narratives provide a close study of spiritual conflict; the heroes of these tales, be they men, animals, or gods, emphasize the survival factor for man in an undeterminable world. Though the trickster-hero may possess wit and cunning, he may, at times, employ benevolent magic in order to survive in an unequal contest.

In a broad sense, however, the prose narratives are calculated to provide moral instruction in proper behavior and to educate the youth in the tenets of group solidarity: respect for the elders and awareness of duties and responsibilities. This educational intention tends to impose moral endings which may, at times, have very little to do with the plot and may sound very farfetched to outsiders, especially Europeans. This may in part be so because the European point of view seeks clearly accountable plot outlines instead of the cumulative effect of a number of episodes which may not in themselves share any observable links. But to stress this functional-utilitarian aspect of the folk tale is not to deny its pure entertainment and aesthetic value. The structure-and-function school, led by the School of Social Anthropology in Oxford,[11] tends to believe that the stories are designed to stress group solidarity. This approach seems to assume that the social structure itself remains locked in its "primitive" integrity. A regular attempt has been made to analyze stories and interpret them as representations and reflections of social reality or as a kind of sociological model of the society. T. O. Beidelman's interpretation of the Kaguru story of how the rabbit tricks the hyena as a Kaguru representation of matrilineal relationship seems to play down the context of the story and its relationship to the whole corpus of Kaguru oral literature.[12]

The most significant characteristic of the folk narrative, as

pointed out earlier, is the trickster character. He shares the primary
essence of Eshu-Elegba. He is amoral and expresses the idea of
opposition to the normal world. He is the instrument of disorder,
the everyman who lives by his wit and cunning. At times, he loses
the contest, but this is hardly relevant since his function in the
world is to prey on it.

The man-animal hero of the tales, legends, and myths is always
equipped with magical powers which he inherits or acquires. The
contest between the hero and forces bent on his destruction provides the stuff of which the heroic monomyth is made of. Monsters, ogres, malevolent spirits try to devour him. The eternal
conflict that the principle of survival entails becomes the source of
the folk hero's role. In the working out of this conflict, man comes
into contact with spirits and operates in a fantasy world that is
coterminous with the waking world itself. The boundary between
spirits and men is thin. The significant point is that in this contest
with spirits and even death, man must come out victorious, aided
of course by deities, ancestors, and benevolent spirits whose essence
is the life force of which man is the most visible and articulate
expression.

By trying to create a typology for poetry, one enters a rather
protean area. What are the criteria? Mine here will simply be based
on content or form, a slight shift from any purely functional
(hardly tenable all the time) approach. In poetry we draw nearer

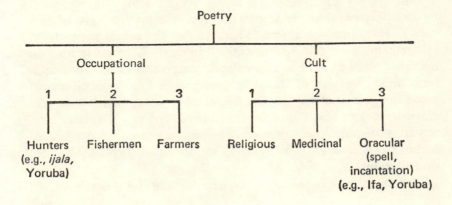

to a more significant dimension of language than can be discerned in the other forms designated ritual drama or "prose." Poetry depends on *voice performance* which has its scope, meaning, and strength at the linguistic level.

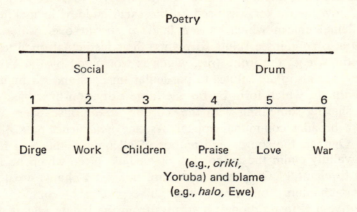

This diagram presupposes both a functional approach at the primary level and a formal one at the secondary level. For example, under "cult" the poetries listed are religious, medicinal, and oracular. These at the formal level share the form of generally being rendered in a heightened voice, functionally being part of magic or prayer and sharing some significant aspect of the occult art itself. At another level, the dirge may share the same formal quality of slow solemnity with some types of *ijala,* the Yoruba hunter's poetry listed under "occupation," since some types of *ijala* are performed at the funeral of hunters.

The group listed as occupational includes poetry that is peculiar and specific to certain trades. To follow a trade means to join a guild or a special group of people who are united by the lore and tradition of that group. Thus, hunters among the Yoruba are bound by their allegiance to Ogun, the god of the hunt, fire, iron, and war, which unites them with blacksmiths and hunters. But hunters also share the lore of animals and the forest; hence, they participate in a more cultic essence of Ogun. In a very comprehensive book, S. A. Babalola discusses the nature of the Yoruba *ijala.*[13] He describes it as a speechlike song chanted at the gather-

ings of the devotees of Ogun. *Ijala* contains imagery drawn from
all aspects of non-human life. It deals with human relations, provides admonitions for ethical conduct, and covers the whole range
of traditional mythology. Its subject matter includes a salute to animals, stressing their attributes, characteristics, or roles in legend,
e.g., how the duiker was used by the earth goddess in making the
medicinal charm which caused land to spread over water. The
ijala also contains a salute to plants, their medicinal qualities and
functions, e.g., the iroko tree, which is worshiped by the Yoruba.
There are also *ijala* salutes to particular lineages and distinguished
individuals, which form by far the largest division of subject matter, sharing something with the Yoruba *oriki* praise poem which
has a broader communal appeal. As one *ijala* artist puts it, "the
god Ogun is the source and author of all *ijala* chants. No hunter
can validly claim the authorship of an *ijala* piece which he is the
first to chant."[14] Of course, there are new *ijala* chants created by
expert chanters from time to time. The process of composition is
intuitive and inspirational; it springs from the innate talents of the
artist. "The spirit, the genre of *ijala*-chanting teaches a master
chanter new *ijala* pieces to chant. The god Ogun, himself, is ever
present with a master chanter."[15] *Ijala* artists undergo intensive
training from late boyhood and grow by imitation and tuition in
medicinal herbs and in the powers of retentive memory. Because
Ogun, like most other deities, is also a cure god, *ijala* artists sometimes become diviner-physicians. *Ijala* is distinguished by rhythm
segments, and the lines (marked by pauses for breath), when in-
toned, sound more like singing than recitation, "yielding the
traditional tonal contrasts or successive segment-ends and the
characteristic antiphonal rhythm."[16] The technical competence of
the performer depends on voice, resonance, nasality, clarity, and
absence of gruffness or breathy guttural tone. The chanter lingers
on final syllables or phrase ends and shakes his voice in the
suspensory pauses. The hunter's drum is usually in accompaniment. The chant's basic poetic qualities include repetition of lines,
digression, word-picture painting—use of ideophones and parallelism—comparison, simile, metaphor, metonymy, allusions, and
epigrams.

Other occupational groups use poetry as an essential aspect of work. These poems go beyond being just mere work songs since they are part of a repertorial accumulation used in specific religious functions pertaining to the group's calling. A good example is the Ewe fishermen's song tradition. These poems—for a song's range is that of the poem—invoke the sea, fish lore, and ceremonies pertaining to specific nets. They are only at times accompanied by drums; they are marked by a quick, almost martial rhythm, which is established by the regular one-two of the march of feet. Each poem itself is led by anyone with a clear ringing voice who, aided by only a little gong, gives the beat and unfolds it. The beat may, however, vary with the quickening tempo that the pulling in of the net suggests. In communities where farming is done on a communal basis, traditions of farming poetry exist: one example is the large repertory of farm poetry among the Ewe of the hinterland, especially of the Ho and Kpando.

Cult poetry covers religious poetry, medicinal poetry, and oracular poetry. Religious poetry includes the praise poems of gods, or what may be called hymns. The Yoruba god Eshu-Elegba, the messenger deity, has his own worshipers who perform his rituals and sing his praise names:

> When he is angry he hits a stone until it bleeds.
> When he is angry he weeps tears of blood.
> Eshu, confuser of men.[17]

Or the praise poetry of Shango, the god of thunder:

> Huge sacrifice
> too heavy for the vulture,
> it trembles under your weight.[18]

It is clear that these praises are sung to put the gods in good humor. Elaborate prayers for good health, plentiful harvest, children, and wisdom follow the praises. Among the Dinka people of the Sudan the same pattern exists—extravagant praise, followed by a quiet reflection on the meaning of life, and then the characteristic demands and complaints:

> Do you not hear, O Divinity?
> The black bull of the rain has been released from the moon's byre.
> Do you not hear, O Divinity?

I have been left in misery indeed.
Divinity, help me!
Will you refuse the ants of this country?[19]

Sometimes the gods are rebuked for failure or persistent malevolence. This, too, is an aspect of worship. The long ceremony of libation among the Ashanti and the Ewe includes a long poem to dead ancestors, who are invoked at important occasions such as birth or death rites to continue to give succor to the living. Some of these poems, generally recited, are interrupted with characteristic yells from the audience to signify agreement and emphasis.

The diviner's art exists within the significant context of a poetry that produces direct revelation of the cure. Disease has both physical and metaphysical dimensions. Gods themselves reveal cure for all ailments. As the Ijaw poet J. P. Clark puts it:

For every ailment in man,
there is a leaf in the forest.

Poetry is invocation of spirits and forces to parley and commune. The elaborate Ifa (Yoruba) and Afa (Ewe) divination is meaningful only in terms of what can be deduced from the poetry loaded with symbolism, allusions, mythology, and a large body of complex imagery. The messages have to be decoded, and it is a rare knowledge of Ifa divination that enables anyone to interpret the poetry. It is normally chanted. Here is a brief example:

The hot birds flew into the palm groves.
The female crocodiles went into the bird forest.
The anago priests are searching for a home
away from storm, and rain and wind.[20]

Or, the Sotho diviner's:

You my white ones, children of my parents
whom I drank from mother's breast,
and you many colored cattle
whom I knew when still on mother's back.[21]

Or:

Sunbird secret and daring,
when you take a bit of straw
and swear you imitate the hammer kop,

it is the bird of those who take a new garment
in the deep waters.[22]

What is impressive is the allusive nature of these poems. Symbolic expressions are used to hide real meaning; each line can bear many interpretations. For this type of poetry, direct or literal interpretation is totally ruled out.

There are a number of cure, or medicine, cults whose art rests very much within the nature of the poetry they engender. Among the Ewe, medicine cults such as Dente, Brekete (which came from the northern parts of present-day Ghana) use an elaborate system of chants and prayers to induce cure. These are not so much divination poems as accompaniments to the art of cure itself. When the herbs and roots are all in place, their efficacy can only be assured through incantations and chants. Closely related is the poetry of magic:

The eagle called the hawk,
"Come let us go try the chameleon."
When they went, they dug till rain fell.
Eagle spread her wings afar,
hawk's flesh was picked clean from its bones.[23]

The primacy of the word in magic is very much emphasized when one looks closely at religious poetry. The word has both the mythical power of inducing confusion in the enemy and of calling down gods into the midst of men. Its sacredness is shown in the nature and function of this type of poetry.

The grouping under social poetry lists six broad subgroups: dirge, work, children, praise, love, and war poetry. Dirge poetry is a very encompassing type. As shown above, within *ijala,* for example, the dirge may occur. In the broadest sense, the dirge is the lament for the dead. The elaborate African funeral, from the wailing and ululation through the first burial and second or final burial, provides occasion for poetry. This type may be described as philosophical, seeking the meaning and purpose of life and has an expected tone of solemnity and sorrow. In the Ewe tradition, the dirge poem has received a tremendous boost through the work of the dirge poet Hesino Akpalu. The Ewe dirge reveals the loneliness and sorrow of death, traditional world views of what the next stage of the journey is, and finally a message or prayer. The dead person is a traveler from the living to the ancestors; he is given intimate messages to deliver to those who had gone ahead. The Ewe dirge is normally performed by women; it is not accompanied by any large orchestra of drums but perhaps with a rattle or a gong. Prominence is given to the words (as in all other chanted poems) over the simple melody which serves only as a vehicle to convey the basic notions and ideas of the poem. Repetition of lines or large segments and of imagery and sounds act to enchance the chorality of the lament. This gives it a persistence that tends to relieve the mourners of the burden of their sorrow. The Akan dirge of Ghana is a famous example of elegiac poetry, chanted mostly by women in a dense atmosphere of sobbing, wailing, and weeping. Among the Illa and the Tonga of Zambia these poems are composed only once, i.e., at the funeral of the person whose death inspires them; these *zitengulo,* or mourning songs, are short. In Akan dirge poetry praise names are invoked. The overwhelming note is one of personal grief in the Acholi dirge of Uganda:

> I wait on the pathway in vain.
> He refuses to come again.[24]

Death is a predatory animal, the warrior who refuses wealth and insists on man:

> The earth does not get fat. It makes an end of all beasts.
> Shall we die on the earth?[25]

So asks an Ngoni song of Malawi. The Akan dirge piece:

> Grandsire, the crab that knows the hiding place
> of alluvial gold.
> What is the matter, child of the spokesman.[26]

The Ewe dirge piece:

> How is it that mother does not answer when I call?
> Are we quarreling?[27]

state the same deep sense of loss and sorrow expressed by the grandchild and the child of the deceased.

Work songs are very commonplace throughout Africa. They

have a directly functional relationship to the activity they accompany. The mine and plantation workers of South Africa are said to have no end of work songs. The work song was a feature of the plantations in the South of the United States during the dark days of slavery. Most of this poetry is simple in form and rhythm. Its hallmark is a rhythmic repetition that tends to relieve the sheer drudgery of labor.

Children's, or cradle, songs can be grouped as one branch of poetry serving a social need. Like lullabies in other traditions, they are simple both rhythmically and in terms of ideas. They cover a number of subjects. Ewe cradle poetry ranges from solemn dirgelike songs of consolation to a brisk type that employs a great many ideophones and plays on words for effect.

Perhaps the largest subgroup under the social poetry group is praise poetry. I have bracketed this with blame poetry, or the songs of abuse, since it is obvious that within many traditions the transition between praise and blame can be swift. Within this group one must mention the Yoruba *oriki,* or praise poems; the *halo* poems of abuse among the Ewe; and the praise poetry of the Zulu, sometimes called heroic recitations. Among most African peoples, praise singing is an art which may be part of a chief's court, as among the Ashanti and the Hausa. There may be professional praise singers as among the Yoruba, the Hausa, and the Wolof. These are strolling performers who follow their patron through the streets, beating out his patronymic salutations and heaping upon him an exaggerated array of praise epithets. They may liken him to the elephant to signify his strength, to the fox for his sagacity, to the cow for her meekness. If the patron recognizes their work and rewards them, he may soon be elevated to the status of a lion, a leopard, or some other noble beast. But if he makes the mistake of ignoring them, he may soon be likened to the red-bottomed baboon or the greedy goat who ate too much at his own mother's funeral and thus befouled the funeral compound.

Shaka, the nineteenth-century warrior-king of the Zulu, utilized praise poems as an essential aspect of war and heroism. They employ exaggeration, and among the Zulu are chanted with a very shrill voice, with the poet beating time with a long stick. Some of these poems may refer to real acts of heroism or to the nobility of particular chiefs and their benevolent reigns. They are mainly figurative, calculated to add color to the ceremonial procession. The man becomes the animal:

> I am the young lion,
> the wild animal with pad-feet and black back,
> whose father gave up home, whose mother wept for long.
> I am the fine elephant of Mathabapula,
> the finest elephant in the Matsark gang.[28]

The emphasis is on allusion in this kind of poetry. "Mathabapula" refers to a lineage whose totem is the elephant. Shaka was

> The thunder that bursts on the open
> where mimosa trees are none.
> The giant camouflaged with leaves
> in the track of Nxaba's cattle.[29]

Some of these praises are addressed to animals, especially among the southern Bantu people, particularly the Zulu, Xhosa, and the Swazi, whose cattle occupy a significant ceremonial and economic role. At times the praises are an aspect of the rites of passage, marking the point of upward movement of a man into the next group. As noted earlier, praise poetry coincides with war poetry at times, especially among the Zulu and other southern Bantu groups. Praise poets occupy important positions in the royal household. They acquire wealth and status according to their success. This type of poetry is very public, being recited at festival occasions like anniversaries or victories. Its scope may include legend, mythology, and history. Its delivery is ceremonial and elaborate.

Closely associated with the praise poems is the poetry of abuse. This second type has become perfected among certain peoples, especially the Ewe and the Yoruba. The Ewe *halo* poetry was a regular feature of Ewe drumming for a long time. Its essence is its verbal agility, exaggeration, and elaborate use of imagery. *Halo* became the instrument through which rival villages settled outstanding differences. Each side commissioned its poets to dig into the history of the other group for all the scandalous details about their leaders, true or false. The ingredients constitute the material for verbal assault on the ugliness of the opponent's leadership, juicy bits about whose grandmother was a whore or whose great-grandfather built a wealth on stolen goods:

> The whore was forgetful; she walked
> like the wandering duck into my song.
> You clutch the earth like a bag;
> on your stem you stand like the porcupine in clothes;
> beneath your back is the hyaena's ravine;
> your chest as short as the red monkey
> on the corn barn.
> Alas, my song shall speak the words of song.[30]

To this the other poet responds:

> He is winding in the air, his anus agape,
> his face like the egret's beak;
> he who eats off the farm he hasn't planted,
> his face the bent evil hoe on its handle.[31]

This poetry tends to dramatize intragroup conflicts and dissipates these in words. Its recitation works at a cumulative level; it indulges in sheer verbal overkill.

Love or erotic poetry has as long a tradition as any of the other types. It exists within the specific framework of the lovers' performances, as among the Ewe, or as an aspect of the *tumbuizo,* or the serenade, tradition of Swahili poetry:

> I want to give a burden to the daughter of the moon.
> Welcome! The crescent shines forth like the full moon.[32]

This is a piece of Swahili love song performed in the *ngoma,* or dances, that are held at night. Young men and women fall in love around these performances. The love poets take a lot of liberty. At times their work borders on the bawdy and ribald. But this is the purpose of it all, to destroy embarrassing bashfulness by open reference to the love act, to establish rapport with the loved one through flirtatious references to her beauteous endowments and to arouse attention from the lover by exaggerating her virtues and those of her lineage. The full moon is the occasion for love poetry. It sometimes states the sorrow of love, the demise of love, and the parting of lovers:

> I am on my way to death's land,
> folk are in tears.

My beloved, weep not,
for it is for you I die.[33]

says an Ewe love poem. Needless to say, love poetry can easily
become banal, since every would-be lover fancies himself an accomplished poet. But tradition quickly separates the real poets
from the pathetic whiners. The love poetry of black Africa is more
abundant in the Moslem areas. This is because of the direct influence of erotic poetry from the Arabic. The romantic love poems
composed by the accomplished poets, however, become swallowed
in the larger tradition. Thus, specific objects of such ardent adoration become readily anonymous. Luo love songs of Uganda are
mostly composed by women. The *aigo* are songs by young women
on the way to visit their young men. They sing them in groups or
singly, awaiting to be entertained by their men by the light of the
full moon.

Call her for me that girl,
that girl with the neck like a desert tree;
call her that she and I will lie in one bed.[34]

goes another Ewe love poem.

The last subgroup of social poetry deals with war. The role of
the Zulu panegyric has already been referred to. War poetry among
the Ewe or the Akan is fast, agile, and brief. It is normally accompanied by a chorus of yells. It is calculated to frighten the enemy,
to instill the spirit of bravery into the hearts of the warriors, and
to recall the heroic deeds of the past. The *asafo* tradition of young
warrior groups among the Ashanti has left a large corpus of war
poetry even though the *asafo* organization itself was banned by
the British at the turn of the century. Here is a short sample:

Hirelings adamant to rain and scorching sun,
members of the Apagya company;
there was a cannon mounted vainly on top of the fort,
the cannon could not break us.
The trusted company that engages in battle
hail the helper.[35]

The Ewe war poetry tradition rests within the war drumming performances such as *atrikpui, kpegisu,* and *agbadza.* The war drums
in ancient times accompanied the warriors to the front:

I shall sleep in the desert land
without moving my feet.
I shall sleep in the desert land.
Guns in our hands we cannot fire,
machetes in our hands we cannot throw.
Without moving my feet
I shall sleep in the desert land.[36]

There is, apart from the defiant voice of bravado and boasting, a generally deep sense of sorrow that anticipates death at the battle-front for the warrior. Today this type of war poetry is heard only on the occasions of the great festivals in which the *asafo* groups perform, e.g., the deer hunt festival of the Efutu of Ghana or on the occasions of the funeral of notables. They also serve as dirges to heroes.

There is one non-oral type of poetry which should be classified as unique. This is the poetry of drums and horns. Drum language plays a very important part in traditional life. In the first place, drums serve as signaling instruments, sending out agreed codes. This function is non-literary. Secondly, drums communicate the tonal system of language and are therefore used as a literary medium. The drum can play refined stereotyped phrases. Among the Tumba and Kele of Zaire, the Ashanti of Ghana, the Ewe of Ghana and Togo, the Yoruba of Nigeria, and many other groups, the use of drums to transmit poetry is widespread. But the delineation of this art belongs primarily to musicology. The material produced is only important when transliterated and its verbal equivalent rendered. This presumes a close knowledge of the language and a keen awareness of tonal variations on individual words. Here is an example of the famous Akan drum prelude called the *Anyaneanyane* (*Awakening*), played at the Adae festival in Kumasi, the Ashanti capital:

The path has crossed the river.
The river has crossed the path.
Which is the elder?
We made the path and found the river.
The river is from long ago,
the river is from the ancient creator of the universe.[37]

Most important, proverbs can be played on the drums. The Akan talking drums are twin drums, one male, one female, the male

being the low pitch and the female the high pitch; an almost infinite variation between the two tones can be achieved through
graduated control of the vellum. The drummer learns his art from
infancy and develops a complex awareness of the minutest details of pitch. The Yoruba *dundun,* or hourglass, drums are also
used for praise-singing (or for abuse). The eulogies are built up
into a repertory, based on a series of praise verses. In fact, any of
the regular *oriki* praise poems can be played on this single drum,
which possesses much variation in pitch, depending on the expertise of the drummer. Drums also tell history, as among the
Ashanti. The names of dead kings, not to be spoken lightly, will
be told through drums.

In order to narrow down the discussion of spoken poetry, I
intend to do a close examination of three samples. I shall also
make reference to types of poetry that have influenced subsequent
stylistic developments in more modern writing in Africa.

Poetry in Africa generally expresses itself in the songs, ritual
incantations, prayers to gods, praise, or salutation to gods and
men. In short, it covers all that ordinary everyday speech does not
express. In everyday life a good deal is performed in the name of
gods. The simplest libation before a meal or a drink is a prayer
and a poem. This poetry, therefore, involves an extremely complicated sense of materials and structures, the manipulation of
multiple elements. Its boundaries are limitless in the sense that the
total world—mythology, legend, music, dance, worship—is embraced
in a feeling for what the late Ernst Cassirer called "the solidarity of
all life." Its folk nature is only discernible within the scope of the
genius of individual poets, both dead and living, whose creative
powers are expressible in the forceful depth and dimensions of the
language in which they work. As stated earlier, it is in the art
of poetry and its immense verbal variability that individual talent
flowers. For the poem is carried by the voice. It is sung, or chanted,
on specific occasions, some of which are part of specific rites and
occupations, as noted. The most significant fact is that the ultimate
realization of this material lies in the *occasion* and *atmosphere*
of its performance.

Our first type of poetry to be examined in full detail is Yoruba
poetry. The Yoruba are one of the largest linguistic groups in west-

ern Nigeria, numbering conservatively ten million. Hunters' poetry or *ijala*, as already noted, is one important Yoruba poetic form. It is, as S. A. Babalola has pointed out in his impressive book already referred to, a speechlike song performed at the gathering of Ogun's devotees. The chanters and performers of *ijala* are also regarded as entertainers who perform on social occasions that may have nothing to do with hunting at all. It is delivered as a "type of speech utterance with rudimentary musical characteristics, rather than a species of song."[38] *Ijala* is also sung during Ogun worship. Narrative *ijala* is rare since the typical *ijala* poem contains almost any theme—forest, birds, animals, human relations, admonitory words for ethical conduct, praise of friends, and traditional mythology. Its poetry lies in the euphony of words, associated rhythm, and emotiveness. Its rhythm is based on tonal variations in the pitch of the vowel sounds and the general levels of mid, low, and high, allowing for an infinite number of variations in between. At the end of the speechlike chant may be a song which is used to mark the end of one segment before the next one begins. The rendition of this tailpiece can be joined in by the chorus and may be accompanied by drumming. Occasions for *ijala* are Ogun festivals, activities of hunters' guilds, festivals in honor of lineage ancestors. *Ijala* covers many subjects. Its subject matter may be salutes to animals such as the duiker, lion, bushbuck, elephant, etc., stressing their attributes, characteristics, or roles in legend. There are also salutes to trees, e.g., the iroko, which is widely worshiped in Africa, or the cassava, the great stand-by food crop. There are also salutes to particular lineages and distinguished individuals and to group progenitors.

Ijala artists include women beggars who perform for the sake of winning the favors of Ogun for the family. There is also a large corps of trained male performers who are part-time artists because they are primarily farmers, hunters, or diviner-physicians. All of them, however, acknowledge the hand of Ogun in the chanting of *ijala*. As one chanter, Adediran Ogunmola, told Babalola:

> The god Ogun is the source and author of all ijala chant; every ijala artist is merely Ogun's mouthpiece.[39]

Ijala artists are supposed to receive tuition from the god Ogun in dreams and trances. Criticism of *ijala* is normally based on the accuracy of observation on Yoruba life, humor, idiomatic expressions, metaphysical turns of phrase, wisdom, and voice. The technical competence of the chanter determines the applause he receives. The singing of *ijala* involves a high degree of nasalization, clarity of rendition, a relaxed effort, absence of gruffness, breathy or guttural tone, and a metallic vocal quality. Babalola describes the language of *ijala* as a formalized version of Yoruba speech, even though much of it is ordinary and straightforward. Such stylistic devices as digression from the main theme or story in order to interpolate comments, on, say, the fickleness of women, are also employed. Repetition is one of its persistent features and is used in returning to the main motif of the poem:

> The tree squirrel is in the forest.
> It has a flossy tail.
> The ground squirrel is in the forest.
> It has a flossy tail. . . .[40]

The audience is encouraged to participate by repeating the refrain.

Repetition may also include listing of items such as diseases, animals, parts of the body. Here is an *ijala* poem addressed to Ogun:

> Ogun kills on the right and destroys on the right.   1
> Ogun kills on the left and destroys on the left.
> Ogun kills suddenly in the house and suddenly in the field.
> Ogun kills the child with the iron with which it plays.
> Ogun kills in silence.   5
> Ogun kills the thief and the owner of stolen goods.
> Ogun kills the owner of the house
> and paints the hearth with his blood.
> Ogun is the forest god.
> He gives all his clothes to beggars: 10
> He gives one to the woodcock—who dyes it in indigo,
> he gives one to the coucal—who dyes it in camwood,
> he gives one to the cattle egret—who leaves it white.
>
> Ogun's laughter is no joke.
> His enemies scatter in all directions.   15
> The butterflies do not have to see the leopard;
> as soon as they smell his shit
> they scatter in all directions.

Master of iron, chief of robbers,
you have water, but you bathe in blood.   20
The light shining in your face
is not easy to behold.
Ogun with the bloody cap,
let me see the red of your eye.

Ogun is not like pounded yam.   25
Do you think you can knead him in your hand
and eat of him until you are satisfied?
Do you think Ogun is something you can throw into your cap
and walk away with it?
Ogun is a mad dog   30
who will ask questions after seven hundred and eighty years.
Ogun have pity on me:
Whether I can reply or whether I cannot reply,
Ogun, don't ask me anything.

The lion never allows anyone to play with his cub.   35
Ogun will never allow his child to be punished.
Ogun, do not reject me!
Does the woman who spins ever reject a spindle?
Does the woman who dyes ever reject a cloth?
Does the eye that sees ever reject a sight?   40
Ogun, do not reject me.[41]

This poem represents a lively acknowledged salute to Ogun, one of
the most colorful gods of the Yoruba pantheon. His divinity encompasses all acts of bravado, of reckless disregard of danger, of
delirious heroism, of death by blood, for he is the lord of the cutting
edge of iron. He is heat and vengeance, a god of excesses who
knows no moderation. His vitality is signified by the deeds of
bloody proportions in which he indulges, from war to circumcision,
and whose ultimate emblem is the sword. He is also at times celebrated by the phallus, by which his aggressive masculinity is
stressed. The Ogun staff, or sword, is shown penetrating the
earth, a striking realization of the male organ in a state of sexual
excitement.

The poem begins with a typical repetitive recounting of the terrible attributes of Ogun. Though he is the god of laughter and
debauchery, he is reputed to possess a terrible temper that sweeps
over every offender without remorse. His laughter disguises his ter-

rible temper. The cumulative listing is ended with the brief but poignant line 5, "Ogun kills in silence." This perhaps attempts to contrast him with the god Shango, who kills in thunder and lightning. His ability to kill at home and in the field connotes the unexpectedness with which iron instruments—machetes, guns, in the days of flintlock guns—inflict fatal wounds upon even their users. Lines 6 to 8 state Ogun's abhorrence of thieves. Workers in iron cannot steal or receive stolen goods, for the punishment from Ogun can be dreadfully severe. It is widely held in areas where Ogun worship still obtains—notably Yorubaland, Dahomey, and Eweland—that the most honest members of the community are the ironworkers. Line 8 emphasizes Ogun's sheer love of blood; his sign is blood, with which, after killing those who offend him, he paints the spot where they fall. Lines 9 to 13 emphasize Ogun's love of colors. He is the most flamboyantly dressed god, next perhaps to Eshu-Elegba, the trickster-god. He is friend to the birds of the forest with whom he shares his clothes. The paradox of Ogun, the god of blood, retaining the purity and innocence of the undyed cloth in its whiteness emphasizes the victorious aura that encompasses Ogun the warrior. This is stressed in the simplicity of line 14, "Ogun's laughter is no joke." Line 15 reaffirms the fearsome awe that typifies Ogun's laughter. He is the god of preternatural vengeance, marked by an endlessly destructive cunning that is expressed through that laugh which is one of mockery and anger rather than of joy. His vengeance is so embracing that he hardly distinguishes those who offend him from his own devotees. The awe in which all men hold Ogun is vividly portrayed through the powerful image of the butterflies fleeing upon smelling the leopard's excrement. Ogun's malevolent addiction to blood, his orgiastic predilection for wallowing in it, is expressed in line 20, "You have water, but you bathe in blood." The god of war is also a god of brightness, an essence of the Supreme God that he shares. But it is the brightness of spears and machetes, weapons of war rather than of pristine innocence. And, like the men of blood, the warrior and the hunter, whose clothes are soaked in blood, it is hard to distinguish the frenzied redness of his eye. Pounded yam of line 25 suggests utter helplessness, the dependence and uselessness that is associated with the pounded yam ready for feasters to knead into any shape. Line 28 suggests the ease and nonchalance with which the beggar tosses a coin into his cap, or perhaps more precisely, the way in which the giver tosses the coin into the beggar's cap. These lines suggest the negative and absolute passivity of the object—the coin or kola gift and pounded yam—which represents the very opposites of the active malevolence of Ogun when challenged. Ogun's lunacy is always emphasized by his addiction to silly games and quarrels, his unpredictability, and his ability to dissemble. He is the god who will punish an offense even after seven hundred and eighty years, inflicting punishment upon the descendants of the offender.

It will be observed that the structure of this poem follows that of very regular *oriki,* or praise poem, to a god. It opens with declarations of the god's capacity for killing which knows no control. Then the poem gives Ogun's attributes from line 9 to line 31. This segment represents flattery and praise, calculated to put the god in a good mood to accept the prayer and supplication of lines 32 to 41. It is in the last segment that the Ogun worshiper reveals his own relationship with the god. He has drawn a picture of an unrelenting, vengeful god. But he asks for a special consideration; his tone is one of humility and reverence. He is the priest of Ogun, Ogun's own child whom the god cannot allow to be punished; he is the lion's cub with whom nobody is allowed to play; he is the spindle of the weaver woman, the cloth of the dyer, and the sight of the eye. In these lines the Ogun priest states his special relationship with his god, a relationship based firmly in a certain interdependence. In other words, Ogun, in spite of his awesome and fearsome temper, is not realizable except through his priests. This underscores the close relationship between a god and his priest, a kind of mutual dependence that gives the priest powers of rebuttal and powers beyond the simple sacerdotal responsibility. The primary reason for chanting *ijala* is to put the god Ogun in good humor, to achieve a needful rapport with him, and to serve effectively as his mouthpiece.

The funeral dirge represents one of the most common types of poetry in Africa. Its scope is that of the lament, and it is characterized by an elaborate use of imagery, symbolism, and allusion. The funeral itself is an elaborate celebration in which elegiac poetry exists as part of the lamentation and the memorial rites. The sorrow and the heavy apprehension that engulf the homestead when death strikes are exquisitely expressed in this Yoruba dirge:

Slowly the muddy pool becomes a river.   1
Slowly my mother's disease becomes death.
When wood breaks it can be repaired,
but ivory breaks forever.
An egg falls to reveal a messy secret.   5
She has gone far.
We look for her in vain
But when you see the kob antelope on the way to the farm,
when you see the kob antelope on the way to the river,
leave your arrows in your quiver   10
and let the dead depart in peace.[42]

The dirge is the preserve of women performers among many groups, and it is important for the full realization of this poem to visualize the atmosphere of mourning, punctuated by the sobbing and the weeping of the women's chorus. This dirge is sung for or by the child of the dead mother. The first line establishes an interim finality of death for the living, but the image of the muddy pool becoming a river suggests continuity and flow of what is the dynamic life force into the spirit world. Therefore, death itself becomes a release from the messy, muddy pool of disease. There is a cleansing that is associated with the river, the representative image here of death. But the consolation and comfort of death as a release of spirit from human bondage change into the lamentation of the next four lines. These lines, especially line 4, emphasize the ultimate finality of death, the simple truth that the living cannot see the dead. The preciousness of the dead one is expressed in the image of ivory; this line, at the same time, stresses the irreparability of the loss:

When wood breaks, it can be repaired,
but ivory breaks forever.

Line 5 stands alone, a suggested throwback to the muddy pool of disease. It stresses the spilling of the life force that hides within its womb the "messy secret" of mortality. But line 6 contradicts this by its insistent reference to the mother, perhaps not revealing the death that killed her. African thought insists on assigning causes to all death. The revelation that comes through oracles and diviners will tell the cause of an illness and prescribe cures. When the cause is not revealed, then the reason of the death that will ensue for lack of proper cure remains a secret. Lines 7 and 8 recall the custom of spirit searching which exists among the Yoruba and the Ewe. On the morning of burial, or even at the moment of imminent death, mourners and priests go to the crossroads of the village where they "search" for the spirit of the departing one. Children of the dead are aware of the possibility of the return of spirits, of a force that binds them to the dead. This bond emphasizes the link between the ancestors and the living. The last four lines of the dirge reveal a piece of mythological lore, and also a powerful use of imagery. The kob antelope is a beautiful and graceful animal. In these lines the dead mother is likened to the kob antelope. But more important, spirits of the dead in their journey into the other world can assume the body and the form of animals. This is part of the mythology that feeds animal totemism. The lament here warns the hunters not to kill the kob antelope, which the dirge singer stresses is the totemic representation of the dead mother.

Sometimes the dirge contains personal references or address to the dead. This is the case in the following dirge piece:

I say rise, and you will not rise.   1
If Olu is told to rise,
Olu will rise.
If Awo is told to rise,
Awo will rise.   5
The newly married wife
will rise when asked,
although she dares not
call her husband by name.
The elephant rises in the morning,   10
the buffalo rises in the morning.
The elephant lies down like a hill.
Alas, the elephant has fallen
and can never get up again.
You say you have neither wealth nor children,   15
not even forty cowries with which to buy salt?
You muffled head, arise![43]

Olu and Awo refer obviously to the relatives of the dead, whose totemic animals are the buffalo and the elephant. The elephant, the great king of other beasts, has fallen and can never rise again.

The funeral dirges of the Akan of Ghana and Ivory Coast represent perhaps one of the most intrinsically complete poetic types in Africa. The dirge, as J. H. Nketia points out, shares the pathos of mortality that the universal fact of death engenders with other general songs and with the poetry of the language of horns, pipes, and drums. This is so because "death is a universal subject of poetic thought, and, second, because there is a place for songs and all vehicles of poetry in Akan funeral celebrations."[44] In these dirges, speech is overlaid with music, sobs, and tears, and conjoined to body movements. As in all performances, the verbal component receives the greatest prominence. "The usual way of performing dirges," Nketia writes, "is for each individual mourner to perform on her own, singing dirges of her choice. In the dirge, the mourner is herself the soloist and the chorus, and must therefore rely on her own resources. The dirge seems to represent, therefore, a most accomplished poetic statement, carrying with it a degree of verbal expectancy." Accuracy is demanded of the performers who may expand or deviate from the repertorial material. However, since the pieces travel from place to place, Nketia insists that the authors of dirges are unknown but the pieces are held by all and recreated by individuals when necessary. The medium is that of the poem. The style is simple.

Here is a sample of a section of an Akan dirge:

Mother, there is no fire in the deserted dwelling   1
from which I could take a brand to light my fire.
My helpful wicker basket that comes to my aid with lumps of salt,
O Mother, I would weep blood for you, if only Otire's child would   4
   be allowed to.
Grandsire, the crab, knows the hiding place of alluvial gold.
What is the matter, child of the spokesman?
Mother has allowed this death to take me by surprise.
O Mother, I am struggling; all is not as well with me as it   8
   appears.[45]

This is one of the specific clan dirges belonging to the Aduna. It was sung by a woman for her dead mother, Nyaako. The earlier lines ask the mother for gifts from *asamado,* the world of spirits; for example:

> Mother, if you send me something, I would like
> parched corn so that I could eat it raw if there
> was no fire to cook it.[46]

Or:

> Mother, if you would send something, I would like
> a parcel and a big cooking pot that receives
> strangers.[47]

Then comes the line:

> Mother, send me something when someone is coming.[48]

The poem itself is replete with allusions to the ancestors, to the clan founders who are saluted in the opening lines. Its emphasis is, however, on the total sense of loss and helplessness that overwhelms the child. The mother in the African world view represents not only the most steadfast person in the homestead, but also the symbol of the eternal giver, the earth itself. When sorrow strikes, our last place of refuge is at our mother's hearth where nothing is refused us. This poem laments more the intense loneliness of the orphan child than it mourns for her mother. The first line expresses the total pathos of the suffering that the mother's absence imposes on the child. The absence of fire in the dwelling connotes both the absence of light, brightness, and warmth and the absence of the usual bustle that goes on around the cooking place and the hearth, the very nerve center of the homestead. But the absence of the fire also means that the child cannot light a brand that will illumine her way in an uncertain and dark world full of pitfalls and snares. The African tropical nights are thick and impenetrable; travelers carry lanterns and torches. Here the child laments the pathetic fact that there is no fire to light her torch. The suggestion can be further made of the lack of the inspirer and pathfinder, the mother, in life's dark and uncertain journey. Line 3 is a cryptic, encompassing expression of the Giver concept. The wicker basket hangs in every kitchen, and in it are stored meat, salt, and condiments for cooking. The imagery of the mother as the kitchen wicker basket is particularly expressive of her function; it is a symbol of the sustainer. Salt is referred to here because in the olden days salt was a very precious commodity throughout all trans-Saharan Africa, especially to those who lived in the forest areas where there were no salt flats or lagoons. The reference to salt also underscores its preserving and seasoning power, a virtue acknowledged in most cultures. The next line, line 4, is the ultimate lamentation expressed in the tears of blood. Tears are not enough. "Otire's child" refers to the mourner. Line 5 refers to the opening salutation of the clan founder, Kwaagyei, whose totem is the crab, whose home is the hiding place of alluvial gold, a very precious metal among the Ashanti. It is only the grandsire who can relieve the suffering of the mourner by showing her the place of gold. The last two lines restate the suddenness of the mother's death and reiterate the notion of the orphan's suffering. Here both the deceased and the mourner meet at the focal point. The closeness of the world of the dead to that of the living is expressed in the simple messages of support that are addressed to the departed mother. The significant point here is that the orphan believes that help will and can come to her from the land of spirits and that her prayers and lamentations will be heeded by both the grandsire and her mother.

It is clear, from Nketia's very comprehensive study of the Akan dirge, that various qualities such as appellations, salutations, bynames, and kinship terms combine with benevolent qualities as the basic features of the departed. The various clans have their specific patterns of address. These include such samples as:

The white fowl spotted by the roving hawk . . .
The mighty tree laden with fruit . . .
Fount of satisfaction . . .
The slender arm full of benevolence . . .[49]

Qualities such as kindness, fruitfulness, bravery, heroism, and strength in magic and herbal knowledge are elaborately expanded upon within the body of the dirge. As stated earlier, the immediate death is not the only focus of attention. The ancestors also are addressed. For it is believed that the dead form a community that is no different from that of the living. In this community the elders still occupy their revered positions and receive the homage and dutiful attentions of newcomers. That is why most dirges contain messages given to the newly dead for those who have gone generations before. (This is also a very significant feature of the Ewe dirge.) The commemoration of ancestry is divided along the specific lines of paternal (spiritual) and maternal (blood) lineage. It is the relationship of the deceased to these two groups of ancestors which defines his place in *asamado* and the nature of his communication with his offspring. As illustrated, the mourner also speaks about herself. Her farewell depicts death as a journey, and her lamentations restate the stock phrases of departure thus stressing her loneliness. But her function is also to affirm a continued bond with the dead whose spiritual essence can be extended to protect her offspring with whom she has established rapport.

Nketia distinguishes four main types of Akan dirge. All are, however, centered on the conventional theme and motif of death, departure, and spiritual communion. There is the first type—which he calls Type A—which is short and marked by unity of reference to just one ancestor; its structure is stereotyped, but it retains possibilities of being varied according to the mourner's choice. The Type A dirge can be divided into four sections made up of an opening, subject, and close, followed by an extension which carries the verbal expression and the lamentation proper of the dirge. Type B, according to Nketia, is made up of a number of short stanzas which are structured according to a conventional pattern. Type C dirges are patterned on cumulative linear stanzas which open with proclamations and statements of a dozen or so lines. Their power lies in the invocation of the ancestral lineage, and they are an expressive vehicle of memorial mourning. The last, Type D (sample quoted above), is more or less the dirge piece that expresses more of individual sorrow and the pathos of death as it engulfs the mourner in her remembrance (the dead person could still be lying in state) of her dead relative. Types A and B are supposed to be very dignified and thus appropriate for royal funeral occasions.

The dirge is performed in a wailing voice, the words receiving absolute prominence at all times. Sometimes the performance may be accompanied by special musical conventions, responses, and

interjections and shrill outbursts from the other celebrants who
serve as the chorus to the whole ritual.

The last type of Akan poem to be discussed is the praise poem.
(We shall talk in some detail about this when the Zulu praise
poem, or the *izibongo,* is discussed.) Ashanti praise poetry is
carried more by instruments, such as horns and drums, than by
mouth. On these instruments are played the patronymics and the
praise names of the king.

Here is an example of Akan horn poetry, which Nketia describes as tending to be lyrical:

> Conqueror of kings,   1
> the great silk cotton tree has fallen down.
> There is a big river flowing in the valley
> but it has no deposits of gold.
> Asono Gyima that never retracts his words,   5
> noble and tall Osafo Gyamfi Agyei,
> Osafo, father of Osei of Amantem,
> Master of the path, I am exposed to fire.
> Master of the path, I am exposed to fire.[50]

The sounding of the appellations and the boastful salutations are
emphasized in the name calling that the poetry indulges in. Besides, it also expresses the cryptic lyricism of proverbs in the image
of the river flowing in the valley and the proclamations of valor
and truth. The last two lines constitute the horn blower's lamentation and prayer for protection.

The second poem is the drum prelude *Anyaneanyane,* mentioned above, which ushers in the Adae festival. The poem begins, according to Nketia, with the drummer's confession of his
lack of mastery over the drum, a signal statement in humility necessary to establish that important rapport between him and his
sacred instrument. The poem then proceeds as an address to the
earth deity, the witch, the cock and the clockbird, ancestor drummers, and finally the Ashanti sacred river, Tano:

> The path has crossed the river.   1
> The river has crossed the path.
> Which is the elder?
> We made the path and found the river.

The river is from long ago,   5
the river is from the creator of the universe.
Kokon Tano,
Birefia Tano,
River-god of the King of Ashanti,
noble river, noble and gracious one,   10
when we are about to go to war,
we break the news to you.
Slowly and patiently I get on my feet.
Slowly and patiently I get on my feet.
Ta Kofi, noble one,   15
Firampon, condolences!
Condolences!
Condolences!
Ta Kofi, noble one,
the drummer of the Talking Drum says   20
he is kneeling before you.
He prays you, he is about to drum on the Talking Drum.
When he drums, let this drumming be smooth and steady.
Do not let him falter.
I am learning, let me succeed.[51]   25

This drum prelude is played on the twin Ashanti talking drums. The piece is set and invariable. The first two lines stress the primacy of the river which symbolically represents life and its continuous flow from the house of creation right back into the spirit world. The path, cut by man, therefore cannot be older than the river, for the

River is from long ago,
the river is from the Creator of the universe.

But the river is specifically the Ashanti sacred river, Tano, which is part of the Ashanti pantheon. Her spirit and its worship has always been a significant factor in Ashanti history. As most Ashanti wars were fought outside the Ashanti homeland, the river goddess herself played an important role in the going and coming of the Ashanti armies. The whole poem is not only a call to worship but also an affirmation of the drummer's humility and the people's dependence on the river deity, Tano. For the drummer's art, like that of the poet, singer, carver, or dancer, can be realized only with the good will of the gods.

Nketia divides Ashanti poetry into four main groups. The first group comprises of a purely oral poetry which is recited and not sung. This poetry, spoken in connection with chiefship, is replete with allusions to martial glories and the victories of a particular chief. The second group is the type of poetry which is half-spoken and half-sung. This covers the dirge and hunters' song of celebration. The references and allusions are grouped around themes such as ancestors, individuals, and the fortunes of families. The third group he describes as lyric poetry-song used as the vehicle to carry worshipful statements, ceremonial utterances, and individual's poetry. It is also used for highly stylized exhortation and didacticism (apart from proverbs, saws, etc.). The fourth type is the poetry of horn and drum, a sample of which has just been discussed. By their tonal pitch, these instruments imitate human speech and serve as vehicles of poetic statements.

Praise poetry has a special place in the oral literature of Africa. It serves as a significant aspect of chiefship and has always been associated with the chief's court. Its quality and use are varied, from the Hausa praise poets of northern Nigeria, who, at times, operate as individual troubadours and strolling praise-singing mercenaries, to Zulu praise poetry which is part of Zulu military history and exploits. The praise poetry of the Bantu peoples of southern Africa, the second type of oral poetry I will discuss in detail, forms a complex and specialized branch of this type of poetry in sub-Saharan Africa. It has been described as a cross between the epic and the ode, what has further been described as a "combination of exclamatory narration and laudatory apostrophizing." It contains narratives of battles, hunts, and the deeds of heroes. But its statement is dramatic, panegyric, marked by a tone of high solemnity and adulation. Figurative and symbolic use of language, poetic praise names, and an exaggerated tone of high praise and boast are essential hallmarks, as is a certain evocative and highly emotive quality. Certain structural devices are used to achieve these qualities, such as repetition, rhyme, repeated final syllables, alliteration, repeated consonant sounds, assonance, and parallelism. Imagery is also an essential ingredient of this poetry.

In Zulu praise poetry Senzangakhona, King of the Zulu, is described as the gate post (*uthi iwempundu*) of the kraal and his son, Shaka, as the ax (*izembe*) of his father, the "fire of the long, dry grass," the "hawk descending from the hills." The stock images include the sun and the sky, sticks and shields, lions and elephants, which are common titles of address of chiefs. Parallelism is described as a variety of repetition that Zulu poetry employs as an effective literary device. It can be in the form of a simile:

> Innovator who overcame the other chiefs.
> Just as Songodo overcame Malusi.[52]

But its most effective use is seen in such lines as these:

> Who when he lay down was the size of rivers.
> Who when he got up was the size of mountains.[53]

Although normally the salutation to nobility, Zulu praise poems also apostrophize objects and animals. Cattle have a central place in Zulu life and thus receive significant attention as the subject of poetry.

Some of the most famous Zulu praise poems center around Shaka and his heroic exploits in founding and consolidating the Zulu nation and empire. A warrior-king, Shaka, through military conquests, united several of the small Ngoni groups under his rule, rising to the height of his power and reign in 1820. The perfecting of the praise poem during his time was marked by its development from simple clusters of praise appellations to a stanza capable of expressing an episode completely. Mazisi Kunene, the contemporary Zulu poet, attributes this development to Shaka's chief praise poet, Magolwane. What had evolved as a collective effort, he had extended and consolidated into a recognizably effective style. (This has also occurred in other poetries, particularly in the Ewe dirge poem and the impact of one poet, Hesino Akpalu, on the earlier form.) The Shakan praise constitutes a stanza in itself, with four recognizable and unified parts: a statement, its extension, development, and conclusion. For example:

> Hawk which I saw descending from the hills
> of Mangcengeza,
> And from those of Phungashe he disappeared.

They said "Hawk, here he is, there he is!"
Whereas he was silent in the forest like the
leopards and lions.[54]

Lines 1 and 2 constitute the statement, while line 3 is the extension of the statement. Line 4 is the development of the statement from the extension. Lines 5 and 6 become the rounding up
or the conclusion. Either extension or the development may be
omitted but not both; the statement and one of the two—extension
or development—together with the conclusion constitute the rigid
structure of the Shakan praise poem. The most essential constituent
of this poem is the conclusion. For certain dramatic effects, the
conclusion may be left out, but its implication is always clear, for
at times it becomes so obvious that it will be unnecessary to restate
it.

Buffalo whose horns are widespread,
they thought it would not cross the Mhlathuze,
thinking they were preventing it by heaps of spears.[55]

While line 1 is the statement, lines 2 and 3 constitute the development. The conclusion is left to the listener's imagination.

The style of the praise poem of the Zulu chiefs (perfected from
around 1750 to 1900) was at its most experimental and innovative during Shaka's reign (1816–28), the period of Zulu consolidation. This is not to suggest, however, that the Zulu form did
not borrow stylistic devices from allied languages of the Natal
Ngoni group, especially from the coastal peoples.

The main topic of the Bantu praise poem is the chief's military
exploits and record on the battlefield. But there may be comments
on his personality and his ancestry and sometimes sly rebukes or
sarcastic remarks about some weakness in his rule. Exaggeration
and hyperbole are essential features of the poem. The fierceness of
a battle is described in this way:

The small herbs were frostbitten in the middle
of summer.
The trees lost their leaves,
the sparrows, the birds that lay eggs in the trees,
forsook their nests.[56]

Figurative and allusive devices describe actions, qualities, and attributes of people. Finnegan writes:

> There is little stress on personal emotions, lyrical descriptions of nature, or straightforward narration. Rather a series of pictures is conveyed to the listener through a number of laconic and often rather staccato sentences, a grouping of ideas which may on different occasions come in a different order.[57]

She cites a short passage first discussed by the late Absalom Vilakazi, a Zulu poet, which is a sample of economic use of imagery to convey a total figurative impact:

> The thunder that bursts on the open
> where mimosa trees are none,
> the giant camouflaged with leaves,
> in the track of Nxaba's cattle.
> he refuses tasks imposed by other people.[58]

Shaka's temper is the thunderstorm that strikes down the mimosa trees. The thunder is the brother of the giant elephant. Line 4 states how he is able to win back the cattle of Nxaba, one of Shaka's generals who fled north. Shaka's intrepid power and unconquerable spirit is summed up in the last line. These poems do not only constitute charged statements on action and valorous deeds; they may, at times, express an inherent lyricism which indicates an attachment to nature:

> The greenness which kisses that of a gall-bladder
> butterfly of Phunga, tinted with circling spots,
> as if made by the twilight from the shadow of mountains
> in the dusk of the evening, when the wizards are abroad.[59]

Or the praise of the blue lizard:

> Blue-throated lizard of the lizards,
> a blue chest I have put on.
> Brown I also have put on,
> I, father-of-clinging of the hillside.[60]

The stress in the Zulu praise poem is on the hero. It is linked up, in its social significance, with the aristocratic nature of the southern Bantu societies. These societies, like most others in western Africa, are based on hierarchical systems of birth and the per-

fected institutions of chieftaincy and its divine dimensions. The
poetic ingredients of Zulu praise poems are drawn from nature—
and from a pastoral life centered around the cattle. But its poetic
significance as a historical literary style rests in its embeddedness
in the military tradition, particularly the Zulu. The Zulu nation,
before its demise in the mid-nineteenth century in the face of
superior military power from Europe, based its militarism on personal bravery, competition among members of the same age group
for honor and glory in the field of battle, or on the hunt where man
pits his brute strength and cunning against those of the beasts of
the great southern African savannas. The desire for fame and
honor extended even into death, as a brave man's memory was
kept alive in these praise poems which, in themselves, served to
consolidate these values. Pride in family, cattle, and clan, in chiefship, in birth, in military achievement, all were aspects of the social
function which the praise poem fulfilled.

The most significant Zulu poems, as pointed out earlier, were
those related to Shaka, his court, and his outstanding military exploits. He rose to the throne in 1816, the son of Senzangakhona.
He and his mother, Nandi, were exiled because of court intrigue.
He succeeded to the throne with the help of Dingiswayo, a powerful Zulu chief, and proceeded to extend the frontiers of his kingdom
through conquest, first over the larger and more significant Qwabe
group. His most spectacular conquest was over the Ndwandwe
under Zwide who had earlier defeated Dingiswayo. These conquests form the subject of the best of Shaka's praise poems. They
are less personal and more national and are described as less ode
and more epic, and they reflect the attainment of nationhood and
a wider political dimension for the Zulu under Shaka. Militaristic
interests are reflected in the stories of conquests, the images of
noble animals such as lions, leopards, elephants, and phenomena
such as fires and thunder; the praiseworthy warrior virtues of brute
strength, ferocity, and rage outweighed diplomacy and subtlety.
Shaka's image through praise poetry therefore conferred the
qualities of arrogance, confidence, and aggressiveness upon the
Zulu people, qualities with which they are identified even today in
spite of the changed fortunes of the Zulu under white fascist rule.
Here is a sample of a typical Shakan praise poem.

Dlungwana son of Ndaba,   1
ferocious one of the Mbelebele brigade,
who raged among the large kraals,
so that until dawn the huts were turned outside down.
He who is famous as he sits, son of Menzi,   5
he who beats but is not beaten, unlike water,
ax that surpasses other axes in sharpness;
Shaka, I fear to say he is Shaka,
Shaka, he is the Chief of the Mashobas.
He one of the shrill whistle, the lion.   10
He who armed in the forest, who is like a madman,
the madman who is in full view of the men.
He who trudged wearily the plain going to Mfene,
the voracious one of Senzangakhona,
Spear that is red even on the handle,   15
The open-handed one, they have matched the regiments.
They were matched by Moju, and Nggengenye,
the one belonging to Ntombazi and the other Nandi.
He brought out the one with the red brush,
brought out by the white one of Nandi.   20
They called him to Mthandeni, despising him,
they said! We cannot compete in dancing with this
Xtungwa from up country,
Whereas he was going to annihilate Phakathwayo in the
return competition.[61]   25

First of all, the statement-extension-development-conclusion structure of the Shakan praise poem can be noted: lines 1 to 4 constituting the statement, lines 5 to 15 the extension, lines 16 to 22 the development, and lines 24 to 25 the conclusion. The poem begins with the salutation and the opening praise expressed in lines 1 to 4. These state Shaka's appellations, Dlungwana, the rager, the ferocious one. The noun is derived from the verb *dlunga,* to rage, by means of which the statement is extended into noun-verb initial link parallelism. Lines 5 to 15 contain most of the simple single-line praises and recall events in the Zulu nation around the time of Shaka's accession. "He who is famous as he sits" in line 5 refers to Shaka's famous praise name "Nodumehlezi," translated as "he who is famous without effort." "Menzi" refers to Shaka's father, Senzangakhona, addressed here as the Creator. Line 10 yokes together two faculties of voice and strength to describe Shaka. The reference to the madman is a piece of historical evidence that links Shaka with the killing of a madman who terrorized the district in which Shaka spent his youth in exile with his mother, Nandi.[62] "Unlike water" (line 6) refers to the invincibility of Shaka; water can be beaten but to no effect, but Shaka cannot be beaten at all. Line 15, "Spear that is red even on the handle" refers to the blood that covers the spear right up to the handle. It is said that Shaka proved his prowess while still a young boy in the army of Dingiswayo, his military mentor and subsequent right-hand man. Lines 16 to 20 constitute a praise stanza referred to as the transitional type (as lines 1 to 15 represent the pre-Shakan style). It consists of the extension and the development. It is the story of how Shaka lured Zwide into Zululand. Noju was one of Zwide's counselors who conspired with Shaka to betray him. Nggengenye was one of Shaka's generals. Ntombazi was Zwide's mother. Lines 19 and 20 refer to Shaka, the white one, and Zwide, the red one. These seem to be references to the colors of the shields of the two men. Mthandeni (line 21) refers to the chief kraal of the Qwabe clan which belongs to the Xtungwa (line 23) branch of the Ngoni-Bantu people just as did the Zulu clan. Phakathwayo (line 24) was the Qwabe chief who allegedly insulted Shaka at a dance, one of the reasons why Shaka was later to destroy him. The last two lines constitute the conclusion of the poem which carries a contrary twist emphasizing Shaka's invincibility. These twenty-five lines, it must be noted, form only the opening part of a long praise poem that runs to 450 lines, the performance of which may last for hours. The section quoted here sets the tone for the Zulu leader's ferocious future career by describing him as a strong youth whose life held a great deal of promise. It reveals the preparations he received as a youth, the provocations and the justifications of his future ferocity already locked in the frightening dimensions of his lineage.

The last type of oral poetry to be discussed in detail comes from among the Ewe of Ghana, this writer's own group. The general remarks made about oral poetry applies in many ways to Ewe poetry too.

Ewe poetry is embedded in the drums. By "drums" I do not mean only the physical entities of leather and wood, rattle, gongs,

and other such instruments which are normally part of the African
musical ensemble. By "drums" I mean chiefly the musical and
poetic styles and content of the various types of drumming performances that abound in the Ewe country. Some of these drums
are historical monuments, repositories of legend and mythology.
Others are expressions of the attributes of occupational groups
such as hunters, cult priests, and deital devotees. Others record as
a matter of course the various facets of Ewe life: war (in the olden
days), love, courtship, funerals, rites, royalty, chiefship, medicine,
and herbalism. It is from these various drums that emerges the
poetry proper of the Ewe. Other poetic forms can also be found
in libations, cult prayers, invocations, the acquisition and practice
of magic and medicine, "name" calling or salutation, and various
other forms of the verbal art.

The language of the drumming songs reveals poetry in its varied
range. In the performance of the famous drums (*atrikpui,
kpegisu,* the war drums; *husago, brekete, yewe,* the medicine, or
ritual, drums; *adzro, kete, sibisaba, tudzi,* the youth and lovers'
drums), the poet, or *heno,* first recites the whole range of the poetry
of the song solo, as if reminding his followers and himself of the
depth and significance of particular words and points. At times he
skips through the poetry at a rapid pace, at times he takes it slowly
and deliberately, soliciting verbal and modal responses from his
followers. The drums are silent. When he is done, the rattles and
gongs and the drums pick up the beat and the *heno* moves into the
center with his fly whisk and, with the whole chorus, gives emphasis
to the words. The first part of this type of performance is *hamekoko,*
the "taking apart" of the song; it is the recitation itself, the statement of the poetry. What follows is the arrangement of this poetic
statement in emphatic structural forms marked out by choral response, dialogue between *heno* and *vuviawo,* or songsters, and the
accompanying sound of the various instruments.

Ewe dirge poetry is naturally slow and funereal, encompassing
and expressing the pathos of loss through death:

  I am on the world's extreme corner.
  I am not sitting in the row with the eminent.
  But those who are lucky sit in the middle and forget.
  I can only go beyond and forget.[63]

The poet laments his own loneliness caused by death, which has torn down the fence around him, exposing him to wind and rain and sun. Sitting on "the world's extreme corner" connotes the concept of being outside the human family. If sorrow strikes, it strikes at those outside the pale of human society. Those sitting in the middle are those who are protected by relatives and wealth and have no fear of disaster. The poet's desire to go beyond, that is, to the land of the dead, is grounded in the African belief that one's ancestors are in the spirit world and will provide comfort and solace to their offspring when life's troubles are over. The poet's lot is an unhappy one. The Ewe are fatalistic; *se,* or destiny, sends us into the world, each with his mission; for some *se* has planted their grinding stone under shady trees, for others in the hot noonday sun. The tone of this dirge also connotes a criticism of the dead ancestors in *avlime,* or spirit world, who should protect their offspring from the buffeting storms of this earthly wilderness called life and obviously do not. The performance of the dirge is a preserve of women; drums play very little part, as the words are given absolute prominence. The greatest dirge poet of the Ewe today is Vinoko Akpalu of the Anlo-Ewe.

Here is another example of an Ewe dirge poem:

> Mother who freely gives of what she has,
> fresh food and cooked meals.
> Mother, who never deserts the hearth.
> Mother, hearken to me.
> The crying child will call after its mother.
>
> How is it that mother does not answer when I call?
> Are we quarreling?[64]

G. Adali-Mortty points out the overwhelming pathos of the last line, "Are we quarreling?"—a question the orphaned child asks the laid-out corpse of her dead mother—as revealing the controlled intensity of the sorrow and loneliness of death that takes away the mainstay of the homestead, the mother. One quarrels with one's father perhaps into death, but with one's mother, a new sun cannot rise over a disagreement. When a mother dies, the Ewe say, she has turned her back upon her children; and it is only your most implacable enemies who turn their backs on you.

Ewe poetry, as pointed out earlier, includes songs of the various occupational groups. A popular fishermen's poem invokes the white swordfish:

Anipaye, Anipaye,
I myself shall stay at the net's end
While you go beneath the testicle.[65]

("Testicle" is a literal translation of *vo,* the last bag on the long seine net.)

The medicine man's art consists of a series of chants and incantations which reflect the trade's groundedness in symbolism and the magic that is part of the function of the *word.* The stanza

I will be under the trees.
Under the trees I will be
And the rain will come and beat me.[66]

from Afa divination states the invincibility of him who has received the particular message which makes him immune to the power of thunder striking tall trees in heavy rainstorms. The medicine drum, which is a cult drum by itself, encompasses the knowledge of herbs and of the conduct of animals stated in heraldic terms. The couplet

When the rams are alive
The ewes cannot perform the weed-off . . .[67]

is an oblique reference to the dominant spirit of man in affairs magical and spiritual. Afa divination is widespread in Eweland and bears close affinity to the Yoruba Ifa from which it may have derived. Diviners are poets in their own right, since the language of the oracle is shrouded in the secret nature of the cult—explainable only in a very complicated language dominated by symbolism and imagery. Here is an example:

The hot birds flew into the palm groves,   1
the female crocodiles went into the bird forest.
I did not think it will be like this.
Great priests, I did not think so.
I never surmised it will be like this.[68]   5

Or another example:

The diviner said it. I have no child.

It was not good for me, the message.
The Dzisa priests are looking for an abode of rest.
To have no one to lean on
is a burden. The anago priests   10
are looking for a home.
The diviners said it, I have no child.
I am lost.[69]

Some of the best type of Ewe traditional poetry came from the warrior organizations. This tradition is reflected in a fierce belligerence which survives into the warrior dances of *atsia* and *agbekor.* The old war drums, *atrikpui* and *kpegisu,* however, are rarely performed today, except at the funeral of very old people. Its modern version, *agbadza,* still retaining something of the brisk *atrikpui* beat, captures the verbal agility of war poetry, full of taunts and boasts, exaggerated verbal gestures, hyperbolic symbols, and sheer verbal play. The war drums are also funeral drums for old and reverent departed ones. They form a tribute to bravery and heroism.

I shall sleep in calico.
War has come upon the sons of men
and I shall sleep in calico.
We have arrived at the bridge head.
Tears fall.
We have arrived at the jetty.
Tears fall.
If you have no heart,
please go home.

I shall sleep in the desert land.
I shall sleep in the desert land
without moving my feet
I shall sleep in the desert land.
Guns in our hands we cannot fire.
Machetes in our hands we cannot throw.
Without moving my feet
I shall sleep in the desert land.
When we move the earth shall split.
War has struck Dahomey.
When we move the earth shall split.[70]

War poetry is marked by yells and wild gestures of defiance calculated to frighten the enemy, recall the bravery of the ancestors, and instill the spirit of daring in the young men. Today, as noted, the war drums are performed only at the funerals of elders and notables, as tributes to their wisdom and sagacity and as a token of respect for these revered dead.

The calling of the poet is intuitive. At times it is hereditary but only in the sense that a son may possess the talent of his father. A poet emerges, he is born, out of the traditions of songs, and he is the bearer of exceptional skill in words and has the talent to weave those words into coherent poetic statements. Among the young men's and women's drumming groups, the *heno* (poet-cantor) will be obvious. He makes up the songs, perfects them, rearranges them, organizes them, and, in turn, teaches his followers in rehearsals, or *hakpa*. His talent is self-evident, immediately recognizable in the association on which the particular drum is based and for which he creates poetry. He may have as an assistant another singer, preferably a woman, whose function is to teach this material to the women and thus provide the female choral counterpart in voice or accompaniment during the *hame-koko*. Female poets also are about, but their role is limited to exclusive women drums, which are not as common as the joint drums. Our young poet, of clear voice and an acclaimed ability to weave words, create allusions, and "speak," may grow from association to association. Some of these may center around old drums, some may be new drums created by the *heno*.

To have the ability to create song, the Ewe believes, is a gift from the gods. So in the Ewe pantheon there is a god of songs, or *hadzivodu*. He is the inspirer and the creator of songs. The poet, or *heno*, is only an instrument in the god's hands. That is why every poet who has a god of songs must pour libation and offer prayers to his god before he appears in public to perform. Singing, like all other aspects of Ewe life, is not a purely secular act. Its sacred nature lies in the power of the god to intervene and take away a poet's voice. In the phenomenon of *halo*, or the poetry of abuse, the *heno* is aware of rival forces marshaled against him. Among these forces are workers in evil medicine. But evil medicine, it is believed, cannot affect you if the gods do not approve. So the poet must be at harmony with both household and public gods.

Many traditional poets do not accept any necessity for a *hadzivodu* in their work. They achieve the spiritual rapport they need only with their household or public gods who are their protectors. Some, however, specifically acquire a *hadzivodu* and make him personal to themselves. The poet, if he means to acquire one, goes to the diviners who establish contact with the god and serve as intermediaries between him and the poet. Through divination and revelation, information is transmitted to the poet as to what kind of objects he must acquire. He acquires a brass pan, white clay modeled into human form, a selection of herbs, a fly whisk, fowls, and drinks for offering. A day is set for the "placing" of the god, a day on which he is to be "established." When the ceremony, marked by offerings of drink and food, and libation is over, the poet goes home with his god image. To this he makes offerings and pours libation at the appropriate season. There may be a few taboos to observe.

Other poets are born poets. But they are aware of the power of the muse. Their song, they may say, comes to them in their sleep and they wake up at the moment of its arrival and record it in their heads. Sometimes if it comes, by the time they wake up it has fled. Then they know they must make offerings to household gods and deities who will see to it that when the muse comes, the song stays. These are born poets, gifted with the power of words, who yet acknowledge the power of a divinity as the essence of song with which they must be in accord.

What is very striking about the Ewe oral tradition is the individuality of the poets. Even though their work has full meaning only within the all-embracing scope of the folk tradition, the individual genius and talent of the poets come into full play, contradicting the popular notion that performers are generally following rigidly laid down patterns in their art.

The dirge tradition, as pointed out earlier, owes its development to the work of Vinoko Akpalu, now about ninety years old. This is yet another example of a whole tradition owing its development and expansion to the work of one man, as was noted in the case of Zulu praise poetry during Shaka's rule. Akpalu's dirge pattern is not very rigid; yet it utilizes certain recurrent forms which reveal a structural regularity. For example, the poem opens with a statement about the mourner's condition or predicament, then moves into a general lamentation, and ends with a message, supplication, or prayer to those gone ahead into the spirit world. As with the other oral poetic forms discussed above, such syntactic devices as repetition of lines or whole segments, parallelism, alliteration, assonance, and pun are frequently used. The dirge also contains imagery drawn from nature, symbolism, and allusions and other regular poetic devices. But the main preoccupation of the dirge poet is himself, for the dirge is more a personal lament, full of self-pity. Here is a typical sample of Akpalu's dirges:

Soon I would be dead and gone from amongst you.	1
This branch will break off.	
The sons of men have gathered in counsel,	
debating how they will deal with Akpalu.	
Death is within my homestead.	5
My mother's children, soon I shall be gone from amongst you.	
This branch will fall.	
Someone find me tears to shed.	
Vinoko says he wished he had some tears to shed;	
a mother-in-law may get back a thing, but not one's tears.	10
I say I wish I had some tears to shed.	
Some people write	
to deny the blood that binds us,	
that Akpalu should be severely dealt with,	
that Agoha's ring should cease.	15
The sons of men are in counsel,	
debating just how to deal with Akpalu.	
The singer's death is not from any distant place.	
Death is within my homestead.	
Children of my mother, soon I would be dead and gone	20
from amongst you.	
This branch will break off.[71]	

The first line, the opening statement, does not refer to the dead person at all, but to the imminent death that stares the mourner in the face. Line 2 refers to the mourner as the branch. This image comes from the Ewe conception of the family as a tree, with the ancestors as the genealogical center, and the principal homestead the trunk, and all the members the branches. This line also indicates that the "you" of the first line refers to the members of the poet's family. This is again stressed in line 5, "Death is within my homestead." The belief is commonplace that the death that kills a man is within his very homestead. This is further explained in the proverb: "The insect that will bite you has its home in your cover cloth."

"My mother's children" in line 6 again refers to the kinsmen. All kinsmen are regarded as sharing the same blood, thus they are symbolically one's mother's children since they can all trace a common ancestry. Line 6 is a variation on line 1, just as line 7 is an approximate repetition of line 2. Line 8 connotes the overwhelming nature of his sorrow and, very obliquely, the burden of the threats being made against him by his own kinsmen. "Someone find me tears to shed" expresses the breathless inability to weep while in the grip of this sorrow. When events are overly painful, the impact is beyond tears. The emphasis here is on the treachery of the kinsmen, which is so painful as to hurt the mourner even beyond the capacity of seeking relief in tears. Line 9 is a repetition of line 8, with a variation achieved through the stress on the poet's own name, Vinoko. Line 10 reveals the power of the mother-in-law in kinship and familial relationship. The mother-in-law can make an unlimited number of demands on the man because she still retains a great amount of power over her daughter. She can ask and receive many things, but in this instance if she asks the poet to shed tears, there will be none forthcoming. This line is a repetitive variation on the lines 8 and 9, which yet forestalls line 11. The whole section from line 9 to line 11, therefore, constitutes a segmented whole. Lines 12 to 17 represent another segment; this describes the activities of his enemies. First they deny the kinship relationship between him and them and ask for stringent measures against him. (It was said that this poem was inspired by a lawsuit that developed between the poet and some of his own relatives; in the process of this suit, Akpalu was brought before the council of the elders charged with defamation and slander in an earlier song.) Lines 16 and 17 are again repetitions of lines 3 and 4. The last five lines revert to the opening lines, emphasizing the closeness of death to the poet and lamenting his imminent departure to the world beyond. The tight structure of this poem is evidenced in the use of repetition of individual lines and of segments and also in the integrity and completeness of the segments themselves in terms of ideas, sentiment, and imagery.

The next poem is a more direct dirge, slightly different from the one discussed above because it relates to the immediacy of a death. The poem above, though cast in the dirge mold and performed at a funeral, is more of a lament than a dirge. In the next poem, however, the poet's own sorrow expresses the deep sense of loss which the death of his only sister engenders.

```
What all else in the land does                              1
turns sour upon me.
I say she should just remain for me
a palm-branch so that when the rainy day comes,
Akpalu might cover his head with it.                         5
There is war at our gate,
Vinoko says there is war at our gate.
There is war from the very heavens.
Akpalu would not plunge his head into it.
Comrades! The bush has brought misfortune.                 10
Poor man, the bush has brought misfortune.
What all else in this land will do
Turns sour on me.
Let even a bad sister just be
a palm-branch with which to cover my head                   15
When the day of rains comes.[72]
```

The principal image here is that of the palm branch. The sister is seen as the palm branch which will be used as cover during the rain. Death has removed the sister, who, it is hinted, was perhaps of no great help when she was alive. This is suggested in line 14. The structural devices of repetition are here; lines 2 and 13 and lines 4 and 15 are examples. War represents death's attack upon the homestead. Lines 10 and 11 are allusions to certain herbs that were used as cures for the ailing sister which turned out to have aggravated her illness and brought on death.

The last poem I will discuss is also in this vein, but expresses in a more passionate manner the poet's loss of his only child. The importance of these "personal" dirge pieces is that they serve very well as instruments of mourning for anyone who falls into similar predicament.

How does this world fit us into it?   1
As for Vinoko, he does not understand.
Death has gone a step too far!
When one possesses an only thing, is it to be taken from him?
Death has poured out my life.   5
How does this world fit us into it?
As for Vinoko, he is so unlucky.
Akpalu's misfortunes
Are not to be compared with anyone else's.
How the beast torments me!   10
I, a sick fowl, perched upon the fence,
Am bypassed by the wolf for a stronger one indoors.
How does this world fit us into it?
Vinoko does not understand.[73]

Here a deep-seated anger is expressed by the querulous and plain-tive tone of the first line. This is stressed again by the total tone of resignation in line 2. Line 3 is a violent outburst against death. This tone of complaint and outrage ends with the tearful query of line 4: "When one possesses an only thing, is it to be taken away from him?" Line 5 brings in a new, startling image of a vessel out of which death has poured the life liquid, which here represents his only child around whom his life centered. The connotation of total emptiness is powerfully suggested in this line. It is as if there is a universal conspiracy against him, a plot to pick on him. The "one" of the poem recalls the folk tale, used also in the Afa divination, of how, though all other animals have litters of two, the lion has one and how the leopard came for the lion's only child one after-noon when the father lion was not at home. Line 6 repeats line 1. Line 10 introduces the imagery of death as a predatory beast. The poet's torment is expressed in the next two lines, a well-structured segment of the whole poem.

What is significant about Akpalu's poetry is his sense of loneli-ness and betrayal and his deep sense of despair. When this writer spoke to him in the summer of 1970, he was alone in his little hut by the lagoon at Anyako in eastern Ghana, his eyesight failing. He was keenly aware of his place in the tradition of the dirge among the Ewe. His worry was what would happen to the style which he had spent his lifetime establishing and perfecting. But it is evident from my own studies that his dirge poetic style is well established, and hundreds of younger poets have followed Akpalu's footsteps in adding more poems and songs to this exciting type of oral poetry.

Two other poets whose work I came into contact with represent another variety of the Ewe poetic medium and, as in the case of Akpalu, significant evidence of the important role of the individual poet. These were the *halo* poets Komi Ekpe and Amega Dunyo. These two poets in their earliest works had been part of the *halo,* or poetry of abuse, tradition, long a feature of Ewe poetic tradition. *Halo* expresses itself in invective, satire, and insults. Two sections of a village or two separate villages may engage in *halo* for years.

The first poet, Komi Ekpe, now an old man, started singing when he was about twenty, just before the First World War. He has a *hadzivodu,* a personal god of songs, from whom he claims he receives poetic inspiration in his sleep. The god was his protector during fierce contests of *halo*. Before he sings or makes a public appearance, he offers his god a drink offering. Ekpe's poetic skill rests in his verbal versatility. He moves from light-hearted poetry full of exaggerated abuse and invective to heavy sorrowful and sententious poetry that borrows heavily from the dirge. This second type of poetry stresses his intense loneliness (he has buried all his children, he says). His abuse poetry is recognized for its vitriolic sharpness. He is a man of wit with a devastatingly wicked tongue. This writer was shown a respectable elder who had moved out of the village of Tsiame because of Ekpe's persistent verbal assaults on him at wakes and funerals. Ekpe has sung widely outside his own home town. His forte is sarcasm, allusion to events which are part of local history to which he makes references in order to clinch a point, and a generally effective sense of humor. Here is a sample of Ekpe's *halo* poetry as translated by this writer:

She with the jawbone of a cow   1
falling upon her chest like sea egret's beak,
Her waist flat,
earlobes hanging, oversize intestines,
it was you who took my affairs to Sokpe   5
and asked him to sing against me.
I do not refuse;
I am not afraid of song.

I shall stay at home; if anyone likes,
let him come; whatever he has,   10
let him say it;
I shall listen.
I was far up north
when Kunye of the mad ram's face
came and insulted me.   15
There is no one. I shall tell
a little tale to the slave;
let him open wide his ears and listen.
They heaped slave-insults upon Aheto's head
and he swore a lengthy oath   20
full of boasts and boasts
that he was not a slave.
Atomi came and said it.
We caught him, sold him to Zogbede.
Zogbede bought him with his own wealth   25
Your grandmother was taken from Yosu
from there she came to Tsiame.
The people of Dagbame, do you wear underclothes?
A small underpant was put upon your grandmother
and she burst into tears.[74]   30

The poem opens with an insult directed against a particular woman member of the opposing side. Lines 1 to 4 are an accumulation of abuse. The images used—the jawbone of a cow, the sea egret's beak —underlie a specific nature of the Ewe insult as it tends to concentrate on such items as lack of good looks, ungainly gait, and ugliness in general. Lines 5 and 6 state the provocation the poet has had. He had obviously been attacked in song by another *halo* poet, Sokpe, at the instigation of the woman. Lines 7 to 12 contain expressions of boast and of patient anticipation of a verbal fight. Another opponent, Kunye, in line 14 is described as a man with the face of a mad ram. Lines 16 to 30 form an important segment of the poem in that it plows into the opponent's antecedents. *Halo* does not concentrate only on the immediate opponents—it extends its insults to the opponent's ancestors. One of the most fearsome insults centers around slavery. As pointed out above, domestic slavery was a feature of traditional Africa. It functioned as a substitute for prisons. Offenders—criminals—debtors especially, were sold into slavery or went into servitude under those to whom they owed money. A chronic indigent might be sold very far from home by his own relatives in order to pay the embarrassing debts which he incurred as a result of profligacy and reckless living. Reference to this becomes an insult to his offspring—a skeleton in the family, or clan, cupboard, as it were—engendering shame and embarrassment. This kind of insult is calculated to shut up an opponent for good. The fact remains, however, that *halo* also depends on inventiveness, and an insult may be based on sheer fiction.

The second poet, Dunyo, primarily a *halo* poet, was also impressive as a poet of the long lament. He had been an opponent of Ekpe in the *halo* during their youth. What is striking about Dunyo is the overwhelming ennui and deep sense of despair which was engendered by the death of a kinsman and a friend called Zanu in most of his work. Dunyo is now about eighty but still an active poet of the *adzima* drumming association which he founded himself. His style is that of the long lament which is highly personal, allusively clear about such wide questions as man and his destiny in the world. Here is an example of Dunyo's work:

```
Our adzima drums have stepped out;                          1
who will listen to the songs of sorrow?
Who put death's rope on the ram's neck
and yet the ram refused to move?
Call the poet's supporters, call his chorus.                5
I do not know what I've done.
We went afar looking for wealth;
Ekuadzi went to the land of spirits
leaving his kinsmen behind.
Mothers of children cried into sobs.                       10
The winds of the grave blow here.
My mother's child died;
Death is adamant, death is very adamant.
Shall I sing the Christian's song
about angels circling a throne                             15
and the heavens opened
so my mother's child shall see the promised kingdom?
The boat has arrived on the other shore.
Who heard the songs of sorrow?
```

Dunyo says not nay; he agrees.   20
Go and tell the elders that
when they go to death's homeland
and see how affairs are,
let them come and inform their offspring.
I will stay till Zanu returns;   25
if it were so, I will await his return.
And so Death locked the door waiting for me,
waiting to come and uproot
what lies in life's field.
I leave the rest to the chorus.   30
I leave the rest to my songsters.[75]

"Adzima drums" refers to Dunyo's own association. Line 2 establishes that this is a lament, a "song of sorrow." This type of an-
nouncement is also commonly heard in the dirge in which the
poet-cantor calls upon his audience to listen to his song. In line 3
the poet sees himself as the sacred ram on the way to the sacrifice.
Lines 3 and 4 ask a rhetorical question. When the death rope is
put on the ram's neck, it cannot refuse to move. The poet is now
the ram on whose neck this rope is placed. His enemies have
planned his death and his ancestors concur, so he cannot refuse to
go. Line 5 is a call to the community who may perhaps insulate
him against the frightening loneliness of his pending fate. Lines
7, 8, and 9 are statements about the meaning of his destiny.
Ekuadzi, his own kinsman, went by foot to *avlime,* the land of
spirits, to seek the meaning of this life. At his death, there was great
mourning, as suggested by line 10. After this brief diversion, the
poem returns to the world of the living, stating the imminence of
death in the line, "The winds of the grave blow here." The inexorable and destructive adamancy of death is stated in lines 12 and
13, with the usual technique of repetition being used in line 13.
There is a hopelessness that expresses itself in the poet's search for
an answer and in the desire to go as far as into the Christian Church
for the knowledge. This segment—lines 14 to 17—shows how ready
the traditional poem is to absorb imagery, ideas, and motifs from
other cultures, in this case Christianity. Line 18 makes a reference
to the Ewe mythology of crossing Kuto, the river that separates
the world of the living from that of the dead. Line 20 is a reaffirma-

tion of his readiness already stated in line 4. Lines 21 to 26 constitute a message to the dead, to the elders who have gone ahead to *avlime*. The message is for the elders to return to the living world to inform their offspring how affairs stand in the land of the dead. Zanu is the poet's close relation who had died and around whom most of Dunyo's songs center. Line 27, "And so Death locked the door waiting for me," expresses the idea of death as the predator, in this case, the slaver who waits inside the locked gates in life's field, ready to strike. The last two lines constitute absolute resignation, a giving up of the struggle.

From the foregoing discussions, it would be seen that oral literature covers a wide field and is diverse in subject matter, technique, and style. What seems to be an important truth is that practitioners of this traditional art possess an individuality and genius of their own, even though their art exists and has meaning within the *Gestalt* of the group. Individual poets suffer from the same, sad sense of loneliness which marks them as sensitive human beings. Their work is realizable fully only within the context of the whole group since their art has its impact within the specific genius of the language, culture, and the system of beliefs and philosophy of that group. This does not mean, as already noted, that types and styles of this literature do not travel farther afield than its own place of origin. Poets, praise singers, and storytellers and the materials they deal with exist in continuous development and flux. A great deal of this literature still exists, for about eighty per cent of Africa is still rural. The social, political, and economic conditions may differ, but the literary or aesthetic outlook remains the same, firmly based in man's infinite ability to manipulate language at a highly complex and sophisticated level in order to communicate the primary sensations pertaining to life, history, men, gods, destiny, and death.

Part III

Contemporary Africa

In Africa, this emphasis [on means of social cohesion] must take objective account of our present situation at the return of political independence. From this point of view, there are three broad features to be distinguished here. African society has one segment which comprises our traditional way of life; it has a second segment which is filled by the presence of Islamic tradition in Africa; it has a final segment which represents the infiltration of Christian tradition and culture of Western Europe into Africa using colonialism and neocolonialism as its primary vehicles.

KWAME NKRUMAH, *Consciencism*

With true independence regained, however, a new harmony needs to be forged, a harmony that will allow the combined presence of traditional Africa, Islamic Africa, and Euro-Christian Africa, so that this presence is in tune with the original humanist principles underlying African society. Our society is not the old society, but a new society enlarged by Islamic and Euro-Christian influences!

KWAME NKRUMAH, *Consciencism*

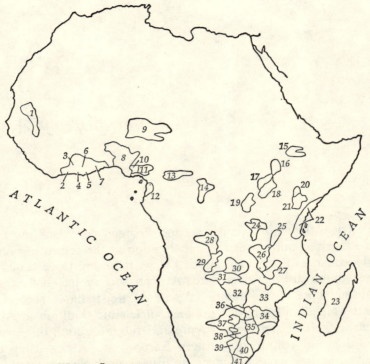

African Written Languages
in Sub-Saharan Africa

1. *Tukulov*	**15.** *Chaha*	**29.** *Lozi*
2. *Nzema*	**16.** *Acholi*	**30.** *Lenje*
3. *Ashanti*	**17.** *Nyoro-Toro*	**31.** *Tonga*
4. *Fanti*	**18.** *Ganda*	**32.** *Ndebele*
5. *Ga*	**19.** *Kwanda*	**33.** *Shona*
6. *Akuapem*	**20.** *Kikuyu*	**34.** *Tswa*
7. *Ewe*	**21.** *Kamba*	**35.** *Tsonga*
8. *Yoruba*	**22.** *Swahili*	**36.** *Venda*
9. *Hausa*	**23.** *Malagasy*	**37.** *Tswana*
10. *Edo*	**24.** *Bemba .*	**38.** *Pedi*
11. *Igbo*	**25.** *Tumbuka*	**39.** *Sotho*
12. *Duala*	**26.** *Chewa*	**40.** *Zulu*
13. *Chaha*	**27.** *Nyanja*	**41.** *Xhosa*
14. *Ngala*	**28.** *Lurale*	

0   500   1000 *miles*

Literature in African languages: Samples of Sotho, Xhosa, Ewe, Hausa, and Swahili literature

The beginnings of modern literature in Africa can be traced to the work of missionary institutions throughout the continent. Most African languages received orthography as a result of missionary work based on the realization of the need to translate the Bible and other holy works of Christian dogma and teaching into African languages. The spread of Islam also gave impetus to literary activity in Swahili and Hausa, two languages most influenced by the Arabic.

The earliest literary works in African languages naturally reflected the religious orientation of the missionaries. In West Africa, languages such as Ewe, Igbo, Ashanti, Yoruba, and Duala were written down by the end of the last century. The Bible and Bunyan's *Pilgrim's Progress* were immediately translated into these languages in order to facilitate the work of the missionaries and to train catechists and teachers. The same thing happened in the case of Sotho, Xhosa, and Zulu in southern Africa. As of now, it is difficult to determine how much literature has actually been produced in African languages as the problem of linguistic accessibility is compounded with that of the multiplicity of languages in Africa, most of which have up till now not been properly classified or documented.

Two sets of examples of vernacular literature will suffice to illustrate the nature of what was being written in these languages. The first set is made up of examples of three indigenous African languages. The impetus, as was stated earlier, came from missionary sources and the direction has remained, even till today, largely missionary inspired.

Sotho, a Bantu language, was the first southern African language into which the Bible was translated. Its earliest vernacular literature was therefore inspired by trained local catechists. The Paris Evangelical Mission in Morija, for example, undertook the publication in Sotho of a fictional work of one of its pupils, Thomas Mofolo, who was employed as a proofreader in the missionary press in 1906. *Moeti oa Bochabela* (*The Pilgrim for the East*) is a convert's book. Fekesi, the hero, spurred by belief in the infinite goodness of the Almighty God, escapes the degraded life of drunkenness, vice, and debauchery to seek the succor of the true God as his dream premonitions directed. He journeys eastward across deserts till he reaches the coast land where he collapses. Thanks to God's divine intervention, he is discovered by some Europeans who nurse him back to health and, aware that he is destined to be a tool of God, take him to Europe where he discovers true happiness—and God. He returns to teach and work among his own people. Mofolo's implicit faith in the Christian world led him to the simplistic theological position that the African world is pagan and satanic and the European world a blissful expression of God's laws and the resultant blessings that come from them. His African world was condemned as godless, barbarous, and lost; salvation lies only in seeking the true God. Two years later Mofolo wrote *Chaka,* a historical novel which constituted an attack on paganism and on Shaka's rule in Zululand. Mofolo was said to have rebelled later in his life against the narrow morality of his missionary existence and have withdrawn to a farm in East Griqualand where he died a broken old man in 1948. *Chaka* remained unpublished until 1925 when, translated into the major languages of Europe, it received great acclaim.

Morija (in present-day Lesotho) became the great center for Sotho literature, which saw a period of great flowering between 1906 and 1912. Mofolo wrote a third novel in this period,

Pitseng, which was an idyllic story of two Christian youths achieving happiness under the benign wings of the Church. Another Sotho writer was Lechesa Segoete, whose *Monomo ke moholi ke mouoane* (*Riches Are Only Mist*) is cast in the mold of the Pauline conversion on the road to Damascus. Still another, Mangoela, who died in 1963, also wrote Sotho praise poems which were direct transcriptions from the oral traditions.

The second significant southern African literature was based on the work of the Scottish Mission in Lovedale, in Cape Province, among the Xhosa. This followed the earlier work of Joseph Williams of the London Missionary Society, who, in the late eighteenth century, had converted Prince Ntsikana to Christianity. Ntsikana was noted for his hymns. But the first Xhosa novel was written by Henry Ndawo, whose *U-Hambo Luk a Ggoboka* (*A Journey Toward Conversion,* 1909) is similar to Mofolo's *Pilgrim for the East.* It borrowed significant features from *Pilgrim's Progress* and certain elements from traditional folklore. Samuel Mgayi, another Christian, whose parents had been converted, wrote *Ityala lama-wele* (*The Lawsuit of the Twin Brothers*) which became a textbook. Mgayi left Lovedale to return to Ntabuzuko, a small village of the Ndhlambe, where he was active in local affairs and wrote praise poems for the Prince of Wales during the latter's visit to South Africa in 1925. Mgayi died in 1945. Another Xhosa writer was Enoch Guma whose novel *Nomalizo* (1918) was translated into other African languages. The present writer remembers reading this slim book in Ewe as a boy. Again, the theme of the triumph of virtue over sin is the central one. Nomalizo, a virtuous, pious, beautiful girl from a Christian home, is abducted by an evil young schoolmate, Nxabanizo, from a pagan household where wickedness abounds. But she loves Rangela, an upright, Christian, young man, with a pious Christian love and spurns Nxabanizo's evil designs on her. Before her marriage to Rangela, her wicked suitor plants stolen goods in Rangela's rooms and he is sent to jail. One of Nxabanizo's accomplices, stricken by guilt and conscience at Rangela's fate, confesses his part in the plot. The Christian and virtuous Rangela is released and the two lovers are united in holy matrimony. The triumph of Christian virtues over dark, satanic, pagan wickedness is again illustrated. The style of this early literature is didactic and stiffly moralistic, because it had to conform to the literary demands of the writers' Victorian missionary standards. Most of the work of all these writers severely ignored the oral literature of their own people, which was still a viable aspect of life, designating it as pagan and undesirable.

In West Africa the story was not much different. The Ewe language, for example, received its orthography through the work of the Bremen missionaries. D. Westerman's *Study of the Ewe Language,* written in 1904, is still the most authoritative study of the language, superseding A. B. Ellis' work in depth and clarity. Before this date, however, the work of the Bremen Presbyterian Mission based in Keta on the Coast and Peki in the hinterland, had been in progress since 1847 and was linked with the church's work in Togo and also in Akwapin in the Gold Coast. The Bible was first translated into Anlo-Ewe dialect, which was later to become the standard written Ewe dialect even though other dialects continued to enjoy currency to some extent, both in the pulpit and in the classroom.

The earliest Ewe literary efforts were in the area of hymn writing, and such great hymnologists as Torsu of Anyako, Banini of Anloga, Aku of Lomé, and Kwami of Amedzofe were also some of the earliest African missionaries who took over the work of the church from the Germans at the outbreak of the First World War and the ensuing hasty withdrawal of the Bremen missionaries. Before their departure, the Germans had compiled, with the help of Ewe scholars, a series of Ewe readers covering subjects such as Ewe folklore, history, and culture and also one volume devoted to such practical things as the manufacture of gunpowder. But the over-all orientation of these early Ewe readers remained religious, though the practical needs of far-flung mission posts were catered to in short essays on such matters as snakebite treatment, honey gathering, farming, animal rearing, and civics. While the earliest Ewe works followed the pattern of this compendium-type writing, there were some writers who began seriously to turn their attention to their own society, and even though they saw it through missionary-tainted spectacles, they did not condemn it as a totally pagan and satanic world with which they could have no dealings. Their own fascination with Ewe culture and life almost took on the exhilaration of new discoveries, and they wrote, albeit apologetically, about them with excitement and pleasure.

One of these earliest writers was Kwasi Fiawoo, who was one of the first Ewe to be educated in America by the African Methodist Episcopal Church. He received his B.A. and B.D. degrees from the Johnson C. Smith University in Charlotte, North Carolina, in 1929 and a Ph.D. later at Roosevelt University in Chicago. His play *Toko Atolia* (*The Fifth Landing Stage*), published in 1937, has become an Ewe classic. Inspired by a vaguely nationalistic fervor, the play attempts to come to terms with African life and the African conception of the world, without any apologetic gestures toward European or missionary norms. In the introduction to the play, he writes (I translate freely): "This little book comes as a messenger from our ancestors. It brings a brief story of their life to us Ewe and to others who would want to learn something about our forebears."

The story attempts to dramatize the theme of crime and how it is punished among the Anlo-Ewe of the southeast coast of present-day Ghana. Again, in the introduction, Fiawoo writes: "In those days, there were no police, soldiers, or prisons in Anloland. But everyone was alert against evil and young people who make crime their work received terrible punishments. Some are fined, others are sold into slavery, while others are executed according to the nature of their crimes." But Fiawoo does not escape his own Christian and a self-imposed moral responsibility; his avowed intent is to correct the youth of his day who, to him, have strayed from the narrow and strict moral paths laid down by the ancestors. Offenses that were severely punished included stealing, burglary, highway robbery, persistent lying, chronic indebtedness, adultery, and murder. Our forebears simply concluded, according to Fiawoo, that the continuity of the group was paramount, and anyone who indulged in these crimes had as his primary aim the ultimate destruction of the group. So the group must exact the severest punishment from such an individual in order to ensure its own survival.

Fiawoo's intention in this play was also to draw attention to the total life style of the Anlo-Ewe, their daily lives, customs, rituals, and ceremonies. But he does not allow these to usurp the legitimate role of his drama. Where cultural events occur, they serve to lighten the dramatic intensity of the plot and to give full body to the theme in its cultural context.

He confesses, as a Western-trained scholar, that his play does not follow the Aristotelian demands and apologizes for using dislocations in time and space, as important requirements for the total realization of the play. He claims that the play follows the principles of English drama of the Elizabethan Age and of our times in sticking to the unity only of the action. His division of the play into acts follows the natural divisions of plot progression; thus, his first act is an introduction to the society in which the play is set. Here we are also introduced to the main theme, the main characters, and are presented the tying of the thematic knot through the outbreak of a quarrel central to the plot. His second act is the further complication of the plot, and the climax comes in the third act when the main character is condemned to death. Then follow the last two acts with the resolution.

The story line is very simple. During the reign of one of the Anlo paramount chiefs, Zanyido, around 1700 or so, there was a great deal of upheaval in the land caused by a group of young malcontents. One of them is Agbebada ("evil life"), the son of Gbadago and Egbo of Dzita town on the west side of Anloga, the royal town. His parents try their best to correct his life, but he is adamant. His evil nature shows itself in the way he manipulates the parents of a girl already betrothed to his age-mate Kumasi, and thus he unleashes a grim family and clan quarrel in the village. Agbebada has a great capacity for dissembling, pretending to be someone other than who he really is; he wins the ears, affection, and respect of the girl's parents. After turning their minds against Kumasi, he himself comes forward to ask for her hand. But the girl is undeceived as to Agbebada's real nature and hesitates to give a straight answer to her parents' request that she marry him. When her indecisiveness drags on and is interpreted as willful disobedience of parental rule, her parents drive her out of their house. Accompanied by a younger sister, she sets out for Odumase in Kroboland where her maternal uncle lives. But on the road they fall into the hands of ritual executioners of the Krobo who, upon learning that the uncle is a friend of their chief, sells the girls to a white slave dealer at Accra instead of sacrificing them to the Krobo god. After quickly patching up their quarrel, Agbebada and Kumasi set out to rescue the girls. But on the way Agbebada breaks away, seeking to rescue the girls singlehanded. But like the coward he is, he hides himself in a grove near Atiteti and after a few days returns home to announce with great solemnity and sorrow that the girls have fallen into the hands of the Ashanti who promptly sacrificed them during a funeral for their chief. Everyone believes him when he tells of his singularly brave but vain attempts to save the girls. He asks for the hand of the youngest of his former loved one's sisters in marriage. The parents tearfully agree to grant the request of this brave young man who almost lost his life in search of their other daughters. Just as the marriage is about to be performed, a respected elder, Amedza, brings a suit against Agbebada for seducing his wife. This is not the first time this charge has been brought against him—his father had become poor as a result of the numerous fines he had paid on his son's behalf on other occasions, and it is because of him that his younger sister is in temporary slavery. The case goes to Anloga. Meanwhile, his rival Kumasi pursues the tracks of the girls and falls among robbers at Goenu. But as luck would have it, the leader of the robbers knows him well and places his and his men's services at Kumasi's disposal in the search for the girls. At the beach at Accra, the white slave trader is getting ready to set sail with the girls. Kumasi, leading the gang of robbers, attacks the slaver and his retinue, rescues the girls, and brings them safely home. There is jubilation. Kumasi is given the girl, Fudzikomele. These developments have exposed Agbebada's lies, and the elders pass the death sentence on him. On the appointed day he is sent to Anloga where he is to be buried alive. Kumasi, filled with compassion for Agbebada and forgiving him his evil intentions, proceeds to the fifth landing stage, the execution spot where Agbebada is already half-buried. Kumasi rescues him and sets him on his way to Seva to begin life anew. In a solemn pledge to Kumasi, Agbebada changes his name to Amegbedzi, which means "obedient to man's word," and swears to lead a good life till the end of his days.

Fiawoo's grasp of the central movement of the dramatic denouement of his story is one of the finest in any language. His understanding and knowledge of Ewe proceeds from a basic confidence that the language is rich and endowed with immense literary potential. At the time he wrote, Ewe was being seriously studied in German universities, and the play was translated into German in 1937 by Reinhold Schober. Fiawoo, unlike others who wrote in Ewe at the same time, does not use the biblical style which tended to be stiff and non-colloquial. He tried as much as possible to capture the cadences of spoken Ewe and stuck very faithfully to the speech patterns of an older language. This faithful adherence to spoken Ewe language was dictated apparently by a certain distaste for the biblical style which uses more a "grammatical," "book"-type language than existed in current speech. His efforts in this direction were not, however, followed by those who wrote after him. All of them to a man wrote a bookish, biblical, or school-type Ewe which sounds artificial and stilted and has naturally been relegated to the pulpit and the classroom. Fiawoo insisted upon a currency in usage; he used words that Ewe has borrowed and absorbed from other languages and this made his work reflect a truer linguistic situation than did any other writer.

The dramatic center of Fiawoo's play lies in the controlled manipulation of character as an instrument in stating a moral position, which, however, does not remain stuffily apostolic and evangelical. Fiawoo's grasp of the demands of the stage is sharply focused by the division of the play into five acts with a number of scenes, with the climax occurring in the third act. The play's main weakness is in the proliferation of scenes and characters. In one act there are about six scenes with unbelievable shifts, which make it move very slowly in production. There are about twenty main characters besides numerous townsmen, executioners, and women who at times serve as commentators on some of the events.

Fiawoo's work, however, did not lead to the great burst of Ewe literary creativeness that was expected. His only other play, *Tuinese* (*Tell It to Fate*), has not even been published even though it was well received when it was first performed in the late 1940s in Keta.

The other very important Ewe writer whose work has become part of Ewe classics is Paul Desewu. His first book, *Le Nye Adaba Te* (*Under My Eyelash*), was a collection of tales, sketches, and satirical pieces, published in 1944. Desewu is a writer of very great and controlled skill, whose style comes close to that of Fiawoo in agile recreation of ordinary speech and the avoidance of the stilted biblical style to which I have already referred. His intention is, like Fiawoo's, to instruct the youth, to draw moral lessons. Typically, the first sketch is about drunkenness. In Desewu's apostrophic mode, drink becomes personified and called simply "That Strong Man." He is described as a quiet unassuming man, who, when in his room, does not even move. He does not seek the company of others. But strangers follow him, seek his friendship, hang around his compound day and night. He in turn loves everyone who loves him, does not discriminate. Desewu's tale continues in this vein until one by one he dramatizes the evil consequences of drink and drunkenness. The second sketch attacks the superstitious notions of witchcraft, teaching simple lessons of hygiene and cleanliness, subjects which the missionaries spent great energy on. Other pieces are comic tales of married life, a chapter on Ewe poets, and a long section on travelers' adventures in Eweland. He loads his tales with proverbs, aphorisms, and wise sayings, but his most refreshing trait is his conversational and relaxed fireside manner. For example, at the beginning of one travel tale he writes:

> To travel is to see wonders, and the child who has never left home always boasts that his mother cooks the tastiest soup. To see the town from afar is not to enter it. The other day, Elder Agbemafle and I took a trip into the interior. . . .

Le Nye Adaba Te constitutes one of the most relaxed moralistic pieces of writing in any language, combining seriousness with a lighthearted and humorous tone that redeems it from sententiousness. Desewu's other work, *Mise Gli Loo* (*Listen to a Story*), is one of the earliest collections of Ewe folktales and has for years enjoyed the status of a classic in the literature of the Ewe. These two books are still read in Ewe schools, as well as by old men and women with some education in Ewe.

Heavy moralism and didacticism characterize a great deal of more recent writing in Ewe. After the non-apostolic and non-evangelical concerns of Fiawoo and Desewu—who, though Christian converts, wrote from a vaguely non-Christian perspective—

Ewe literature returned to the narrow missionary concerns. One of the most prolific of the relatively younger writers is Sam Obianim, whose novel *Amegbeto* (*Man*) is very well known throughout the Ewe country. His works include short studies in Ewe grammar, customs, and culture. *Amegbeto* is dedicated to the Ewe Presbyterian Church. In the rather heavy and moralistic introduction, he writes, and I translate very freely:

> Since the day we are born into this world, we begin our life's journey home which is heaven, and the day we die and are buried in the grave is the end of that journey. Each one has his life's road, and no one's resembles that of another. For some the road is short, for some long; for some it is wide and full of happiness, contentment, and good fortune; but for others it is narrow, and suffering, poverty, unhappiness, and sorrow cover it. For some the journey begins well and ends disastrously. For others it begins badly and ends well. But whatever our road is, it is known to God, who brought us into this world and who follows us on our journey and arranges everything before it happens. If things are good for us, we must know that it is God's will; and when things go wrong, we must be aware that it is His plan. Nothing is hidden from Him, for He plans everything.

From the tone here it is quite obvious that this will be a tale of suffering and Christian submission to God's will, how man accepts suffering and yields himself to God, who leads him into eternal life.

The story deals with the rise of a slave, Agbezuge, to a position of eminence through hard work, humility, and acceptance of his fate, and how he fell from the exalted position given him by his master through the evil machination of supposed friends. Beloved of his master, whom he serves until he dies, he inherits his wealth. Envied and hated, he is attacked by his enemies who inflict grievous wounds on him. He survives, but sorrows strike him one by one. Like Job, however, his faith in God remains unshaken. He is accused of murdering a child of one of his friends. Tormented by his accusers, he is saddled with the task of burying the murdered boy. He is finally exiled from the village, all his wealth taken away from him. When the verdict of exile is given by the emissaries of the elders, Agbezuge proclaims:

Where will I go? Where shall I turn? From whence will a light appear and lead me through life's dark valley?

One of his friends says to him:

Put yourself in the hand of God and leave everything to Him, and He will lead you on this stormy sea of life better than any light, so that your boat shall arrive safely on the shore and you will be home. Take heart even if the night is frightful. Take heart, a good day shall dawn.

In a tearful farewell to his wife, Agbezuge laments:

I shall wander through the wide world because I have no home; whenever I arrive and life's evening falls for me, I shall rest there, whether it is a thick forest, a desert, in water or in fire, I shall give up my spirit to its maker. Every death is death, the death of the poor and the rich is one. If I die in the wilderness, the wild beasts and the fowls of the air will bury me. My life was full of sorrow. My soul shall leave this wicked world to seek its resting place. And when we meet beyond the river, there will be joy. I shall call upon my God and ask Him why did He adorn my earthly days only with suffering.

Amegbeto is a sentimental story of man's suffering in a wicked world and his undying faith in God. It is also the story of a journey from rags to riches and back to degradation and sorrow. Agbezuge is the heroic, humble, persevering, trusting Christian man, who in spite of brief moments of doubt accepts the faith of the Church and the irrevocable and implacable nature of his destiny. Pitted against him are his neighbors, wicked men who smile on him but plot his downfall because he is so trusting. Christlike, he accepts the humiliations that are heaped on him, because he knows that there is a better place beyond the river. When he starts upon his road into exile, into an unknown future as a wanderer and a vagabond, only a handful of neighbors shed tears for him. But the story has a happy ending. After years of wandering and going through further suffering, he finally arrives among his own kinsmen, from among whom he had been snatched and sold into slavery. At the end, the man who planned evil against him comes to confess his crime. He is Hotoenyame, the father of the child Agbezuge was accused of murdering. He confesses to the killing of his own child. He asks for forgiveness and dies, to Agbezuge's utter sorrow that he was not able to do a kind deed for him.

Obianim's work is not limited to fiction. He has also written a comprehensive book on Ewe culture and life which continues to be widely read. He writes within the strict Christian tradition. His style is more ornate and studied and follows the rotund non-colloquial style of the Bible and the hymns. It owes very little to spoken Ewe, which is agile and more prone to the use of metaphors and complex images. He uses proverbs, but they stand elegantly aloof from the general tenor of his story and serve specific didactic purposes. Unlike the work of Fiawoo and Desewu, Obianim's work lacks that tough and earthy humor and wit which is characteristic of the Ewe language, speech, and conversation. His moral concerns are very high pitched, and therefore his style remains severely stiff.

Other Ewe writers include Bidi Setsoafia, an accomplished dramatist, Necku, Kofi Nyaku, and many others. Like most of the literatures in the other African languages, Ewe literature is severely handicapped by the absence of a vigorous local publishing industry. The influence of the churches, which had taken earlier interest in publishing, is today greatly diminished, and there are no local publishing houses to take up the challenge of these literatures. So, even though the readership for Ewe literature increases every year, since the written language is taught up to the high school level, the literary output remains small and sporadic.

Hausa literature goes back to the early Islamization period of northern Nigeria, with the rise of *ajami,* religious poetry composed by Islamic learned men, or *malaams,* using Arabic meter. This literature defined the rise of Hausa nationalism. It derived from strict Koranic studies. Mohammadu Gwari, one of its earliest practitioners, who lived at the time of the founding of the town of Sokoto in the early nineteenth century, was educated at Timbuctu during the reign of Usman dan Fodio, whose son and sister also lent their support to the genre. Aliyu dan Sidi, onetime Emir of Zaria, wrote a long poem when Lord Lugard arrived in the country at the end of the nineteenth century. It was a poem in praise of himself and his reign, how peaceful and prosperous it was. He then launches into a diatribe against European intervention and the evil of allowing the white man to take over the country. He was said to have been deposed and exiled to Lokoja, far to the south by the British. His work established *ajami* as a dominant Hausa literary form that replaced the Arabic form entirely. Shehu na Salga also wrote at this time; his epic poem, *Bagauda*, celebrated the founding of Kano. He was said to have done much to rid Hausa of Arabic.

Another Hausa writer, Ibrahim Nalado of Katsina, wrote short poems on the importance of education, using the prophet Mohammed's call to the people to seek knowledge. He was an innovative user of alliteration and his influence is still felt today in Hausa poetry. Most of the literature of this period dealt with the theme of religious and cultural purity and the corrosive and destructive influences of European rule and life style. Nagwamatse, another Hausa writer, composed poems on the theme of the struggle between the Europeans and the emirs, lamenting the gradual liquidation of the Islamic faith.

A significant innovation in this century was the introduction of the Roman alphabet into written Hausa to replace the Arabic. This did not, however, affect the Islamic cultural orientation of the literature. Sa'adu Zungur, one of the most prolific of Hausa writers, is the poet who brought the conflict, tensions, and the confusion of the Islamic north of Nigeria into sharp focus. His *Maraba da Soja*, a Hausa classic, employs a traditional form to deal with the theme of a soldier returning from the Burma campaign after the Second World War, the dislocation of his world, the demise of old values, the horrors of war, and the isolation of a past shattered by the European presence. Writing about the use of the atomic bomb, the poet laments:

Kai, what this atom bomb has done to the city of Hiroshima!
The outbreak of its fire reached from Wakayama as far as Yokohama,
and to the north of Fujiyama, then to Tanega, and Kagoshima,
like the tongue of fire from Hell.[1]

Aliyu na Mangi's work, also contemporary, is in a more traditionally Islamic mold, reflecting a popular style. His poem *Wakai*

Imfiraji is well known and a classic available in both Arabic and Roman-script Hausa:

> In the name of God, the most generous,
> I intend to sing a new song,
> in praise of the beloved messenger,
> the saviour at the day of judgement.
> Who loves him will never suffer.[2]

The poem contains twelve books, each of which deals with subjects such as the Prophet, general problems of life, bribery and corruption, and praise.

Hausa literature is still receiving great impetus with the active encouragement and teaching of the language, through the work of the Gaskiya Corporation and also from the radio.

Swahili literature, in East Africa, like Hausa literature, also owes its beginning to the spread of Islam and goes back for more than three hundred years, some dating from the sixteenth century. Like Hausa literature, Swahili poetry started by being religious, but later became secularized. *Hamziya,* a poem of 460 stanzas in praise of the Prophet, and *Herakali,* a poem of 1,150 stanzas, are samples of the early Swahili poetry, both showing their Arabic derivation even though they are said to be metrically based on Indian models. *Inkishafi* is an eighteenth-century poem of seventy-nine stanzas describing ancient Swahili culture as seen in the ruins of the old city states. It draws attention to the glories of the past in order to admonish the people to lead virtuous lives and point the moral that decay and ruination are the wages of sloth and vice. The transitory nature of things and the need to do Allah's bidding form the central theme:

> Where are the palaces of the Emirs?
> Where are the court rooms of the Grand Viziers?
> Where are the offices of noble Peers?
> They are all dead and buried in the dust.[3]

Religion is the center of early Swahili poetic tradition. The brotherhood of Islam, love of neighbor, prayer, fast, communal ties, obedience to Allah, and the teachings of the Prophet combine to form the primary focus of its expression. The poetry also warns that money and other earthly goods are hindrances on the road to

Paradise and points to the virtues of almsgiving and Allah's ordained sufferings for man in diseases and poverty. Morality is the
main concern of this poetry, whose sacred nature excludes any
concern with the mundane or secular. Pietistic, its only descriptive passages refer to the moral beauty of the Prophet, from whose
face the light of Divine Wisdom shines forth, the longed for light
of Paradise and of Allah.

The later secular poetry in Swahili exists in the form of *shairi*,
which is very similar to European lyrical verse. Its origin is traced
to the word, or poetry, contest performed at the *diriyi*, the festive
occasions sponsored by rich merchants who were also patrons of
the arts. The townspeople are invited to these contests to listen
to two competing master poets. The metric system of the *shairi*
is used now for all non-narrative poetry. Most of the *shairi* that
accompany the *ngoma,* or dances, are influenced by Indian and
Oriental speech style. It is couched in flowery language replete with
erotic references:

> I want to give a burden to the daughter of the Moon.
> Welcome! The crescent shines forth like the full moon.
> When she wears colored cotton she fancies herself;
> better in blue calico, like rain clouds.[4]

Blue calico, the cloth of married mothers, signifies fertility, which
in turn is linked with rain clouds. Or:

> One day in the virgin forest I found a pomegranate tree.
> Reaching high I could pick a fruit with my hand,
> but a worm had bored his way through its fresh flesh.
> I turned back never to see the forest again, never
> to remember.[5]

These lines refer to the lovely woman who harbors a venereal
disease.

The narrative poems in Swahili form the largest body of the
literature. They vary in length. The shortest is said to be not less
than a hundred stanzas of four lines each. The longest is over
six thousand stanzas. Some of these poems are of great epic
quality, dealing with heroes of early Islamic history and focusing
attention on the life and death of Mohammed the Prophet, his
son-in-law Ali Talib, Abu Bakr, Omar, and their successors.

These poems are also replete with details of battles against in-
fidels and the struggles of heroes against monsters and satanic
demons:

> They swooped down like vultures on their prey,
> condemned to death.
> They were like ferocious buffalo angered by a
> pack of jackals,
> ready with their mighty horns to rend the bodies
> apart.
> They were like the spotted leopard, swift and
> deadly with his claws,
> hitting in one swing and not missing.[6]

Swahili love poetry, written in four lines, started in the nineteenth century and is a popular form. Shaaban Robert, a Swahili
poet who died in 1962, is said to be the most outstanding modern
writer. It was he who expanded and modernized the vocabulary
and generally mapped out the literature's future path of growth.

Swahili, a combination of Arabic-Islamic and indigenous African
languages, illustrates the powerful cultural assimilation which
Africa underwent over the centuries. Today it receives great impetus as an instrument of cultural nationalism in East Africa, particularly in Tanzania where it is the official language. Its spread
westward followed the ancient trading routes from the Indian
Ocean to as far as Katanga province in the Congo (modern-day
Zaire), and now there is a move for its adoption as a national
language in other East African countries. Its vitality as a mixed
language enables it to enjoy territorial expansion, and of all languages of Africa south of the Sahara, it has the greatest possibilities
of growth. The impetus Swahili receives from the new literature
of Tanzania is shown in the work of a large number of poets,
dramatists, and novelists who now use it in writing for a growing
reading public. Julius Nyerere, the President of Tanzania, himself
translated Shakespeare's *Julius Caesar* into Swahili. It continues to
enjoy great currency and widespread support as one of the most
important languages of black Africa, capable of uniting diverse
groups that speak little-known tongues and can only reach one
another through English.

The problems confronting the written vernacular literatures of Africa today are enormous. First, there is the primary question of uniformity for the languages themselves. Missionary attention seemed to have been focused on selected dialects to the neglect of others which form the linguistic units. The written language must reflect broad usage and be accessible to each of the dialectal groups. This will require careful study and the laying out of ground rules on questions such as usage, vocabulary, syntactic patterns, and morphology. Written Ewe, for example, even though primarily based on the Anlo dialect, has been able to achieve this neutralist position to a certain degree and is therefore accessible to all the major dialectal groups in the West African areas where Ewe is spoken or read. The case is said to be not nearly the same with, say, Igbo. But, again, dialectal differences can be exaggerated and made to look as grave obstacles to intelligibility. This is where the contribution of trained linguists is needed.

The other major question is the accessibility of the literature to a wide readership. Book production and distribution have been the preserves of missionaries and, lately, governments. These bodies, especially the latter, have not been keen enough on the literature possible in the vernaculars to make adequate provision for it. Some governments have deliberately set out to minimize the importance of this literature in the name of national unity. To most of them, to promote literature in regional languages will undermine national unity. There is also the problem of the accessibility of this literature to critics and commentators who cannot speak or read the languages. This can be circumvented by translating into other languages material already available in the original.

The fact remains, however, that the vernacular literature of Africa is increasing rapidly in direct proportion to the growing number of people who can read and write their own languages.

Literature in the received languages, Negritude, and the black literary revolt

The African writing that first became known outside of the continent was done in the received languages of Europe, namely, English, French, Spanish, and Portuguese. It represents aspects of Africa's contact with Europe and her effort to define herself in cultural terms.

In a generally intelligent survey, *A History of Neo-African Literature,* the German bibliographer Janheinz Jahn traces the ancestry of this literature to the pre-Islamic era, discussing Afro-Arab writing, such as *Mo'allagat* and the work of Antar, who founded a whole school. Antar, who died in 615, was the first known writer of African descent and wrote poetry called the "Antar romance." The English commentator Cedric Dover describes this as the first classical work concerned with color prejudice. Antar was followed by Abu Ibn al-Djaun, who lived in Bagdad in the eighth century, and Ziryab, the black singer-poet who was said to have made great contributions to the evolution of Andalusian music. All these writers were slaves, the first *déracinés,* who wrote in the language of their enslavers, having forgotten, or been made to forget, their mother tongues.

This group was followed by displaced Africans in the Christian kingdoms of Spain and Portugal. The most important of these was Juan Latino, who personified the rich tradition and history of the

Moorish conquest of Europe. Highly educated, he proclaimed himself *"hic scriptor nec fuit orbe satus, Aethiopum terris venit"* ("this author was not born in the region, he came from the land of the Ethiopians").[1] As a slave of Elvira, daughter of the Spanish soldier Gonzalo Fernandez de Córdoba ("El gran Capitán"), Juan learned Latin and Greek with Elvira's son, the Duke of Sessa, and entered the University of Granada. In 1546 when he took his B.A., he was already an accomplished Latin scholar, lutist, guitarist, and wit. He became a professor at the university in 1557 and in 1565 delivered the Latin address to open the university year. His main work, the *Austrias,* written in Latin, is a praise poem celebrating the victory of Don John of Austria at Lepanto in 1571. His verse was said to show the academic style of the period, revealing his love for the Catholic Church and for Spain, his foster country. He also commented wittily on color prejudice:

> If our black face, O King, seems to your ministers odious,
> Ethiops find your white faces no more to their taste.[2]

And he referred to himself as the "fly in the milk." To Cervantes, he was an erudite writer full of linguistic sophistries.

Two hundred years later a group of displaced African writers emerged in the United States and the West Indies. These have been described as the "guinea pigs," products of the eighteenth-century European's experimentation with Africans to find out whether they could be educated like white men. Francis Williams of Jamaica, one of the first "guinea pigs," was selected for such training by the Duke of Montagu. He attended English schools and then went on to Cambridge. When Brigadier General George Haldane became governor of Jamaica in 1758, Williams celebrated the event in a Latin poem. Sancho, another "guinea pig" was born on a slave ship and became protégé and butler to the same Duke of Montagu; his *Letters,* published in 1782, were described then as a work of great charm and literary merit. Abrasu Hannibal, an Abyssinian African slave educated at the court of Peter the Great, became a man of great military prowess in Russia and was allegedly the great-grandfather of Alexander Pushkin. Other African scholars of the period included Wilhelm Amo, philosopher and poet, and John Capitein, author of a learned treatise in defense of slavery, who returned to Ghana as a missionary and was said to have "reverted to idolatrous habits." Phillis Wheatley, born in Senegal and brought to Boston as a slave in 1761, when she was seven, learned to read and write English. By the age of seventeen she had achieved considerable fame in Boston as a prodigy and as the author of many popular poems. One poem was an ode to George White-field, the English preacher, and when Phillis was taken to London in 1773 she stayed with Whitefield's famous patroness, the Count-ess of Huntingdon. A collection of Phillis' poems was published in London the same year, to wide acclaim. She returned to Boston, but after the death of her owners she fell into obscurity and died in 1783.

Phillis Wheatley's style was an Augustan, neo-classical one, rotund and tediously sententious. For General Washington, who admired her poetry, she wrote:

> Proceed, great chief with virtue on thy side,
> Thy ev'ry action let the goddess guide.
> A crown, a mansion, and a throne that shine
> With gold unfading, Washington! be thine.[3]

Her early Methodist training was reflected in the poem *On Being Brought from Africa:*

> 'Twas mercy brought me from my Pagan land,
> Taught my benighted soul to understand
> That there's a God, that there's a Savior too:
> Once I redemption neither sought nor knew.
> Some view our sable race with scornful eye:
> "Their colour is a diabolic die!"
> Remember, Christians, Negroes, black as Cain.
> May be refin'd, and join the angelic train.[4]

Most of the African writers of this period were torn from their homelands when very young and educated to reflect the ideas of their owners and to produce letters and poems in their received language. Two other early African writers in English are worth mentioning, since their works have been reissued in our times. These were Olaudah Equiano of Essaka, Nigeria, and Ottobah Cuguano of Ajumako, Ghana. They were kidnapped and sold into slavery at the very early ages of ten and twelve around 1735.

They were educated, albeit sporadically, in the New World but ultimately settled in England. Their writing is autobiographical, containing fascinating accounts of their African origin and life. Equiano's autobiography is a moving record of his African origin, the customs of his people and rituals, and his own transplantation as the result of a slave raid. It tells of his wandering between the West Indies, Philadelphia, and Western Europe; of his life as a deck hand and a ship's gunner, his adventures as a freed slave, his settlement in England, and his involvement in the abolitionist's work, which led to his ultimate entanglement with the British Parliament.

Other Africans in exile at this time who were writing in English were Briton Hammon from Massachusetts; John Marrant, a sailor and adventurer; Prince Hall from Barbados, who started a lodge for black Free Masons in Massachusetts in 1787; and Jupiter Hammon, a lyric poet from Long Island, who wrote a strong rhythmic verse. There were other writers who worked in the Portuguese Alvarenga of Brazil, studied at Coimbra University in Portugal between 1773 and 1776, and returned with Ph.D.s to Brazil to play prominent roles in that country's literary life, creating pastoral poems of romantic beauty. Of these poets, Barbasa, born on a slave ship between Angola and Brazil in 1738, is perhaps the most important. Educated by the Jesuits, he founded an academy of fine arts and wrote his best poems in Lisbon, where he died in November 1800. His popular songs possess musical qualities that are said to be of African origin. They were reported to have become very popular forms in Brazil.

There was a flowering of writing among the growing community of displaced Africans down the ages, although the African memories of some of them were wiped out, and their culture, in basic terms, did not define itself in any pure African context. Wherever the black diaspora occurred, wherever Africans were taken, new rhythms, sounds, and literatures emerged as the result of the amalgamation of the African soul with new forms, both a gesture of defiance and an act of survival. Gradually, however, the memory of Africa disappeared. But yet Africa remained as a distant spiritual homeland for the exiles. In the West Indies and South America, where large plantations existed, the distorted yet vibrant

magic of the African continent, with its customs and manners, its
music and dance, lingered on, even though its languages and details
of daily life had vanished, leaving only vague traces behind. No
violent alienation resulted, because the problem of survival could
only be solved by painful modes of adaptation to the new environ-
ment. What was left was the spiritual link with the African continent, the nirvana of black souls, Guinea, the place where the
dead returned and rejoined the tribe and the ancestors. In North
America, the puritan ethic and the smaller and more rigid plantation system destroyed the finer fabric of this folk memory, and in
its place were erected large cultural patterns based on the Christian
Church and the vaguely perceived ethical and survival system of
slavehood.

This coincided with the era of colonialism in Africa, and the
introduction of European culture and education into what was
essentially a vast sea of complex yet unified cultures, customs,
and peoples. By the nineteenth century, missionary work had
started producing African converts, men and women who believed
the notions of their own inferiority as a people. These converts
were persuaded to accept European man and his ways as something ordained by the Christian God. We have already seen the
impact of this on the vernacular literature in selected areas of
Africa.

In the twentieth century the features of colonialism became
more clearly defined in terms of European imperialism and eco-
nomics all over the globe. What had been a sporadic historical
phenomenon became systematic and well defined by the end of the
nineteenth century with the implementation of the conclusions of
the Berlin Conference of 1884. The close cultural impact of the
colonial experiment was not to be evident until the first two decades
of this century and the First World War, the first global war in
many senses and one into which Africa was also drawn. It can be
safely suggested that Africa's thrust into modern times began from
this period, with her massive economic participation and territorial
involvement, since the combatants in Europe were also on her
shores. The questioning of colonialism can be traced to the rise of
an African elite, educated men and women who, through the traditions of European liberal democracy, were inducted into the acade-

mies and universities of Europe. The meaning of the two great revolutions of the United States and France and of the democratic ideas of Jefferson, Paine, Rousseau, and Marx was not lost upon the black world. W. E. Du Bois wrote in 1903 in *The Souls of Black Folk* that the greatest question of the twentieth century was going to be one of the color line. Post-First World War awakenings led to the massive reappraisal of the African question by the colonizing powers, who shortly after Versailles began preparing for the next round of colonial conflict, this time political, in which Africa's destiny would be largely involved. The rise of an elite class in the Asian colonies, particularly India and Ceylon, was to sharpen the edges of the sword of the coming confrontation between the colonized and the colonizer. Gandhi, as far back as 1914, a young lawyer, was championing the cause of the Indian "coolies" of South Africa and preparing himself for his great historical role in India. In Africa the mission schools were turning out trickles of malcontents who were without platforms until the eve of the Second World War. A few professional men—Atoh Ahuma and Casely Hayford of Ghana and Herbert Macaulley of Nigeria—were beginning to pit their strength against the imperial giants. Alienation is a fundamental vehicle of discontent, and in cultural terms, the European presence in Africa had begun to create an army of alienated and displaced people, produced in the image of the conqueror and yet bereft of the instruments of power that define this conqueror.

But it was to take the permanent exiles, locked into the cultures of America and the Caribbean, to make the literary statements about this alienation. Those who complained in Africa expressed their complaints by crude political pamphleteering. In 1925 Casely Hayford, addressing the National Congress of British West Africa in Bathurst, Gambia, proclaimed the political battle cry:

Today, where two or three of our race are gathered, the thought uppermost in their minds is how to attain African emancipation and redemption. . . . Let no one make the mistake to think that the general disabilities of our race in the four corners of the earth do not concern us.[5]

The political debate of the post-Second World War years was anticipated in the ringing rhetoric of this challenge. Sons of Africa were learning in the universities of America and Europe. They were acquiring, in Martiniquan poet Aimé Césaire's words, those "miraculous arms" with which to defeat their naïve conquerors. The issues of race and culture had been clarified by the deal at Versailles, where Du Bois and his Pan-Africanist comrades had pleaded in vain for African emancipation.

But the roots of the revolt, which began as a cultural phenomenon, were much older. Slavery, colonialism, alienation, dispersal, blackness—these were to become the essential aspects of the legend of Negritude. The word itself, coined by Césaire, has its genesis in that sudden racial assertion and defiance which the historical factors of slavery and colonialism were to engender. The sad sense of loss during slavery was echoed in the unified experience of colonialism, both inside and outside Africa. It was not only economic, it was also cultural. So Negritude became the intellectual black man's literary response to what was a loudly proclaimed monologue of white supremacy. The exiled African was the bearer of the burden of this new awareness on behalf of his African brothers. Negritude was the self-assumed mantle of his exilehood. The publication of Césaire's *Cahier d'un Retour au Pays Natal* in 1939 marked a development from the literary-political renaissance inspired by Toussaint's revolution in Haiti and the Afro-Cuban *negrisimo* movement, backed by the harsh realities of colonialism and the remembered insults of slavery. The *Revista d'Avance* of Cuba was the first articulate journal of the Negro revival. The Afro-Cuban movement influenced poets such as Ramon Guirao, Nicolas Guillen, and the Puerto Rican Pales Matos in the late twenties. In his *Ainsi Parla l'Oncle,* Price Mars, in Haiti, proclaimed: "Oh, I know the wall of repugnance against which I am striking by daring to speak to you of Africa and things African." The African romance had begun. Haiti, the first black republic, had been born in the revolutionary songs of liberty (the lessons of the French Revolution were well absorbed), pride in one's color, and a nostalgic longing for Africa. In his *Cahier* Césaire made the first articulate proclamation and issued the manifesto inspired by the memory of Haiti and the promises of Africa. It was the beginning of the season of new madness on the part of the black man marked by vile renunciations, of "the restoration of the umbilical cord to its fragile splendor," and a new rendition of the Catholic missal heard today in the African tones of the Congolese *Missa Luba*. It is the resurrection of the dead mythology, quickened to existence by the swinging phallic aggression of the new black consciousness. Césaire asserts it in the lines:

> My Negritude is not a speck of dead water on
> the dead eye of earth.
> My Negritude is neither a tower nor a cathedral
> it thrusts into the red flesh of the soil
> it thrusts into the warm flesh of the sky
> it digs under the opaque dejection of its
> rightful patience.[6]

The "droite patience" of this poetry is fed by the memories of slavery. For Martial Sinda, the Congolese poet, there is no escape from it. In his *Clarté de l'Aube,* he writes:

> Négrier,
> Plaie incurable au poignet de l'Afrique
> L'odeur des chicottes;
> L'odeur de corde au cou
> Suffoque les vagues furieuses de ma pensée.[7]

The affirmations of Negritude were to feed a lasting thirst. In the words of Césaire:

> c'est pour la faim universelle
> pour la soif universelle
> la sommer libre enfin
> de produire de son intimité close
> la succulence des fruits.[8]

Thus Negritude self-assertion was based on self-evident truths and on a vaguely familiar political platform for equality and liberty. The agonizing search for the proper black self created the African Golden Age before the transatlantic trade. In this age were the nubile girls, the eternal fires, the tribe at peace, the priests in communion with the gods. The African dove would rise again.

Negritude as a literary and philosophical movement was the direct result of the insistent policy of assimilation of French colonialism. This policy invoked from the new black citizens of France the earliest responses that found expression in the pages of the two journals published in Paris, *Légitime Défense* (1932) and *L'Étudiant Noir* (1934–40). These became the vocal organs of the young intellectuals from France's colonies in Africa and the West Indies. Léon Dumas' *Pigments,* antedating Césaire's *Cahier* by two years, made the first poetic declarations. It was poetry that expressed itself in a simple litany of irritated complaints and owed a great deal to earlier black American poetry of the Harlem renaissance. In Paris the Afro-Antillean intellectual *déraciné,* twice removed from his authentic African self, met his ancestral blood brother from Africa; he too, detribalized to some degree, participated in the new culture of France which he was told was also now his. The two sets of exiles, one permanent, the other temporary, shared that peculiar burden of having had Gallic ancestors, blond and blue-eyed. It was in the metropolitan homeland that the self-discovery that would lead to total alienation was born. These young men, products of French culture, suddenly felt their collective alienation from the white world that had so far made only gestures of acceptance to them and also from their birthright culture. The Africans were less radically cut off, but they were also victims of the same colonial program of assimilation. To both, the "return" to Africa was to be a romantic move. Ennui, disaffection, frustration, and self-hate drove them to delirious dreams of Africa. This drive, demonic and tormented, was to create a summation of all things African upon a totem pole of imaginary and real black virtues, to create a mystique based on the innate qualities which the black man alone possesses. It was to formulate a system of their own understanding of the world, nature, events, and history into a new ontology. And Damas from Guyana, Senghor from Senegal, and Césaire were the fashioners of the aesthetics of this new ontology.

Senghor, perhaps the most consistent and articulate voice of the movement, enunciates its philosophy based on rhapsodic assertions about the black man, definitions of the African soul and mentality, his world and mystical systems. In his essay, *L'Esthétique Negro-Africain,*[9] he defines Negritude as "l'ensemble des valeurs culturelles du monde noir." This ensemble defines the black man's estate, describes his lingua-ontology which feeds all things, deriving itself from a divine origin, dominating the mythology of the African and defining his entire world. On the basis of a sensual perception of the world, Senghor concludes that the predominant trait of the black man's soul is his sense of the divine. This encompasses philosophy, aesthetics, ethics, and politics. The *Weltanschauung* becomes anchored in a basically metaphysical understanding of man and the world. The idealized situation of its philosophy partakes of the existentialism that is rooted in the Earth Goddess, in the interrelation between the inside and outside being in man's participation within the cosmic force, in the communion of man and man, and beyond that with all things. It becomes, in Senghor's mind, the ultimate truth which alone will save a world gone mad through the overwhelming impact of science and technology, and the dessicated rationalist thought that is its main support.

Celebration is Negritude's essence. Black blood, festival, blackness, all were to generate and project what Sartre calls "that effective attitude towards the world." The ancestors and the dead, the eternal guardians of the black nirvana, are recalled to partake of the ultimate festival of the senses. The mask, the transfiguration of the ancestral essence, is the basic instrument of achieving a new awareness for man. In their jointly edited anthology of African poetry, Senghor and Césaire proceeded to establish this knowledge through participation. The girls of the northern mists, the goddesses of natural beauty, shy, nubile, dancing to the primordial beat of the tom-tom are the familiar inhabitants of the Negritude landscape. They are united with the masks and the ancestors. The chief celebrant is the Black Woman, the Earth Mother, the anthropomorphic symbol of primal sensuality.

The romanticism of Negritude poetry was already encountered in the poetry of Claude Mackay and the Harlem renaissance and its search for release to sing forgotten jungle songs. This romanticism is restated in Sartre's introduction to Senghor's 1948 anthology. Africa was

the hemisphere far down, making the first of the three concentric circles—the land of exile, colorless Europe; then comes the dazzling ring

of the islands and the childhood that dances in circles around Africa.
Africa makes the last circle, navel of the world, pole of all black
poetry. Africa bright, burning, and oily like a snake skin. Africa of
fire and rain between being and becoming more real than the end-
less boulevards of pleasure but destroying Europe by its black invisible rays beyond arrest; Africa, imaginary continent.[10]

The need to revitalize the black self means the rejection of Europe,
to establish in Sartre's words an "anti-racist racism." He saw this
as the "weak stage of a dialectical progression: the theoretical and
practical affirmation of white supremacy in the thesis, the position
of Negritude as an antithetical value, is the moment of negativity."

To equate Negritude with Marxism, Sartre seems to be saying,
is to misunderstand its dynamics, for though embracing an essentially egalitarian principle, it is marked by an all-pervasive racial
consciousness, which contains the power, by its active combatant
spirit, to destroy global racism. Its *Gestalt* was an orphean descent
into the tormented and wounded depths of the black soul. The
black man, after grappling with the objective reality of his being
and the subjective dimension of the sustaining force, will *disalien-
ate* himself. It is a journey to reclaim the Eurydice of the black
soul from the destructive embrace of white Pluto. This will be
achieved only through the total reversal of white values. The poet's
instrument is surrealism, an aspect of the miraculous arms of the
revolt. It is a means of reversing the human and social order imposed on him by white rationalism, of which total freedom and
rhythmic celebration and the dance of the naked feet constitute
a negation. On the other hand, it calls for the creation of a new
and different order, based on the values of the essential man, for a
full-blooded being, an integral personality resting within the African ontology. Suffering and rhythm are elements of its fulfillment,
one the erotic response to the world's woes, the other the primary
passion of blackness. Emotion is its primary impulse. For Senghor,
it is linked with the drums, what in Sartrean terms "cements the
multiple aspects of the black soul." Senghor writes, in an essay on
religion:

> The African's contribution to the religious sense lies in his faculty
> of perceiving the supernatural in the natural, his sense of the trans-

cendental and the active self-abandonment that accompanies it, the self-abandonment of love.[11]

It is less in the theme than in the manner. Its center rests in the sensuality of the black woman; the self-abandonment of love is part of the rhythm and the emotivity, in the rhythmic beat in jazz, and in the swaying flamboyance will of the Negro vision. These all will emerge to save the world. Senghor in a well-known poem proclaims this view:

> New York! I say to New York, let black blood
> flow into your blood
> Cleaning the rust from your steel articulation
> like an oil of life
> Giving your bridges the curve of the hills, the
> liana's suppleness.[12]

After the philosophy, the agonized soul searching, and the proclamations, it was David Diop, the younger Senegalese poet, who expressed the absolute anger of Negritude. Rejecting Senghor's Roman Catholic pardon for the oppressor and his ambivalent love for France, Diop, the cultural mulatto par excellence, writes, addressing a black dancer in Paris:

> Around me the wigs of learning
> In great fires of joy in the heaven of your steps
> You are the dance
> And burn false gods in your vertical flame.[13]

For him the carnival was over. The task was to "sharpen the hurricane for the furrows of the future." Diop died too young for his poetry to mature beyond this distilled anger.

Negritude has been attacked by a number of English-speaking Africans, particularly by the Nigerian dramatist Wole Soyinka, and Ezekiel Mphahlele, the South African novelist and critic. Their rejection of Negritude is perhaps motivated by an understandable irritation with what, outside its historical condition, looks like an inductively quaint system designed to perpetuate European myths about African simplicity, sexuality, communal sense, and all the other clichés of nineteenth-century "noble savage" anthropology. Vague mystical values for Africa in this century, they contend, constitute only a stupendous alibi for sloth, backwardness, and a supine acceptance of the condition of economic servitude which the so-called "developed countries" continue to impose on Africa. "What I do not accept," writes Mphahlele, "is the way in which too much of the poetry that is inspired by it [Negritude] romanticizes Africa as a symbol of innocence, purity, and artless primitiveness. I feel insulted when some people imply that Africa is not also a violent continent" (*The African Image*).

Some African political thinkers, particularly Kwame Nkrumah, have rejected Negritude as a sociopolitical set of principles that are hardly relevant for an emergent continent with a long history of external interference. He talked of the need for Africa to jet-propel itself into the twentieth century without leaving behind its humanism. The problems of Africa, it is argued, do not admit of mysticoanthropological assertions about the black soul. Negritude's atavistic posturings deny a legitimate place for the continent in today's community of nations and peoples.

As a historical phenomenon, Negritude was a legitimate revolt, a meaningful assertion of the black self. Its ontological system was an expected response to centuries of European racism and downright arrogance. Yet there was something elegantly dilletantish about it, its contradictions exposed in the political sterility of Senghor as the President of Senegal, where French commercial and cultural power is still paramount. In these contradictions are revealed the basic emotional nature of Negritude—the eternal exile's designation of himself. Non-rationalist philosophy has to admit as its basic antithesis a rationalist outlook which was responsible for pragmatic solutions to simple questions of survival, shelter, food, and politics in the African world long before the European presence. Neo-symbolism and surrealism are elegant literary concepts that may have nothing to do with the black man's *real* estate in our times.

10

Negritude poets: Aimé Césaire, Léopold Senghor, David Diop, and Tchicaya U Tam'si

Negritude poetry, in spite of the definitions, slogans, and the proclamations that seem to frame the ideology and shroud it at times in Senghorian mystery, emerges as some of the finest poetry from modern-day Africa. Its affinities are with sound, rhythm, and the music of the word. Though it receives impetus from the French language, the poetry retains a fresh African thrust which astounded Bréton and Sartre. It celebrates at a primary level the mysteries of language and symbolism shared by the very essence of African artistic expression. It strives to achieve a unity of being through the invocation of smell, suggestion of movement and gesture, form, texture, and the very life force of the total African mythic landscape. The symbols explode the sense, the ritual is embedded in the movement. Tone itself delineates the subtle nuances in the ritual movement.

Aimé Césaire, from Martinique, a fiercely political man, remains Negritude's finest poetic voice. He was born in Martinique in 1913, into a family of modest means. His poetry is based in a strong recall of that childhood period of poverty, a period of great imbalance between the poor and the rich, the worst conditions of a plantation colonial situation. He later came to represent Martinique in the French Assembly and also serves as the mayor of St. Fort-de-France the capital. His *Cahier d'un Retour au Pays*

Natal (*Return to My Native Land*) is a poetic political testament
that created the imagery, landscape, and the needful spiritual center of the black revolt. Its indignation and righteous anger was fed
by the humiliation and suffering that have been heaped upon the
black man through the ages. Denial of humanity for the African
heralded the period of loss and alienation of the race and nour-
ished the universal hunger of the black man:

> For his voice sinks in the swamps of hunger. . . .
> Nothing but the hunger which can no longer
> climb to the rigging of his voice
> a heavy and slack hunger,
> a hunger buried in the depths of the hunger
> of this starveling hill.[1]

The great fearful night that was unleashed upon the black world
was a terrifying nightmare out of which he must awake:

> Here the parade of contemptible and scrofulous bubos,
> The gluttony of very strange microbes, the poisons
> for which there are no known alexins, the pus of very
> ancient wounds, the unforeseeable fermentations of
> species destined to decay.[2]

It is Césaire's own personal sense of loss, alienation, and non-
fulfillment as a *déraciné*, a black colonial man poised on the verge
of returning to a native land that remained inscrutable and mysterious in its sorrow, that overwhelms the opening passion of the
poem. This sense of loss transcends the purely lyrical agony of the
man and expresses itself in the traumatic agony of the race. The
restoration of his land was not done

> with wide sweetness but with tormented concentration
> of fat breasts of hills with an accidental palm tree[3]

but saw the blazing march of hurricanes of September, the sugar
cane burning of October, and the blooming desires of the pome-
granate of December.

One of the great centers of *Cahier* is its attachment to and expression of the magic of place, within the march of time. The
hungry West Indies "pitted with smallpox" is reduced in scale to
the brawling city, inert, passive, flat, sprawled, baffled, and mute.

The city becomes the battleground of inordinate passions and agonies, peopled by a desolate crowd, lepers: then the hill blood-drained and bandaged, a bastard and a starveling. These places are in themselves symbolic objects of the poet's mind, the veritable features of a disfigured and abused landscape. Remembrance of former joy and the memory of the place bring him to the house:

> . . . a broken-backed street dives into a hollow where
> it scatters a few huts; an indefatigable road runs
> at full speed uphill, and is at once swallowed by a
> puddle of houses, a foolishly ascending, daringly
> descending road, and that wooden carcass, which I
> call "our house," comically perched on small feet
> of cement, its iron coiffure corrugating in the sun
> like skin hung up to dry, from the bare boards of
> the living room shine the hobnails, while the
> ceiling is striated by pine-joints and their
> shadows, the chairs of spectral straw, the gray
> light of the lamp, and the varnished, rapid glimmer
> of roaches tripping about.[4]

There is suffering and degradation here; but here also is invoked a tenderness and a nostalgia disguised by the squalor and the roaches; the ironic tone does not overcome the sad melancholic attachment to this place, which is yet the final testimony of the degradation imposed. It is in seeing this squalor and sorrow that the tenderness bursts forth, stronger than the anger and the bitterness. The depths of Césaire's poetic passion are normally seen by critics only as recesses of hate and agony. Beyond these is the gentleness and the joy muted by the silent love, which lie in the Negritude return to the mystical sources of life.

From the melancholic subdued sorrow of the places, the poet leads us to the little church, amiable and benevolent. It is the spirit house of the tribe, where music of the rites of the dispossessed will be heard. Into the huts the festival food is brought and laid out:

> Wine to drink, and there are sausages. . . . the soft
> kind tastes of thyme, the strong red-hot spice,
> there is burning coffee and sugary anise, punch
> with milk, and the liquid sun of rum.[5]

The Christmas celebration is prepared in a "burgeoning of vague dreams," for it is the season of restoring the umbilical cord to "its fragile splendor."

The poem bursts into the Negritude celebration, into the rhythmic sway of the dance and the song, building into the frenzied moment of the ascent of the spirit:

> And not only the mouth sings, but also the hands,
> feet, buttocks, sexual organs, the whole being
> is liquefied in sound, voice and rhythm.[6]

It is the moment of release from the fears, when joy bursts like a cloud, and the songs "roll now anxious and heavy past the valley of fear, the tunnels of anguish, the fires of hell." The liberation of spirits is achieved in the magic of dreams, of song, sleep, smell, bells, and rain. This is the magic moment. Even though it passes swiftly, it yields to the expression of the primal unity of the poet's being, his shared essence with the universe:

> I should say river. I should say tornado
> I should say leaf. I should say tree. I should be wet
> by all rains, made damp with all dews. . . .
> Whoever would not comprehend me would not comprehend
> the roaring of the tiger.[7]

His instrument of containing this whirling vastness is words; in the evocation, his desire is to contain the earth, the land whose mud is his flesh.

This is the moment of return to the specific place, the ritualistic act of renewal of faith with the native land after the universal self-identity. But this earth shares of the essence of the black earth everywhere, of Africa, Guadeloupe, Haiti, and Florida, the territories of death and nakedness. These are the geographical and spiritual entities that define for him his revolt against the white world, celebrated in the triumphant revolt of Toussaint L'Ouverture, who was later destroyed by Napoleon's treachery:

> A single man imprisoned in white
> A single man defying the white cries of white death.[8]

The frenzy of his death constitutes the denial of his conquerors' victory, the flaming madness cancels their vicarious triumph. From the depth of the Congo, the primeval splendor of forest and animals will hurl the "bolt of anger" and defiance in a delirious march to the lynching tree. But it is against this designation that the poet's heart bursts forth, that his cries, unified with the sounds of waters and jungles, are raised. The period of silence is over.

So the poet departs, he leaves Europe. "Wracked with cries," he claims a new knowledge and awareness of self. But there are memories of blood, suffering, and corpses. But liberation is here, expressed in the jazz, in the Lindy Hop, heaving him over the "gentle waters of abjection." Reversing the order, his proclamation of victory is for the vanquished; in the ironic praise song of "hosanah for the master and the castrator of Negroes," he hurdles over the burden of his imputed ugliness. The vision moves. Horses gallop from the depths, black men, urinating, dropping magnificent dung, "superbly limbed," while the shrewd dealer struts around. It is a vision of slavery, the historical era of debasement that turned a race of princes, warriors, architects, and wise men into dishwashers, shoeshines, and "conscientious sorcerers whose only incontestable achievement has been the endurance record under the lash." The memory of slavery and the horrors of the middle passage are invoked to fuel the agony of the present anger. We hear the whip and the lash and the cries of the slaves:

> I hear from the hold below the curses of the chains,
> the hiccups of the dying, the splash of someone thrown
> into the sea, the baying of a woman in labor.[9]

Slavery was the pristine degradation, of men sleeping in their excrement and the white world calm in its obedience to the will of God. The rejection of the poet's *assimilé* role was epitomized in the humiliation that results from his laugh at the ugly Negro he sees on the Parisian train. In him and his ugliness he sees the tormenting features of the history of his race, something he had denied all his life and to which he has come with a deliriously rude awakening. The realization is the celebration of Negritude:

> Eia for the royal Kailcedrat
> Eia for those who invented nothing
> for those who have never discovered

for those who have never conquered
but, struck, deliver themselves to the essence
of all things.[10]

This does not represent a naïve assertion, as some critics will have us believe. It is the denial of the dessication of Western technology and the rejection of the conquering feats of colonial empires as the legitimate basis of twentieth-century man's existence. It is a cry for humanity, humanism, and compassion, which have been banished by machines and the robotal conquering rulers of a despoiled world. It connotes the refusal to conquer, to join the lunacy of the "master" race. The essence of things is the unity of the world, "the reconciled exultation of the antelope and the star," the harmony of forces expressed in the cosmic dance and the mystery of the flesh. The inflexibilities of blue steel are overthrown by the mystic flesh vanquished, yet resurrected, in the great festival of joy, love, and grief.

In this joyous moment, Césaire expurgates hate from his system, as it constitutes anathema to the condition of spiritual and physical unity, to the moment of total celebration of the real humanity's festival. From him will emerge the controlling power that will chain evil and the burgeoning of the seed. The universal hunger and thirst will be quenched and his unique race shall produce out of its intimate knowledge of things "the succulence of fruit." Hate is replaced by love and acceptance:

I accept. . . . I accept . . . totally without reserve.

But the acceptance is ironic in its recall of the details of earlier racial humiliation, redeemed by the breathing of new life transmitted by the driving force of the cyclones and the volcanoes of his native land. These destructive elements have been turned around to achieve the needful rejuvenation and rebirth, close identity and communion with the geographic mysteries of the islands. This unity of man and place is a signal of renewed hope for humanity: "For it is not true that the work of man is finished" —a denial of the racism of European civilization, in the simple assertion which seems to be lost on most readers of Césaire's poetry, that "no race has a monopoly of beauty, intelligence, strength. And there is room for all at the rendezvous of conquest."[11] The ultimate focus is the man, not the country or the place, the erection of the totem pole of human unity. The achievement of this rests in the raising of the "poor old Negro," who will stand upright:

> upright in the cabins
> upright on the bridge
> upright in the wind
> upright under the sun
> upright in the blood
> upright and free.[12]

The black man's redemption is achieved in the rising of the dove of fraternity, mounting to heaven, emerging from the great black hole of despair (Negritude), leaping into the unity of all.

In *Cahier,* Césaire sets the most lyrical tone of the Negritude literary revolution. Nature is the informing source of his mystical imagery and symbolism, a sturdily delirious rhythm reminiscent of the ritual celebration at sacred festivals and a unified sensibility that derives from an unforced surrealistic style, which in itself defines the poetry. The alleged Césairean absolute hate is denied in the final proclamation for man, a voice which has also been heard in the work of the Senegalese poet Léopold Senghor, his comrade. Césaire's vision becomes central to the Negritude philosophy as it sweeps across and takes in the history and geography of the black man's estate and links these inexorably with the essential man of Europe, whom he forgives his dual disabilities and invites to the final "rendezvous of conquest."

Senghor's poetry creates the geographic focus of Africa as the sustaining spiritual force that will nurture the human festival at the ultimate rendezvous of all men. But for Senghor, as for Césaire, the point of departure was a painful quest for self-identity and for redemption from the strangulating embrace of French assimilation. In *Totem,* the poetic statement is made in a brisk succession of eight lines:

> I must hide in the intimate depths of my veins
> The ancestors storm-dark skinned, shot with
> lightning and thunder
> And my guardian animal, I must hide him

Lest I smash through the boom of scandal
He is my faithful blood and demands fidelity
Protecting my naked pride against
Myself and all the insolence of lucky races.[13]

This search for identity connotes a spiritual return to Africa, to
the mythical landscape populated by the dead ancestors, the
memorials of childhood, and the presence of the mother, the fashioners of the ultimate Negritude reconciliation. In *Nuit de Sine*
the poet invokes the black woman, the maternal principle, who is
at the center of the return to the African world:

Woman, lay on my forehead your perfumed hands,
hands softer than fur
Above, the swaying palm trees rustle in the high
night breeze
Hardly at all. No lullaby even.[14]

The song of the beating dark blood, the recounting of the tales
at evening, the children asleep on their mother's backs, and the
weaving feet of dances invoking the hour of ultimate night, all
state the magic of this black mythical moment of existence in
sharp contradiction to the opaque description of the light of Europe. At this hour, at the call of the woman, the Earth Mother,
the ancestors gather to talk to their children. The unity between the
living and the dead enforces the eternal links that feed the poet's
being:

Let me breathe the smell of our Dead, gather
and speak out again their living voice.[15]

It is this same woman, naked, clothed in black sin, who expresses
the principle of beauty, dazzling like the flight of eagles. She
shares an affinity with the firm-fleshed ripe fruit (image of her
breasts), the raptures of black wine, the rhythmic beat of the tom-
tom, and the solemn contralto of the spiritual song. The poet
strives, through the delirium of recapturing the features, voice, and
rhythm of the black woman, to encapsulate her passing beauty
against the destructive power of jealous fate.

Alongside the woman, the dead, and the ancestors, Senghor
invokes the spiritual power of the ancestral masks which, in their

ritualist roles, are aspects of the divinity of man's being, the visible symbolic link between the dead and the living. He shares a being with the masks, for it is they which fashioned

> this portrait of my face bent over
> the altar of white paper.[16]

The divine role of the mask is to quicken the being of African man to prepare him for the task of teaching the world:

> For who would teach rhythm to a dead world of
> machines and guns?
> Who would give the cry of joy to wake the dead
> and the bereaved at dawn?
> Say, who would give back the memory of life to
> the man whose hopes are smashed?[17]

The African, despised and abused, will serve as the "yeast which the white flour needs." Senghor and Césaire achieve a unified outlook which is the bedrock of Negritude in this concept. The rebirth and the new strength can only be arrived at through the presence and the impulsive dance of the black man.

In a long poem, *For Koras and Balafong,* a lament, Senghor exploits the rhythmic beat of drums, music, and dance. The poem opens in a quiet tone, recalling the predance silence, that Jungian somnolence which precedes the outburst of the drums. The paradise of peace is also the poet's African childhood, the Edenic period of softness and twilight. There is something pastorally idyllic about this world, of

> sleek companions decked in bush flowers
> . . . .
> the herdsmen's flute piped to show movements of the cattle.[18]

The dead and the forefathers supervise the drums beating the rhythms for the line of dancers. The African world is juxtaposed against the world of Europe represented by the thorns and signs of Verdun. This process of placing Europe against Africa becomes one of the commonplace features of Senghor's poetry, as it is in Césaire's; it creates the opposition of night and day, of black and white, and of rhythm and silence, the violent outburst of tropical forests and "snowy graveyards." The drum is the center of the

Negritude celebration: "Drum, drum, hear the drum." The rhythm
takes over in the long sweep of sounds:

> I have chosen the verse of streams and of winds and
> of forests
> The assonance of plains and rivers, chosen the rhythm
> of blood in my naked body
> Chosen the tremulsion of *balafongs,* the harmony of
> strings and brass that seem to clash, chose the
> Swing swing yes chosen the swing
> And the far-off muted trumpet, like the plaint of a
> nebulous star adrift across the night
> Like the summons to Judgement, the burst of the trumpet
> over the snowy graveyards of Europe.[19]

In this long poem of nine movements, cluttered with the music of
the *kora* and the *balafong,* Senghor makes the choice to be black,
washed clean of all contagions of civilized men, to identify with
the black toiling peasant whose sweat enriched the cane and cotton
fields, whose life is the abandon in delight to the great universal
power, the Césairean essence of things, and to love "that moves
the singing worlds." The last movement is the ultimate affirmation
of the Negritude outlooks:

> African night my black night, mystical-lucid black-
> brilliant
> You rest at one with the Earth, you are the Earth
> and the harmonious hills.[20]

Toko Waly, the feminine principle of Africa, is the lioness of dark
beauty. Night, the magical part of man's being, the essence of the
primal rhythm of blackness locked in mysteries and mystical, delivers the poet from arguments and sophistries of European civilization, from calculated

> hatred and humane butchery
> Night dissolving all my contradictions, all contradictions
> in the first unity of your blackness.[21]

Senghor, like Césaire, believes in universal reconciliation of all
men; but unlike Césaire, he does not arrive at it through the fury
and agonized frenzy of self-knowledge only as a black person. It

is about France that Senghor is particularly concerned, and his Roman Catholicism delivers the pardon. For France Senghor bears an inexplicable love:

> I have need of Maytime murmuring at Montsouris,
> of the splendour of the Tuileries at the end of
> Summer
> I need the pure quoin of the front of the obelisk
> and the Place de la
> Concorde to help me find again beneath brushwood
> and liana, my own obelisk.[22]

It is ironic that this quotation comes from a poem called *Elegy for Midnight,* a denunciation of summer and the light of Europe.

Night, death, childhood are unified in his poetic landscape and share the essence of Africa, the ancestors, the dead, the mother, the dance, the drum, and the blood of life. In *Elegy for Waters* the summation of the universal reconciliation is achieved:

> Lord, harken to my voice. LET IT RAIN. It rains
> And you have opened from your arms of thunder the
> cataracts of forgiveness
> Rain on New York, on Ndiongolar, on Ndialakhar
> Rain on Moscow on Pompidou on Paris and suburbs
> on Melbourne on Messina on Morzine
> Rain on India, China . . . four hundred thousand Chinese
> are drowned, twelve million Chinese are saved, the
> righteous and the wicked
> Rain on the Sahara and on the Middle West, on the desert
> on the wheatlands on the ricelands
> On straw heads and wool heads
> And life is born again colour of whatever is.[23]

Senghor has been accused of being a poseur and, at best, a mediocre poet. His reading of some of his poetry to African musical instruments, such as the *kora* and *balafong,* has been dismissed as a bogus and forced attempt to yoke two disparate cultures together. But his mastery of French has been acclaimed and it is not for nothing that he is a respected member of the French Academy. He has illustrated very well in his poetry the thematic concerns and mannerisms of Negritude. If perhaps lacking Césaire's clarity and surrealistic imagistic precision or the fury of his voice, Senghor

illustrates the essential music of French in an unconventional poetic mold. It is he who created the magic of that African world,
with its kingdom of childhood, an innocent yet preternaturally
aware state of mind, the pastoralism of a lost Eden, which he
fondly believes is out there in Africa. The sense of loneliness and
isolation that characterized Césaire's work is here, but, unlike
Césaire, Senghor strives for a community with living and ancestral
comrades as a testimonial to the grandeur of the past and the promise of the future. He is the poet of two vicarious experiences, a
veritable sample of Africa's own history. Senegal was colonized
over three hundred years and the Serer, Senghor's people, became
one of the most Europeanized groups in West Africa, accepting
Roman Catholicism. At an early age he moved from the *lycée*
at Dakar to the Sorbonne in Paris, to the *agrégation* based on a
study of Baudelaire, and to a German prisoner-of-war camp. Europe was a happy and at times, sad experience. His poetry is the
attempt to fashion out of the European experience a language and
testament that will constitute homage to his African past. While
for Césaire Negritude has been one of repudiation and renunciation of his so-called "Negro" past and its historical designation,
for Senghor it is the affirmation of the values of his past and the
lamentation of what has been lost, an assertion of an African outlook and perception of the world. For him Negritude becomes a cultural instrument of fusion, fashioned for the survival of man in
a world gone mad with machines and industry. Basing a great deal
of his thinking on the work of the French Jesuit philosopher Teil-
hard de Chardin, Senghor affirms the need for the achievement of
the final human evolution through the pulling together of disparate
and, at times, opposing elements into the unity of this revolution.

David Diop, a much younger poet than Senghor, died tragically
in a plane crash in 1960. Born of a Senegalese father and a Came-
roonian mother in Bordeaux, he spent his life moving between
France and an Africa that he never really came to know. Like
Senghor, he exhibits a passionate attachment to his African heritage and, like Césaire, a virulent anger against Europe that defies
control. His poetry is a litany of crimes committed against Africa
by European conquerors, the sorrow and tears of Africa's suffering.
The contempt and oppression of centuries heaped upon Africa led

him to protests and violent accusations. Unlike Senghor, he rejects any reconciliation.

His reputation as a poet is based on only one volume, *Coups de Pilon (Pounding)*, which appeared in the 1950s. Its basic impulse is the rejection of the Senghorian synthesis and the denial of even a possible balancing polarity between the two historical positions of Africa and Europe. For him, the feeding source is an agonized hatred of Europe and all it stands for. Across the centuries of hate and bitterness, Diop proclaims the millennial dawn to which Europe has contributed nothing but darkness and sorrow. In his poem *The Vultures* the agony and frustration of this overwhelming "historical" position soars to the liberation of the last line. The same idea of Africa, supine, offering a thousand sacrifices, but yet preparing itself in hope for the ultimate salvation is again expressed in the poem *Africa:*

> Is this you this back that is bent
> This back that breaks under the weight of humiliation
> This back trembling with red scars
> And saying yes to the whip under the midday sun
> But a grave voice answers me
> Impetuous son that tree young and strong
> That tree there
> In splendid loneliness amidst white and faded flowers
> That is Africa your Africa
> That grows again patiently obstinately
> And its fruit gradually acquires
> the bitter taste of liberty.[24]

Slave labor, slavery, and the massacre of Africa were part of history. Diop claims these elements as aspects of his individual poetic revolt. It is a voice yet imbued with tenderness and a deep sense of sorrow, indulging an appeal for comradeship in sorrow. Brotherhood of the black world will nourish the new strength. In *Listen Comrades* he states this in the revolution of blood, achieved through the companionship of the chain. After a litany of sufferings, the poet pauses:

> But no
> For there rings out higher than my sorrows
> Purer than the morning where the wild beast wakes

The cry of a hundred people smashing their cells
. . . .
It is the sign of the dawn
The sign of brotherhood which comes to nourish the
dreams of men.[25]

It is poetry of one-dimensional impulse, of certitude revealed
through the energy of its own conviction. *Listen Comrades* revives
the history of the rape of Africa, a familiar theme in Negritude,
in the clamor of the slaves in the middle passage, in the agony
of Mamba, the personification of Africa, the prisons, and death.
Yet there is a sustaining warmth of hope:

And his smile despite agony
Despite the wounds of his broken body
Kept the bright colors of a bouquet of hope.[26]

Hope is the eternal light that beams through the struggling centuries for Mamba, old aged man of dignity

Who ten times poured forth for us milk and light
I feel his mouth on my dreams
And the peaceful tremor of his breast
And I am lost again
Like a plant torn from the maternal bosom.[27]

But liberty is won through the smashing of cells and chains, in
the revolt of the wild beast held in chains. The revolt is both
physical—heard in the smashing of cells and chains—and spiritual
—in the self-discovery of the blood, the spiritual elemental bond.
The will to be free nourishes the hope of freedom, making Diop
the most politically direct of all the Negritude poets. Before the
outbursts of present-day apostles and prophets of the black diaspora, the Diop cry was heard for black brotherhood on both sides of
the Atlantic.

But he is also the Negritude poet par excellence, with attachment to the mystical motherland where magic and blood reaffirm
for him, in exile, the spiritual bond. In *Your Presence,* a poem inspired by a return to Africa, is stated the renewal of faith in the
tangible power of blood. Addressing the mother and lover, he
writes:

In your presence I rediscovered my name
My name that was hidden under pain of separation.[28]

The separation is exile and absence; awareness and return are a recovery from illness:

I rediscovered the eyes no longer veiled with fever
And your laughter like a flame piercing the shadows
Has revealed Africa to me beyond the sorrows of
yesterday.[29]

The exile period was filled with illusion, shattered ideas, sleep made restless with alcohol, suffering "that burdens today with the taste of command." But it is this suffering that typically opens the flood gates and "turns love into a boundless river." The memory of the poet's blood, the primary elemental bond to his birthplace, is basic to the discovery and awareness of the mother, adorned in precious beads and necklaces of laughter. The last line of this poem is again Diop's affirmation of hope of the future of liberty and redemption in "days sparkling with ever new joys."

In *Renegade* Diop attacks the man who deserts his father, his people, his race. He is the sell-out, the Uncle Tom, the member of the black elite who believes that salvation lies in his total submission to and unquestioning acceptance of white values and his surrender to the humiliations that the so-called "master race" heaps on him. This man, Diop points out, scorns his origins, acquires the civilized mien of his oppressor, and in immaculate evening dress screams, whispers, and pleads "in the parlors of condescension." He deserves only to be pitied, this man for whom his "grandmother's hut brings blushes to [his] face that is bleached by years of humiliation and conscience." The bitterness gives way to pity without compassion, summed up in the last line, "Oh I am so lonely so lonely here." *Africa* is the Negritude writer's poem, without the upright patience, without conciliation, evoking the nostalgic dreams of Africa. He is the exile for whom the land where his grandmother sings on the banks of the distant river is not real: "I have never known you," he says. In spite of this, there is a bond forged in blood, the center of Diop's poetry:

But your blood flows in my veins
Your beautiful black blood that irrigates the fields
The blood of your sweat.[30]

Africa is the symbol of the old man, his "back trembling with red scars and saying yes to the whip under the midday sun." But Africa is born anew from the loins of the aged man, an

> Impetuous son that tree young and strong
> that tree there
> In splendid loneliness amidst white and faded flowers.[31]

The "white and faded flowers" symbolize the decaying civilization providing the manure and the nurture for the trees and the son "that grows again patiently obstinately."

Europe is the obsolescent putrefaction, the vulture, the parasitic dunghill bird that hovers and devours everything in its way. In his poem *Vultures* Diop recreates the chain gangs, the greed and rapacity of vultures in the suggested violence of words like "blood-stained" and "talons." The prayers of the faithful are heard in the paternoster that "drowned the howling of the plantations." The rape of women—the bitter memories of extorted kisses, promises broken at the point of a gun—by people

> who did not seem human
> Who knew all the books but did not know love.[32]

But who are we? In lines reminiscent of Césaire, Diop proclaims "we are those whose hands fertilize the womb of the earth." In *A Black Dancer* Diop, the sensitive poet of anguish, hate, and celebration of liberty, achieves a new dimension as a sensualist wallowing in the dance of the naked joy of the dancer's smile, in the ritual offerings of breasts and secret powers, and the great festival of marriage: "You are the dance by the golden tales of marriage nights," he proclaims. The dance, the symbol of primal life and of Africa, is the dance "of giddyness, by the magic loins restarting the world" during the festival of primal sensuousness when the myths, hypocrisy, and cant of the white world will be burnt away. It will be the occasion, too, for burning false gods through the innocence of the initiate and the childhood that must be regained so that the ultimate salvation can be achieved:

> You are the idea of All and the voice of the Ancient
> You are the word which explodes
> In showers of light upon the shores of oblivion.[33]

It is through this sensuous reclamation of the primary functions of life, symbolized by the magic of the dance, the achievement of the state of trance, the harmony of sound, rhythm, and movement, that expiation can be won for a rebirth and renewal of faith with *la vie même*. In *Nigger Tramp* the central figure is a battered, tattered, and trampled Africa in whose humiliation the poet reads the forgotten legends of Africa's heroes. The cotton plantations and the mines are the geographic landscapes of this humiliation; but the noble princes Soundiata and Shaka will rise again. In an apocalyptic vision, he recalls the past, in the agony of bellies burst open, in the fear that crouches in the entrails of cities. The vision is one of total dispossession, a devastating alienation, of toil and tears. It is in these that he finds voice for his own *assimilé*'s impotence: "But what was I doing on your morning of wind and tears?" he asks. He was, alas, seated upon his clouds. In the tramp's sorrow and suffering he confesses his own inaction and impotence:

Forgive me Negro guide
Forgive my narrow heart.[34]

The ultimate is founded upon hope, springing anew; the carnival of hate, suffering, and derision over, he will

sharpen the hurricane for the furrows of the future
For you we will make Ghana and Timbuctu.[35]

Diop is the Negritude poet of the political resurrection and the restoration of liberty for Africa and all peoples of African descent. For him the poetic voice of the movement assumed a passionate delirium of the trance, out of which the cure, the liberation, and the salvation will emerge. Things remain simple and one-dimensional—history, Africa, Europe, the past, and the dreams deferred from yesterday blossoming tomorrow. In essence his poetry stands unique in its single-minded clarity and simplicity, a homage to his restlessness as a cultural mulatto and an African exile of all time.

Among the younger contemporary African poets in French, Tchicaya U Tam'si stands out. A selection of his poems has been made available in English in a handsome translation by the critic Gerald Moore. U Tam'si's work has been said to be heavily influenced by surrealism, Césaire, and the whole Negritude manner. Senghor has described him as bearing manifest witness to Negritude. Of his own role as a committed revolutionary, he writes: "The revolution does not guarantee a public place for the writer." He is obviously the private, anguished fashioner of awareness, yet limited by audience and, in the African sense, by language.

In U Tam'si's work it is clear that the most persistent influences are French symbolism and surrealism, an overwhelming attachment to Catholic imagery, and a persistent return to a Congolese landscape as the ultimate focus of his inspiration. Even though aware of race, his poetry does not anchor itself in the racial memory of Negritude's atavism. It seeks what in essence is a voice to articulate an individual rather than a collective agony. In this sense, he is closer to Césaire than to Senghor, whose poetry tends to make large and expansive gestures rather than the poignant personal assertions like Césaire, locked in the purgatory of French civilization. Having gone to Paris at an early age from Brazzaville, Tchicaya carried away only vague memories of Africa, which become merely the points of racial reference in an anonymous French existence. When the Belgian Congo's drama of the early 1960s was being enacted, he became closely identified with the Lumumbists and shared the frustration and despair that became Zaire's subsequent history. These experiences alone were enough to impose a political and racial awareness on his work without his necessarily making proclamations for race and continent in the loudest of the Negritude tradition. He has published five books of verse: *Feu de Brousse, A Triche-Coeur, Épitomé, Le Ventre,* and *Arc Musical.* The most persistent idea in his work is a search for the self. U Tam'si's search is an individual rather than a racial one:

> body and soul naked
> I am the man without history
> One morning I came up black
> Against the light of setting suns.[36]

His poetry attaches itself to the Catholic ritual in which he at times sees himself as the crucified Christ, accentuating the legend of betrayal in which he launches his present sense of agony and loss.

In a short poem from *Feu de Brousse* (*Brush Fire*), the familiar landscape of U Tam'si's poetry is firmly established. In it is the river, the source of life. In reality, the Congo River is the eternal nourishing source, an extension of the sea, and, in time, the very limbs of humanity flowing to the heart, the seat of the most pure human passion. It is this river of birth that energizes the poet and others to whom he addresses his verse. "My race" is the Negritudist focus, the sufferer even in triumph. The combination of the river, wet and cold, and the fire and flames brings to birth the brooding, the loneliness of those sitting by the side of a river warming themselves by a fire. They are members of the poet's race, tormented, lost, waiting, the race that remembers "the taste of bronze drunk hot." U Tam'si's greatest talent is for yoking two opposites together to highlight his ultimate poetic thrust—solitude. In *Dance to the Amulets,* a poem celebrating life and a festival of abundance in the midst of suffering and decay, are found

> gestures and stabs of sickly hands
> curving then unripping of conception.[37]

"Stabs," "unripping," "blood," the rope at the neck, the harsh explosion existing within the idyllic setting in which fairies and fawns are summoned to dance where "our grass is rich," where the dreams of men are rainbow-colored, where the morning is supple. Within this pastoral revelry is solitude, the only boon the poet receives from his mother, and the flint he is promised in this festival. In *Still Lives,* a touching poem of self-identity, the image of a tree on which bodies hang becomes the totemic symbol of birth and death, revealed in the fish and carcasses introduced by the dead sister. The adoration at the foot of the cross where the Christ image hangs links the devouring act with the fast, the hunger, and the dispossession of his blood, the Negritude bond and link. The last lines establish the surrealist scene of the father who does not know the name of the mother of his children, a statement in total alienation, emphasizing the devastating denial of recognition for the mother, the symbol of the earth through which the river of life flows. A liberation of spirit and final awareness is achieved in the epiphany of suffering in

> I have often seen
> carcasses in the air
> where my blood burns[38]

with sharp imagistic symbols of the sacrifice and the self-immolation, the passionate anger of blood burning, and the certitude of the end of the fast.

U Tam'si's poetry escapes the one-dimensional impulse of the most recognized Negritude verse, asserting an essentially personal poetic sensibility that is at once illusive and sharp. In *A Mat to Weave* the search for and assertion of self-identity, the statement of alienation, and the acceptance of one's destiny are the elemental ingredients of a poem of great depth and sadness. The humanity of the poet seeks answers to the questions of

> Why crystals in his blood
> Why globules in his laughter.[39]

Poised and ready for an answer to these questions:

> someone called him
> dirty wog.[40]

The pain and the hurt of the insult do not disturb for "still he is left with the gentle act of his laughter." The tower of strength is in the giant tree, in the nobility of the beasts reflected in the giant tree with living cleft, the symbolic features and elements of his country whose memories are still left to him. Besides, there is the stream, the river, which is

> the safest of cups
> because it was bronze
> because it was his living flesh.[41]

Through alienation and the despair will come the knowledge that his life is not a poem; the land, the tree, the water, and the stones are the elemental objects that emphasize for him the priest-diviner and the prophet's role, that of the sufferer and carrier. The attempt to partake in the romantic flight of doves, in the tenderness of mothers, must yield place to the harsh realization that he is nothing but "a dirty wog." The poet moves us into the visionary dimensions of self-awareness, into the magic of the bush, the abode of lost souls, the confused terrain where night and day are one, where the miracle of time remains unrealized. He also leads us into a world of surrealistic memories when even the sea, the sustaining force for his rivers, becomes a gull, a bird of flight and fancy, the fictitious inhabitant of the shore he cannot recollect. For here, in this territory of haze and doubt, is re-enacted the terrible dance of animals, symbolizing the fall when the harmony of nature itself collapses:

> All standing upright tooth to tooth
> against the spume of a deadly dance.[42]

In this scene the leafy tree and the tender bark are consumed in the fire. After this, "what more to say." Even the escape route from the agony is shut "for there was absinthe in the wine," the wine of infinite resignation. The re-creation of the memory of the past, like the memory of the sea, in the restoration of the scene of canoers and crocodiles on the stream, is no longer important. The inability to revive such dreams of the almost tender dawn of his own non-awareness and the crashing of those half-remembered dreams are the "grains of sand between the teeth." The poet must withdraw into himself, must savor his cup, for there is no avenue of escape. There is the despair that Césaire talks about, of race and alienation, stated here in passionately private and personal tones. It was for U Tam'si the reality of being a "wog" and the subsequent withdrawal after the rejection into the safety of his stream—"the gentlest cup, his most living flesh." It is the same Fanonesque awareness, the putting together of the fragments by another self. For U Tam'si, it is made manifest only after the shattering of the dream, the regurgitation of the romance of his river, his tree in the burning forest, after which nothing more can be said.

> Here begins the poem of his life
> He was trained in a school
> He was trained in a studio
> and he saw roads planted with sphinxes.[43]

The sphinxes are the eternal symbols of the inscrutable, answering no questions, offering no explanation for the way things are, the blank impassive faces that lack the animation of the brush fire, the tree, the river, and the stream: "But he hangs to the secret of the sun." He still possesses the magic of his gentle laughter, he has the tree, the water, and the leaves stored in the privacy of his blood:

> That is why you will see him
> The marching canoers have raised once more

against haulers of French cotton
Their cries
This flight is a flight of doves.[44]

He is the marching canoer on the river; he is the hauler of cotton, the eternal toiler, carting cotton for the leeches who cannot know the bitterness in his blood, cannot understand the communal anguish now poured in blood and carried in his cup. The persistent image of the cup that is drunk refurbishes a completion of the wine image, now full of absinthe, and restates also the image of Christ on the cross suggested in the tree. That cup, the purest and safest, is the affirmation of his humanity—it is his Congolese head and his Congolese blood. The levels of statement in this poem do not lend themselves to easy identification. But the passion of it, its despair, has a ringing resonance that makes it one of U Tam'si's best.

The river is again the central symbol of *Epitome* and *Le Ventre* (*The Womb*), nourishing the search, the rebirth, the restatement of the mannered theme with "arborescent madness" dictated by the events that gripped the Congo in the early 1960s. In a sensitive celebration of blackness, the poet revels in the black salt, the leaven, and the black blood, the incarnative spring fountain. Nakedness, a natural state of being, is the stripping away of the trappings of alien culture for a return to the primal source, which, being black, is not a corporeal malediction. It is the moment of assuming responsibility for his ancestors, his mother, his friend Sammy, and all men. In the love act he finds the febrile co-ordinate of self and race:

I have the claws of a woman in my flesh
I bleed for her delight in love.[45]

—a co-ordinate that is destructive and dislocating; the image of her god—the fakir, the Arab, the grinning Negro—desalts his soul. If that god is hidden,

then let the ferns
hold in the earth
the freshness of a patch of violent water.[46]

"Violent water" is an echo of black blood which must run like the rivers and streams of earlier poems—its assertion is its freshness and aggressive nakedness, its warmth, and its rejection of any act of servility and submission. There is the Césairean anger and the cry for life. In a fragment that contains one simple act of contempt, spitting into the Seine, this anger becomes the impotent rage at the events that gripped the Congo while the world floated gently by unconcerned. The poet is being driven out of his mind and clamors to no avail for the moon and stars—the former inhabited by himself, the rapt surrealist, proclaiming a benediction. But he is not at one with the stars in his levitation, in that hour when the moment of eminence and of flight arrives, like the patient woman who sits in the corner and

> knits a blue stocking for the violated night
> it kindles hell in the black flames
> it ends the purification of my sinful swan
> which once fixed a halo of pollen.[47]

The "violated night," "hell in the black flames," "sinful swan" are the symbols of passive suffering, the pollen, the source of new life for the tree whose sacredness was once fixed upon the brow of the race. But reason is crazy, deliriously upset in spite of its focal identification with stars and moons, with the universal which alone is the romantic reality. In the bunch of withered flowers in his letter box, a rage is born at the normality of life in Paris, including his own, while the trauma of the Congo deepens, like the lunacy of the insane at moonrise:

> On the head of the lustful black crab
> My reason makes me difficult and faithless
> in the abstract of my passion.[48]

The impotence and rage yields nothing:

> My prick is not even a root of the tree,
> to speak as that tree rustles
> would give a rustic perfume
> to the game of my flight
> and put less blood on the hands of my quest.[49]

The tree image, central in U Tam'si's poetry, is given a new force through the absence of root in the impotence of the prick, its inability to infuse blood into the source of life. The disasters mount, like the play of children, and childhood memories distant now yet loved in that state of impotence and inaction. There are those who have taken flight, indistinct now in the grayness:

> and a grey rain serves all our dreams
> forcing me to become a forger
> and holy assassin
> despite the equinox
> despite myself
> despite the sorcery of the smiles
> of my obedient black brothers.[50]

Despite his fanatical cause, his infidelity and impotence are total. The silence is unanswerable, his defeat is complete:

> And then what would you have me say of this silence
> Squatting beside my own conscience?[51]

The theme of silence called faith in the humiliation and rejection surges into the search for an abode of refuge.

> They give you what they have eaten
> and what they have not known how to keep.[52]

The poet talks with another black man in the streets of Paris and takes some consolation in a kindred spirit whose impotence is also his and with whom he will conspire to say his last prayers in a dark corner. The identification is through the soul, in the dance of his compatriot in that moment of sadness because and in spite of it. At another level it is through blood which is here presented in the image of the oil of the lamp, burning out and overflowing. Darkness will envelop them. This darkness will signify the hush hour in which they must make their prayers and confess their sins before the ultimate catastrophe. It is a return to the silence, the impotence now "reeking with iodine" for those who have awkward Congolese heads.

The Scorner is a poem of return to the ancestral gods, to the God that fuses in the crucifixion image the sadness of Christ. Sadness is the underlying keynote of this poem, and it is this that the poet celebrates—the exile, the promise, do not yet occur:

> What wine shall I drink to your jubilee
> In this country which has no vines
> In the desert all the bushes are of cactus

> Shall I take the crop of flowers
> for flames of the burning bush of your desire
> Tell me in what Egypt my people's feet lie chained.[53]

The sacrament of the holy eucharist is meaningful only in terms of the supreme sacrifice and suffering of Christ. The poet at once is Christ and Moses who will lead his people out of Egypt. He will receive the sacraments at the precincts of the burning bush, the epiphany occurring only in the desert where all the bushes are cacti —the thirsty desert plant. The desert is the symbol of the African and the black condition; its sterility echoes the impotence of the poet. It is in the fusion of these Christian images that the identification with Christ is introduced. For his god, too, is a sad god; his path lies through a desert, his people lie in chains in Egypt. Emboldened, the poet relishes in the agony of Christ with whom he is one:

> Christ I laugh at your sadness
> O my sweet Christ
> Thorn for thorn
> We have a common crown of thorns.[54]

The passion is the final act of sacrifice after the identification of the mother, the father, and the betrayer, it is the slaying of the pascal lamb and the asking for forgiveness. Over the dead of the Congo whose bellies are ripped open, he mourns in the awareness of the ultimate atonement which their blood has achieved:

> They are dead
> so that no evil grass may spring.[55]

It becomes his own death, that summer. But there is a promised purity, resurrection, and rebirth which become the prize of the Congo. Christ becomes the focus of his agony, as in his name much blood has already been shed. The historical and contemporary act of betrayal deepens his own despair; it is in the water in the communion wine, the absinthe and gold in the wine of joy. In the Christ image is seen the body of the mutilated Lumumba, the supreme martyr whose belly, and the Congo's, is ripped open. Sacrificed like Christ in the company of his two companions, the prophets fall, "their bellies to the sky."

A poet of passionate and limitless consistency, U Tam'si's work represents one of the clearest aspects of the self-assured individual voice that contemporary poetry of Africa carries. There is nothing sentimental or insincere in the feeling, which is uniquely matched with a great passion for language. The whole world is his roving ground; history, the past, Roman Catholicism, and political events provide the feeding sources for the nourishment of the strong images of rivers, the tree, blood, and the sacrifice. Louis Aragon's *"cri de l'esprit qui retourne vers lui-meme"* informs U Tam'si's surrealism. For him it is no frivolous exercise in verbal and imagistic agility. His Negritude retrieves itself from public affirmations and returns to a private personal agony in which a catatonic array of emotions, episodes, images, and symbols is pressed into service to explode his poetic madness and silent agony. His master is Césaire who provides the inspiration, the surrealists—Bréton, Aragon—and the passion of his own poetic and musical ear supplying the unification and thrust in his verse. He may be a Negritude writer, but with an immense difference.

11

Older poets
of English-speaking Africa

The earliest poetry of English-speaking Africa followed a different path of development from the work of the Negritude writers. The first impetus in writing came from the missionaries, and the emergence of writing in the vernaculars became the most significant aspect of the Churches' contribution to the expansion of African culture.

The work of the first West African poets, now characteristically referred to as "pioneer poets," was also heavily influenced by the Victorian poetic traditions and a hymnological structure. It must be remembered that the first poets of English-speaking Africa came from West Africa where British colonialism was more entrenched. They formed part of that early community of detribalized Africans who represented eloquent copies of the English society which colonialism tried, however, haphazardly, to establish. It is one of the most interesting ironies of history that English colonialism aroused the earliest nationalistic sentiment and anticolonial rhetoric on the African continent, as witnessed in the work of politicians like Casely Hayford, Edward Blyden, Atoh Ahuma, Herbert Macaulley, and a host of other West African professional men and women. These English-speaking Africans did not go through the blinding program of assimilation, but in the best tradition of liberalism were exposed to what in today's terms represent some aspects of pan-continental, or regional, ideas. Ideas of liberty, pride of race, morality were aspects of the African renaissance period of the early part of this century.

Some of the English-language poets of West Africa were Benibengor Blay of Ghana, Crispin George of Sierra Leone, Roland Dempster of Liberia, Gladys Casely-Hayford of Ghana and Sierra Leone, Raphael Armattoe and Michael Dei-Anang of Ghana, Dennis Osadebay and Nnamdi Azikiwe of Nigeria. They wrote during the period from the rise of popular journalism in the Sierra Leone *Weekly News* in the 1860s to the West African *Pilot* of the late 1940s. The mid-1920s saw the rise of nationalism in the wake of the work of the National Congress of British West Africa.

The preoccupations of the poets were race and nationalism, themes which became the main focuses of their writing. It would be obvious, too, that these poets were not interested in the fine questions of technical competence. They wrote what can be described as poor English Victorian verse, vaguely imitating eighteenth-century Augustan and neo-classical poetry with its heavy reliance on rhyming couplets and borrowing liberally from nineteenth-century hymnology, especially what came out of Methodism.

As poets they formed a community of detribalized African intellectuals, culturally British, yet politically, though modestly and urbanely, rebellious. Their fathers were the first African converts, African missionaries, colonial clerks, or merchant princes who could afford to send their children to England for an education, which in fact only frustrated them. These young men and women came face to face with tail-end English Victorian bigotry and nineteenth-century racism in an England that was supposed to be their mother country. So, like the Negritude poets of a later date, they rebelled against the stranglehold of this alien society. Unlike them, they were not impelled to make philosophical postulations on the question of race. And unlike their French counterparts, their European models did not come from the best poetic traditions of their received literary culture.

Four of these early English-language poets' work are worth examining at close quarters. The first is Gladys Casely-Hayford, daughter of the famous Ghanaian lawyer-politician. Educated in England and Wales from the age of fifteen, she returned to Freetown, Sierra Leone, where she taught school till her death in 1950. Deriving her background from an upper-middle-class African society in both Accra and Freetown and from an English education, she was fiercely aware of her color and race and possessed, like the other poets of her period, a moralistic and didactic tone which was reminiscently Victorian. In a poem called *Rejoice,* she makes a simple-minded proclamation of race pride:

Rejoice and shout with laughter
Throw all your burdens down,
If God has been so gracious
As to make you black or brown.
For you are a great nation,
A people of great birth
For where would spring the flowers
If God took away the earth?
Rejoice and shout with laughter
Throw all your burdens down
Yours is a glorious heritage
If you are black or brown.[1]

Blackness becomes a rallying point of joy, for the African is the very earth that feeds the flowers. "Burdens" recall the agonies of slavery and colonialism and is also an echo of the Christian religious burdens of the world of flesh. But this is obviously a secular poem written in the form of a hymn and can perhaps be sung to a popular church tune, especially with the positioning of the last four lines which constitute a reprise of the first four lines. There is a joyous, soapy, evangelical swing to the poem. In a descriptive poem about Freetown, the poet's awareness of God as a Creator fashioning the very features of the town is the center of her deep love for it:

Freetown, when God made thee, He made thy soil alone
Then threw the rich remainder in the sea.[2]

After He created the inlets, the Atlantic deep,

He scattered palms profusely o'er the ground
Then grew tall grasses, who in happy mirth
Reached up to kiss each palm tree that they found.[3]

God, after his creation, whispered: "This is my gem!" This is poetry distinguished neither by its ideas nor by its language. Her poem *Nativity* is a fiercely Christian poem about the birth of Christ, couched in a rather pompous Miltonic language:

> Within a native hut, ere stirred the dawn
> Unto the Pure One was an Infant born.[4]

But there are Africanisms like "lappah" (cloth), "home-tanned deerskin hide," "spirits of black bands" in attendance at the holy birth. Mary is black, the baby is black, black women are present at the birth. But the setting of the poem remains biblically pastoral, with palm fronds, pink lilies, "frangipani blossoms." This is tropical Africa, and not a cold wintry land; the birthplace is a warm "native hut." This poem represents one of the earliest attempts to turn round a major Christian event into a race statement.

Raphael Armattoe of Ghana was also educated at an early age in Europe where he studied to be a doctor. In the early 1950s he became involved in politics, particularly in the cause of the unification of the Ewe of Ghana and Togo. He was a prolific writer, a nationalist, a researcher interested in the use of African herbs in Western medical practice, a historian, and an anthropologist. His two volumes of poetry were *Between the Forest and the Sea* and *Deep Down the Black Man's Mind,* both published privately in Londonderry in 1950. Even though he wrote in the conventional manner of his contemporaries, dealing with the large themes of race and nationalism, his poetry expressed a superb lyricism which was very reminiscent of Wordsworth. In the poem *The Lonely Soul,* recalling Wordsworth's Lucy poems, a sad somber tone is struck in very simple and melancholic mood:

> I met an old woman
> Talking by herself
> Down a lonely road.
> Talking to herself,
> Laughing all the time,
> Talking to herself
> Down a country road.[5]

The woman's mood is engendered by "showers of sorrow." This sad mood, as the poet confesses, is also his. In another poem, *A Little Child,* Armattoe echoes Blake's *The Lamb:*

> Little child, what ails thee
> In a world so tiny?
> Why are thy sweet lips cross
> Thy pearly eyes so dim?[6]

One of the most obvious weaknesses of the pioneer poets is the imitativeness as illustrated here. In copying Blake's *The Lamb,* Armattoe picked upon a trivial theme—the soiling of a child's smock—and thus falls into using false poeticisms such as "sweet lips," "pearly eyes," and such exclamations as "what odds." He wrote a few political poems which state his own early frustrations at the confusion of the political direction, goals, and climate of the Gold Coast in the late 1940s. *Servant-King* is an angry poem of political frustration, revealing his own haughty pride and impotence, hardly distinguished in style:

> Leave them alone,
> Leave them to be
> Men lost to shame,
> To honour lost!
> Servant kinglets,
> Riding to war
> Against their own.[7]

In one of his longer poems, *The Way I Would Like to Die,* Armattoe's ear for lyrical verse and his astounding simplicity are shown in a style which is entirely his own:

> I would like to go while still young,
> While the dew is wet on the grass;
> To perish in a great air crash,
> With a silver plane burning bright.
> Like a flashing star in the night.[8]

The poet sees his death in the image of a crashing plane, fiery, blazing across the firmament, dissolving, and becoming part of the "eternal mind of God." This romantic death wish is again an aspect of his restless petulance, refusing mourning, vowing to live only in the memory of his mother. There is a desire to reach a state of purity, to be, in spite of the Blakean echoes,

> Cleansed now of all impurities
> By the red all-devouring flames.[9]

Dennis Osadebay is the African political hymnologist par excellence. He was very much involved in the political agitational phase of Nigeria's history. A trained lawyer, he was also, like most of the well-known politicians of Nigeria, a noted journalist who used his literary writings as instruments for his propagandistic work. His collected verses, *Africa Sings,* contains a large variety of nationalistic verse, moralistic and didactic hortatory poetry addressed to the youth, men, and women of Africa. There is a great deal in his work that brings it closer to that of the Negritude writers, especially in its tone of racial protestation and lamentation of Africa's lot under the colonial yoke. Young Africa's soul, in his poem *Who Buys My Thoughts,* is described as

> The soul of teeming millions,
> Hungry, naked, sick,
> Yearning, pleading, waiting.[10]

The urgency of the last line is repeated in another section about the life of restless youth

> who are born
> Into deep and clashing cultures,
> Sorting, questioning, watching.[11]

In Africa he sees the spirit of the age, the restlessness of the youth in their struggle for a direction hemmed in by the two cultures of Europe and Africa. But there is a mood of rebellion expressed in the

> unquenching fire that smoulders
> And smoulders
> In every living heart
> That's true and noble or suffering;
> It burns all o'er the earth
> Destroying, chastening, cleansing.[12]

Osadebay, in the best Negritude tradition, also calls for a reconciliation of the two worlds of Africa and Europe. In the poem *Young Africa's Plea,* he pleads for his life to be taken over by the white man's ways, in a mood that suggests that he was rather ashamed of his own customs, and, working with the black man's brain, he will

rise a better man
Not ashamed to face the world.[13]

His direction is toward a synthesis of the best of both worlds that will give him strength as history's new man. In one of his rousing nationalistic poems, *The Women of New Africa*, Osadebay swings into vague rhyming poetry characteristic of the fighting mood of all anthems:

God bless you, Mothers of our Race,
God cause to shine on you His face;
And give you strength and all you crave
To bring forth sons and daughters brave.[14]

Michael Dei-Anang of Ghana has remained one of the active workers in the field of African culture and history, whose creative talent has been expressed in both drama and poetry. He has published two plays, *Cocoa Comes to Mampong* and *Okomfo Anokye's Golden Stool,* and two volumes of poetry, *Wayward Lines from Africa* and *Africa Speaks.* He is one of the leading lights of the pioneer poets, sharing with them a deep Christian upbringing, a European education, and a great awareness of himself as an African and a nationalist. In a poem, *Dear Africa,* Dei-Anang conceives of Africa as a virgin lover to whom all Africans must give their love and devotion:

Awake, thou sleeping heart!
Awake, and kiss
The love-lorn brow
of this ebon lass,
Dear Africa.[15]

The language is rather highly derivative and inelegantly archaic. But in an elegiac poem, Dei-Anang's lyrical powers come to full play. *Let's Live in Peace* is a poem of calm, possessing a certain lyrical tone very suitable to the theme of the transience of life and the wastefulness of strife:

Let's live in peace,
For here, like tenants
In thatched huts we dwell;
Soon, too soon, the tropic storm

Will outblow the flick'ring lights
Of human life
Our huts will fall
In frailty upon the earth.[16]

The theme of decay and corruption, obviously Christian-derived, is
stated here in such simple melancholic lines that, while revealing
some archaic tendencies, yet retains a hold upon the sadness of the
mood.

The pioneer poets of English-speaking West Africa were all politically motivated poets with no great passion for language or original
style. It also never occurred to them that they could turn to their
own oral traditions for poetic forms, imagery, and style. Their education, fiercely English and missionary, did not prepare them, as
in the case of the Negritude writers of French expression, for very
original poetic careers. But with the Negritude writers they shared
a passion for race and Africa even though their models remained
vaguely English and indistinctly Victorian. The Negritude poets
turned to the French symbolists and surrealism for style and language into which they pushed vaguely familiar African concepts.
The English-speaking poets were united in their attachment to what
looks like a string of mediocre English models which were not very
contemporary. So their style was archaic and hymnal. But their
burning nationalism was not diminished, and it was clear that in
their frustrated search for a voice they achieved rare moments of
lyrical beauty in their verse.

12

Contemporary samples
of English-speaking African poetry

Modern poetry from Africa has also focused, like all the other genres, on the tension between the traditional and the modern world. Its themes have ranged from Negritude's race proclamations to the hymnal verse inspired by the patriotic sentiments raised by the anticolonial struggle of the postwar years. Most of the poets took their direction from external sources; as we have seen, Negritude borrowed heavily from French symbolism and surrealism, while the English-speaking poets of the immediate postwar generation borrowed from Victorian verse and Methodist hymnology. The later poetry in English-speaking Africa derives from Yeats, Pound, Eliot, and the modern imagists, who make up the English and American literature syllabuses of the new African universities.

A few of the poets, however, owe their growth in style and language very largely to the genius of traditional oral poetry. One of these is the Zulu poet Mazisi Kunene, who has worked both in his native Zulu and in English. He insists upon a communal and oral quality in his work, which he sees as flowing directly from the Zulu oral poetic tradition. The Zulu poetry perfected during the reign of Shaka in the first half of the nineteenth century is an example of the Bantu oral traditions that have been largely preserved in spite of the brutal assault made upon the Bantu societies of southern Africa by white supremacist regimes. Special institutions such as competitions in the art of storytelling enabled the poets to continue their work within the fold of the community. Mission schools with their Christian dogma failed in their attempts to discredit the calling and art of poets as part of a disgustingly barbaric age when the people knew not the "true" God.

In the introduction to his collected poems, first written in Zulu and later translated by him into English, Kunene writes: "These are not English poems, but poems directly evolved from a Zulu literary tradition."[1] Kunene's use of that tradition embraces the techniques of the poetry and the philosophical features of its thought. In one of his earlier poems, *Elegy,* his use of the Zulu epic form and dependence on ideas taken directly from his vernacular poetic tradition are intricately woven into the beginnings of his own personal style. It is, however, impossible to think of him as anything other than a Zulu poet whose art, even though written, owes its impact to the oral traditions.

The poem *Elegy* captures those elegiac feelings, expressed in understatements, calculated to disguise the intense sense of loss which the death of a particular man engenders and the meaning and impact of the symbolic death that the clans have suffered:

O Mzingeli son of the illustrious clans   1
You whose beauty spreads across the Tukela estuary
Your memory haunts like two eagles
We have come to the ceremonial ruins

We come to mourn the bleeding sun   5
We are the children of Ndungunya of the Dlamini clan
They whose grief strikes fear over the earth
We carry the long mirrors in the afternoon
Recasting time's play past infinite night.

O great departed ancestors   10
You promised us immortal life with immortal joys
But how you deceived us!

We invited the ugly salamander
To keep watch over a thousand years with a thousand sorrows
She watched to the far end of the sky   15

Sometimes terrorized by the feet of departed men
One day the furious storms

One day from the dark cyclone
One day in the afternoon
We gazed into a barren desert   20
Listening to the tremendous voices on the horizon
And loved again in the epics
And loved incestuous love!

We count missions
Strewn in the dust of ruined capitals   25
The bull tramples us on an anthill
We are late in our birth
Accumulating violent voices
Made from the lion's death
You whose love comes from the stars   30
Have mercy on us!
Give us the crown of thunder
That our grief may overhang the earth
O we are naked at the great streams
Wanderers greet us no more.[2]   35

Kunene's debt is more to the elegiac tradition than to the epic one, even though the latter also comes into play. The poem begins with two lines of praise to the dead man, Mzingeli. The "illustrious clans" of line 1 establishes the dead hero's ancestry firmly in the tribe; line 2 describes his beauty, employing the typical Zulu style of linking the abstract concept with natural phenomenon, here the Tukela estuary, which suggests the brightness of waters and their many arms spread at an estuary. Line 3 links him heraldically with the eagles, brave predatory birds of dazzling strength. Line 4 emphasizes the desolation that has swept over the place of ceremonies, suggesting that when a sacred abode is destroyed, the ultimate abomination overtakes the people. Mzingeli is seen as the "bleeding sun," red with blood at its setting. So far, all the images, as in traditional Zulu poetry, are derived entirely from nature, emphasizing the link between man and the universe. In these images the related aspects of nature do not retain their own autonomy, but exist as elaborate features of the man they represent. Ndungunya is the immediate ancestor of the mourners of the Dlamini clan. Note that throughout the poem the poet uses the "we" of the traditional poem. "Where individualistic societies read 'I,' this philosophy [traditional

Zulu thought] requires one to read 'I on behalf,' "[3] Kunene states, insisting upon the communality of the poet's work. Lines 6 to 9 express in very visual and dramatic terms the image of the mourners in their fearful grief reflecting in their sorrow the "infinite night" of despair and dispossession. The mirrors reflect the sorrows of the past beyond the afternoon. This concludes the first section of the poem, illustrating an adherence to the Shakan form of the statement, its extension, development, and conclusion, as it deals here with the elegiac theme. Lines 10 to 12 use the voice of chastisement for the departed ones, a voice very common to the poetry of prayer and libation, which is independent of the dirge but tends to be incorporated within it, as can be seen in the Ewe dirge. These three lines are treated as a separate segment within the poem; it, however, leads to the fourth segment to which it is united by the reference to the departed men. This segment, lines 13 to 20, stresses the sorrow. The "ugly salamander" shares the myth of creation, resistant to fire and storms. The segment also recalls in its sweeping images the journey of the Zulu across vast expanses to their present homes under the supervision of the totemic salamander. Lines 17 to 19 illustrate the use of parallelism, a feature of the oral Zulu style; here employing the simple technique of repetition to create the parallels. The "voices in the horizon" refers to the voices of the departed men who accompanied them on this journey, emphasizing for them the primordial bonds of blood (incestuous love) and the heroic dimensions of their history. The fifth segment picks up again the theme of the desolation, employing now more precise images again drawn from nature. Line 25 suggests the after-scene of a battle, destruction and carnage conjured vividly in the image of the bull elephant trampling the people upon an anthill of line 26. The mourners see themselves as the latecomers after the battle is over, men born into a world that only bears the signs of destruction that has been; "violent voices" are shouts and sounds of mourning; the "lion's death" refers again to the particular death, that of Mzingeli, who is now seen as a lion, the symbol of heroism. Heroism, desired even into death, is the essential element of ancestorhood. The stars in Zulu thought express, along with the moon and the sun, the "nature of distance and the quality of light while also being symbolic of power."[4] This power will be expressed now through the benevolence that will give those left behind the "crown of thunder," whose voice, like the rainbow, will "overhang the earth." The last two lines of the poem return to the concept of desolation, which is poignantly expressed in the image of being naked at the stream. Yet this line also carries a sense of cleansing and rejuvenation, emphasizing for the suppliants, naked and weak, the blessed regenerative powers of the "great streams."

Of such wanderers or travelers in Zulu culture, Kunene writes:

> Many romantic stories and myths are associated with travelers, who in old days were very common. The traveler acquired a special place in the culture both because many people were themselves likely to travel (*unyawo alunampumulo*—the feet know no rest), and also because the traveler puts to test what was one of the important ethical demands, namely, generosity. Unless you had been generous to a stranger whom you may never have met again, your generosity was still in doubt. This gave rise to a number of idioms like "never shut your door to a stranger, 'no hill is without a graveyard.' "[5]

There is a series of short poems by Kunene that reflect a pre-Shakan technique of putting statement, extension, development, and conclusion in single lines. One very successful poem in this vein, using the imagery of the homestead and war, is *The Day of Treachery:*

> Do not be like the people of Ngoneni
> Who rushed with warm arms
> To embrace a man at the gates
> And did likewise on the day of treachery
> Embracing the sharp end of the short spears.[6]

This poem is didactic, a moralizing aspect of oral literature. The image of embrace within the content of Zulu culture is extended from the embrace of a man, signifying brotherhood and kinship, to "embracing the sharp end of the short spears," the price for treachery. The reference to the people of Ngoneni will be obvious perhaps to a Zulu listener for whom the treachery of the people of Ngoneni is apparently part of local history.

In another poem, *Gifts Without Recipients,* Kunene recaptures the same elegiac voice that marked *Elegy,* pushing into nine lines the same pathos and sense of desolation that characterized the longer poem.

Where were you the day we arrived with Nomalizo
Coming to bring ours and others' gifts?
Why did you not leave the imprints of your hands
So that we may count the fingers of the years,
Saying he has not departed like a river
Which leaves with the silence of death.
Alas! You left ruins as big as mountains
Haunted by the hubbub of bats
Who mocked us with their wings.[7]

Nomalizo is the bride accompanied by gifts and the bridal procession to the lover's homestead, only to meet with the ruin and
desolation that have overtaken him. The "silence of death," the
haunting sound of bats who are a symbol of decay, the image of the
departed river, all emphasize the desolation. The exaggeration of
"ruins as big as mountains" is a feature shared by oral poetry, in
its intrinsic dependence on hyperbole for an awesome effect. It is
meaningful also in terms of the nature of the Zulu country marked
by mountains and hills.

In *Sadness on a Deserted Evening* Kunene's sense of loneliness,
using the same structure as in the other poems, becomes personalized. While *Elegy* mourns the death of a community, this poem
expresses the intense agony of the individual poet, even though in
the oblique manner which is characteristic of the Zulu tradition:

O Mantantashiya
Your child is crying
Alone, after the devastation of the earth.
Listen to it departing
With all the lion winds
That are pierced with spears.[8]

In a typical praise poem called *Sons of Vulindlela* Kunene captures the aurality of the Zulu poetic chant which uses the common
technique of repetition in order to achieve a cumulative effect: there
is a narrative quality in the repetition of the deeds of Vulindlela's
sons until the last two lines which represent, in the Shakan style,
the conclusion, drawn from the statement of line 1 and the extension of lines 2 to 9.

Happy are the sons of Vulindlela   1
Who are armed with swords of thought
Who cut the roots of an unknown plant
Who begin from the beginning of beginnings
Who upturn stones lurking with scorpions
Who shout at the running buck   5
Who return a hundred times with tales
Who stood stretched into the horizon
Who rushed above with a thousand years
It is they who will not be shaken
Who have no fear of the hostile winds.[9]   10

Kunene's most ambitious poem, *Anthem of Decades,* utilizes
the style of the long Zulu epic poem which at times runs to five
hundred or more lines. What appears in his collection *Zulu Poems* is
only an extract of 186 lines. This epic, he writes, "does not aim
at narrating mythologies of the past, but at projecting the conceptions of life and the universe according to African (Zulu) belief
and interpretation. I have used the story of the origin of life and
added my own detailed descriptions according to the dictates of
Zulu culture."[10]

In *Anthem* Kunene endeavors to create deities out of the Zulu
mythological idea of the female and male thunder (a concept
present in Ewe mythology also), allying them with Nomkhubulwane, the Zulu goddess of plenty, and the concept of the universal
creator, Unkulunkulu, the very earliest progenitor. Somazwi represents the concept of evil, the opposing force which concludes the
contradictory but complementary system of the universe. He does
not represent evil per se, since the idea is not prevalent in most
African philosophies, but rather, like Eshu-Elegba of Yoruba myth,
represents the opposing force, that in its intrinsic nature embodies
the power to elicit only what is good and harmonious from his
innate oppositional actions. The epic characterizes the victory of
one force over another; the victor, representing a higher morality
and will, triumphs not because he is good and the other is evil; in
his victory will be shown his humility dramatized in the act of
cleaning the vanquished combatant's wounds. As Kunene points
out, the characters are not gods, but personalized ideas, representing anthropomorphic conceptions of the universe as embedded in

Zulu philosophy and thinking. Imprecise, the Zulu concept of the deity or Supreme Creator shares a pantheistic nature that is clouded in vagueness and mystery.

The poem opens with Zulu creation myth, which significantly begins with the birth of time. Then comes the description of the earth which heaved "like a giant heart," the "crooked mountains," and the stars thrusting out "their swords of light." Then, the Creator, tearing away the blanket that covers the mysteries,

> Created heaven and earth
> Filled this planet with the commotion of beasts.[11]

He himself walked the paths of the skies, looking at the mountains, the racing of great rivers and spacious oceans. The primeval era of the creation is marked by carnage, the lion and his allies feeding on those not ferocious, as

> Life must continue
> And good things must feed the ruthlessness of
> appetites.[12]

The Creator's messengers were Sodume, the male thunder whose essence is fertility, Sino, the essence of limits, Nodume, Sodume's wife, whose personality softens the ferociousness of her husband's thunderings across the heavens and whose pet was the bluebird; and Nomkhubulwane, the "source of all life," "giving abundance to the earth." These functionaries performed the Creator's bidding, in preparing the world for the beasts, and the birds of the air. What was left to be created was man:

> He who will bind all things of existence.
> A great shepherd who excels with wisdom.[13]

Then there was Somazwi, the essence of evil, "who speaks with the vehemence of fire" with his entourage of praise singers. His power is opposed to man, to his knowledge which will excel all created things. He predicts for man an unfulfilled tomorrow and a predilection for building dreams "that will never be fulfilled," a condition of vagabondage and despair. A debate ensues between Sodume and Somazwi as to the need for creating man. Nomkhubulwane intervenes, with the argument that

> Creation must always create
> Its essence is its change.[14]

And to love its greatness is not to question it. For man, yet to be created,

> shall derive his power
> From the very struggle of incomplete power
> Which alone will rouse his mind with the
> appetite of wisdom.[15]

Sodume endorses the creation of man. When the debate was over, with the gathering also airing its views, mainly in support of the princess of creation and Sodume, a feast was held at the house of Somahle, the source of all pleasure; much beer was drunk, as Sodume threw fire balls across the heavens, displaying lightning in the horizon:

> Its flashes making paths in the sky
> Those who like to play sped down on them
> Swinging from ray to ray as they descended to the earth.[16]

Kunene writes of this poem: "As the epic develops there will be no Satan banished into limbo and made to suffer eternal damnation. Such an action would damn the victor and show him as weak."[17] It seems that in this poem Kunene attempts to unite the principles of creation and of the struggle between forces as contained in Zulu thought. The material is completely derived from Zulu cosmology. It is obvious also that the poem is suggested by *Paradise Lost,* even though its denouement presents a vision totally different from that of the Christian epic. Its predilection for abstractions seems obviously to be based upon an attempt to achieve for it a preciseness. But the language and style are based in Zulu imagery. The principles that inhabit the landscape of the poem share of the Zulu conception of the world and express its creation myths.

Kunene's work on traditional Zulu poetry has been significant in that he determined the historical features and development of the oral poetic art before and after Shaka's rule. It is obvious that his own poetic center is firmly fixed in this tradition. It should be remembered that the impact of these poems rests in their being heard aloud, in the atmosphere of drama, the excited participation, and in the native Zulu sounds.

Perhaps a fuller illustration of the use to which African writers put the oral tradition will be drawn from discussion of my own poetry which depends heavily upon the Ewe oral tradition. My earliest days were spent within a society that still practiced the oral art. Even though missionary education (Roman Catholic and Presbyterian) tried to draw me, like all other African children, from this world, its hold was strong and binding. Born into a community of drummers, dancers, and singers, my earliest recollection of Ewe oral poetry became the basic inspiration of my earliest writings.

The Ewe dirge has fascinated me as a complete poetic form. Its use of the elegiac tone, statement, exhortation, and prayer combine into a totally effective poetic medium. The expression of philosophical concerns is incidental to the total mood of sorrow. The Ewe dirge, as already stated, is the preserve of women performers. Its present-day form owes its nature to the work of Vinoko Akpalu, whose work I have already reviewed. The Ewe dirge establishes a relationship with the dead in order to emphasize the loneliness that death engenders for the living. It expresses the pathos of death, its desolation, and the accompanying sense of loneliness.

Some of my earliest poetry was an attempt to take over from the dirge a series of segments or individual lines around which to create longer pieces that still express a close thematic and structural affinity with the original. As stated earlier, Akpalu's style has affected greatly the present-day Ewe dirge form. An element like repetition of lines or whole segments is of course a commonplace feature of the oral poem. The translations from which I worked at the earlier period were unpolished and retain a crudity which reflects not only an incomplete grasp of the English language, but perhaps an effective rending of typically Ewe idioms into English. One of my very earliest poems, *Songs of Sorrow,* attempted to incorporate the features of the Ewe dirge, borrowing liberally from Akpalu's work (much of which has entered into the public domain), into a song of lament. The emphasis here is on the personal sense of loss expressed through the opening statement of the lament which is expanded through four stanzas, by a litany of woes, the remonstration against clan enemies and the dead, and the prayer and message:

Dzogbese Lisa has treated me thus 1
It has led me among the sharps of the forest
Returning is not possible
And going forward is a great difficulty
The affairs of this world are like the chameleon feces 5
Into which I have stepped
When I clean it cannot go
I am on the world's extreme corner,
I am not sitting in the row with the eminent
But those who are lucky 10
Sit in the middle and forget
I am on the world's extreme corner
I can only go beyond and forget.

My people, I have been somewhere
If I turn here, the rain beats me 15
If I turn there, the sun burns me
The firewood of this world
Is for only those who can take heart

That is why not all can gather it.
The world is not good for anybody 20
But you are so happy with your fate;
Alas! The travelers are back
All covered with debt.

Something has happened to me
The thing is so great that I cannot weep; 25
I have no sons to fire the gun when I die
And no daughters to wail when I close my mouth
I have wandered on the wilderness
The great wilderness men call life
The rain has beaten me, 30
And the sharp stumps cut as keen as knives
I shall go beyond and rest.
I have no kin and no brother,
Death has made war upon our house;

And Kpeti's great household is no more, 35
Only the broken fence stands;

And those who dared not look in his face
Have come out as men.
How well their pride is with them
Let those gone before take note 40
They have treated their offsprings badly
What is the wailing for?
Somebody is dead. Agosu himself
Alas! A snake has bitten me.
My right arm is broken 45
And the tree on which I lean is fallen

Agosu if you go tell them,
Tell Nyidevi, Kpeti, and Kove
That they have done us evil;
Tell them their house is falling 50
And the trees in the fence
Have been eaten by termites;
That the mortals curse them.
Ask them why they idle there
While we suffer, and eat sand, 55
And the crow and the vulture
Hover always above our broken fences
And strangers walk over our portion.[18]

The imagery is drawn from observed life, following closely the imagery suggested by the oral dirge. Dzogbese Lisa of line 1 refers to the Creator God, the reproductive essence of Mawu, the Greater Than All. The emphasis here is on the belief that he accompanies man at the point of his creation into the world and serves as his mission or destiny. He is also known as *se*, similar to the Igbo *chi* or the Akan *okra*. He represents immutable Fate, appointing and working out his destiny for man on earth. Among the Ewe if a man succeeds or fails in life, it is said: he brought his good fate with him. The poet here in the first stanza laments the nature of *se*'s selection for him. His fate is one of total hopelessness, wandering restlessness, and non-fulfillment of every hope he had ever cherished. This is emphasized by the image of the man led into a newly cleared forest full of sharp stumps of the slender undergrowth. It is further enforced by the image of the wanderer lost in the primeval African forest, unable to find the path that leads forward beyond the bush or the one on which he has just come in order to retreat. The image of the lost wanderer in the thick impenetrable forest is further sharpened by line 5. The chameleon in Ewe mythology shares the essence of the Creator God. She is Lisa, the Earth Mother, and her nature is one which changes (yet never changes), emphasizing the unpredictable aspect of her being. The chameleon features prominently in important medicines. In many places she is the messenger of the earth *vodu*. But the impact of this line is in the emphasis placed on the abominable stench of the chameleon's feces. The affairs of this world are the chameleon's feces in their stench. There is no possibility of eliminating the odor when you step into it. These lines illustrate the manner in which the oral poem yokes together two or more disparate ideas in order to create out of them a sharp and concrete image. The relationship between Dzogbese Lisa and the chameleon's feces may not be apparent to a non-Ewe listener, but yet the clarity of the image of the affairs of this world is self-evident.

Line 8 recalls the pre-Renaissance idea of the world being flat and marked by corners, a concept not alien to Ewe thought, in the sense in which it is employed to create the image here. Here, "extreme corner" connotes the idea of being outside the center where there is protection and warmth. The poet laments the absence of helpers on all sides, those who hem you into the center, thus protecting you from wind, rain, and storm and, above all, from the predatory animals and clan enemies. Line 9 is a statement on his poverty, which is yet an index of low status in the community. The poor man spoke words of wisdom, an Ewe proverb states, and they said his cloth was smelly; the rich man spoke a lot of nonsense and everyone said what a wonderful man of wisdom he is. "Lucky" of line 10 recalls his fate, the absence of good fortune, a destiny of grinding poverty and bewildering suffering and sense of confusion which had been so clearly stated in the first stanza. Line 13 is a statement in fatalism. There is some comfort for the sufferer in life beyond the grave. The idea that we will exist in a spirit world at our death and thus escape the agonies of the flesh is a persistent one in the Ewe dirge. (Most of Akpalu's poems end on this note.) "Forget" here connotes more of the idea of release from the sorrows of our earthly existence than of oblivion or of cessation of being, as expressed in Western romantic poetry. It can be noted that the second stanza uses repetition of the line, "I am on the world's extreme corner," to pull sharply together the notion of suffering of lines 9 to 11 and focus the hope of release expressed in line 13.

The third stanza opens with the dramatic voice of address, recalling the raconteur, the storyteller at the fireside about to tell his tale of woes: "My people, I have been somewhere." The lines that follow restate the Ewe belief that life is a wayside farm or a market place from where, after we sow and harvest our crops or sell our wares, we shall return home.

There is a restless hopelessness in the fate of the protagonist expressed in the very blinding fury of the elements as they lash at him carried in lines 15 and 16. Lines 17 to 19 suggest that the world is a forest into which we have all come to gather firewood for our hearths at home in the Creator's house. Those who can gather any must be strong of heart and firm of spirit. Some, lacking these qualities, return home at sundown empty-handed. The image here vividly recalls what every Ewe child knows, the experience of collecting firewood for the household. The use of this image to focus an abstract philosophical thought again illustrates the reliance upon the commonplace experience or the blatantly obvious for poetic statement, a characteristic of the oral literary tradition. In line 20 the protagonist turns upon those who are his enemies, the boasters, who, because of instant success, happily flaunt their wealth, until their fate, or *se*, turns malevolent and they come home "all covered with debt."

The fourth stanza opens with a more intimate statement of lament, the overwhelming sense of personal loss which is "too deep for tears." Not only is the protagonist alone in the world because he is an orphan, but also because he has lost his children. So, at his death there will be an unnatural quiet in his homestead. Lines 26 and 27 recall Ekpe and Akpalu's preoccupation with the silence that will mark their going away when they themselves had spent their lives adorning the funerary rites of others with their songs. The ideas expressed in lines 15 and 16 are again picked up in lines 28 to 31. Here the world is seen as a wilderness of sharp stumps (echo of line 2) and of buffeting rain, a picture which is a reversion to the opening parts of the poem. The image of the desert plays a very persistent role in Ewe dirge poetry, as it recalls an earlier era in folk memory, the period of their journeys from the east across sections of what obviously is the Sahara. It emphasizes the desolation, suffering, and sense of despair that marked those unsettled periods, leaving in the memory of the tribe an almost totally atavistic recall of the desert even when they had been settled in their present homes among rivers, creeks, and lagoons for hundreds of years. Line 32 is a variation on line 13, more definite in its resolve of going beyond, and this time to rest. It is as if the desert wanderer is called home to a warm hearth, to food and sleep after the desperate agonies of the wilderness. Line 34 comes as a startling recall of the death that stares him in the face and foreshadows the last stanza of the poem. Death, in the Ewe imagination, is seen as a warrior, a predator who refuses money and all other things and insists upon man. He is also known to be persistent in pursuing his enemies; in collusion with a malevolent fate or at the instigation of an angered deity, he declares war upon a household and does not stop until he reduces the homestead to ruins. Line 32 states the declaration of this war.

The next stanza opens with the straightforward statement:

And Kpeti's great household is no more,
Only the broken fence stands . . .

The war is over, and the result is ruin and decay. Lines 37 to 39 pick up the idea already expressed in lines 21 to 23, but this time with a venomous anger that lashes out in the sarcasm of the tone: "How well their pride is with them." Remonstration with the ancestors, and sometimes outright verbal assault on them, is a characteristic aspect of the dirge or of rituals saluting the dead on important occasions. The protagonist launches an attack on his ancestors. The living expect the dead to act as guides and protectors against suffering and sorrow. The fate of the living rests in the hands of their ancestors with whom they are in regular communication through offerings, prayers, and libations. When the ancestors provide this help, they are amply rewarded with more sacrifices. When they fail, they are chastised. This attitude extends to deities. Gods have been known to fail a people, and the result has always been that they were chased out of the land or destroyed completely. This occurs when a deity turns malevolent, refusing to be placated, and indulges in senseless carnage and destruction for their own sakes.

In line 43 we are told for the first time that this dirge is elicited by the death of an important personage, Agosu. Death is seen in line 44 as a snake, a venomous creature from whose poison the protagonist cannot escape. Agosu, the dead man, is the "right arm" of line 45, the strong arm of work and survival. Without it the man is helpless. He is again the "tree" on which the protagonist leans. The "tree" here recalls the "broken fence" of line 36 and foreshadows the "trees in the fence" of line 51.

The last stanza picks up the theme of chastisement, this time couching it in the form of a message which Agosu will carry to those who have gone ahead. The whole stanza restates the frustration and sorrow that the lot of the living encompasses. In a series of quick lines, we are hurled through the falling homestead, the trees of the fence having been "eaten by termites" and the crying curse of the mortals. Lines 54 to 58 constitute the summation of the lament. Eating sand is the ultimate in destitution and, symbolically, also restates the death agonies of the living. The crow and the vulture are the birds of death, the scavengers of the desert, predators who hover over the dying animal ready to snatch the fallen corpse. Where they abound, there must be death around the corner. The impact of these last lines is in the fact that these birds are hovering over ruins—"broken fences"—desolation. The last line completes the scene of total collapse of the homestead with the introduction of strangers who take over the ruins and the protagonist's and his people's portion.

My fascination with the Ewe dirge enabled me to begin to use its style, themes, and general tone in a large number of my earlier poems. This was a deliberate act of falling back upon a tradition which has been ignored in our missionary education and whose practice has been labeled paganistic by our Christian mentors.

In another poem, *A Dirge,* I create a lament that borrows thematically from the Ewe dirge but uses mood rather than a succession of images to achieve its effect:

Tell them, tell it to them   1
That we the children of Ashiagbor's house
Went to hunt; when we returned
Our guns were pointing to the earth,
We cannot say it; someone say it for us.   5
Our tears cannot fall.
We have no mouths to say it with.
We took the canoe, the canoe with the sandload
They say the hippo cannot overturn.
Our fathers, the hippo has overturned our canoe   10
We come home
Our guns pointing to the earth.
Our mother, our dear mother
Where are our tears, where are our tears?
Give us mouth to say it, our mother.   15
We are on our knees to you
We are still on our knees.[19]

In many ways this is a more personal poem than *Songs of Sorrow*. Ashiagbor is the founder of my lineage. This poem tells of the desolation that has overtaken the family. Line 4 tells the story of how, when the hunters return from the hunt without any trophy, their guns point to the earth as a sign of lament. But the emphasis here is that not only do the hunters return empty-handed, they were also witnesses to strange events in the forest. What they saw emphasizes their sense of indescribable sorrow; they cannot say it because their mouths are sealed with grief, they cannot weep because it is beyond tears. Line 8 is a reference to my grandfather Nyidevu, whose totem is the canoe-upsetting hippo; this line recalls his death when I was a child. "Our mother" of line 13 refers to the earth who alone understands the burden of our sorrow and gives us the power to articulate it. As the sorrow overwhelms the protagonists, they kneel upon the earth, assuming the posture of suppliants in front of the household shrine. What they ask for is an illumination of the meaning of their sorrow.

In a perhaps more ambitious poem, my dependence upon and derivation from the Ewe oral poetic form becomes more clear and self-assured. In 346 lines, I tried to capture a more total mood of the Ewe lament, its stock images, its flow and direction, its ability to digress into other areas expressing, say, humor, and above all its consistent preoccupation with the human condition. The elegiac mood, I dare suggest, does not flag. But the realization of this poem (it was written for both radio and stage performance) lies in the use to which the Ewe dirge music is put, serving as background to the voice. The poem, *I Heard a Bird Cry,*[20] was first composed in the Ewe and then translated into English. It contains snatches of oral verse as I knew it, but its power, I believe, rests in the way in which what may on the surface appear as fragmented pieces are united by a thematic flow and by linguistic variability.

The poem is a long lament by one person, who obviously bears the responsibility of a poet and thus sings on behalf of the group, for he is the one with the gift of songs. The poem opens by establishing the mood of desolation by using the image of the single tree.

> There was a tree which dried in the desert
> Birds came and built their nests on it.[21]

One of the most persistent images that runs through the poem is that of an orphan child. The orphan child shares some aspect of the widow. He is alone. Overwhelmed by this sense of loneliness, he is a figure that flits through the village at sunrise and sundown. At times he is seen by the roadside, his hands over his head, a sign of his orphanhood.

The tone of the poem is not one of total lament. There is a raging anger directed at the pretensions and the moral turpitude of a world gone greedy and cruel. In the flow of funeral songs, there are rebel gods

> Marching to the dunghill
> With fetish bells in their hands.[22]

This tone of rebellion and outrage is again stated in the following lines:

> Though they said
> The prince should not hasten for the stool
> and the young leopard
> Should not be in haste to walk
> There are noises in the air.
> The young leopard should stand up against
> the tree.
> And the prince should run for his father's stool.[23]

The defiance is also emphasized in those sections when the protagonist rejects the European world in order to return to the rites of his fathers to achieve knowledge and understanding:

> That day we killed the sacred ram
> And the thunder drums sounded
> I was there.
> I put down my white man's clothes
> and rolled a cloth
> To carry the ram's head
> And go into the thunder house.
>
> When you started the song
>
> I put my hand in the blood pot with you.[24]

The last line emphasizes the communion that is achieved through the sacred ram's blood and the rite of the eaten meal from the same pot. The communal feast is still an active aspect of Ewe religious rites. It affirms and renews the bond that unites men, families, and clansmen; it eliminates ill will and bad blood; it emphasizes the unity between the living and the dead in its open communication with the dead through accompanying propitiatory rites; above all, it affirms the living force of the community as it is expressed in the drumming, dancing, and general atmosphere of feasting. Here, the protagonist uses this as a return to the primal source of his being; it is an occasion for renewing a pledge made to the ancestors, signifying his dependence on them and his reliance upon their support.

In a short scene preceding the pledge, the protagonist conjures a picture of his people, battered into bloody submission, limping toward the sacred hut. His role is one of inspired admonisher of the seer, and the prophet who stands aside, touched deeply by the agony of his people and from his intimate knowledge of the spirit world, prescribes a series of ritual actions.

> My people, what has happened
> And you bear many cudgel wounds
> and rope marks cover your naked bodies?
> Wipe away your tears
> And knock the door of the sacred hut
> The gone-befores are waiting for you.[25]

He returns them to the original home of their being, the sacred hut,
where they can plead for help with those gone ahead of them. These
lines suggest also that the people are lost through their own fault,
and they are paying the price for the neglect of the ancestral shrines
by suffering the bitter agonies of spiritual neglect and physical pain.
After a number of boastful statements calculated to humiliate his
enemies, the protagonist returns to his own condition of loneliness:

> I am the bird on the dunghill
> The birds flew and left me behind.[26]

But there is a mood of resolve and a desire to undergo the same
cleansing and propitiatory rites that he prescribes for his people:

> I too shall carry the fetish bell
> and start towards the sacred hut
> I will shout and call the ancestors . . .[27]

The ancestral neglect of allowing him to be bitten by the evil snake
draws a veiled criticism from him. The dirge poet has a lingering
desire to cross beyond into the spirit world.

> Look for a canoe for me
> That I go home in it,
> Look for it.
> The lagoon waters are in storm
> And the hippos are roaming
>
> But I shall cross the river
> And go beyond.[28]

The river is Kuto, the river that separates the living from the dead.
In spite of the turbulent state of the river and the roaming hippos,
he wants to cross over into *avlime* where alone is rest. After a long
digression into the world of the priests and fishermen, he returns
to the image of himself as the beggar child in the market place; he
is the wanderer in strange lands, a man who followed the "trancers"
to another land which cannot give him food to eat. His nakedness
and helplessness is again reiterated in the lines

> Under the trees, under the trees
> I will be under the trees
> And the rain will come and beat me.[29]

The voice of defiance is heard in the last line of

> Some say we must cover our heads
> With our hands, and burst into tears.
> But I will not cry.[30]

He rejects his orphanhood, his pathetic helplessness. He refuses to play the role of the whimpering orphan child any longer. This regenerative defiance leads him to the realization that he shares, as a poet, a nature of the gods:

> The singing voice I have
> I have it from the gods
> Those who cannot bear my songs,
> Let them patch their ear holes with clay.[31]

But the mood shifts again to one of sorrow, of awareness of his human condition, an emphasis on the dirge and the song of sorrow. He is again the vulture who, because he has no relatives, shaves his own head in anticipation of his burial rites. There is a return, however, to the feast, the note on which the poem ends:

> It was in the season of burning feet
> And the feast is ready for us.[32]

"Burning feet" recalls the hot desert of his desolation.

I Heard a Bird Cry, as I said earlier, attempts the total impact of the dirge, even though it moves into the large landscape of the Ewe oral poem. It not only employs ideas, but also attempts to capture the rhythm of the Ewe language through translation.

Apart from the dirge, the Ewe war poem has also appealed to me as a very fruitful poetic medium. The war poem is an intrinsic aspect of the drums that were part of the warrior tradition, now heard only at the funerals of important men. Its form is less elaborate, its images more direct. Its appeal is in its simple use of language, agile phraseology, and brisk rhythm. One of my earliest poems using the form, language, and rhythm of the war poem was written at the experimental period to which *Songs of Sorrow* belongs. *Song of War* owes its existence to a number of Ewe war poems from which I borrowed ideas and motifs in order to create one single poem. The war poem is not only a poem proclaiming bravery and heroism, it also anticipates death at the battlefront; and so it encloses within its outer fabric of heroic recitation a deep sense of mourning and a sharp awareness of death.

I shall sleep in white calico;   1
War has come upon the sons of men
And I shall sleep in calico;
Let the boys go forward,
Kpli and his people should go forward;   5
Let the white man's guns boom,
We are marching forward;
We all shall sleep in calico.

When we start, the ground shall shake;
The war is within our very huts;   10
Cowards should fall back
And live at home with the women;
They who go near our wives
While we are away in battle
Shall lose their calabashes when we come.   15

Where has it been heard before
That a snake has bitten a child
In front of its own mother;
The war is upon us
It is within our very huts   20
And the sons of men shall fight it
Let the white man's guns boom
And its smoke cover us
We are fighting them to die.
We shall die on the battlefield   25
We shall like death at no other place,
Our guns shall die with us
And our sharp knives shall perish with us
We shall die on the battlefield.[33]

It should be obvious that the rhythm of this poem is brisk and agile, in contrast to the slow funereal rhythm of *Songs of Sorrow*. The poem opens with a short statement of intention. To "sleep in white calico" means to die at the battlefront and to be brought home wrapped in white calico, the symbol of victory and heroism. "The white man's guns" refers to the guns mounted by the British on

Fort Prizenstein in Keta, where the Ewe fought a series of battles in a war against British occupation in the nineteenth century. Line 11 refers to self-confessed cowards who are enjoined to stay at home and protect the homestead while the braves went to war. But they are also admonished to keep away from the wives of the heroes. If they are found interfering with the wives, they will "lose their calabashes." "Calabashes" refer to heads, and this comes from the old Ewe tradition of drying enemy heads, for use as ceremonial drinking vessels by the warriors on great occasions. Lines 16 to 18 suggest the protection that the child receives as he walks in front of his own mother. The "snake" here is death, and the mother is the earth who protects her children from death that accompanies war within their very huts. The final stanza recalls sheer bravado and reckless daring.

In another poem, *At the Gates,* I used the war poem as the outer crust within which to push not only its own traditional ingredients but also aspects of the dirge and the lament poems. The first stanza is the lament of the warrior, besieged by war and a host of woes: "I do not know which god sent me" is an attack upon his *se:*

> to fall in the river and fall in the fire
> these have failed.[34]

Every means by which he attempts to remove his own life in order to end his agony fail. Marked by his *se,* the warrior complains of following his own brothers, yet

> bearing upon our heads nothing
> save the thunder that roars.[35]

The third stanza places him outside the gates, fleeing from the malevolence of the world outside, pleading to be let in:

> Open the gates, my mother's children,
> and let me enter.[36]

He is among those who have slept in the desert land, helpless stragglers from a lost battle,

> guns in our hands we cannot fire,
> Knives in our hands we cannot throw.[37]

Death stalks them in this desert, walking behind them as they stum-

ble toward the homestead only to find the gates barred against
them. The same stanza states the acceptance of his *se*'s bidding; its
gift to him is a calabash of poisoned wine which he cannot refuse.
From the mood of acceptance, he sees himself as the bachelor, the
object of every evil tongue and gossip, the one whom no one trusts
with any responsibility. The fourth stanza slides back into the dirge
mood, this time lamenting the death of an only daughter:

> Don't cry for me over
> My daughter, death called her.
> She is an offering of my heart.[38]

His daughter becomes the sacrifice he has made to his god, but it
seems, as suggested in the closing part of this stanza, the offering is
unacceptable to him: "A snake has bitten my daughter" suggests a
negation of the principle of maternal protection. The last stanza
states a mood of resignation and acceptance of his fate, but still
retains the tone of the dirge and the lament:

> Uproot the yams you planted
> for everything comes from God
> it is an evil god who sent me
> that all I have done
> I bear the magic of the singer that has come
> I have no paddle, my wish,
> to push my boat into the river.[39]

The first line of this stanza suggests a giving up, expressed in the
idea of uprooting the yams, for there cannot be any good harvest
if they are allowed to stay in the earth. The third line is a final
statement on the nature of his god, who it seems is malevolent for
no reason. But there is something that the warrior achieves in a
life that has turned very sour; he has the magic and the voice of the
poet; his words are his only source of hope. And the infinite
resignation expresses itself in the last wish to cross the river without
a paddle. His boat is his song on which he will cross Kuto into
avlime and to well-earned rest.

My own work as a poet owes a great deal to the oral tradition
out of which I grew. My dependence on it has primarily been motivated by a desire to give this much-neglected poetry a voice and to

bring into focus the theme of cultural contact, conflict, and resolution for the modern African.

Christopher Okigbo, the Nigerian poet killed in the 1967 civil war, was perhaps the most eclectic African poet of our time who wrote in English. A graduate of the University of Ibadan, he was part of the new community of African writers who did not study abroad and therefore escaped, to a large extent, the alienation and frustration of the earlier generation. Educated entirely in Africa, even though within the rigid framework of the colonial pattern, he was exposed to the best in colonial education in English and American letters. Thus the literary influences on him were varied and numerous. A few of these new writers, as illustrated earlier, also took their literary direction from the oral traditions which, given the half-hearted cultural intentions of the British, still had great influence on some of them. The important thing is that the writers were free to choose their models.

Okigbo was one of the leading poets of this generation. Educated first in Roman Catholic mission schools, he read classics at the University of Ibadan. He confessed to a predilection for the most esoteric and original voices in modern English and American letters and arts. Of his poem *Lament of the Silent Sisters,* inspired by the death of Lumumba and of Chief Awolowo's eldest son, he writes:

> The "Silent Sisters" are however sometimes like the drowning Franciscan nuns of Hopkins' *The Wreck of the Deutschland,* sometimes like the "Sirènes" of Debussy's *Nocturne*—two dissonant dreams associated in the dominant motif "No! in Thunder" (from one of Melville's letters to Hawthorne). This motif is developed by a series of related airs from sources as diverse as Malcolm Cowley, Raja Ratnam, Stéphane Mallarmé, Rabindranath Tagore, Garcia Lorca, and the yet unpublished Peter Thomas.[40]

The words that sum up Okigbo's poetry are ordeal, agony, and cleansing. His poetic growth came through a unified consciousness and awareness of other cultures. External sounds and internal music coalesce into bursts of poetic brilliance. He was in essence a restless, tormented soul whose poetry assumed high-pitched, prophetic resonance and clarity. In his work he combines the choral

voice of Greek classical verse, the litanic cadence of the mass, and
the ritualistic pattern of traditional poetry. Since he was a poet of
the sacred journey, the pilgrimage, his poetry sets out through its
strong images on a trip to the land of awareness. The accompanying
voice is marked by anguished cries of supplication, at times defiance, and at times ironic sarcasm and boyish petulance. At an
early age his journey was toward death, toward the explosion in
the ultimate self-awareness.

His first poem, *Heavensgate*, opens with a short fragment he
calls "the passage," and we are introduced to the suppliant acolyte.
It shows in a flash the various strands that Okigbo pulls together:

BEFORE YOU, mother Idoto,
naked I stand;
before your watery presence,
a prodigal
leaning on an oil-bean,
lost in your legend . . .
under your power wait I
on barefoot,
watchman for the watchword
at Heavensgate;
out of the depth my cry
give ear and hearken . . .[41]

Idoto is the sacred stream in the poet's home town. Overwhelmed
by the legend and power of this goddess, he confesses his primal
nakedness and powerlessness. He stands ready for the ritual cleansing that will yield him knowledge. Of the whole Heavensgate,
Okigbo writes:

Heavensgate was originally conceived as an Easter sequence. It later
grew into a ceremony of innocence, something like a mass, an offering
to Idoto, the village stream of which I drank, in which I washed as
a child; the celebrant, a personage like Orpheus, is about to begin
a journey. Cleansing involves total nakedness, a complete self-
surrender to the water spirit that nurtures all creation. The various
sections of the poem therefore present this celebrant at various stations of his cross.[42]

The dying lines of the poem come from the Book of Common

Prayer. But the singularly powerful image is of the naked suppliant leaning on an oil-bean, one of the totems of Idoto's worship. Elsewhere, Okigbo reveals that the function of priest and guardian of this river fell to him, and even though he was not required to be present at all times, it was expected that he show up now and then to renew his own pledge. This awareness as a priest, and therefore of the carrier, as the ultimate supplicant on behalf of the people is at the center of his whole poetic career. It is to this singular passion and knowledge he owes the sense of deep and agonized search and unquestioning self-abandonment and abasement that amount to self-sacrifice. In this poem, the sacrificial self-offering is evident. The creative impulse and the vision will be achieved in it. He waits for the impulse, vision and the knowledge; this constitutes the overture, the statement of the wish, and the prayer.

In the third movement, "Watermaid," is stated at one level the moment of awareness in the opening of eyes to the receiving of the terrible secret. This he shares with the elemental forces and covers up with the beach sand. There is the protective rain clouds over a beach drenched in sunshine and over two lovers in the sex act upon this beach. The creative elements erupt at the end of the act stated in

Shadow of rain over man with woman.[43]

There is a world of dazzling light in which things are washed clean in the brilliance of an after-expiation. In "Watermaid" a woman, Orphean companion of the searcher, emerges from the sea. She is the woman of the sea, the watermaid and spirit of West African mythology. Here she is a lioness crowned with moonlight and escorted by waves, dressed in white light. She makes a tormentingly brief but dazzling appearance; in that epiphany a point of contact is established with the poet, but only briefly. Then she vanishes beneath the waves. But she had brought the sanctity of the secret which she shares with the poet. The poet laments the abandonment:

AND I WHO am here abandoned,
count the sand by wavelash abandoned
count her blessing my white queen.[44]

He awaits the return, still naked, after the departure of the stars.

In the fourth movement, "Lustra," the poet moves upon his way in search for the ultimate abode of cleansing, to hills, springs, fountains, to a hilltop where he places a newly laid egg and a white hen, his humble offerings for the cleansing. Alongside are five fingers of chalk. He waits amid the booming of drums and cannons for the ultimate moment of truth. He is now in the abode of interminable mystery waiting for an immersion. The landscape is again one of shadows and blinding light, a place of infinity. The green bowl is the sacrificial bowl in ritual offering which gathers the dew upon the herbal and medicinal plants; the light that results from the voice of the god at the hour of epiphany blinds the heron, who is the poet. In this state he achieves unity now with the watermaid, the moonman, and the singer (himself). The act of connection is vaguely established in "Sacrifice," in the moment of the ascent of the spirit; here the drums summon for him the primordial hour of the coming of gods and deities. It is the timeless moment of spiritual unity, the flashpoint of trance that draws him nearer his nirvana.

In the fifth movement, "Newcomer," the time for the worship has come. He wears his own mask. Humility and petulance coalesce in

> Anna of the panel oblongs
> protect me
> from them fucking angels
> protect me
> my sand-house and bones.[45]

Over the bridge, the unifying arch of the real and spiritual worlds, he stands now between the two universes, disconsolate, spiritual, yet vulnerable to the tidal waters, sharing the magic of incense and the laughter of waters, waiting. The prophetism of this poem is not complete. Throughout we are aware of a journey, of pain, sacrifice, and self-disbursement conducted in an austerity and poignancy of passion. At the bridge, the connecting point, he arrives in a religious sense, at the link in the voices; the newcomer, the seer arriving at the bridgehead, the smell and sounds of sacrificial fires still in his nostrils and ears, still awaiting ultimate acceptance and redemption.

Of *Limits,* perhaps his most ambitious and also most derived poem, Okigbo writes:

> *Limits* and *Distances* are man's outer and inner worlds projected—the phenomenal and the imaginative, not in terms of their separateness but of their relationship—an attempt to reconcile the universal opposites of life and death in a live-die proposition: one is the other and either is both.[46]

Its opening poem stands out as one of Okigbo's most complete short poems, diving into the traditional landscape for very effective images and expressing his most original voice as a poet. Again the sacrificial priestly role is stated. There are moments of frenzy accompanying the attempts at the supplication in which the poet is a talkative weaver bird.

> Suddenly becoming talkative
> like weaver birds
> Summoned at offside of
> dream remembered
>
> Between sleep and waking,
> I hang my egg shells
> To you of palm grove,
> Upon whose bamboo towers
>
> Hang dripping with yesterday's upwine
> A tiger mask and nude spear . . .
>
> Queen of the damp half-light,
> I have had my cleansing,
> Emigrant with air-borne nose,
> The he-goat on heat.[47]

The rest of *Limits* never achieves the authenticity of voice as revealed in this opening segment. The elements that cloud the subsequent movements range from such weak images as "shrub among poplars," "low growth among the forest," and "green cloud above the forest." It is in sections of "Limit II" and "Limit III" that echoes

of T. S. Eliot, are heard especially in the refrain: "And the mortar
is not yet dry." Such lines as

> Silent the footfall,
> Soft as the cat's paw,
> Sandaled in velvet in fur[48]

show a strong lack of originality, exhibiting a mellifluously Swin-
burnian roll that rings false. The rest of this movement contains
distinct echoes of *East Coker* and *The Waste Land*. In "Limits V–
XII" Okigbo swings into statements that carry an obvious fascination with classical Egyptian and pagan legend; in long sweeping
sections utilizing the choral voice, his poetry flags in such lines as

> Eunice at the passageway,
> singing the moon to sleep over the hills.[49]

It is in his last poems that Okigbo begins to regain, in a more
confident way, elements of his earlier original voice, especially in
Path of Thunder, poems prophesying war. In these the obvious
derivatives are missing, and the poet, firmly in control, speaks with
an urgency that is as raw as it also shares his prophetic role. *Elegy
of the Wind* recaptures his early prophetic and priestly voice in

> The chief priest of the sanctuary has uttered
> the enchanted words;
> the bleeding phallus,
> Dripping fresh from the carnage cries out for
> the medicinal leaf . . .
>
> O wind, swell my sails; and may my banner run
> the course of wider waters.[50]

The lyrical tone of the last two lines does not dissipate the voice
of prayer for salvation in the historical moments of carnage and
blood revealed in the paradoxical image of the raw wounds of the
circumcision. *Come Thunder* foreshadows the great upheavals of
Nigeria's recent sad history:

> And a great fearful thing already tugs
> at the cables of the open air.[51]

The catastrophe seems to hang over the whole country; homesteads, rural farm land, the "deserted corn cobs," and the birds witness the coming deluge:

> The arrows of God tremble at the gate of light,
> The drums of curfew pander to the dance of death;
>
> And the secret thing in its heaving
> Threatens with iron mask
> The last lighted torch of the century.[52]

This is poetry of clarity of thought and great lyrical power, unsagging at any point, registering the slow, heaving, inexorable march of a nation toward disaster. In *Hurrah for Thunder* Okigbo tells the story of his own imminent death. The central image is the elephant, once powerful, but now the fallen victim of the hunters' weapons:

> Alas! The elephant has fallen—
> Hurrah for thunder—
>
> But already the hunters are talking of pumpkins:
> If they share the meat let them remember thunder.[53]

This poem reveals Okigbo's own political frustration and restlessness. The petulant resignation of the last two lines underscores both this and the self-prophecy of his own end:

> If I don't learn to shut my mouth I'll soon go to hell,
> I, Okigbo, town-crier, together with my iron bell.[54]

In *Elegy for Slit-Drums* Okigbo deliberately returns to the traditional dirge form, weeping and mourning the death that surrounds him at the onset of the Nigerian civil war. It is a poem that owes its impact almost entirely to the use of a traditional idiom and motif, employing the techniques of repetition, proverbs, allusions, and extensive animal imagery borrowed entirely from the Igbo world. After each poetic segment, consisting of parabolic and proverbial listings, is interpolated a choral voice which follows the voice of the lead as in some types of traditional oral poetic forms:

> condolences from the twin-lips of our drum
> parted in condolences

the panther has delivered a hare
the hare is beginning to leap
the panther has delivered a hare
the panther is about to pounce—

condolences already in flight under the
burden of this century.[55]

The poem is to be read to the accompaniment of rattles. In the train of mourners are the myth-maker, the hornbill, and the poet who gives voice to the rattles. The persistent central image is again the elephant who ravages the jungle, tramples over other animals —the snake, squirrel, mongoose—only to be felled himself by thunder. The dirge mounts in intensity after the fall of the elephant, achieving the silent fury of mourning in

from our bruised lips of the drum empty of condolences:

trunk of the iron tree we cry *condolences* when we break
shells of the open sea we cry *condolences* when we shake.[56]

In *Elegy for Alto,* the war is on and death is near. The eagles, robbers, politicians are the despoilers armed with cannons, bombs, and mortars. His choice is to give up himself as the ultimate sacrifice; his journey as the priest, seeker, supplicant is over; and like the carrier scapegoat, he will offer himself in order that the cleansing be complete:

So let the horn paw the air howling goodbye . . .

O mother mother Earth, unbind me; let this be
my last testament;

Earth, unbind me; let me be the prodigal; let this
be the ram's ultimate prayer to the tether . . .

AN OLD STAR departs, leaves us here on the shore
Gazing heavenward for a new star approaching;
The new star appears, foreshadows its going
Before a going and coming that goes on forever . . .[57]

Okigbo's best poetry has come to be identified, in his quick maturing, with the best tradition of contemporary African writing in English. An apprentice poet whose path to poetry began with a fascination with the masters of English and American verse and with myths other than his own, he quickly became his own master, gaining power as a poet who returns in his ideas and technique to the oral sources, and combining the function of the poet and the priest, he grew into a clear-voiced diviner whose role as a poet in old Africa has always been taken for granted.

Experimentation with older forms becomes the central concern of the poets discussed here. They are however aware of English poetic tradition. But it seems that their voices gain and express greater authenticity as they return to the oral poetic form for both patterns and ideas. As was shown above, Kunene owes a great deal of his artistic skill to the mastering of the Zulu manner, whilst Okigbo even though he began as an imitative poet of particularly T. S. Eliot and Ezra Pound, returned to a spectacular Igbo voice for his later work. The tragedy is that this new-found voice, self-assured and ready to burst forth, was sadly silenced by the Nigerian civil war.

Amos Tutuola and Yoruba folklore

Amos Tutuola, the Yoruba writer, stands alone as the only African writer of our time whose art owes its significant impulse and impact to the total use of folklore and mythology. His work, derived from an analphabetic culture which expresses itself in its myths, legends, and folk tales, is a recapitulation in the written form of what is essentially the great common soil of literature.

To understand his work there are a few facts that must be pointed out at the onset. Tutuola is a Yoruba, firmly based in the Yoruba tradition of storytelling. The Yoruba number several millions of people occupying the western part of present-day Nigeria. Culturally, they are close to the Benin to the east (center of ancient Ife culture), and to the Fon and Ewe of Dahomey, Togo, and Ghana. Yoruba religion with its conglomerate of gods is still an active aspect of Yoruba life in spite of Christianization. Secondly, there is a large body of written literature in the Yoruba language itself. The most important writer in the Yoruba language, Chief Fagunwa, died only a few years ago. Thirdly, Tutuola's education in English is rudimentary. This has resulted in an original style which European critics have labeled "quaint," "naïve," "young English," and "amusing."

Tutuola has published six books. These are: *The Palm-Wine Drinkard, My Life in the Bush of Ghosts, Simbi and the Satyr of the Dark Jungle, The Brave African Huntress, Feather Woman of the Jungle,* and *Ajayi and His Inherited Poverty.* All of these works are linked together by the single device of a journey on which the heroes or heroines who set forth, each journey a variant of the mythical quest, a significant feature of the folk mythology.

Tutuola's works, therefore, because of their clear antecedents, cannot be discussed as novels, but rather as romances which base themselves on the Yoruba folk tale. Cast in the mold of what Northrop Frye calls the "naïve quest romance," the stories follow the pattern of the folk story in which the man or animal hero or heroine departs in order to acquire knowledge, wealth, food, and the wherewithal for survival in an uncertain world. The features of the quest are the trials, labors, revelations which the hero experiences on his journey.

What is very significant in Tutuola's work is the way in which he links a number of folk tales together by creating for them a singular hero and also by extending the aspects of the quest through more than one story. The Yoruba myths and conception of the world are also revealed in his work. Men and spirits exist in a unified cosmic territory. In this world, the physical and metaphysical coexist, or rather have one single entity; magic and ritual are instruments of harmonizing those forces that may be opposed to the weak natures of men who remain firmly at the center of this cosmic order. Man's contests, therefore, are with malevolent spirits and forces which are bent on his destruction. His conquest of them provides him with knowledge with which to come to grips with the question of life. Besides, his acquiring an insight into the very dynamics of life, gained through suffering, provides him with power and perception which will enable him to help others. His achievements, possible only through the rigorous trials of the rites of passage, are not for himself or his immediate kinsmen only, but are placed at the disposal of all humanity.

In the first book, *The Palm-Wine Drinkard,* the hero's quest is for his tapster in Deads' Town. Each episode is taken directly from a folk tale; the "crucial struggle" is therefore well spread and repeated by the episodic re-enactment of the contests from one stage of the journey to another. His first major contest is with death who lives a few hours march from the village and tends his own patch of ground. The story here is a variant of the popular African story of how death came into the world. The significant stress here is on the contest between man and death, a contest which man won, thus achieving total mastery over death, and yet, paradoxically, bringing into the human world the destructive power of death. In the framework of the quest, however, the importance of this story lies in man's ultimate victory over death by his ability to achieve a spiritual state that creates a transcendent power beyond death itself. But as the "drinkard" brought death into the world, the price of physical decay must be paid by the human family:

> So since that day I had brought death out from his house, he has no permanent place to dwell or stay, and we are hearing his name about in the world.[1]

Through this story the successful point of departure is established for the hero, who, at this stage, has achieved a superhuman quality through his conquest of death, to proceed upon his journey in order to accomplish his appointed destiny. It is to be noted that even though this was not the first task the drinkard performs, it marks the significant point of his departure on the journey that indicates the nature and purpose of his quest.

The Palm-Wine Drinkard, even though made up of individual folk tales, achieves a unity which is owed to Tutuola's storytelling genius. It is obvious from a close examination of each folk tale that the stories in themselves represent a quest, thematically conforming to the structure of the heroic monomyth of departure, imitation, and return. For example, the story of the disobedient daughter represents one single naïve quest tale; the drinkard pits his wisdom, cunning, and magic against that of the skulls and risks his life in order to rescue the girl. The concept of descent into the nether world is strongly carried across through his access to the skulls' house which "was under the ground." The story of the conquest of death also possesses the features of the cycles of the monomyth. But Tutuola's linking of these stories does not destroy their individual mythological or folkloric integrity. He uses them in order to intensify the demands made upon the hero, who becomes the link for the various stories as they flow into one another.

Moreover, their structure restates in segmented units the ultimate impulse of the whole story. The first story, about returning the "right thing" from the blacksmith, ends with

> So the blacksmith gave me the bell; after that I returned to the old man with the bell and when he saw me with the bell, he and his wife were surprised and also shocked at that moment.[2]

Tutuola, in order to lead us into the next ordeal, more ominous and demanding than the first, continues in the next paragraph:

> After that he told his wife to give me food, but after I had eaten the food, he told me again, that there remained another wonderful work to do for him . . . He told me to go and bring "Death" from his house with the net.[3]

When the task of bringing death was completed, Tutuola ushers his hero into his next adventure by making the old man, who had promised to tell him the whereabouts of the tapster, run away.

> Then I left the town without knowing where my tapster was, and I started another fresh journey.[4]

This new departure led him to the adventure in the house of the skulls where he went to rescue the disobedient daughter of the new town. No story stands alone as a completed quest story per se, but each becomes integrated into the framework of the story of the larger quest of the drinkard's for his dead tapster. Tutuola weaves the single stories into the pattern which lends momentum to the total impact of the drinkard's adventures. The conquest of death itself connotes a complete mastery over the spirit world and all that death signifies, a reversal of the life force. With this conquest behind him, the drinkard can proceed upon his major task, with the assured confidence of a god. The story of the disobedient girl and her rescue also affords him further information upon which his greater search can be pursued. His exploits against the skulls and his ability to outwit them enable the father of the girl to give him a companion: "This is how I got a wife." The purpose of the task, of course, was not to win a bride. But it enables the hero to go through a short period of rest or recuperation, an idyllic interlude, in order to face the journey ahead. These pauses seem to be designed to stress new climacterics in the story and strengthen the unity between each story as it leads to the greater purpose of the search for the dead tapster. Some of these other pauses are the story of the Wraith Island[5] and Faithful Mother;[6] their folkloric significance lies in the stress on the pre-fall situation of man, a primal Edenic era in which there was no toil or death. They are designed to remind man of what he has lost; they are used in *The Palm-Wine Drinkard* as brief respites from the relentlessness of the tasks confronting the hero. Yet again, they are periods that in themselves engender sloth and may lead to evil, for forgetfulness of the primal purpose of the journey leads to possible abandonment of will. The pause also illustrates almost a total regaining of the prejourney state for the drinkard, with a wife to minister to him and be his companion. In order to break this pause and to enable the protagonist to pursue his primary objective, Tutuola introduces a new story, which is a logical result of the honeymoon and rest period.

> I noticed that the left-hand thumb of my wife was swelling out as if it was a buoy, but it did not pain her. One day she followed me to the farm in which I was tapping the palm-wine and to my surprise when the thumb that swelled out touched a palm tree thorn, the thumb burst out suddenly and there we saw a male child come out from the thumb, he began to talk to us as if he was ten years of age.[7]

This is the story of Zurrjir, the *enfant terrible,* who, in himself, constitutes another ordeal to the drinkard and his wife. Thus a link is forged between the story of the disobedient daughter and the next adventure, the escape from the evil child, which in itself is a continuation of the search and the breaking of the period of the lull.

The story of the terrible child is by itself well integrated, even though it serves to break the pause and precipitate the continuation of the journey. The parents decide to kill him by fire. The child emerges after the house was burned down on him, as a half-bodied baby on the journey to Deads' Town, insisting on being carried by his parents up and down, eating them out of house and home, until they were relieved by three benevolent characters, Drum, Song, and Dance:

> But as the [half-bodied baby] came down from my head he joined

the three creatures at once. When "Drum" started to beat himself it was just as if he was beaten by fifty men; when "Song" started to sing, it was just as if a hundred people were singing together, and when "Dance" started to dance the half-bodied baby started too, my wife, myself and spirits, etc., were dancing with "Dance" and nobody who heard or saw these three fellows would not follow them to wherever they were going.[8]

The half-bodied baby danced into the dwelling of the creatures, and thus the parents escaped his torments finally. It is after this ordeal that the drinkard takes stock of his predicament, recollects his spiritual attributes as a god, attributes which enable him to turn himself into a big canoe to be used by his wife to ferry people across the river for money. Again, this constitutes a minor pause which enables them to prepare themselves to continue their journey; it serves also as a useful link between the story of the half-bodied child and the story of their arrival (by air) at the town where his father-in-law had said his tapster had gone to.

When reaching there, I asked from that town's people about my tapster who had died long ago in my town. But they told me that [he] had left over two years. . . . I was told that he was now at "Deads' Town" and they told me that he was living with deads at the "Deads' Town."[9]

From here, the drinkard and his wife enter another bush, which promises to be more ominous than the first. Here they encounter the white creatures who were a quarter of a mile long, resembling white pillars.

The links are well worked out, in order to enable what in the folkloric sense is an autonomous adventure to flow into the next one. This enables the quest motif of each tale to be suspended and to remain unresolved.

It is quite obvious that Tutuola, as suggested earlier, has made ample use of Yoruba stories as he knew and heard them. He claims to have heard some of these stories from an old man who lived on a palm tree plantation in his home town, Abeokuta. But it must be assumed that as a boy he was familiar with each single story as it exists in the Yoruba folklore. Besides, these stories are the stock in trade of West African folklore as a whole. It is impossible to determine the purest version or the origin of any of the stories. Any effort to determine these is a fruitless venture and will add no further illumination to the way in which Tutuola uses them in his work.

One of the most significant and commonplace stories in *The Palm-Wine Drinkard* is that of the disobedient daughter who marries a skull. In M. I. Ogumefu's *Yoruba Legends,* Barbara and Warren Walker's *Nigerian Tales,* E. Dayrell's *Folk Stories of Southern Nigeria,* and Alta Jablow's *Yes and No: The Intimate Folklore of Africa* variants of this story occur. Besides, variants exist in Ewe and Ashanti folklore and perhaps for other groups too. Two versions appear in Ogumefu's collection alone. In both, the girl is lured away by a handsome stranger. But in these versions, the handsome gentleman did not rent the parts of the human body, but borrows them. In the Ewe version, too, he borrows instead of rents them. It seems the borrowing concept is more in line with traditional custom and usage than the renting. In Ogumefu's versions the girl escapes at the point when the handsome gentleman gives up his borrowed legs and thus could not pursue her. In Dayrell's version the girl is blown home by a wind summoned by her anxious mother. In Jablow's version she is helped by the skull's mother who arranges for her to go home on a friendly wind. Tutuola's addition seems to be in the elaboration on the stranger's beauty. This significant extension is entirely his own, just as in the mouths of the individual storyteller each story acquires additional qualities that owe their impact to the fertility of his imagination.

> I could not blame the lady for following the Skull as a complete gentleman to his house at all. Because if I were a lady, no doubt I would follow him to wherever he would go, and still as I was a man, I would jealous him more than that, because if this gentleman went to the battle field, surely enemy would not kill him or capture him, and if bombers saw him in a town which was to be bombed, they would not throw bombs on his presence, and if they did throw it, the bomb itself would not explode until this gentleman would leave that town, because of his beauty.[10]

The exaggerated and glamorized picture which Tutuola paints of the gentleman's beauty is designed, I suggest, to increase the shock of the discovery later that he had borrowed the parts in order to look beautiful. None of the variants that this writer came across lingered on the man's beauty, as attention would be focused on the basic moral of the story and the punishment (fear, anguish) that is attendant upon the act of disobedience on the part of the girl. The rich details and the dramatic elaboration are Tutuola's storytelling art, the capacity to elaborate segments, events, or characters that get hold of the individual storyteller's imagination, what in essence distinguishes his *style* from that of another storyteller even within the same vicinity. The storyteller is not expected to follow a rigidly handed down or "correct" version, since there is no such thing as the "correct" version of any story. Witness Tutuola's almost personal injection of himself into the story when the drinkard says,

> I ran to a corner of the market and I cried a few minutes because I thought within myself why was I not created with beauty as this gentleman, but when I remembered that he was only a Skull, then I thanked God that he had created me without beauty . . .[11]

No variant that I know of possesses this incredible and imaginative digression. At times he may change significant details, rearrange the sequence, elaborate events to enable him to place his own emphasis. It is obvious that Tutuola knew the barest skeleton of this story, and his telling of it does not create a variant or constitute an "improvement" on any particular version. What is apparent here is his acute imaginative technique.

The second very significant story is that of the terrible child. In Itayemi and Gurrey's collection *Folktales and Fables,* he is conceived on the big toe. In an Ewe version he is conceived as a boil on the mother's private parts, and when the boil is incised, the terrible child is born. In the Ewe version he is named "He who knows more than the chief." He was also a great dissembler. He waits until his parents go to the farm when he rises from his mat (on the same day he is born), takes his father's hunting weapons, and does an old hunter's dance. When he hears the footsteps of people, he quickly puts down his hunter's clothes, jumps into bed, and cries like a baby. When he is finally caught, he offers to go and ensnare death. He brings death into the village as his vengeance upon the people. In the Itayemi and Gurrey collection, he kills his father and forces his mother to eat his liver. The story of the evil child is prevalent throughout West Africa. He is the inescapable destiny of parenthood, and the plague that at times comes as punishment for crimes or sins committed by the forebears. In Tutuola a terrible picture is painted of him fighting the whole village, eating every scrap of food cooked for the next day. He could flog more than a hundred men, was as strong as iron, and, in short, became the ruthless ruler who terrorizes everyone. Tutuola uses this story as one more ordeal for the drinkard, to set him once again upon his journey after the brief honeymoon.

Another significant story in *The Palm-Wine Drinkard* is the tale of the magic egg. The story of the boon won, through humility, obedience, and preparedness to undergo suffering, is a commonplace one in West Africa. In *The Palm-Wine Drinkard* it becomes the ultimate boon (apart from the awareness and knowledge the drinkard acquires) which he wins from the Deads' Town. There he and his wife meet the dead tapster. But he cannot come back with them to the world of the living.

> But when I thought that he would not follow us to my town, and again, my wife was pressing me too much to leave there very early, when he came, I told him that we should leave here tomorrow morning, then he gave me an "EGG." He told me to keep it as safely as gold and said that if I reached my town, I should keep it inside my box and said that the use of the egg was to give me anything that I wanted in this world, and if I wanted to use it, I must put it in a big bowl of water, then I would mention the name of anything that I wanted.[12]

The motif varies within a number of folk traditions. In the Itayemi and Gurrey version the Yoruba animal folk hero, the tortoise, wins a magic ladle after a long ordeal. In Dayrell's version it is a magic drum, just as in the Ewe version, which tells the story of two sons of rival wives searching for food during a great famine. One, obedient and humble, collects palm kernels. As he begins to crack them, each nut jumps into a hole. He decides to follow them. In the hole he comes upon a tumbledown house inhabited by a smelly old woman who forces him to give her a bath. As he is scrubbing her back very hard, it caves in. And in the hole there are many drums. The old lady orders the boy to take one drum. As a well-brought-up and not greedy child, he takes the smallest drum. The old woman tells him to beat it any time he wants food. He takes it home and uses it to feed his family. Out of jealousy and envy, the rival wife drives her own son away from home to go and look for the old lady who gives out magic drums. He also collects palm kernels, and even though they don't jump into the hole when he attempts to crack them, he pushes them in and jumps in after them. He meets the dirty old lady whom he mocks for being so smelly. When asked to give the old lady a bath, he derides her, but because he wants a drum, he gives her a bath. Her back caves in and naturally he takes the biggest drum he could set eyes on. He goes home to his mother, who, in her greed, collects all her children into a room and beats upon the drum. Out come diseases like yaws, leprosy, smallpox, and other dreadful ailments which attack them. They flee their hut and the diseases follow them, attacking anyone they come across. That is how these diseases came into the world—through greed.

This variant underscores the most important motif which Tutuola stresses: the overwhelming destructiveness of human greed. An Ashanti version places the contest between Ananse the spider and his own son who did not inherit his father's senseless greed. The Yoruba version of Itayemi and Gurrey turns the magic ladle that produces food into a whip that lashes the whole community when it turns greedy. In *The Palm-Wine Drinkard,* the people, after having been fed by the egg, start to wrestle and, as a result, break the egg. The drinkard patches it up, but it refuses to produce food. When the people are hungry for four days, they heap insults on the drinkard:

> So one day I went to my room and regummed it [the egg] securely, then I commanded it as perhaps it might produce food as usual. And to my surprise, it produced only millions of leather whips, but immediately I saw what it could produce I commanded it to take the whips back and it did so at once. . . . I went to the King and told him to tell his bell ringers to ring the bell in every town and village and tell the whole people that they should come to my house and eat. . . . I put the egg in the middle of them, after that I told one of my friends to command it to produce anything it could for them,

then I entered my house and closed all the windows and doors. When
he commanded it to produce anything it could, the egg produced only
millions of whips and started to flog them all at once.[13]

After the egg performs the final act of punishment, it vanishes, and
the famine which the drinkard had come back to after his travels
continues with increased fierceness. This story, together with that
of the disobedient girl, constitutes the most moralistic and didactic
pieces used by Tutuola in the whole book. While the first story,
that of the girl, deals with an individual's disobedience and places
the stress on filial duty, the second story swings back to the community which the drinkard's tapster has served at the beginning
of the book and which, even at that stage, exhibits a characteristic greed which is the hallmark of all freeloaders.

Perhaps it would be easier not to point to a resolution in *The
Palm-Wine Drinkard* development and to suggest that the whole
tale is purposeless and without focus. As stated earlier, Tutuola
seems to be fascinated by the over-all impact of the whole adventure which he loads with significantly well-chosen folk tales
that underscore the theme of a search, suffering, and the gaining of
a boon. One disagrees with Gerald Moore[14] when he says Tutuola's affinities, in terms of projecting an effective vision, are
Bunyan, Dante, and Blake. The religious and eschatological preoccupations of these writers are decidedly absent in Tutuola's work.
The individualism of perception and creation which marks these
writers as Christian is not present in Tutuola. His creative impulse
does not express itself in the visionary outlook that concerns itself
with man alone, suffering, but with the community on whose behalf
he endures pain in order to win the boon of wisdom with which
to serve.

The resolution which seems to be the final knot that ties all
the stories together may be regarded as the sacrifice offered to
heaven at the end of the book. Tutuola ends the whole tale in
this manner:

I called the rest of the old people who remained and told them how
we could stop the famine. We stopped the famine thus:—We made
a sacrifice of two fowls, six kolas, one bottle of palm-oil, and six
bitter kolas. Then we killed the fowls and put them in a broken pot,

after that we put the kolas and poured the oil in the pot. The sacrifice was to be carried to heaven.

BUT WHO WOULD CARRY THE SACRIFICE TO THE HEAVEN FOR HEAVEN? First we chose one of the King's attendants, but that one refused to go, then we chose one of the poorest men in the town and he refused to go, at last we chose one of the King's slaves who took the sacrifice to heaven for Heaven who was senior to Land and Heaven received the sacrifice with gladness. The sacrifice meant that Land surrendered, that he was junior to Heaven. But when the slave carried the sacrifice to heaven and gave it to Heaven he [slave] could not reach half-way back to the earth before a heavy rain came. . . . But when for three months the rain had been falling regularly, there was no famine again.[15]

Moore rightly stresses the fact that the resolution of the drinkard's individual quest is linked with the restoration of harmony between man and his gods and that it is his new understanding "won by hard way of adventure which enables him to settle the cosmic quarrel through which man is suffering." However, to accept this as the most final gift he achieved connotes an existing disharmony between man and gods, for the conflict was one between two gods, and men are inevitably caught in the ensuing contest. It also plays down the role of the magic egg which dramatizes the eternal conflict between men engendered by greed and other evil forces that exist purposely to assert this conflict. If we accept the Yoruba concept of the necessity of conflict in order that balance and harmony can be achieved, the community greed only attempts a dramatization of an essential folk philosophy. One can go further, to suggest that in the Yoruba thinking, therefore, the god that creates the mischief among men on the one hand and between the two gods on the other is Eshu-Elegba, the trickster-god who in effect awaits the benefits of the sacrifice sent to heaven. Further, it may be suggested that the drinkard himself, in his role as the trickster, magician, and god, who pits his strength against supernatural elements, defies boundaries, breaks taboos, and upsets predetermined orders in the spiritual world and shares the single essence of Eshu-Elegba, represents the deity of disharmony whose paradoxical role is to ease the process of balance and harmony. As suggested earlier, the folk tale and the concept of the trickster-

hero owe much to the trickster principle of this god, whose equivalents exist in traditions other than Ewe, Fon, and Yoruba. On
that basis, the quarrel between the gods might have been en-
gineered to test the wisdom and awareness of men toward their
gods whose fates are inextricably bound with theirs. The African
religious process is deeply embedded in the principle of sacrifice
which stretches from the daily meals and drink to the more elaborate sacrifices ordered by the priests for specific propitiation or
enjoined in periodic rites and ceremonies. The sacrifice, therefore,
becomes an automatic gesture of ensuring that succor and protection continue to flow from the gods, and forgiveness is being
asked for sins unknowingly committed by one or by members of
one's household.

Tutuola's other book worth discussing at length is *My Life in
the Bush of Ghosts*. It is in this work that he achieves a fantastic
unity between his folkloric sources and his own inventiveness, which
tends to be syncretic and dependent on his observation of Western
or European institutions, norms, and practices.

My Life in the Bush of Ghosts continues the quest motif, exhibiting the same faithful adherence to the folkloric style and
utilizing the significant details of this genre. The idea of a deliberate quest is, however, missing, the suggested purpose being the
process of development into manhood, a significant stage in the
rites of passage. The narrator, a boy of eight, existing in a state
of innocence, has begun to learn the meaning of evil as the helpless
victim of domestic rivalries sometimes prevalent in a polygamous
household. It is significant that he acquires the knowledge of evil
before good. The forced quest for a unity of life seems to be the
purpose of his journey.

In the confusion of a slave raid, the protagonist is abandoned
by his relatives:

> Now it remained me alone in the bush, because no brother, mother,
> father or other defender could save me or direct me if and whenever
> any danger is imminent.[16]

The point of danger drives him into the bush, a place of ghosts
and spirits. We have already encountered the bush in *The Palm-
Wine Drinkard;* there it exists alongside the normal world of

towns and villages. Though yet a place of mystery and fear, it shares the attributes of the waking world. In *My Life in the Bush of Ghosts* the totality of the spirit world, or world of alienation for the human person, is prevalent.

> But as the noises of the enemies' guns drove me very far until I entered into the Bush of Ghosts unnoticed, because I was too young to know that it was a dreadful bush or it was banned to be entered by any earthly person.[17]

His search for safety and salvation and escape from being sold into slavery becomes the point of departure into new experiences, into a world where the protagonist will acquire knowledge and awareness.

The basic ingredients of the folk tale are again here; transformation into other objects in order to escape persecution and suffering intensified by the protagonist's slave status are aspects of a more closely knit and better dramatized story than that of *The Palm-Wine Drinkard*. The protagonist's meeting with the smelling ghost, the epitome of evil and the ultimate in scatological embodiment of man's corruptibility, the kingdom of smell where "All the babies born the same day were also smelling as a dead animal," a town in which "they had an Exhibition of Smells," putrescent beyond imagination, the metamorphoses into monkey, lion, horse, camel, cow, often a horse for the smelling ghost, and the way in which Tutuola weaves these materials into an even-flowing narration show a firmer grasp of style and use of what in *The Palm-Wine Drinkard* seems to be a profusion of folkloric material.

Again, there are a number of important stories derived from Yoruba folklore which Tutuola takes over almost wholesale and in which he adds his own characteristic elaboration and expansion. One of these is the story of the Super Lady. This is a variant of the animal or demon lover story, a commonplace of West African folk tales. Barbara and Warren Walker, in their *Nigerian Tales,* record the story of a hunter who marries a deer woman. She leaves him, after retrieving her deerskin from the attic, because her co-wives have taunted her with her animal origin. There is an Ewe version which is close to this, except that the cause of her departure is her husband's referring to her animal origin in one of those frequent marital quarrels. In most West African myths, men, especially hunters, have met animals in the forest and, because of the comeliness of these creatures, had entreated them to change into women. Many had brought home these animal lovers, who became wonderful matriarchs and founders of clans in legendary times. It is a myth that perhaps illustrates the bond between men and animals, signifying the source of animal totemism. It also recalls an Edenic golden age when there was a real relationship between men and animals. For men claim, in most "folk" cultures, to have learned the knowledge of herbs and cures from animals, and ultimately from gods. Here is the confrontation, in *My Life in the Bush of Ghosts* between the antelope and the hero:

> Though it was clear to me that she was an antelope in form at the first time that I saw her running to that tree. Again I was surprised that it was in my presence she took away the antelope skin from her body and hid it inside a hole which was at the foot of that tree. . . . After that she came to me for herself and asked "Will you marry me?"[18]

She is endowed with powers of self-transformation, her mother and father being witches. Her house contained a parlor, mirrors, fine clothes, drinks of all kinds, "costly decorations," all "made with supernatural power":

> Before she woke me up early in the morning, she had put out the water and soap which had a sweet and lofty smell . . . that the sponge which was as fluffy as cotton, she put them in the bathroom, which was as clean as a food plate.[19]

Super Lady represents one of Tutuola's most integrated "characters" in that her attributes are basically those of a European lady, with her parlors, her mirrors, sweet-smelling soaps, fluffy sponges, easy chairs, cushions, maids, and servants, even though she is entirely derived from Yoruba folklore.

The other very significant story in *My Life in the Bush of Ghosts* is the one in which the hero molds an arm out of mud for the king's one-armed wife, who stood in danger of losing her life as an "amputy" who has dared to marry a king. In Itayemi and Gurrey the woman has no teeth and receives a new set on her mother's grave while her accuser's teeth fall out. A variant of this story occurs among the Ewe with a comic effect. The story is of the spider man who climbs the king's fence to steal his beans. In the course of climbing the fence, the spider's buttocks are ripped by the sharp spikes. In order to catch the thief, a general inspection of buttocks was necessary. The spider wriggles out of this by threatening the village that, since he is a special attendant and ally of the sky god, if his buttocks are inspected, the god shall withhold rain and dew from falling upon the earth and famine will ensue. Tutuola, using the tragic variant of this story, builds up the drama of the inspection of the arms by asking each of the king's wives to pound corn in public.

The third story, significant in the sense that it plays a major role in the return of the hero to the world of the human family, is that of the Television-handed Ghostess. The role of mirrors in magic in West African lore is well known. Important medicines (fetishes) such as *tigare* and *sibisaba* and masks such as *ogungun* utilize mirrors which are expected to reflect the spirit world. It has been suggested that the mirror was introduced into West African religious practice as an important talismanic item from Islamic sources. Its antecedent is water. Water divination is still widely practiced. Tutuola's use of this motif is made more effective by the way he brings together two conflicting and opposing phenomena; one, the aspect of the "ghostess" which is repulsive, covered with sores which the hero is asked to lick, and the other, the picture of his native homeland with visions of his family, a place he has been searching to return to for twenty-four years. The Television-handed Ghostess is one of the most repulsive ghosts the hero encounters:

> She was not more than three feet high. Immediately she entered she went direct to the fire, she spread the mat closely to the fire, and then sat down on it without saluting or talking to me. So at this stage I noticed carefully that she was almost covered with sores, even there was no single hair on her head, except sores with uncountable maggots which were dashing here and there on her body. . . . She was crying bitterly and repeatedly as if somebody was stabbing her with knives. . . . When I could not bear her cry I asked her—"By the way what are you crying for?" She replied—"I am crying because of

you!" Then I asked again—"Because of Me?" She said "Yes" and
I said—"What for?" Then she started to relate her story thus:

> I was born over two hundred years ago with sores on my head
> and all over my body. . . . I have been to many sorcerers to know
> whether the sores would be healed but every one of them was telling
> me that there is an earthly person who had been lost in this Bush
> of Ghosts . . . and the sorcerers said that if you will be licking the
> sore every day with your tongue for ten years, it would be healed.[20]

The ghostess, as a form of subtle blackmail, shows him his town
where he sees his mother, brother, and all his playmates, and in
payment for licking the sores, she promises to return him there.
He is relieved of the horror of this task with the help of the same
television which shows him his mother preparing an herb to heal
the sore on a baby's foot. He cures the ghostess of her affliction
within a week. In recompense, she transports him back to his
hometown:

> She opened her palm as usual, she told me to look at it, but to my
> surprise, I simply found myself under the fruit tree which is near my
> hometown. . . . It was under this fruit tree my brother left me on
> the road when he was running away from his enemies' guns. . . .
> This is how I got out of the Bush of Ghosts which I entered when
> I was seven years old.[21]

Bernth Lindfors[22] makes the very important point that though
Tutuola has been compared to Bunyan, Dante, and Blake, it is
with Chief Fagunwa, the Yoruba writer, that Tutuola has a close
affinity. In the use of scatological detail, Tutuola comes close to
Fagunwa with whom he shares a typical Yoruba sense of the
bizarre. Fagunwa's repulsive creature, Egbin, in *The Forest of a
Thousand Daemons: A Hunter's Saga,* has some aspects of the
characteristic ugliness of the Television-handed Ghostess:

> All his toes were pocked with the jigger. . . . The sores on his legs
> were numerous and he covered them with broad leaves for the small-
> est of them was at least the size of my palm. . . . Egbin never
> cleaned his anus when he excreted and crusts of excrement from some
> three years back could be found at the entrance to his anus; while
> he rested worms and piles emerged from his anus and sauntered all
> over his body. . . .[23]

The performance of unsavory tasks related to sores and filth is a commonplace of West African folklore. It is invariably an aspect of the task imposed upon heroes and heroines who are known to be sensitive to smells. It is also demanded as part of filial duty from the youth whose responsibility it is to care for the aged, the infirm, and those who generally cannot help themselves. The emphasis in this motif is on the virtuousness of those who, without complaint or any sense of revulsion, perform these duties. Gods themselves are known to have come into homesteads covered with sores and tormented by flies to ask for a place to sleep, a drink of water from the cleanest bowl, and the chance to put their hands into the communal pot of the family. Families or homesteads who receive them without showing any revulsion and allow them their wishes have been known to have received great wealth, health, longevity, and, at times, magical powers and secret knowledge. Lindfors' point that the two writers' heaping of olfactory image upon image is Yoruba-derived is well borne out when we consider Yoruba or any other West African myth as possessing no distinct sense of demarcation between the acceptable and the bizarre or the grotesque, as both exist side by side in the folk imagination.

My Life in the Bush of Ghosts represents a better structured work in its use of details, its smooth flow, and its less episodic nature than the other Tutuola romances. The last quality is due more to the fact that the quest here is imposed. The story itself ends from where it began by stating simply, "This is what hatred did," which signifies the end of the initiation into the nature of good and evil.

One of the book's most significant qualities is Tutuola's ability to weave into his folkloric material imagery and motifs drawn from the European contact with Africa. He introduces us to a wedding ceremony at which Rev. Devil officiates, to a baptism by fire and hot water, to a Methodist church, to a doctor trained in England, and to such countless other details as he knows of European life style in Lagos. After a fantastic gala day by the river ghosts, the hero and his hosts "flew by air to the twentieth town, the seat of H. M. the King of the Bush of Ghosts."

Another of Tutuola's works, *Simbi and the Satyr of the Dark Jungle,* tells the story of a girl born to wealth who feels that she must go through suffering in order to pay for the comfort of her existence. Here the theme of the quest undergoes a change in that the heroine believes that the experience of suffering and abasement constitutes a way of understanding life, renewal and regeneration. There is a compensatory scale which is calculated to balance the experience of poverty and sorrow against that of the wealth and easy life into which the heroine is born. She escapes this world in order to experience "poverty" and "punishment" because she has never known them. It can be said that the quest here is for a fullness of life, for a totality of knowledge, self-imposed but no different from what drove the hero of *My Life in the Bush of Ghosts* into the world of spirits. The heroine's first act on the road to seeking this knowledge is to consult the Ifa oracle against the wishes of her mother. The Ifa priest advises her to prepare a sacrifice which she must place at "the place where three paths meet." It is from here that Dogo, the terrible monster, snatches her and carries her onto the Path of Death. From there her adventures into the knowledge of poverty and punishment begin. Her ordeal, voluntary as the palm-wine drinkard's, brings her into contact with the Satyr and his empire. Her final conquest of the Satyr, by turning into *iromi,* a water fly, through magic and flying into his nostrils and killing him is the point of her salvation. The main adventure centers on the dark jungle, which she arrives at through the Path of Death and by which she must return.

Tutuola's later works follow the same pattern. The ingredients are the same. The style undergoes some change, either at his publisher's insistence or because his language becomes more polished.

The structure of the tales, however, remains strongly embedded in the oral tradition. They consist of episodes which are in themselves loose. There is no effort to structure them into chapters. Most are set off from each other with closing formulas, and a few have etiological endings: "This was how I got a wife." "This is how I brought death to the old man." "This is what hatred did." All these formulas signify to the audience that this is the end and serve in a didactic capacity by formulating the basic moral of each story, a task which Tutuola could not neglect in his use of the folk tale. The etiological endings are more didactic. Here is an example from *The Palm-Wine Drinkard:*

Since that day I had brought death out from his house, he has no permanent place to dwell or stay and we are hearing his name about in the world.[24]

Or,

Since that day nobody could see the three fellows [Drum, Dance, Song] personally, but we are hearing their names about in the world.[25]

Tutuola's strength as a writer rests in his keen awareness of the Yoruba folkloric tradition and his ability to expand what in themselves constitute autonomous tales into the scope of the mythology of the search. He embellishes his direct borrowings with proverbs. *The Brave African Huntress* has every chapter opening with an appropriate proverb, quoted again in the story to emphasize its didactic nature. *Feather Woman of the Jungle,* the most episodic and folkloric of his romances, is told as a series of nightly entertainments. One suspects here a direct influence from *The Arabian Nights* in the mode of its narration. But it conforms to type, the drama of the folk tale being "staged" every night to the accompaniment of palm-wine drinking, drumming, and dancing.

Tutuola's style is derived essentially from the oral tradition. There is an orality in the written form marked by a sequential flow with *ands, buts,* and *thens.* At times it is quite obvious that he is translating from the Yoruba. The opening of *The Palm-Wine Drinkard* illustrates a typical Tutuolan style derived from the Yoruba speaking voice:

I was a palm-wine drinkard since I was a boy of ten years of age. I had no other work more than to drink palm-wine in my life. . . . My father got eight children and I was the eldest amongst them, all the rest were hard workers, but I myself was an expert palm-wine drinkard. I was drinking palm-wine from morning till night and from night till morning.[26]

His style elicited a great deal of controversial response from both his critics and his admirers. What European critics found as "quaint," "young English," and "naïve" owes much to the fact that Tutuola's English is rudimentary. His early works present almost a pleasant reflection of this fact, in producing sentences such as "Something is smelling, I can hear it," or the string of sentences all beginning with "then." This style is due more to a deep-seated knowledge of the language of the original stories and to the writer's facility in it than to any elaborate effort to sound quaint or revolutionarily refreshing. His style is, therefore, not a conscious development, but based on the transference of Yoruba syntactical structures into English. He is less conscious an artist in this particular sense. This style, without control, can easily bore since only the speaking voice with its ranges of modulation can eliminate a natural monotony. The stories will come to life when read aloud or when performed.

The most significant talent Tutuola shows in his work is his ability to take the oral tradition and, like the good storyteller he is, expand it into long tales which possess their own rhythm and autonomy as written works of art. Imagery, exaggeration, horrendous details are typically his own creation. Besides, true to the syncretic nature of the material he works with, Tutuola adds images and items from another culture, one which it seems he was not even very familiar with—items such as floodlights, umbrellas, television, buoys, Technicolor, and conveyor belts serve as details of his fantastic landscape. A creature's eyes close and open as if a switch is being flicked off and on, some creatures use the language of church bells, the huntress uses the never-dying eye of a monster she kills as a miner's helmet. In the ghosts' town, the hero's body is "transparent" like an X ray when the silverish ghost's light falls on his body. When the hero shakes hands with a ghost it is "as if I touch a live electric wire." One other ghost is equipped with "various voices as a motor horn." In *My Life in the Bush of Ghosts* there are chapels, hospitals, banquet halls, parlors with mirrors, and a whole life style reminiscent of Europe. When these Western concepts are not serving just as ingredients of a particular imagery, they are made to appear as part of the bizarre. In the nameless ghost town inhabited by the Super Lady, ghosts drink tea. In all cases, Europe or the West is part of a fantasy realm where its technology imposes a clumsy ghostlike, if at times desirable, world order. In most African myths, overseas, mainly Europe, is also the land of spirits.

It has been suggested by a number of critics including Ulli

Beier[27] and Bernth Lindfors[28] that Tutuola owes some debt to Chief Fagunwa, the Yoruba novelist, the author of *The Forest of a Thousand Daemons*. It seems on the basis of the evidence, that even though Tutuola might have read Fagunwa, and at times borrowed, as Lindfors amply illustrates, a large body of details from him, Tutuola remains very much his own master. Beier makes the very important point that Fagunwa was very much influenced by the Christian tradition in the over-all impact of his moral position. Beier writes:

> Fagunwa is a much more Christian writer. . . . he loses no opportunity to moralize and to improve his reader. He can also be sentimental and sloppy. There is nothing very Yoruba about Fagunwa's naïve somewhat tearful sentimentality. . . .[29]

Fagunwa's world view, I suggest, shifted from the Yoruba religious world into a world of the obviously Christian Almighty God and angels, without losing its traditional focus. After all, moralizing and didacticism are not limited to the Christian world view. Tutuola's work retains the robust and simple-minded morality of the folk myths; no details are too insignificant for him to relish. This is not to suggest that Fagunwa's outlook is not Yoruba-derived. His description of Egbin, or death, obviously influenced sections in Tutuola's *The Palm-Wine Drinkard* and *My Life in the Bush of Ghosts*. Fagunwa exhibits the same exaggerated attachment to detail, the same ebullience, the same visuality of language which is the genius of Yoruba, the same humor, and the total manner and tone of his storytelling. But until all Fagunwa's works—nine novels —are available in English for non-Yoruba-reading critics, it is futile to attempt to determine to what extent Tutuola's work owes its inspiration to Fagunwa. Suffice it to say that both writers, being Yoruba, exhibit the same stylistic qualities that are very much part of the language's genius.

Tutuola has definitely been aware of traditions other than his own. Even though he was a man of limited formal education, it is possible that, like every child who attended missionary schools in his time, he must have read Bunyan's *Pilgrim's Progress* in its Yoruba translation. The influence of Bunyan on his work, it can be safely said, does not lie in the total impact or in any theological preoccupation. Tutuola takes no obvious theological position. He emphasizes the moral or ethical system of a tradition based in mythology and folklore. His debt to Bunyan may be traced to the details of description of creatures, for example, the Redfish in *The Palm-Wine Drinkard* which comes close to that of Apollyon in Bunyan. In short, Tutuola's moral system is inexact and locked within the framework of the story where it is not allowed to take over in any theological manner. In fact, it can be said that Fagunwa owes more to Bunyan than Tutuola. Harold Collins, in his book *Amos Tutuola,*[30] reports that Tutuola read Edith Hamilton's *Mythology* which "has lots of tales very like his [Tutuola's] own episodes in the novels." But no evidence is produced to show whether Tutuola had been influenced by Hamilton or not, especially in his early works. These remain as derivative as the telephones, electric wires, and such other obvious borrowings from Western life style. There is no doubt that from the point of view of style alone, Tutuola's later works have shown none of the happy linguistic abandon of the earlier books. His language becomes more and more conventional, and, from the point of view of the critical acclaimers of his "young English," loses that effective touch of ungrammatical and syntactical originality. There is an obvious falling off in the dramatic intensity and in the evocation of horror and even the humor in the subsequent works, qualities that are owed to the genius of the West African folkloric tradition which allows for adaptation and adoption of ingredients and motifs from, at times, totally different worlds.

In what could have been one of the most informed books on Tutuola, Harold Collins establishes one of the most clear cases for the importance of Tutuola's artistic talent. Collins, however, weakens his thesis of the quest motif by treating Tutuola's work as naïve quest romances when he falls into error by looking at Tutuola's work in terms of the realistic novel. Collins writes of *The Brave African Huntress:*

> Her escape from the pigmy town where she has been trapped by a rock slide is perhaps *admissible,* though the means—lassoed, reluctant gorilla hauling her up through a tree fallen over the cliff—is not altogether *credible.* Certain episodes would seem to be clearly superfluous. . . .[31]

This is the critic who earlier established for Tutuola "a really correct genre name" and described Tutuola's world as that of the "naïve romances," using Northrop Frye's criteria as put out in his *Anatomy of Criticism* even though allowing Tutuola's use of the picaresque as the only deviation from Frye's structural principle which organizes the incidents. But even then, the episodic nature in a naïve quest is perfectly acceptable given the ordeals or tasks undergone by the hero or heroine. In his genre, there cannot be an insistent call for narrative progression, realism, or characterization. The world of the folk tale and myth is a timeless agglomeration of folk experience and fantasy and, contrary to Collins' belief, has no linearity.

Using the quest motif as propounded in Joseph Campbell's *The Hero of a Thousand Faces,* Gerald Moore compares Tutuola's drinkard to Orpheus, Gilgamesh, Hercules, and Aeneas who all follow the heroic monomyth of departure, initiation, and return. Stith Thompson's *Motif-Index of Folk Literature* buttresses the argument for this approach even if Campbell's ideas insist on creating a somewhat universal philosophy and religion out of all myths and thus endowing all mythological systems with a singular motivation. Yoruba mythology does not obviously observe Campbell's four functions as "properly operating" mythologies do, namely, through its rites and imagery, to awaken and maintain in the individual a sense of awe, gratitude, and even rapture, rather than fear in relation to the mystery both of the universe and of man's own existence within it; to offer man a comprehensive, understandable image of the world around him; to support the social order through rites and rituals; and, most important, to guide the individual stage by stage through the inevitable psychological crises of a useful life. But beyond these, it can be said that mythology also creates for man that needful balance between himself and other men, between himself and nature, upon which his very survival depends, and, above all, provides an assurance of some type of immortality for him beyond the grave. African myths have served exactly these functions and, unlike the Campbell model, do not place the emphasis on the individual but on the community. Tutuola's transference of those myths into written form, releasing them from their folkloric oral structures into a written system, serves only as a continuation of the old art of the storyteller of folk tradition.

Tutuola's work, however, ends in a blind alley. Geoffrey Parrinder's[32] prophecy that Tutuola's writing is "a beginning of the new type of Afro-English literature" has not exactly been realized because of his high individuality of style which remains inimitable. The task of total assimilation was performed by such writers as Chinua Achebe and Wole Soyinka. Tutuola's achievement rests in his going into the roots of Yoruba folklore to rediscover the great common soil of literature. This common soil yields nothing within the range of scientificalness or realism, but bases itself in magic, fantasy, mystery, and the blatantly monstrous, expressing the most bizarre and incredible as the commonplace creations of man's imagination.

14

Chinua Achebe and the rise of modern African fiction

Chinua Achebe's career as a novelist started in 1958 with the publication of *Things Fall Apart,* a novel that can be described as having achieved a remarkable assimilation of African and European features. It not only brought into fiction in English an integrated African world, but also achieved the feat of presenting that world in its entirety in an unrelated language. Achebe's debt to the oral tradition is expressly in his creation of a new English style that follows and derives from his own Igbo African vernacular, idiom, rhythm, and tenor of speech. Above all, he exhibits a remarkable grasp of the proverb, which constitutes for the Igbo the "palm-oil with which words are eaten." These proverbs are intricately woven into the fabric of his style, completely absorbed to the extent that they constitute one of the most significant features of his totally African-derived English style.

Achebe has published four novels between 1958 and 1966: *Things Fall Apart, No Longer at Ease, Arrow of God,* and *A Man of the People.* Of these four, the first and the third are set completely within the so-called tribal world, even though there was juxtaposed to this world the tentative yet ominous presence of the European. The second and the fourth are set in both the African rural village world and the European-influenced urban areas.

Asked about the genesis of his first novel by this writer, Achebe replied, "It was to set the score right about my ancestors." He claims that *Things Fall Apart* was written in response to Joyce Cary's *Mister Johnson,* a novel set in colonial Nigeria. Cary's novel is a grotesque caricature of a semiliterate Nigerian civil servant, endowed with delusions of grandeur and an overwhelming *joie de vivre.* A typically Calibanesque character, he is the servant of the King of England whose praises he sings in the African bush. He regards his wife, for whom he pays an exaggerated bride price and whom he showers with gifts of high-heeled shoes and European clothes, as a government lady who has a place in the ranks of the position-conscious white officials' wives. Johnson's world is one of drunken happy innocence. An African *déraciné,* the product of colonial illogicality, and a buffoon, he is a rebel for whom no code of honor exists. And blissfully, his innocent rebellion leads him to the colonial gallows. The overwhelming caricaturist nature of this novel offended a number of Africans including Achebe. Ezekiel Mphahlele, the South African novelist and essayist, writes:

> I flung away *Mister Johnson* with exasperation when I tried to read it for the first time in South Africa. I had seen too many journalistic caricatures of black people . . . too many to find any amusement in Johnson's behavior.[1]

Achebe's *Things Fall Apart* seems to have been inspired by a need to respond to what seemed to be Cary's sniggering laugh at Africa, whose image of filed teeth and bones stuck in the nose has scarcely receded in the Europe of Cary's colonial experience. To Achebe, the African world before the arrival of Europe was a well-integrated one, with dignity and honor. This story had to be told, and told from an *African* point of view. What emerges in *Things Fall Apart* is a superb homage to Achebe's Igbo ancestry. As a story of the tragic encounter between Africa and Europe, it is an attempt to capture and restate the pristine integrity which has been so traumatically shattered by that confrontation. But his Africa, too, is full of contradictions. Its dynamics are too often determined by rigidity and an overextended system of masculinity. The Igbo, like most African peoples, place great store on the manly virtues as depicted by the wrestling matches and the continuous warring between the various clans. Gods are headstrong and at times willfully malevolent. But the rhythms and beliefs of the society enable men to take a hand against the gods themselves. Some are burned and chased out of the land; but the search goes on inexorably for that fundamental harmony on which their cosmic destiny rests.

The story of *Things Fall Apart* is set in the Igbo country around the middle of the nineteenth century, the period of the gradual extension of the Pax Britannica inland beyond the creeks and swamps of the Niger Delta. Umuofia, the fictional Igbo village, is a collection of nine clans held together by common ancestry and kinship. This community, governed by its well-tried mores, laws, sanctions, and taboos, is well integrated, a living structure, an organism animated with the life and movement of its members and gods. Apart from this society, there is the persona of the protagonist, Okonkwo, who embodies all the virtues and excesses of this society. He is a wrestler, a leader, an intrepid farmer, a man of wealth, unyielding in the pursuit of the ways of his fathers. Achebe draws for us, at a quick stroke, two integrated levels of his Igbo ancestry, with one resting firmly within the other. Around Okonkwo is heard the rhythmic beats of Umuofia's heart. The festival of New Yam is not only a thanksgiving but an occasion for affirming the group ethos, of communion with the ancestors and the gods, and a renewal of faith in the primal life force itself. There is a dramatic tautness that depicts the strength and the cohesion of Umuofia, expressed in the community of interests that binds families and homesteads together. But Achebe suggests faintly that there is something strangulating about this cohesive force, for its demands on the individual are ruthless, its insistence on allegiance and respect for its laws, gods, and customs constituting the stranglehold that breaks the weak. By its very rigid nature, the society creates its own rejects: disgruntled elements who will readily flee into the arms of the Christian church, the *efulefu*, those whom Okonkwo contemptuously refers to as worthless men who throw their machetes away and wear the sheaths into battle.

In the very analysis of the society, Achebe gives us a rhythmic and almost processional journey of the hero himself to his final collapse. His destiny will be as tragic as that of those rejects he so contemptuously scorned. But there is grandeur in his fall, a singular heroism of the type which great tragedies are made of. The very gods whom he strove to obey and serve drove him out of his fatherland because of the inadvertent killing of a clansman, just when he was ready to acquire the highest title in the land, marry his daughters off to deserving suitors, and initiate his sons into their first manhood groups. For him, the virtues that the society had taught him to despise—gentleness, pity, and love—will forever prove illusive. He commits one offense after another till he is exiled. All his three offenses are against the Earth Goddess, the mother to whom he symbolically returns when he goes into exile in his mother's village and whom in the end, after he returns from exile, he defies by committing the final abomination of taking his own life.

Order and coherence are followed by that slow, imperceptible and disguised process of destruction and decay. It is during his exile, when the Christians come to Umuofia, that the seeds of havoc are planted. His own son, Nwoye, flees to join their swelling ranks. And the Church of Christ, armed with the righteousness of its theology and the pigheadedness of its moral superiority, proceeds to dismantle Umuofia. The missionaries preach against the worship of sticks and stones. They openly defy the gods Amadiora, Idemili, Otakagu, Ekwensu, all the terrible gods of the land who had held Umuofia together since the dawn of history. For a brief moment there is that ominous confrontation for which Okonkwo has so much wished, when the blood of Umuofia would rise again to silence once and for all the desecraters of their ancestral shrines. But Okonkwo, back from exile, knows that Umuofia as a community can never be the same again. With the Church has come the courts, the police, and the handcuff. When some of the people burn the church down after the Christian convert Enoch unmasks an ancestral spirit in broad daylight, titled men are openly brutalized and beaten and shorn of their hair. When an ugly assembly gathers to discuss the next line of action, the District Commissioner sends his African orderlies to break it up. Okonkwo, in the belief that the hour has come for Umuofia to go to war, strikes off one orderly's head. The people of Umuofia, stunned and unready, flee. The tribe is no more. Okonkwo goes home and hangs himself.

Achebe has contrived to give us not so much as the death of one man, but of a whole way of life. The austere dignity and the economy of the story recalls the anguish and incomprehensibility that has marked tribal Africa's relationship with "civilized" Europe. Okonkwo's final act of rejection falls into pattern with the traditional rejection meted out to gods that fail.

Achebe is a more conscious artist than Tutuola. His preoccupation with creating an "authentic" African voice is more deliberate and studied than Tutuola's felicitous accidents of language. If Tutuola's work is described as derived wholly from the African tradition, Achebe is the direct articulate product of the European presence in Africa. In one of his pronouncements on the question of language and literature, Achebe writes:

> What I do see is a new voice coming out of Africa, speaking of African experience in a world-wide language. So my answer to the question, Can an African ever learn English well enough to be able to use it effectively in creative writing? is certainly yes. If on the other hand you ask, Can he ever learn to use it like a native speaker? I should say, I hope not. . . . The African writer should aim to use English in a way that brings out his message best without altering the language to the extent that its value as a medium of international exchange will be lost. He should aim at fashioning out an English which is at once universal and able to carry his peculiar experience.[2]

On the question of theme, Achebe's preoccupation was to re-create out of the despised history of Africa the story of its dignity and integrity:

> African people did not hear of culture for the first time from Europeans; their societies were not mindless but frequently had a philosophy of great depth and value and beauty, they had poetry and, above all, they had dignity. It is this dignity that many African people all but lost during the colonial period and it is this they must regain.[3]

Achebe, by the choice of a theme dealing with the historical disintegration of the African people in their unequal contest with Europe, has decided to recreate the world of the African past and present, its austere dignity, and its integrity. He imposes upon himself the task of re-educating the new generation and creating a new sense of awareness through what he considers will be "applied art" committed to the task:

> I would be quite satisfied if my novels, especially the ones I set in the past, did no more than teach my readers that their past—with all its imperfections—was not one long night of savagery from which the first Europeans acting on God's behalf delivered them.[4]

Achebe's trenchant commitment demanded from him the cultivation and perfection of an authentic African voice with which to play his role as the artist of the new Africa. The development and adoption of a *style* become important aspects of the founding of this voice.

Achebe was educated at Government Secondary School at Umuahia and later at University College in Ibadan where he came into close contact with the European literary modes and cultures. In developing his style, therefore, Achebe had the opportunity to select his own way of growth and, more important, his own themes. He has been accused by more than one reviewer of writing novels more distinguished by their anthropological preoccupation than by their adherence to the classical characteristics of the genre. But every novel will reflect the anthropology of its milieu. This is particularly true if the work deals with the past. But anthropology cannot be allowed to usurp the proper artistic function of a novel, which will attempt to dramatize the lives of men in their daily communion with one another and with the world around and beyond them. Achebe cannot be said to be guilty of allowing the anthropological definitions of his ancestors—minute description of their lives and mores—to become the dominant preoccupation in his novels. Where this anthropology exists, it is subordinated to the greater and more dramatic interest of the theme and the passions that it is intended to throw into bold relief. Insisting on maintaining credibility for the writer, Achebe goes farther by calling for the creation of a true picture, notwithstanding the imperfections, of this past. Details of life were intricately woven into the fabric of the novels and possess their dynamism and significance within their total impact.

The first part of *Things Fall Apart* presents a complete picture of this world in a style that reflects the very idioms, rhythms, and

manners of Igbo culture. His narrative is rich in proverbs and metaphors drawn directly from the life he writes about. At the opening
of the novel, speaking about Okonkwo, Achebe writes:

> Okonkwo was well known throughout the nine villages and even be-
> yond. His fame rested on solid personal achievements. As a young
> man of eighteen he had brought honor to his village by throwing
> Amalinze, the Cat. Amalinze was the great wrestler who for seven
> years was unbeaten from Umuofia to Mbaino. He was called the Cat
> because his back would never touch the earth. It was this man that
> Okonkwo threw in a fight which the old men agreed was one of the
> fiercest since the founder of their town engaged a spirit of the wild
> for seven days and seven nights.[5]

There is a straightforward direct simplicity about the language in
this passage that recalls the raconteur's voice. At the very onset
we are given Okonkwo's personality firmly based within the tradition, a man "whose fame has grown like a bush fire in the harmat-
tan." There is a total evocation of the African world, achieved
through an obvious transliteration of Igbo idioms and rhythm of
speech. In another passage Achebe presents to us the dramatic use
of proverbs, "the palm-oil with which words are eaten." Okonkwo
visits Nwakibie, an elder, in order to borrow yam seedlings for his
new farm:

> "I have come to you for help," he said. "Perhaps you can already
> guess what it is. I have cleared a farm but have no yams to sow.
> I know what it is to ask a man to trust another with his yams, es-
> pecially these days when young men are afraid of hard work. I am
> not afraid of hard work. The lizard that jumped from the high iroko
> tree to the ground said he would praise himself if no one else did.
> I began to fend for myself at an early age when most people still
> sucked at their mother's breast. If you give me some yam seeds I
> shall not fail you."[6]

The thematic emphasis on manliness and survival becomes extended through the yam, the "king of crops," a "man's crop." Okonkwo's effort to assert himself through success as a yam farmer is
firmly based in an ontology that insists on man's masculine role
as the provider of support for the family. Contrasted with this and
illustrating the society's insistence on manly virtues is the picture

created of Okonkwo's father, Unoka, a man known "in all the clan for the weakness" of his machete and hoe.

The most prevalent motif in the novel is the concept and dram-atization of the *chi*. B. I. Chukwukere describes *chi* as an indi-vidualistic principle, which is a pervasive trait in Igbo culture, approximating a "personal god." There is a fusion of *chi* and God which does not abnegate the underlying principle of individualism which the concept of *chi* connotes. Chukwukere traces the dra-matic manifestations of hostility between the Igbo and other ethnic groups in Nigeria to the deep-seated, atomistic, competitive, and egalitarian features of Igbo culture and temperament. The basis of Igbo religion, he affirms, is the *chi* concept. It rationalizes achieved status with its attendant features of individualism. The largest political unit in Igbo society, Chukwukere points out, is the village group, made up of a number of villages that can trace their genea-logical connections several generations back. This village group possesses a guardian deity in the same way that each village, family, or individual has one. Along with E. E. Evans-Pritchard who based his study of the *chi* concept on a study of Nuer religion, he draws the conclusion that religious thought bears the impress of the social order, the existence of an atomistic organization of gods, each manipulating its relationship with Igbo mortal beings in order to secure more power and influence, in the same way that those same human beings manipulate their own social relationships for material and spiritual benefits.

Chi shares an essence of the Supreme Being. It is a sort of guardian deity represented by a piece of carving from a "sacred" tree or one plant in front of one's house. (In this sense, it is close to the Legba of the Fon and the Ewe, conceived more as a per-sonal or household deity than a communal one.) In this form, it is reputed to be a guardian or benevolent ancestral spirit, every human being possessing his or her own *chi*. Chukwukere con-tinues:

> Since the Igbo do not have a clear-cut picture of an operational hier-archical ordering of deities, the relative proximity of *chi* makes its value as a primary source of knowledge regarding some of the mys-teries of the supernatural or invisible world priceless. In this sense,

chi can easily take on the role of an *agent provocateur,* thus establishing a relationship of manipulation between itself and its owner.[7]

He pursues this point by establishing that in the conflict that ensues in this mutual manipulatory relationship, the Igbo strongly believes that it is he who strikes the tune and expects his *chi* to keep time. If he fails, he expects to alter things through sacrifices prescribed by diviners or oracles.

The emphasis is on the individualism of man as expressed by his *chi. Chi* assumes a ubiquity in the daily life and life cycle of man. The proverb, "Where one falls, there his *chi* pushes him," illustrates this overwhelming bond between man and his *chi.* This stresses further the point of *chi*'s capacity to turn against its owner. Its manipulatory nature is widened to embrace all other supernatural beings or powers and extends even to ordinary social relationships. Donatus Nwoga, writing on the same subject, suggests that the personal *chi* is only a refraction of the universal force, a personification of its allotted role in the universal motion toward the ultimate. Each person has a good or bad *chi,* according to whether that person's appointed role enhances or diminishes his position in the scale of values which are consonant with his society's ultimate goal:

> A person exerted himself to achieve the promise of his good *chi.* If he did all in his power and yet made no progress, he could take consolation in being resigned to his own *chi.* And there is no contractual relationship between a person and his *chi.*[8]

Nwoga's stress seems to be placed on the non-manipulatory nature of *chi,* a concept that connotes a desperate sense of fatalism, one's impotence before one's predestined fate which one will seek to relieve in extremes through the expression of hope that what follows a constant stream of reversals will be benevolent. But one has no power to know or control it. Nwoga dismisses as untenable the concept of *chi* as a god that serves as a mediator between the person and other deities to which *chi* is superior in its different nature.

The concept of *chi* in the two studies quoted above can be simplified and defined as the basic operative attributes that are related to the personal god. It is agreed that *chi* is a personal god or man's deital expression, the ultimate mission brought by man from the creator's house, a deity that marks each man's unique personality or being. This concept occurs among other African peoples, notably the Akan who call it *okra*. Of *okra*, W. E. Abraham writes:

> The *okra* is the guiding spirit of man, the bearer and instrument of his destiny, that in a man which antecedently to the incarnation takes its leave of God. The *okra* is also that whose departure from the living man means death, and marks the completion of his destiny. . . . The *okra* is capable of appearing time after time on earth in different bodies, and it is the crucial factor in personal identity. That is what encourages the Akan to talk of a person's real self. . . . The *okra*, by being the bearer of destiny, lends its name to signal good luck and signal bad luck. . . . When either takes place, one says it is the person's *okra*.[9]

Abraham refers to the *okra* distinctly as mission, an immutable force whose attributes and dictates (innate) for man must be played out to the finish.

The Ewe *se* shares of the same essence as *okra* or *chi*. This divine essence is linked more closely with the creator god, whose expression he is. Each person, the Ewe believes, has been sent by *se*, each with his own mission. There is an infinite possibility of changing what *se* has decreed. Propitiation, magic, charms, and other acts that ask for help are designed to blunt the sharp edges of *se*'s allotment for man. There are benevolent spirits which may intervene, but *se*'s determination cannot be totally diverted.

Achebe's thematic construction and the dramatization of the conflict in *Things Fall Apart* utilize the *chi* concept. The structure of the novel is firmly based in the principles that are derived from this piece of Igbo ontological evidence. Okonkwo's life and actions seem to be prescribed by those immutable laws inherent in the *chi* concept. It is the one significant principle that determines the rhythm and the tragic grandeur of the novel. Okonkwo's rise and fall is seen in the significant way in which he challenges his *chi* to battle.

Okonkwo's fate is dominated by the contest between him and his *chi*. His father, Unoka, the dismal failure, is said to have had "a bad *chi*, or personal god, and evil followed him to the grave, or rather to his death, for he had no grave." He even died of the swelling disease which was an abomination. But his son, Okonkwo, is cast from a different clay. His *chi* is decidedly made for great things. As Nwakibie says, looking at Okonkwo, you can tell a ripe corn by its looks. At a kindred meeting, Okonkwo, at the height of his early success, calls Osugo a man who obviously was not as successful as he was a woman. An old man present "said sternly that those whose palm-kernels were cracked for them by a benevolent spirit should not forget to be humble." Then Achebe launches into the philosophical basis of the whole novel:

> But it was really not true that Okonkwo's palm-kernels had been cracked for him by a benevolent spirit. He had cracked them himself. Anyone who knew his grim struggle against poverty and misfortune could not say he had been lucky. If ever a man deserved his success, that man was Okonkwo. At an early age he had achieved fame as the greatest wrestler in all the land. That was not luck. At the most one could say that his *chi* or personal god was good. But the Igbo people have a proverb that when a man says yes, his *chi* says yes also. Okonkwo said yes very strongly; so his *chi* agreed.[10]

The benevolence of Okonkwo's *chi* is in sharp contrast to that of his ill-fated father, Unoka, whose *chi* was a malevolent one. Okonkwo's rise to fame, even though attributable to the strength of his arm, is explained entirely in terms of this benevolent *chi*. From a struggling youngster saddled with an improvident father and the burdens of early failure as a farmer, he rises to a position of eminence in the clan. During the tragic year of the bad harvest, when many farmers wept as they dug the miserable and rotting yams, Okonkwo survives by sheer will power:

> It always surprised him that he did not sink under the load of despair. He knew he was a fierce fighter, but that year had been enough to break the heart of a lion.[11]

He begins to believe in his indomitable will:

> "Since I survived that year," he always said, "I shall survive anything." He put it down to his inflexible will.[12]

This success, owed, he has come to believe, to his unconquerable spirit, is sharply contrasted with his father's dismal failure, emphasizing the singularity of fate as it pertains to each man, whose failure and success is his alone. This success, measured in terms of a full barn, a big household of wives and children, a revered position in the councils of elders, titles, and respect due to his position, becomes the factor that defines Okonkwo, gives him respect in the eyes of his clansmen:

> And not only his *chi* but his clan too, because it judged a man by the work of his hands. That was why Okonkwo had been chosen by the nine villages to carry a message of war to their enemies. . . .[13]

This success has earlier been defined in terms of his physical prowess as a wrestler, a man whose fame "had grown like a bush fire." It defined his relationship with his clansmen and with his own household. He is naturally a man of smoldering temper and fierce anger. Anyone who crosses his path comes to taste the edge of his scorn and his proverbial physical strength. He possesses the virtues that the clan lays great store by. His life becomes the exemplar of what a man, by the dint of his own labor, can become within the fold of his community.

As a result of this success, Okonkwo is beginning to develop traits that would go against the benevolence of his *chi*. His natural abhorrence of failure, directed against his own father (whose name he had never mentioned for as long as he lived), is also directed toward men less successful than himself:

> "Looking at a king's mouth," said an old man, "one would think he never sucked at his mother's breast." He was talking about Okonkwo, who had risen so suddenly from great poverty and misfortune to be one of the lords of the clan. The old man bore no ill-will towards Okonkwo. Indeed he respected him for his industry and success. But he was struck, as most people were, by Okonkwo's brusqueness in dealing with less successful men. Only a week ago a man had contradicted him at a kindred meeting which was held to discuss the next ancestral feast. Without looking at the man Okonkwo had said, "This meeting is for men." The man who had contradicted him had no titles. That was why he had called him a woman. Okonkwo knew how to kill a man's spirit.[14]

This intolerance of failure and contempt for lesser men marks his dealings with his own father, a behavior which men in Umuofia find unnatural. His father's words and long talks are a trial to his patience. It is his father's failure that pushes him demoniacally to his great heights:

> But he threw himself into it like one possessed. And indeed he was possessed by the fear of his father's contemptible life and shameful death.[15]

The fear of failure drives him to tempestuous deeds, "the fear of failure and of weakness, fear of himself lest he should be found to resemble his father." This fear extends back into his childhood when a playmate called his father *"agbada,"* a word meaning not only woman but also used for someone who had taken no title. His hatred of everything his father loved, gentleness and idleness, informs his heavy-handed dealing with his own household, with his son, Nwoye. It explains his inability to refrain from bearing a hand in the ritual murder of Ikemefuna, the boy-hostage who lives in his household and has come to call him "father" and to look upon him as such.

The headiness of his early success leads him to a series of offenses against the Earth Goddess, Ani, and provides the impetus for his ultimate exile. During the Week of Peace, the week ordained by the forefathers of the clan for cleansing, prayer, and the banning of any display of anger under whatever provocation, Okonkwo beats his youngest wife, Ojiugo, for neglecting her household chores to go and have her hair plaited. While he is beating her, his two other wives in utter alarm plead with him that it is the sacred week. And Achebe, in a cool ironic way which belies the mounting conflict between Okonkwo and his *chi*, writes:

> But Okonkwo was not the man to stop beating somebody half-way through not even for a fear of a goddess.[16]

The following day Ezeani, the priest of the Earth Goddess, appears at his door with his sacred staff:

> "The evil you have done," he says, "can ruin the whole clan. The Earth Goddess whom you have insulted may refuse to give us her increase and we shall all perish."[17]

Okonkwo pays the traditional fine and is inwardly repentant. But he exhibits an external pride that indicates to his neighbors that he doesn't care:

> He was not the man to go about telling his neighbors that he was in error. And so people said that he had no respect for the gods of the clan. His enemies said his good fortune had gone to his head. They called him the little bird *nza* who so far forgot himself after a heavy meal that he challenged his *chi*.[18]

The contest between Okonkwo and his *chi* seems to be based not only on his neighbors' opinions of him, but also of Okonkwo's own readiness to forfeit the goodwill of the same gods in whose names he is eager to commit murder and to bear arms.

Okonkwo's forced flight into exile is in payment for the female, or accidental, crime of desecration he commits again against the Earth Goddess, Ani, when at the funeral of a clansman his gun kills the son of the deceased. But it can be suggested that perhaps by the very nature of his character, Okonkwo was trying to overreach himself in the public display that accompanies the firing of cannons and guns to salute the dead. So at the height of his achievements and on the verge of achieving greater glories, the gods single him out for humiliation and destruction. His *chi* certainly lends a hand and by this time has turned against him. Exile means that his ambition of becoming one of the great lords of the clan is curtailed:

> That had been his life spring. And he had all but achieved it. Then everything had been broken. He had been cast out of his clan like a fish on to a dry, sandy beach, panting. Clearly his personal god or *chi* was not made for great things. A man could not rise beyond the destiny of his *chi*. The saying of the elders was not true—that if a man said yea his *chi* also affirmed. Here was a man whose *chi* said nay to his own affirmation.[19]

This passage emphasizes the individuality of the *chi*, operating outside the orbit of its owner. It also links the owner closely with destiny, an independent force that determines man's fate. At best benevolent, it yet can become capricious and malevolent. It operates like *hubris* in Greek tragedy, leading its unsuspecting ally or owner on to a certain doom. There is an insistence in Igbo ontology upon a strong bond of harmony between the individual and his *chi* which is maintained through humility. It enables the *chi* to look out for its owner and protect him from mishap, as was the case of those women of Abame in the novel whose *chi* were wide awake and brought them out of the market when the soldiers opened fire on the market in retaliation for the killing of the white missionary. Okonkwo achieves a measure of success even in exile thanks to the benevolence of his mother's people (whom he held in a mild contempt). His yam farms prosper.

> As the years of exile passed one by one it seemed to him that his *chi* might now be making amends for the past disaster.[20]

Okonkwo, believing that his spate of ill luck is ended and his *chi* has assumed a more benevolent posture, begins to plan a great return to his fatherland:

> He would rebuild his compound, on a more magnificent scale. He would build a bigger barn than he had before, and he would build huts for his two new wives. Then he would show his wealth by initiating his sons into the *ozo* society. Only the really great men in the clan were able to do this. Okonkwo saw clearly the high esteem in which he would be held, and he saw himself taking the highest title in the land.[21]

The reversal he suffers through the episode of his own son, Nwoye, fleeing to join the swelling ranks of the Christians is to be repaired by this triumphant return.

But his exile period is also a period of great change in his village, Umuofia. It is as if the gods have conspired to have him removed from the scene while great and disastrous changes are being wrought in the land. The greatest change is brought about by the Christian Church which has led many astray:

> Not only the low-born and the outcast but sometimes a worthy man had joined it.[22]

Apart from the Church, there also comes a government armed with a court of law and policemen, between whom and the people of Umuofia a great enmity develops. The changes are deep and traumatic, hitting at the very existence of the way of life of the people. The suffering that these changes engender through the overthrow of their legal system based on age-old concepts of right and wrong, principles of justice, and customs about land tenure, the brutality that the new dispensation visits upon them at the slightest provocation, these compound the deep agony that grips Okonkwo when he hears about these things in exile. Yet he believes that there is still an avenue of amelioration and for restoring things, once he returns home in triumph among his people. He suspects that the clan has lost its fiber, its moral and physical backbone, that the older people have abdicated their traditional responsibilities.

When he arrives home, his return, which he had dreamed of in exile as a triumphant one, is hardly noticed by anyone because of the tremendous changes that have taken place in Umuofia's life.

> The clan had undergone such profound change during his exile that it was barely recognizable. The new religion and government and the trading stores were very much in the people's eyes and minds.[23]

The splash he had planned to make does not materialize because on top of these dramatic changes, it is the wrong year to initiate his two sons into the *ozo* society. In the face of these disasters, Okonkwo is gripped by grief:

> And it was not just a personal grief. He mourned for the clan, which he saw breaking up and falling apart, and he mourned for the warlike men of Umuofia who had so unaccountably become soft like women.[24]

This grief, signifying tragic resignation, feeds his waking days until the final catastrophe. When the convert Enoch unmasks an *egwugwu* in public, thus heaping abomination upon the desecrations caused by the Christians and their way of life, Okonkwo comes to life briefly. Then follows that terrible night when all the masked ancestral spirits of Umuofia assemble in the market place and carry out their swift and terrible retribution against Enoch and proceed against the church which they reduce to ashes. This is intended to represent the final symbolic manifestation of Umuofia's traditional valor. For Okonkwo it is a time of elation.

> The clan which had turned false on him appeared to be making amends. . . . Okonkwo was almost happy again.[25]

The arrest and humiliation of the six elders, including Okonkwo,

by the British administration exemplifies the relentless nature of
the fate that has overtaken Umuofia. Okonkwo's compound, the
symbol of his authority as a clan elder and the head of a large
household, once bustling with activity and full life, is now deserted.
His *chi,* it seems, has finally decided to desert him. But the divinity
reserves the final act of betrayal for the end. At the gathering of
the clan, after they have ransomed the six elders, to plan their next
line of action, the District Commissioner sends his hated messengers
to break up the meeting. In a terse dramatic moment, Achebe
creates a powerful scene in which his hero's fate is sealed:

> In a flash Okonkwo drew his machete. The messenger crouched to
> avoid the blow. It was useless. Okonkwo's machete descended twice
> and the man's head lay beside his uniformed body. . . . He knew
> that Umuofia would not go to war. . . . He wiped his machete on
> the sand and went away.[26]

He goes and hangs himself, committing the final act of abomination and defiance against the gods, in particular the Earth Goddess,
Ani, to whom suicide is a desecration. A man who commits suicide
cannot be buried by his clansmen.

Achebe is perhaps the first writer from Africa to use a significant
African philosophical principle as the chief determinant in the
construction of a novel. The theme of a man alone, dogged by
jealous fate and baited by unreliable gods, is not a new one. But
in *Things Fall Apart,* its derivatives are based in Igbo philosophy.
It becomes the concept around which every other image in the
novel centers. The most persistent image is that of the wrestler.
Okonkwo is the great wrestler who throws Amalinze in a fight
which the old men agree was one of the fiercest since the founder
of their town threw a spirit of the wild for seven days and seven
nights. This is extended into Okonkwo's contest with his *chi;* he
was the little bird, *nza,* who challenged his *chi* to a match after a
heavy meal. It is the last contest, which he is destined to lose, like
the great wrestler who, after having defeated all men, went into the
spirit world and was confronted with a small wiry spirit who
smashed him on the stony earth.

In order to buttress this theme, Achebe creates a style and language which derive almost entirely from the Igbo world, from its

rhythm of speech. Through the use of proverbs, he creates a style that harmonizes with the processional development of his tragic theme. Most of these proverbs are concerned with achieved status, an aspect of the *chi* concept amply illustrated in Chukwukere's essay, cited above: "The sun will shine on those who stand, before it shines on those who kneel under them." "If a child washed his hands, he could eat with kings." "A man who pays respect to the great paves the way for his own greatness." "The lizard who jumped from the high iroko tree to the ground said he would praise himself if no one else did." "You can tell a ripe corn by its look." "I cannot stand on the bank of the river and wash my hands with spittle." "As a man danced, so the drums were beaten for him." These are samples of proverbs that are woven into the fabric of Achebe's story. They point up the significant aspects of the novel, those that deal with the Igbo value system, status, and achievement and the role of each individual being's life, the expression of harmony or disharmony between him and the gods and in particular as it reflects the disposition of his personal deity, mission, or destiny in this world.

Achebe's second novel, *No Longer at Ease,* represents a historical jump into near-contemporary times. Set in the mid-1950s, it tells the story of Okonkwo's grandson, Obi, educated in England and newly returned to a top civil service post. It dramatizes the conflict between the old world of Umuofia, its traditions and outlook, and the European world represented by the urban societies of cities like Lagos, Accra, or Nairobi. The conflict of cultures has always been a fascinating subject to most African writers, dramatizing the move of agrarian societies and cultures into the world of cities, industries, machines, and the attendant overthrow of the systems of values and mores that animated the older world. The dramatic collapse of the old world of Umuofia had already been presented in all its tragic grandeur in *Things Fall Apart.* In *No Longer at Ease* Achebe attempts to present the warring passions of both worlds, how they both conspire to break their unsure products. The ascendance of imported European materialism (materialism was also a significant feature of the African political system, contrary to what many may believe, but kept in check by the spiritual demands of the religious order) over the African conception of balance between materialism and spirituality becomes the most significant thematic concern in his subsequent books. Did things actually fall apart and the center just not hold? There was confusion and despair. But the old society survived, for survival is its central outlook. There is despair and alienation however. The new generation of Africans, like Obi Okonkwo, is caught between the anvil and the hammer and is being forged into a new, complex, and incomprehensible instrument. The gods themselves seemed to have abdicated, overwhelmed by the odds marshaled against them. They seemed to have abandoned their responsibilities and taken flight.

The burden of Achebe's argument in *No Longer at Ease* is that Obi Okonkwo, a product of the contact between Europe and Africa, lacks the moral rectitude and the austere dignity of his grandfather. His world is one of confused values and of unrealizable ideals struggling in a frightening jungle of a new material culture. Obi, as a result, is vacillating, weak, and lacking any moral center whatsoever. The great resolves of his early days after his return from Britain, his idealistic desire to fight the corroding powers of bribery and corruption in the Nigerian Civil Service, his determination to marry Clara, the girl he loves, against the dictates of a rigid Igbo code that defines her as an untouchable, all collapse when he comes face to face with the crippling demands and ambiguities of his situation as a *déraciné*. For he must yet respect the laws of his older society, as an African holding a European post, a member of a new club whose greetings to one another is "How is the car behaving?"—a man, in short, beset by the basic need to just survive in a world determined by new economic laws that were not his making; he must respond to new values. Unlike his grandfather, he does not attempt to challenge his *chi* to contest; he even lacks the will power to do this.

The novel mirrors two worlds. One, European-oriented, confused, and unsure of its direction, yet brazenly new and arrogant, the world of Lagos, the night clubs, and the British Council. The second world, the world of the village, changed by the Christian Church and the new mercantilism, yet clinging tenaciously to its own beaten path. In writing about the latter, Achebe uses a style that echoes the language of *Things Fall Apart*. Proverbs, wise say-

ings, similes, and metaphors drawn from nature still form a significant aspect of conversation. But the total purity of language
heard in the mouths of old Umuofia in *Things Fall Apart* is missing.
Instead, there are echoes of the Bible, as heard in the speech of
Obi's father, Isaac Okonkwo, the Nwoye of *Things Fall Apart*. The
villagers, too, have changed their tune as the elder Odogwu says
when introducing Obi, newly returned from England, at a wel-
coming feast held for him:

> Titles are no longer great, neither are barns or large numbers of wives
> and children. Greatness is now in the things of the white man. And
> so we too have changed our tune. We are the first in all the nine
> villages to send our son to the white man's land.[27]

As Odogwu proceeds, reeling off proverb after proverb, the most
recurrent sentence in his speech is: "As it was in the beginning, so
it will be in the end." When Isaac Okonkwo, the catechist father
and a first-generation Christian convert, hears that his son intends
to marry an *osu*, an outcast, his speech is a combination of Christian imagery and Igbo idiom. Speaking of Clara's father, Josiah
Okeke, he says:

> I know him and I know his wife. He is a good man and a great
> Christian. But he is *osu*. Naaman, captain of the host of Syria, was
> a great man and honorable, he was also a mighty man of valor, but
> he was a leper.[28]

Mr. Ikedi, another elder, at the ceremony to mark Obi's departure
for England, makes a long speech which illustrates the conjunc-
tion of the two worlds, even though one, the African, dominates in
its love of the long speech and colorful imagery. Turning to a young
man on his right, he says:

> In times past, Umuofia would have required of you to fight in her
> wars and bring home human heads. But those were days of darkness
> from which we have been delivered by the blood of the lamb of God.
> . . . We are sending you to learn book. Enjoyment can wait. Do
> not be in a hurry to rush into the pleasures of the world like the
> young antelope who danced herself lame when the main dance was
> yet to come.[29]

But the theme of tragedy of the type that Obi suffers does not lend

itself to the treatment that characterized *Things Fall Apart*. However, the same bitter ironic tone is here. Achebe is too much
involved in the character of Obi to be able to achieve that dispas-
sionate grandeur that marks his first hero. One senses the author's
restlessness with Obi, his desire to abandon him for more noble
and austere subjects. This is exactly what Achebe does in *Arrow
of God*. The dramatization of the conflict between the old and new
society and their value systems is too easy; it denies Achebe his
aim of presenting the great integrity of the past.

Arrow of God, Achebe's third novel, is set in a period about
twenty years after the period which *Things Fall Apart* deals with.
The fact that Achebe returns to this period of an integrated African world reveals his primary fascination with the destiny of his
ancestors. The result is his most controlled and balanced work
artistically. The period the novel deals with is the era in which the
lineaments of colonialism were settling. The British Empire has
long been a fact of history. The confrontation between Europe
and Africa in the previous generation was brutal. *Things Fall
Apart* dealt only with the *action* of this confrontation. There
seemed to be no men of contemplative thinking in the African
world. Obierika, Okonkwo's close friend, even though a thinker,
like all his contemporaries was too closely affected by the tragic
nature of this confrontation to be able to achieve a self-withdrawal
necessary for thought. The weight of the sorrow was too great to
grant the protagonists and combatants any respite. But Achebe
was aware that it is to those men of accommodation and compromise that Africa owed her present condition, men who, faced with
the inevitability of change, were ready and willing to deal with it.
These thinkers were the real heroes of the African past. Those
who remained pure and firm of heart in the earlier world, those
who refused to bend to the revolutionary tide, like Okonkwo, were
broken like reeds and cast aside. In *Arrow of God* the traditional
intellectual hero assumes his proper place in the tempo of events.
Besides, Achebe felt that he must dramatize the inner conflicts that
tear at the very heart of traditional Africa itself; the rivalries between men, clans, villages, and even gods provide another point of
conflict that was by itself independent of and yet affected by the
external factor. At a more sophisticated level, *Arrow of God* is the

story of man's relationship with his god, the agony of the priest who interprets his own vengeful will as that of his deity and is destroyed in the process.

The same rhythms are here. The organization of the society retains a remarkable closeness to that depicted in *Things Fall Apart*. But the European presence is a cruel reality. We witness this in the British intervention in the war between Umuaro and Okperi. Winterbottom, the district officer in the area, descends upon the "malcontents" and breaks all their guns on his powerful knees.

Ezeulu, the chief priest of Ulu, the guardian deity of all the villages of Umuaro, is a man of pride and of truth. He took the side of the enemy and gave evidence against his own village in the firm belief that Ulu does not fight a war of blame. For this he earns the animosity of a section of the village led by the Izidemili, the priest of Idemili, the python god who has lost his seniority since the founding of Ulu. But Ezeulu is also a lonely man, like all proud men. Aristocratic in his principles and personality, he has little patience for lesser men. Aloof and overbearing, he is capable of smoldering anger that blazes like a forest fire. Half man, half spirit, he has come to believe in the strength of his divine authority. In the end he appropriates for himself the attributes of his deity.

Set against Ezeulu are the European district officers led by Mr. Winterbottom, an old colonial type who claims knowledge of the customs of the people; his deputy, Mr. Clarke, a young man fresh from Oxford who has had the call to serve in the wilds of Africa; and Mr. Wright, the whip-swinging, sadistic road engineer who institutes forced labor in the belief that the roads were being built for the good of the "bloody" Africans anyway.

Ezeulu is caught between two sets of incomprehensibilities and resentments. His pride is unbending. Winterbottom, knowing that he is a man of honor, sends for him in order to confer the title of warrant chief on him in fulfillment of Lord Lugard's indirect rule policy. Ezeulu contemptuously rejects the offer. And for making a fool of the empire, he is clapped into jail by Clarke who is deputizing for Winterbottom. The period he spends in jail prevents him from eating the sacred yams that will signify the time to bring in the harvest. He decides to punish his people for neglecting him at the time he was put into jail. He insists on following the cycle of new moons, after having missed two, until he has eaten all the sacred yams. Meanwhile, the harvest is rotting in the earth, and famine hits the land. During the contest of wills between Ezeulu and his people, his favorite son, the handsome and palm-wine-addicted Obika, dies after running a terrific race of the death mask. When the book closes, Ezeulu is on the verge of losing his mind. He is seen holding a broom trying to sweep the compound, a task reserved for women. He is led away into his hut.

The central theme in this novel is one of the priest of a shrine and his relationship with his god and people. The most significant concept here, which is entirely African-derived, is that of the priest, the man who by his divine office stands between man and the deity. Ezeulu believes rightly that he is the instrument of Ulu's divine power. The duties of the priest in African religions, John Mbiti, the Ugandan scholar and African theologian, writes,

> . . . are mainly making sacrifices, offerings, and prayers, conducting both public and private rites and ceremonies, giving advice, performing judicial functions in some societies . . . caring for the temples and shrines . . . and above all fulfilling their office as religious intermediaries between men and God.[30]

All studies of the priest and his function in African societies reveal his role as spiritual leader, intermediary between men and the deity, and, above all, divine spokesman and bearer of all the people's spiritual burdens. It is he who undergoes cleansings, fasts, purifications, and self-denials; he maintains a state of spiritual purity on behalf of the people. He is in close contact with the deity and maintains a rigid regimen of spiritual preparedness that enables him to transmit the deity's will to his people. His ministration is required at all stages of man's rites of passage. His training as a priest is in many societies very rigid and may last for years. His personality, at the height of his priestly powers, becomes defined in terms of the very attributes of the god he serves. There are minor priests as there are minor gods.

In the particular sense in which the priest is at the center of the spiritual life of the community, he is more of an intellectual, a man of contemplation rather than of action. He is also a man alone:

> He was used to loneliness. As Chief Priest he had always walked
> along in front of Umuaro. But without looking back he had always
> been able to hear their flute and song that shook the earth because
> it came from a multitude of voices and stamping of countless feet.[31]

One of the most persistent images that runs through *Arrow of God*
and what gives it its title is the principle of the priest being the
"arrow of God." At the point when, after his return from jail,
Ezeulu contemplates the problem of the two wasted moons and
the question of the New Yam, Ulu interrupts his thought:

> "Ta! Nwanu!" barked Ulu in his ear, as a spirit would in the ear
> of the impertinent human child. "Who told you that this was your
> own fight?" Ezeulu trembled and said nothing. "I say who told you
> this was your own fight which you could arrange to suit you? . . .
> Beware you do not come between me and my victim or you may
> receive blows not meant for you. Do you not know when two ele-
> phants fight? . . . Go home and sleep and leave me to settle my
> quarrel with Idemili. . . ." After that there was no more to be said.
> Who was Ezeulu to tell his deity how to fight the jealous cult of the
> sacred python. It was a fight of the gods. He was no more than an
> arrow in the bow of his god.[32]

His role as the "arrow of God" imposes upon him the heavy burden
of the decision to eat or not to eat the sacred yams. At no time
does he see himself as separate from his god. Five years after someone threatens, during the war with Okperi, to unseat Ulu if he fails
to fight in their war of blame, Ezeulu says: "We are still waiting,
Ulu and I, for that beast to unseat us." This close relationship enables him to hear his voice. His friend Akuebue stresses this link
between men and god:

> "I am your friend," Akuebue said, "and I can talk to you as I like;
> but that does not mean I forget that one half of you is man and the
> other half is spirit."[33]

Being the "arrow in the bow of his god," half man, half spirit,
Ezeulu is also the carrier of the god's truth, the man, like the traditional scapegoat, who bears all the sins of the people and undergoes purification and cleansing in order to avert disaster. In

intimate contact with his god whose very essence he shares, he is in position to prescribe sacrifices for those who seek succor in the shrine of Ulu.

One of the important functions of the priest-medium in most African societies is the running of the sacred race, a duty that vividly underscores the scapegoat concept and at the same time emphasizes the priest's divine role and his sharing of the essence of his god. The priest's apparent immunity to the severe visceral angers of his god is revealed in this race. It also symbolizes his struggle on behalf of his deity against malevolent forces that are bent on undermining the god's benevolent work and place in the community. The priest maintains an eternal spiritual state, a condition of purity at all times, which enables him to receive and transmit regular messages and interpretations of events past, present, and future. This spiritual state expresses his readiness to be "used" by the god; induction into states of trance, of somnolent suspension, of spiritual dying in order to be reborn with knowledge and affirmation of the god's purpose for man, emphasizes the bearer or carrier concept. In essence, the priest, even though the supervisory agent in divine affairs, is the one who makes himself available for the symbolic sacrifices that are demanded regularly by the deity. On the occasion of the great festivals, the priest's spiritual role is the carrier, the bearer of terrible truths. Publicly, on behalf of the people, he bears the sacrifice and undergoes the purification and the vigorous prayers and runs the symbolic race.

One of the most dramatic realizations of Ezeulu's central function as a priest achieved in *Arrow of God* is in the Festival of the First Pumpkin Leaves. The town crier has announced the appointed day, and the whole village has assembled on the Nkwo market day:

> Soon after, the great Ikolo sounded. It called the six villages of Umuaro one by one in their ancient order: Umunneora, Umuagu, Ummezeani, Umuogwugwu, Umuisiuzo, and Umuachala. As it called each village, an enormous shout went up in the market place. People began to hurry through their drinking before the arrival of the Chief Priest.[34]

To the background of the throbbing Ikolo, the ancient drum in the

hands of the master drummer, Obiozo Ezikolo, Umuaro gathered
for the festivals. Heralded by the *ogene,* Ezeulu enters the market:

> The left half of his body—from forehead to toes—was painted with
> white chalk. Around his head was a leather band from which an
> eagle's feather pointed backwards. On his right hand he carried Nne
> Ofo, the mother of all staffs of authority in Umuaro, and in his left
> he held a long iron staff which kept a quivering rattle whenever he
> struck its pointed end into the earth. He took a few long strides, paus-
> ing on each foot. Then he ran forward again as though he had seen
> a comrade in vacant air; he stretched his arm, and waved his staff
> to the right and to the left. And those who were near enough heard
> the knocking together of Ezeulu's staff and another which no one
> saw. At this, many fled in terror before the priest and the unseen
> presences around him.[35]

On an occasion like this, there is no longer any doubt in his mind
about his own divinity. His power transcends that of the "child
over a goat that was said to be his." Then he proceeds to reenact
the first coming of Ulu, "and how each of the Four Days put
obstacles in his way." The processional journey retells the first
rites of Ulu, as the deity first makes his epiphany, and the establishment of the power of his priest. Miracles take place. Obstacles give
way. Days recede before the terrible power of Ulu:

> I passed, and the sun came down and beat me and the rain came
> down and drenched me. Then I met Nkwo. I looked on his left and
> saw an old woman, tired, dancing strange steps on the hill. I looked
> to the right and saw a horse and saw a ram. I slew the horse and
> with the ram I cleaned my machete, and so removed that evil.[36]

Before the prayers offered by Ugoye, Ezeulu breaks into his ritual
race.

> The Ikolo drum worked itself into a frenzy during the Chief Priest's
> flight especially its final stages when he, having completed the full
> circle of the market place, ran on with increasing speed into the sanc-
> tuary of his shrine, his messengers at his heels. . . . The mounting
> tension which had gripped the entire market place and seemed to send
> its breath going up, up, and up exploded with this last beat of the
> drum and released a vast and deep breathing down. But the moment
> of relief was very short-lived. The crowd seemed to rouse itself

quickly to the knowledge that the Chief Priest was safe in his shrine, triumphant over the sins of Umuaro which he was now burying deep into the earth with the six bunches of leaves.[37]

The sustaining theme of *Arrow of God* is this remarkable dramatization of the role of the priest and his relationship with his community and with his god. By making this the central theme, Achebe was able to centralize the theological arguments that emerge in an African religious situation which outsiders may think is devoid of intellectual debate. Ezeulu's position, Achebe attempts to point out, is made difficult and confused not only by his confrontation with the European protagonists of the novel, but largely by the internal debate that rages around him and his role as the arrow of the guardian deity Ulu. When at the end, believing that he is interpreting the will of Ulu, he refuses to eat the two remaining sacred yams and thus unleashes famine upon the land, Ezeulu is pursuing his spiritual function to its logical conclusion. For the harvest is no longer Ulu's. The Christian Church opens its doors and blesses the harvest: "Thereafter, any yam harvested in the man's field was harvested in the name of the Son."

To the people of Umuaro, Ulu had clearly decided. Ezeulu's favorite son, Obika, collapses and dies while carrying the *ogbazulobodo* in the ritual race for a dead elder. The blow was terrible and decisive:

> Why, he asked himself again and again, why had Ulu chosen to deal thus with him, to strike him down and cover him with mud? What was his offense? Had he not divined the god's will and obeyed it? When was it ever heard that a child was scalded by the piece of yam its own mother put in his palm. . . . But today such a thing has happened before the eyes of all. What could it point to but the collapse and ruin of all things. Then a god, finding himself powerless, might take to his heels.[38]

Achebe alludes to the *chi* concept in this novel too, though he does not make it the main determinant in the denouement of the tragedy. The emphasis here is on the spiritual powers of the priest confronted with the will and power of his own god, who it seems is ready to strike him down. Ezeulu's pride and intellectual hauteur impose a loneliness upon him which he, being half man, half spirit, believes provides him with an instrument of understanding and expressing *in toto* his god's will. His existential awareness of himself as a man apart, even though enabling him to achieve a tragic grandeur in splendid isolation, creates barriers between him and other men: as a man he was unbending and proud; as a spirit he was inadequate.

As in *Things Fall Apart,* Achebe builds up the drama of this austere tragedy by a wonderful adherence to Igbo idiom and speech pattern which permeate every aspect of the traditional life he describes. Proverbs, metaphors, and idioms drawn directly from the Igbo world give the style the same freshness that was exhibited in *Things Fall Apart.* When Obika carries *ogbazulobodo,* the language in which Achebe reproduces his incantatory speech is a close reproduction of Igbo speech:

> The fly that struts around on a mound of excrement wastes his time; the mound will always be greater than the fly. The thing that beats the drum for *ngwesi* is inside the ground. Darkness is so great it gives horns to a dog. He who built a homestead before another can boast more broken pots. It is *afo* that gives rain-water power to cut dry earth. The man who walks ahead of his fellows spots spirits on the way. Bat said he knew his ugliness and chose to fly by night. When the air is fouled by a man on top of a palm tree the fly is confused. An ill-fated man drinks water and it catches in his teeth.[39]

This language illustrates, in translation, the Igbo dependence on allusion, symbolism, and colorful imagery and, above all, on proverbs in ordinary speech and in invocatory prayer and incantation accompanying protective magic. It also illustrates the poetry of self-praise and boast and a certain predilection for extravagant speech and exaggeration. There are also a number of central proverbs used to dramatize significant aspects of the novel. When Ezeulu is invited by his "friend" Winterbottom, his arch enemy, Nwaka, urging him to go, says:

> Did not our elders tell us that as soon as we shake hands with a leper he will want an embrace?[40]

On describing Ezeulu's predicament, he adds:

> A man who brings ant-ridden faggots into his hut should expect the visit of lizards.[41]

Arrow of God is decidedly Achebe's most balanced and finished novel. The theme of conflict between two cultures is not here exploited per se. Around this theme, however, and operating at a more dramatic level is the theme of man and god. This theme, as indicated, is borrowed entirely from the African theological thinking. The Europeans are also instruments in the hands of the gods; each moment of Ezeulu's confrontation with his enemies, his friends, and his god breathes the authenticity of that history and that past whose dignity Achebe has promised to restore. But as an artist, he goes beyond the mere restoration, creating a story of tragic grandeur, based firmly in a culture and owing its strength to the re-creation of the very idiom and language of that culture.

Achebe's latest novel, *A Man of the People,* owes very little to any theme or principle derived wholly or in part from his African world. It is the story of African decline, the collapse of those dreams raised by the dawn of independence. What marks it is its satirical quality, its journalistic accuracy, and its peculiarly restless inability or refusal to confront the heart of the political malaise by creating an almost hopeless political situation and a group of naïve leftists who mistake their own self-interest for political motivation. *A Man of the People* is a modern novel that points to the larger questions of the future, especially as it deals with the theme of political growth and direction. It points to the future both in theme and style more than any of the earlier novels, with the exception of *No Longer at Ease* with which it shares a common ground. More realistic, it ushers the reader into the contemporary African predicament. The dismal world of the abortionist clinic and jail evidenced in *No Longer at Ease* decays further into a world in which traditional public virtues are replaced by a code of conduct that elevates self-confessed thieves into leading positions in the community. It depicts a world in which corruption and political banditry become the basic principles of survival.

Chinua Achebe is perhaps the most influential novelist to have come out of Africa since the late 1950s. Unlike Amos Tutuola, his work, which shows his firm grasp of the structure of the novel, creates new directions for younger writers to follow. In fact, his style and thematic preoccupation have inspired a whole new school of writers who may be referred to as the "clash of cultures" novelists. The novelty of his work lies in his use of African themes, in the creation of an African past, dignified yet unromantic, and in his fresh Igbo-derived English style. His success as a novelist is owed largely to these innovative approaches. No doubt, as is obvious from the novels, Achebe's teachers were Joseph Conrad, Graham Greene, Joyce Cary, and E. M. Forster—all masters of the colonial novel. He obviously learned a great deal from Thomas Hardy's naturalism and overwhelming sense of tragedy. His debt to his own traditions and culture, however, seems to be the principal point of his creative departure as a writer. As a man who set out to redress the balance and tell the African side of the story, he has done more than a propagandist's hack job. He created a new novel that possesses its own autonomy and transcends the limits set by both his African and European teachers.

15

James Ngugi, Ferdinand Oyono, and the anticolonial novel

James Ngugi (Ngugi wa Thiong'o) almost single-handedly has carried the burden of contemporary East African writing in the area of the novel. Born in 1938 in Kenya, he grew up in the deep shadow of the gathering storm of the revolt that the world came to know as "Mau Mau." His education was interrupted. But in spite of these impediments, he attended Makerere University in Kampala, Uganda, where he obtained a degree in English, and later on received a master's degree at the University of Leeds in England. With three novels to date to his credit, Ngugi has also published plays and numerous short stories. His novels, *Weep Not, Child, The River Between,* and *A Grain of Wheat,* established him as the foremost East African writer whose work constitutes an important part of the literary renaissance in East Africa.

Ngugi's novelistic preoccupation is the question of political power and the movement of history as the essential comment on the use of this power. But it seems his greatest fictive symbol is the land. In political conception, land forms the most solid source of power, and its alienation is the basic cause of political conflict. Land ownership is the source of conflict in East, Central, and South Africa in the convulsive relationship of white European settlers and the African peoples. Kenya became the center of this conflict at the turn of the century, with the British colonial policy that established the so-called "white highlands" in the heart of Gikuyu country.

By 1900 and during the first decades of this one, large tracts of Gikuyu land in Kenya were set aside for white settlement. It was an extension of policies already successfully tested in southern Africa, particularly in South Africa and the Rhodesias. The white settlers in Kenya took the most fertile land away from a group whose population was increasing and depended on land and agriculture for its survival. Large armies of landless men were forced to sell their labor to white farmers on their own ancestral land which had been appropriated by law. The white settler element also slowly entrenched itself politically through devious deals concluded with the metropolitan government. Thus about sixty thousand Europeans became the holders of political power in Kenya, while about seven million Africans including the Gikuyus had every single aspect of their political aspirations thwarted, frustrated, and ignored. The Africans existed only to serve the European's economic program of exploitation. Political frustration, genuine land hunger, the immediate discomfiture resulting from the Second World War, in which many Kenyans served, in Burma and the Far East, all led to the beginnings of revolt. Organizations such as the militant Gikuyu Central Association, organized by Harry Thuku in 1923, gave way to the Kenya African Union in 1945, in which old Gikuyu Central Association stalwarts like Jomo Kenyatta became the most articulate spokesmen. This later became the Kenya African National Union, the main ruling political party of Kenya today.

One of the most significant factors in the so-called Mau Mau revolt was the African's conception of land. Land was not merely an economic commodity, it was, more importantly, a sacred entity. The earth represents in most African myths the mother principle which is central to the survival and continuity of the group. That is why land is still communally held in most parts of Africa and not regarded as a commodity that can be parceled out and sold at will. In the pantheon of African gods, the Earth Goddess is an important benevolent spirit upon whom man depends for food and sustenance and to whom he returns at death. Her sanctity as the natural principle is recognized in a number of taboos and abominations which cannot be committed against her. The sanctity of the earth is recognized in ceremonies that mark the clearing of virgin forests for farming and the preparation of new plots for building. Land, thus, is the center of the community's life. The numerous first-fruits ceremonies constitute homage to the Earth Goddess, who blesses crops and yields the abundance of her bosom for her children. All human beings, the African believes, are all children of the earth; but the earth of our native soil, of our village or town, becomes the bond of the community's cohesiveness. It is for this we fight when strangers want to dislodge us. It is the place where our umbilical cord is buried, and our link stretches through her to our ancestors who were buried in her womb. It is this great sacred force that was behind the Gikuyu uprising. It informed every fierce act of heroism and bravado.

Weep Not, Child is the story of the era preceding the revolt. It is the story of Ngugi's own youth, of his growing up in a world that was changing very fast, whose older values were being replaced by others from Europe. It depicts a world of violence—both physical and psychological. It dramatizes the division that Europe through Christianity visited upon the people. The society depicted in the novel is divided by group fears and the excesses of the colonial conquest, as well as geographically.

> The plain, more or less rectangular in shape, had four valleys leading into or out of it at the corners. The first two valleys went into the Country of the Black People. The other two divided the land of the Black People from the land of the White People.[1]

Between the divided Africans and the Europeans were the Indians. Within the theme of African unrest and frustration is worked the subtheme centered upon Njoroge, the hero, his growth and development from boyhood into manhood. The ways of the people are being forged into new molds; for Njoroge, education is the key to a better life.

The symbol of the land dominates every phase of the novel. It is the land which Murungu at the dawn of Creation gave to the first parents of the Gikuyu people, Gikuyu and Mumbi:

> This land I hand over to you, O Man and Woman
> It's yours to rule and till in serenity sacrificing
> Only to me, your God, under my sacred tree. . . .[2]

The novel presents the tensions and the anguish of the dispossession in the dreams of Ngotho, Njoroge's father, who like thousands of other Africans is forced to become a squatter on the land of his ancestors. Old now, he waits for the fulfillment of the prophecy of Mugo wa Kibiro, the great Gikuyu seer, which foretold the departure of the Europeans. There is a religious fervor with which the old Gikuyu people saw the regaining of the land as their deliverance from Egypt and the arrival in Canaan. But it is Boro, Ngotho's restless son and Njoroge's brother, who fought in Burma, who carries the fire of that coming redemption. It is his alienation that creates the Land Freedom Army. Ngotho belongs to the older generation, impotent, humble, suffering in pain and withdrawal, given to dreams, while Boro carries the impatience and the restlessness of the new generation that will set the land ablaze with the revolution and fire its first shots.

Drawn sharply against Ngotho is Mr. Howlands, the British farmer who had escaped a Europe ravaged by war to seek both an Eldorado and a Shangri-La in the wilds of Africa. For him, too, the conquest of the "jungles" of Africa, the taming of its earth, was a dream and later a challenge in which he invests his whole heart and soul, believing, too, in the continuity of his line long after him to carry on the heroic struggle. For him there is no other realization except conquest and victory over this land. He cannot comprehend that the bond between the old African farmer in his pay and the soil which he tends with such loving care goes beyond the physical world.

> They went from place to place, a white man and a black man. Now and then they would stop here and there, examine a luxuriant green tea plant, or pull out a weed. Both men admired this *shamba*. For Ngotho felt responsibility for whatever happened to this land. He owed it to the dead, the living and the unborn of his line, to keep guard over this *shamba*. Mr. Howlands always felt a certain amount of victory whenever he walked through it all. They came to a raised piece of ground and stopped. The land sloped gently to rise again into the next ridge and the next.[3]

Their futures, it seems, were intertwined—one, the expatriate colonial conqueror and master taming a wild strange land among strange people; the other, a tenant and a meager wage-earning farmer on his own ancestral land he now tills for a stranger.

In the shadow of the coming storm and mounting tensions, Njoroge, a member of the newest Gikuyu generation, goes to school to seek other horizons. Education becomes the gateway that leads to the recovery of lost lands, a passage through which to escape old conditions. For Ngotho the dreams are forged on the anvil of his own anguish for his sons: Kamau the carpenter's apprentice, Njoroge the schoolboy, and Boro the restless one.

Set against Ngotho is Jacobo, the African with some education, the representative of the native group that identifies itself with the conqueror. He is an object of fear, envy, and intense hatred. It is against him that the revolution will lift its hand first because he has betrayed his blood, his ancestors, and his people. He has brought disaster upon them only in order to satisfy his own greed. He is a man against whom the Earth Goddess herself will raise a hand.

In this gathering storm of tensions, dreams, and fears of the adult world there develops a love bond between Njoroge and Mwihaki, Jacobo's daughter. Meanwhile, the political restlessness deepens as the prophecy of Mugo is re-examined and placed again before the people by orators such as Kiarie.

Ngugi divides the book into two parts, "Waning Light" and "Darkness Falls," providing an interlude between them which marks a lyrically powerful twilight period in which all the events are cast, and introduces the explosion through a poetic, dramatic, narrative style.

In the meantime, the messiah has arrived in the person of Jomo Kenyatta. He is the man of the old prophecy who will lead the people from bondage to the Promised Land:

> Njoroge listened keenly as they talked of Jomo. Already he felt in-timate with this man. For Njoroge was sure that he had read about him in the Old Testament. Moses had led the children of Israel from Misri to the Promised Land. And because black people were really the children of Israel, Moses was no other than Jomo himself.[4]

Kenyatta expresses for the dispossessed the promises of redemption and a great future.

A deep rift develops between Ngotho and his son Boro just as the former's doubts about the movement deepens. He refuses to allow his son to administer the oath to him. To Boro, his father's impotence is more painful than open betrayal.

Fear now stalks the land in the form of repressive laws, curfews, arrests, and death:

> No one could tell when he might be arrested for breaking the curfew. You could not even move across the courtyard at night. . . . It was said that European soldiers were catching people at night and having taken them to the forest would release them and ask them to find their way back home. But when their backs were turned they would be shot dead in cold blood. The next day this would be announced as a victory over Mau Mau.[5]

The white man's religion, essentially an insidious factor in the dispossession, becomes the ironic focus for a group of African Christians who preached against the movement and the coming confrontation. The same Bible that provides the vision of Moses and the redemption also provides eloquent arguments in the mouths of old African converts, catechists, and evangelists against change and rebellion. In religious revivalism and Christian ambiguity, some sought escape from the inevitable conflict.

Njoroge's life as a growing boy, sheltered for a time by school, a period of confidence and security, enters into the center of the storm. The destiny of his family at home is also his. Like thousands of other Kenyan schoolboys, he was dragged out of school for questioning and sometimes imprisonment for concealing knowledge of his father's and brothers' whereabouts. In the climax of the story Kamau is arrested, Boro surrenders after killing Howlands, and the uncertainty of Njoroge's future becomes a tiny comment upon the historical directions and fortunes of the revolution.

Weep Not, Child is a young man's work, presenting a touching record of the brutality that characterized British rule in Kenya. It is a story of dramatic events simply told; Ngugi's greatest influence seems to be the Bible which he uses to weave the tale of a lost people. He draws from it the story of Israel and Moses in Egypt, to which he adds Gikuyu legend and myth. Its major weakness is in the love between Njoroge and Mwihaki, which was perhaps meant to dramatize the rift between their parents and the opposing forces in the land but remains sentimental and mawkish, never becoming a real focus in the denouement of the tragedy of Kenya. The attachment between these two naïve lovers is vague and hazy; their protestations leap straight out of cheap, sentimental women's magazines. Over-all, *Weep Not, Child* suffers from excessive melodrama, childlike heroics—like Boro's confrontation with Howlands, a scene out of a bad Hollywood movie, or Ngotho's death—which destroy the fervor and the promise of the writing. But there is something powerful and forceful in the way Ngugi draws the women, Njeri especially and Nyokabi, Ngotho's two wives, and in the lyrical quality of his prose which escapes now and then from vague Africanism (Patonesque) to strong clear poetry controlled in its fury, leaping to life at moments. But it is essentially a young writer's work, full of false poses, melodrama, and an oversimplification of relations, reflecting an immaturity that dulls the urgency of the theme.

His *The River Between* picks up the story of the first parents, Gikuyu and Mumbi, and here launches us into the life, in modern times, of the hero, Waiyaki, the son of Chege, who has, by the predestined hand of fate, absorbed the spirit of the land and must fulfill the prophecy of the old seer Mugo Kibiro. His father, Chege, "knew the ways of the land and the hidden things of the tribe. He knew the meaning of every ritual and every sign." Waiyaki is the chosen one. But he must go through the initiation rites; he must be born a second time. Already there is a light in his eyes, a power in his voice which bursts through at moments. He believes that he comes from Demi na Mathathi, the giants of the tribe who lived at the beginning of time. At the holy place, he hears his father's voice:

> Arise, heed the prophecy. Go to the mission place. Learn all the secrets of the white man. But do not follow his vices. Be true to your people and to your ancient rites. . . . Learn all the wisdom of the white man. And keep on remembering, salvation shall come from the hills. A man must rise and save the people in their hour of need. He shall show them the way, he shall lead them. . . . A time will come when they shall cry for a saviour.[6]

Waiyaki is assailed by doubts. Was this only an old man's dream? But he has been changed from boy to man in the holy place where he stood with his father. So that the prophecy must be fulfilled, he went to Siriana to the mission school. In another household, the Christian household of Joshua, a girl is going through a period of doubt, a period of self-examination and growth. Muthoni, Joshua's younger daughter, is passing through a spiritual crisis. She wants to be circumcised, but she is a Christian and the Church has preached against the practice. Soon she comes to the end of her doubt. She will run away from home to her aunt at Kameno, and there she will go through the ceremony when the season comes. But her father is a man of God who believes in the salvation of the Gospel of Christ and in the unerring wisdom of the white man. For him the Gikuyu god Murungu is a prince of darkness, and those who serve him serve Satan. To him the rites and ceremonies of his ancestors are things of abomination in the sight of the Lord. When Muthoni dies from an infection following her circumcision, Joshua is openly jubilant about the Christian God's vengeance.

The novel traces a rather tortuous change of fortunes for the hero, Waiyaki, his love for Nyambura, opposition from Kabonyi who is his rival for the group's loyalty, and his final betrayal and rejection by the people. It suffers, however, from the same weaknesses as *Weep Not, Child*. The hatred and jealousies that Waiyaki arouses are without motivation. The plot is weak, the prophetic vision of Chege as the thematic center becomes clogged. The kidnapping of Nyambura is a melodramatic and inexplicable complication. The final accusation against Waiyaki is not even strong enough to emphasize the theme of the betrayal of yet another Gikuyu prophet. The weakness of the writer's grasp on the details of social and political reality cripples this novel. For example, too much is attributed to the Kiama, the traditional council of elders as a forum of antiwhite feeling. Waiyaki, at first its secretary, resigns. But it is the Kiama that at the end of the book grants him some influence. The change from Christian zealot to a defender of Gikuyu ways in Kabonyi is only reported and we are told nothing that relates the apostasy to the forces at play in the society. Like most of the other characters, Kabonyi makes sudden moody decisions. Even Muthoni's decision to be circumcised, though well motivated, is not unfolded fully. This decison, however, springs upon us a reasonable plausibility of action. Her story, therefore, becomes the most successful part of the novel. Her death becomes the rallying point of conflicting emotions and attitudes of both the traditionalists and the Christians. Ngugi attempts a reconciliation between Christianity and traditional ways, but in the death of Muthoni he rejects this as totally impossible in the prevalent atmosphere of Christian rigidity and hypocritical righteousness typified by Joshua and traditional bigotry and fanaticism represented by Kabonyi.

It is in *A Grain of Wheat* that Ngugi comes of age as a writer. His grasp of plot and motivation is firmer, revealing a remarkable understanding of men and their affairs in a particular historical condition. The fumblings of *Weep Not, Child* and *The River Between* give way to a powerful story of betrayal and suffering.

The story is about Kenya on the eve of independence. The struggle is over; the fighters have come back home to burned villages and memories of torture. Those who survived the brutality and the nightmare of the concentration camps are granted a brief period of lull to reassess their struggle, count their losses, and nourish hopes of the coming dawn of freedom. The Europeans are packing their bags. The new African politicians are getting ready to take their places. The heroes and martyrs are being remembered. But this is the time, too, for seeking answers to questions that were baffling in the heat of battle and to search out those who betrayed their comrades and mete out justice.

The central story revolves around Mugo, a hero of the revolution. His name is linked with that of the great patriot and martyr Kihika, who was betrayed. A deputation goes to Mugo's house to ask him to be their spokesman on the day of honoring the heroes. This request takes him and the story back into the past, into the details of the freedom struggle in a series of brilliant flashbacks.

The struggle has come full cycle, from the great seer Mugo wa Kibiro, from the voice of Murungu to his children, the ancestral parents, to Waiyaki, Harry Thuku, who led a revolt in 1923, and Jomo Kenyatta, who is the messiah.

The war has affected Mugo; he is withdrawn, silent, and apart. But his heroism is remembered. An orphan at an early age, he has known deprivation, hunger, and wandering. Ngugi re-creates the world of the warriors Gikonyo and Mugo, General Russia,

Lieutenant Koinadu, who are still thirsting for revenge for the betrayal of Kihika, and the world of Karanja, who represents those
who helped the white man.

Ngugi weaves into the central story of finding the traitor a sub-
plot concerning the anguished relationship between Gikonyo and
his wife, Mumbi, who is Kihika's sister. As a wandering boy from
Thabai with his mother, Gikonyo had arrived in these parts, learned
a trade as a carpenter, and married the beautiful Mumbi, snatch-
ing her from many other suitors, especially Karanja, his most persistent rival. Arrested during the Mau Mau emergency, Gikonyo
spends six years in concentration camps, nourishing dreams of returning to his wife. The war and the emergency come to an end.
Returning home, he finds that Mumbi has had a child with his old
rival Karanja. In a blind rage, Gikonyo almost murders Mumbi.
He decides to devote his life to his work and abandons the prison
dream of carving a stool for his wife.

Karanja is the archetypal liege to the foreign invader, like Joshua
and Jacobo of the earlier novels. He has revealed that he had taken
the secret oath of the rebellion and thus betrayed his people. He
believes the white man is too powerful to be dislodged by rotted
pangas and spears. The white man has come to stay and his destiny
is linked with this man. Karanja is made a chief during the emergency and takes part in torturing his people and in carrying out
mass arrests, burning down villages, forcing the villagers to dig
trenches, and enforcing the brutal laws of his beloved masters. It
was at this time, at the height of his power as a functionary of
the invader that he entices Mumbi into his house and sleeps with
her. The emergency draws to a close; Karanja is reassigned as an
assistant at an agricultural and research station in Githima. He
is still at his post on the eve of independence, unable to believe
what is happening, devoted to his master, John Thompson.

In this novel, the Europeans emerge with greater clarity than
in the earlier ones. John Thompson, who as district officer was responsible for the death of eleven Africans at Rira Camp (the
Hola Camp incident in 1959), is a broken man on the eve of
independence. The country for which he and other Englishmen
had given their loyal services no longer wants them. It was a dream
formed in his days at Oxford, the dream of a multiracial British

nation, to which Britain would give guidance and protection. They did their bit at their posts with a singularity of purpose that defies any romanticism, bore every indignity and hardship on behalf of Britain. Now Britain has let them, her own sons, down. With him is his wife, Margery, a neglected, empty-headed, typical colonial wife, who seeks temporary pleasure in the drunken love-making of a Dr. Dyke, who is promptly killed in a car crash. She now devotes her last days in Africa to tending a rose garden and wondering what will happen to her flowers after she is gone. The British are caught in a state of utter disbelief and shock—they cannot accept that the mission of the empire is over, that they are to lay down the white man's burden and go home in retreat, that the Africans, bloody savages, are to take over. Caliban, alas, is to reinherit his land, and Prospero must set sail for home.

In the working out of these various strands of the novel, Ngugi achieves a remarkable artistic unity which was missing in his earlier work. Some of the most moving parts of the novel are set in the concentration camps, where we are brought face to face with raw human suffering and the undying energy of men caught in the vise of senseless mass cruelty in the name of empire. One story is of Gatu, the humorous old man who, after telling jokes and creating laughter among the inmates, goes and hangs himself.

But the thrust of the novel is the tentative journey into the crash of dreams after independence. In a short preface to the book, Ngugi writes:

> The situation and the problems are real—sometimes too painfully real for the peasants who fought the British yet who now see all that they fought for being put aside.[7]

There is doubt which weighs on the minds of the people, revealed in the story of the African M.P. who refuses to guarantee the co-operatives a loan and turns round to buy a departed white farmer's land for himself. But the theme of postindependence disillusion is only hinted at, faintly underscored in the larger theme of betrayal which is central to the novel.

The betrayer of Kihika must be found. The independence celebration continues, but Kihika must be avenged. Karanja, everyone is certain, is the one. A plan is hatched to bring him to Thabai, the village on which the main action is placed. Mugo, the hero of the revolution, has told the deputation that he cannot appear at the celebration. In a dark night Mumbi leaves her husband's house in order to persuade Mugo to come out to receive the acclaim of the people as the best surviving comrade of Kihika, her brother. In a frenzied scene, Mugo tells an incoherent story of how he, Mugo, betrayed Kihika.

It is Independence day, 12th December 1963; a wet stormy night preceded it. The sky has cleared, though the crops are damaged—"The rain had stopped, the air was soft and fresh, and an intimate warmth oozed from the pregnant earth." Mugo makes a public confession. He must pay the penalty for his treachery. The story ends with a reconciliation between Gikonyo and Mumbi and the promise of the stool renewed.

The canvas of *A Grain of Wheat* is cluttered with many events told in a series of montage sequences and there is an overwhelming array of characters. But its outlines are bold and clear. Its tensions are dramatic and breathtaking. The world of each character is revealed with artistic eloquence; the personal dramas play to a close; a finality is achieved in the roundedness of events and situations. Its weakness is a certain lack of a proper sense of selection which denies the work a degree of depth. But there is authenticity in the journalistic use of fiction in the history and history in the fiction, in the bitterness of the memory of warriors who refuse to forgive or forget, in the pathetic hollowness of victory, and in the unclear and frightening future that lies ahead for heroic combatants who are no longer sure of what they had fought for. Ngugi's style has matured considerably, leaving behind the banalities and melodrama of his earlier work. His use of a biblical style is superbly integrated into the body of his main material, legend well assimilated into history. Control is the ultimate virtue that is shown in the creation of characters, and in the dovetailing of one event into another.

In the fiction of the French-speaking African writers, we enter into new areas of literary style, into new experiences and new awareness. It will not be wrong to state that the novel in French-speaking Africa restates perhaps with deeper insight and a firmer artistic focus the case for Negritude, the case against colonialism and European intervention in Africa. What the poets tried to articulate in tortuous surrealist statements and lyrical bombast is said in the novel with a great deal of control and a saddened humor.

Guinea's Camara Laye's novel *Radiance of the King* moves into greater symbolism already suggested in his *Dark Child,* a nostalgic tale of mystery and infancy, recalling the magical childhood that Senegal's Senghor is so fond of. In *Radiance* the important question of the relation between Europe and Africa is shifted onto the spiritual plane. Laye's art borrows from surrealism and the conceptualization of dreams into Jungian symbolism that interprets history and cultural attitudes. He is also an anticolonial writer, like Hamidou Kane and Sembene Ousmane, with whom he shares certain intellectual trappings and a concern for politics and institutions of change for the common man.

Ferdinand Oyono, who has much in common with his countryman Mongo Beti, can be described as a naturalist whose art stems from more atavistic frustrations than anything else. Born in the former French Cameroon about forty-three years ago, Oyono, like most of his literary contemporaries, had a French colonial education and went through the assimilative program and later to France to study. He has since become a diplomat after a brief career on stage and in television.

Oyono's writing represents a direct confrontation with the foibles, some tragic, some comic, and senselessness of the whole colonial era. He does not explain anything, nor does he pause to make fierce and virulent proclamations on behalf of Africa. His villains are the Europeans, the French colonial adventurers—priests, administrators, prison commanders—who are in Africa for a set of confused reasons. Both the institution of colonialism—whose tacit basis is *la mission civilisatrice*—and the men who run it are the main focus of what Oyono projects as the monstrous tragedy of the whole colonial nightmare, both for its architects and its frustrated, brutalized, and frightened victims. There is contact between the races, not in the realm of ideas and concepts, but at the level of interaction between two sorts of human beings, one domineering, haughty, and implacably stupid, the other lost, confused, and frustrated at every point. Where Chinua Achebe's co-

lonial types were clichés of imperialist ideas, Oyono's Europeans
are human beings caught in the gigantic web of their own institutional nightmare. They go through the various motions as if
they were the Creator's most noble work of all. His immediate
concern is with the tragicomedy called the French Empire in which
he himself was an actor. His greatest achievement is in the use of
satire, a devastating sense of humor, a sardonic and pathetic por-
trayal of his people caught in the grips of something terrible and
inexplicable. Caricature and irony are weapons of his satire.

Boy is the story of the united operation of the various organs of
French colonial power; in the ultimate realization of this power,
the African becomes the object of the generosity, anger and sadistic
brutality of the European missionary, road builder, commandant,
and jailer. In Oyono's work we come face to face with the essential nature of French colonialism without alibi or excuse. Here
the paternal benignity of English colonialism is missing, together
with its blundering high-mindedness. Instead, we are introduced
to a process of brutalization based on a peculiarly French genre
of racism. Our hero, Toundi, is himself the symbol of that misguided Africa who ran without thought to the European invader
in search of sustenance and an excitingly newer way of life which
was to degenerate into a bad dream for him. Writing in his diary,
he states:

> I caught myself thinking I was like one of the wild parrots we used
> to attract in the village with grains of maize. They were captured
> through their greediness.[8]

Toundi is the young African entranced and ensnared from his
village into the European urban world. Oyono aptly portrays the
process in the language of bird catching:

> He [the missionary Father Gilbert] threw the little lumps of sugar
> to us like throwing corn to chickens.[9]

Toundi has run away on the eve of his initiation, signifying
an important break in his processional journey in the rites of passage. The spiritual rebirth that he needs to enter into manhood
never occurs. Instead, he turns his back upon that rebirth and becomes, by his acceptance of a new way of life, lost forever. He

never even sets foot in his village again. His isolation from his family and people is complete; he ends up in a world in which he has dreamed he would achieve fulfillment and acceptance. Rejecting his own world, he identifies himself with the missionary Gilbert and later the French commandant. For him a journey has been made into another world from which no return is possible. But in spite of the rejection of his own people and his identification with the Europeans, Toundi retains an ironic insight which enables him to evaluate his mentors for exactly what they are. Oyono's novelistic strength shows in the sharp and, at times, pained realization that is forced on the hero at every turn of events, however much this is dressed in levity and humor. Speaking of Father Gilbert, Toundi says:

> I had a look at his diary. Ah, it is a grain store of memories. These white men can preserve everything. In Father Gilbert's diary I found the kick he gave me when he caught me mimicking him in the sacristy.[10]

Upon hearing that he is going to work for the commandant, the leader of the Europeans, Toundi exclaims:

> I shall be the Chief European's boy. The dog of the King is the King of dogs.[11]

The first thing that his new master, the commandant, asks Toundi is whether he is a thief. He brings into the service of his new master a pair of thick knees, the ability to write, a smattering of French, and an unbounded confidence in the European and his ways. Father Gilbert's kindness has fortified Toundi in his original belief in the goodness of the white man, in spite of the brutality of Father Vandermayer who whipped and bullied the African section of the household.

When his old master, Father Gilbert, dies, Toundi's grief is overwhelming:

> I ran towards the ambulance, towards the stretcher. The white man who had been everything in the world to me lay there. I collided with a white man with a long neck, then with another, a yellowish man. They pushed me back one with the whip he always carried; the other feinted a kick.[12]

Even in his genuine grief, he is still the victim of physical abuse which becomes more pronounced during the funeral. But his docility and naïveté is shared by all. "I am not a storm. I am the thing that obeys," he writes. As the "thing that obeys," he receives the first dosage of his new master's power when he shows up on the first day for work:

> From the sitting room, his sharp voice came demanding a beer. As I ran to serve him my cap rolled across the floor to his feet. In a flash I saw his eyes grow as small as a cat's eyes in the sun. I was turning to go to the refrigerator when he pointed to the cap at his foot. I was nearly dead with fear.
> "Are you going to pick it up?"
> "In a moment, Sir!"
> "What are you waiting for?"
> "I will bring you your beer first, Sir."
> "But . . ." Then he said gently, "Take your time."
> I took a step towards him when I came back towards the refrigerator. I could feel the Commandant near me, the smell of him getting stronger and stronger.
> "Pick up your cap."
> Feebly I bent to pick it up. The Commandant grabbed me by the hair, swung me round and peered into my eyes.
> "I am not a monster . . . but I wouldn't like to disappoint you!"
> With that he shot out a kick to my shins that sent me sprawling under the table.[13]

It is this brutality that is peculiar to French colonialism. Raids by the French police on the African population were regular aspects of daily life. In *Boy,* Gullet, chief of police, leads a senseless raid in search of illicit liquor, a pretext for terrorizing the people and eating Toundi's sister's bananas.

The only African character in *Boy* who knows the white man and repays in kind his treatment of her, which is with disdain and contempt, is Sophie, the mistress of the district engineer. Annoyed with herself for losing an opportunity to rob him, she sneers at Toundi who assails her with naïve reasoning appealing to love and loyalty. To Toundi's charge that she wants to stop the engineer from going back to France, Sophie bursts out:

> Fuck his country and fuck him. It makes me sick when I think of

all the time I've been going with the uncircumcised sod and what have I made out of it? Now today comes my real chance and I miss it. . . . I must have mud between my ears instead of brains.[14]

Her anger and frustration mounts up and crashes in the scene on the truck when her lover introduces her as his cook. Her woman-hood, always insulted, now revolts, but only in a pathetic cry, "Christ. What have they got?" Her tears are futile. Her revenge in the end—robbing the engineer clean—was her only hope of per-sonal salvation. The irony of it is that her achievement of this release and satisfaction is the event that leads to Toundi's de-struction.

But it is not so much Sophie's theft which is the turning point in Toundi's life as it is the fact that he possesses the knowledge of the commandant's wife's infidelity and is naïve enough to share his master's discomfiture ten times over. His crime of knowing and al-legedly sharing the ugly secret with his comrades is punished by tor-ture and prison. But here was a boy who has included this woman in the glorious order of beautiful things. She was his beautiful egali-tarian queen for whom he was prepared to give his life. When she offers him her hand in greeting, Toundi breaks into ecstatic poetry:

My happiness has neither day nor night. I didn't know about it, it just burst upon my whole being. I will sing to my flute, I will sing on the banks of rivers, but no words can express my happiness. I have held the hand of the queen. I felt that I was really alive. From now on my hand is sacred, and must not know the lower regions of my body.[15]

The woman at first treats Toundi at least as a human being, asking about his family and his affairs. But when Toundi confides in her that he has not married because he could not afford to support a wife and children in the manner and style of the whites, she accuses him of having "delusions of grandeur":

My poor fellow, you have delusions of grandeur. Let's be serious. You know that wisdom counsels everyone to keep in his place. You are a houseboy. My husband is a commandant. Nothing can be done about it.[16]

Her sweet paternalism is not less brutal than the open hostility and physical violence which Toundi suffers every day in the service. It is this which makes him apprehensive and afraid of this "ray from the setting sun" whose smile "is refreshing as a spring of water."

Madame's arrival introduces us to the European community in Dangan, a motley of vulgarians masquerading as civilizers, of degenerates, and outright sadists, of sexually impotent men and their army of horse-faced women. Their world is one of moral turpitude, trivia, and malice. But they are provided with victims on whom they can vent their diseased perversions after they have torn at one another in venomous abuse, backbiting, and gossip. It is in this atmosphere that we come face to face with the insanity of the colonial administrators' existence in Africa. Inadequate as human beings, they are united in their dislike and shabby treatment of the people among whom they have come to serve their country.

When the storm breaks on Toundi, we witness the combined fury of this colony of sick people. Toundi, in his infinite naïveté, cannot sense the proper direction of the gathering storm and, in spite of Kalisia, the maid's warning, stays on. The story of his torture, in spite of the protection emanating from that invisible solidarity among a colonized people that is offered by the African people, is only the climax of a whole history of suffering microscoped in the destiny of one young African boy:

> "I vomited blood," he wrote. "My body has let me down. There is a shooting pain through my chest like a hook caught me in my lungs."[17]

> "I felt cold. Even in the strong sun, my teeth chattered. A numb weariness filled me. I felt light, a thousand pains of bellows quickening my breathing. My thoughts came to a stop."[18]

Toundi is later discovered dying in the neighboring Spanish colony to which he fled, convinced that it was his own greed that has brought him to this end. There was the agonized query which is Oyono's on his lips: "What are we black men who are called French?" The first narrator who found his notebook remarks:

> Spasms seized him. He shuddered and expired. He could not be kept till morning and they buried him directly, that night. He was already rotten before he died.[19]

Oyono's *Boy* is one of the most painful novels to have come out of Africa. Its lyrical delineation of suffering is achieved at the expense of no significant detail and observation. The technique of short flashes of narration helps to move the events themselves at a quick pace; through the eyes of Toundi we see the tragedy of Africa—from a naïve acceptance of European mores to a period of total loss of independence. The theme of the individual's loss of identity in this brutal confrontation is dramatized in the revelation of the real nature of colonialism *à la française*—a combined exhibition of white supremacy, racial bigotry, and malevolent stupidity that pass for a benevolent, liberal, civilizing mission. Toundi's naïveté, punctuated at times in sharp observations on the real nature of his rulers, is a continental and a historical naïveté. He hangs on to the end; it is not he alone who became the victim of blind racism but the whole African community of Dangan, treated like sheep and goats, beaten at the slightest provocation, and persecuted with varying machineries of torture and death which European civilized man has perfected. The combination of touching pathos, irony, and caustic humor carries the book beyond a simple sentimental tale of persecution, torture, and death. Even dying, Toundi winks at his helpers as if to say, "I know you know I am a fool, but please have pity on me."

Oyono's *The Old Man and the Medal* does not tell of the tragic consequences of French colonialism in personal or epical proportions. Here, there is still the humor, the satirical situation, and the caricatures. The theme is still European and African confrontation. Oyono's sympathy for Toundi in *Boy* is total and unyielding in its intense compassion. For Meka, this sympathy is still there, but its edges are muted by Oyono's restlessness with him. This African victim, even though old enough to understand some aspects of the motives of colonialism, does not have the insight to grasp its generally pernicious nature. Meka is as naïve as Toundi, but unlike Toundi, he is a grown-up, long matured before the whites came; rather he assiduously acquires some of colonialism's most ludicrous trappings and becomes more of a tragicomic character in his suit of European clothes and in his pathetic belief that because his children had died for France and he had given land for the Church, Frenchmen will recognize and respect him as a brother in the symbol of the medal pinned upon his chest. Meka, unlike Toundi, has always been well integrated into the traditional society of which he is a leading luminary. He is a mature man who could be described as wise in the ways of his fathers but a fool in others. But Meka too, like Toundi, has embraced the Roman Catholic faith and the white man's ways, perhaps not with the same reckless abandon as Toundi, but rather with the deliberation and maturity of a grown-up who knows what he is doing. Oyono seems to be saying that the tragedy of the Mekas of Africa rests in the fact that they knew who they were, whose descendants they were, and yet succumbed to the blandishments and flirtations of the colonial adventurer.

The news that Meka was to receive a medal raises his status among his own people, stressing therefore the African's attachment to symbols which in the European context meant absolutely nothing. The apprehension that marked the first invitation to see the commandant is revealed in such short opinions as:

> You cannot come before a white man with an empty belly. You must not show your feelings in front of a white man.[20]

He envisages for himself and all members of his large extended family a new position of respect and honor in the eyes of the French. His kinsman Moogsi points out to Meka's brother-in-law:

> If anything happens to you, all you have to do is to tell the Commandant that you are the brother-in-law of the man the white Chief came to give a medal to. . . . Your family, your friends, and your friend's friends from now on will be privileged people. All they will have to say is "I am friend of a friend of Meka's brother-in-law" and all doors will be open to them.[21]

The second part of the novel throws open the ironic situation in which the colonialized African who identifies himself completely with the whites finds himself. The fourteenth of July, the day of the storming of the Bastille in 1789, will be for Meka a day to commemorate the spirit of fraternity and equality, ideas on which, with the principle of liberty, the great French Republic was built. On this day will be fulfilled the promise of honor, glory, and elevation. The commandant had said ceremoniously:

You have done much to forward the work of France in this country. You have given your lands to the missionaries, you have given your two sons in the war where they found glorious death. You are a friend. The medal that we are going to give you means you are more than a friend.[22]

Meka, on the great day, stands in the hot noonday sun for hours, afflicted by a chronic and desperate need to urinate. But they had made a circle in which he must stand till the chief of the whites arrives to pin the medal on his breast. His new shoes are pinching. He offers a prayer which constitutes the central argument of the whole novel:

"Almighty God," he prayed to himself. "Thou alone seest all that passeth in the hearts of men; thou seest that my dearest wish at this moment as I wait for the medal and for the white Chief, alone in this circle, between two worlds . . . between two worlds, O God, which thou hast made utterly different from each other, that my dear wish and great longing is to take off these shoes and to have a piss . . . yes, a piss."[23]

This was the man who had made his choice, to the point of being upset when a white man walks in front of him with half his buttocks showing. The torture he suffers in the circle is one of humiliation and mental agony, a sense of desperate emptiness. But he will not cry because at his circumcision, he did not. The sadness of his condition hits him when he realizes that the whites do not suffer with their shoes. They wear pith helmets and are young. But in the midst of all these feelings, a transfiguration occurs in him when the medal is finally pinned on his chest. His fantasies of the future, of his election to high status among his people, of the glory of his choice to serve the whites, all come to him now in the hour of his final triumph and make the agony of the hot sun and a full bladder seem inconsequential affairs. But this was the moment when his wife, Kelara, is listening to the jeering remarks being made by members of the African audience. She realizes the untenable position her husband is in and leaves the celebration completely humiliated.

When, after the celebrations marking the giving of the medal, a drunken Meka sleeps and later gets arrested as a night prowler, is manhandled and hauled before the police chief, and vehemently protests that he is a friend of the governor and of the French, everyone laughs in his face. He does not possess the requisite papers that should entitle him to be in the European part of town. By now he is chastened by his experience and by the blows that were rained on him by the other allies of the whites. Brought before Gullet, the police chief, after a night in jail, tired and weary, he simply pleads through an interpreter:

> I feel very tired; so tired that I have nothing to say to Gullet. They can do what they like to me. He asks me who I am. Tell him I am a very great fool, who yesterday still believed in the white man's friendship.[24]

The Mekas, the "lion men," the "thunder men," the "sky men"— "incarnations of strength [who] ruled the sky and the earth"— have been reduced to nothing. Darkness engulfs him, lighting his memories and past years, his remembrance of the first white man. That was the day he became a slave, he says. The journey home from jail is a spiritual journey, undertaken in the state of rebirth and the regaining of awareness. At the onset, happiness envelops him. At every step he makes toward the African township, as the European residence recedes into the distance, the indefinable weight that has been pressing down on him lifts. He says a prayer and stubs his big toe and knows he will find a good meal at home. A panther rat runs across his path. He pronounces the ritual words of good fortune. He bursts through the forest like an elephant on the march. It crackles around him. The path has almost vanished in the great storm of the previous night. Trees have crashed, bushes form barricades across his path. He relieves himself on a type of grass which, it is believed, when watered by a man's urine can restore to him his first virility. A little further he picks up two *essesongo* leaves to ward off ill luck. Some bird droppings fall upon his head, a sign of good luck. He becomes lighthearted and sees a sow that fed on excrement:

> Where had he seen that profile before? He gasped with laughter. It almost swept him off his feet. "The world indeed comes from the hand of God. . . . I see now," he panted. "Why didn't I think of it before? It is the profile of the chief of the whites."[25]

But in spite of this levity in his heart, he is greeted with mourning and lamentation in his household. His kinsmen, afraid that some mishap had occurred since he did not come home the previous night, have gathered to mourn. This atmosphere returns Meka to his recent humiliation. After a great bout of drinking during which sporadic quarrels erupt, Meka's resignation is summed up in the sentence, "I am just an old man now," underscoring the impotence of the African community. Amalia and Kelara sing a dirge, while Essomba gives the final verdict:

> Our ancestors! They have deserted us. I don't know any more where these whites are going! Nothing which we respect has any importance in their eyes. Our customs, our stories, our medicine, our men of judgment, all that is just something to do with their houseboy and now they set traps for us like rats.[26]

The theme of traps, already introduced in *Boy,* seems to be fully exploited here, where to the Africans the invitation to receive a medal is only a trap to humiliate Meka and his people.

Oyono's art in this particular novel owes its impulse to a significantly controlled anger measured in bitter ironic strokes. The wanton abuse of African trust by Europe is delineated with great feeling, sympathy, and pathos. There is still laughter and satire, but there is a deep-seated sense of sorrow which places *The Old Man and the Medal* on the same thematic level as *Boy.* Violence, his favorite theme, is still prevalent, but it extends into the psychological rather than the physical realm. His interest in the integrity of the African, his way of life, and the incomprehensibility of his contact with Europe places him side by side with Chinua Achebe as novelists of the colonial experience. His Africans do not escape his criticism, anger, and annoyance. But these emerge from a deep sense of identity and sorrow that underlie his great concern for his people.

The modern novel in Africa has moved at a speedy rate from a period of one-dimensional anticolonial argument to the 1960s which began to concern itself with the theme of the disintegration of the great dream of independence. In Chinua Achebe's fourth book, *A Man of the People,* which came out in 1966, the novelist, untormented by any ideological visions of excellence, yet agonized by the tragic events that held his country in thrall, becomes almost a chronicler of lost dreams and shattered opportunities. Nigeria, the giant of Africa, Britain's constitutional show piece by 1965, as a model of the Westminster style two-party democracy, had degenerated into a mass of confused alliances. Political unions broke down as soon as they were made, and the English schoolmistress' anthem, proclaiming unity for the federation, had become a bad joke. By 1965 civil order broke down completely in the western region and private armies were let loose upon that area. In *A Man of the People,* Achebe wrote:

> The trouble with our new nation is that none of us had been indoors long enough to be able to say, "to hell with it." We had all been in the rain together until yesterday, then a handful of us—the smart and the lucky and hardy over the best—had scrambled for the one shelter our former rulers left, and taking it over barricaded ourselves in. And from within, we sought to persuade the rest through numerous loudspeakers that the first phase of the struggle had been won, and that the next phase—the extension of our house—was even more important and called for new and original tactics. It required that all argument should cease, and the whole people speak with one voice and that any dissent and argument outside the door of the shelter would subvert and bring down the whole house.[27]

The contemporary novel in Africa seems to be locked in an agonized search for a vision of political excellence on that continent. But this is merely a reflection of the social realities of the politics of Africa. Perhaps the African novelist has not yet been able to achieve a break from the cycle of anger and frustration. The Malian novelist Yambo Ouloguem and the Ghanaian novelist Ayikwei Armah seem to epitomize this era of intense despair. But in a basic sense, these writers are also eternal exiles, removed from a basic perception of the African scene more than most of their own contemporaries by years of overseas living and education. The South African novel is coming into its own in the agonized writings of Ezekiel Mphahlele, its most lyrical representative. Exile, protest, and alienation continue to be the great themes of this writing. The novel in Africa, as much as the poetry, responded to the political events and continues to be the genre through which political statements will be made.

The modern drama of Africa

Modern drama and stagecraft in Africa owes its basic impetus to the introduction of European dramatic technique. Many of the contemporary dramatists writing in English and French have also been involved in experimental theater work in the African universities. The plays attempt a synthesis between traditional dramatic material and the Western stage and production technique.

A few of the dramatists have, however, returned to the traditional ritual for material and inspiration. What was growing up alongside the colonial drama influenced by organizations like the British Council can be described as "folk opera." It was based on biblical themes, stories taken out of the Gospel and adapted to the stage. The actors worked in the vernacular and possessed no basic training in theater technique. They played in school compounds for audiences made up largely of the semiurban or rural community. In Ghana, where the performances were called "concert parties," these groups were trios. The leader of the trio was the major factotum, combining the role of business manager and producer with that of lead actor; the other two actors played both male and female parts and doubled as costume manager, musician, and dancer. The "plays," unscripted, were like the morality plays of medieval England. The emphasis on morality was taken both from the folk tale tradition and missionary influence. In Nigeria this same type of indigenous theater grew during the early 1940s with the work of veteran entertainers such as Hubert Ogunde whose fame covered the whole West African coast. Unlike his Ghanaian counterparts, he did not use female impersonators. He began by using women actors, and when he found the problem of keeping them in the team becoming difficult, he married the thirteen of them himself, thus ensuring stability. According to Ulli Beier, he secularized Yoruba theater by moving away from biblical themes; he also introduced themes from politics.

This type of indigenous theater began to explore African stories and legends for dramatic purposes. In Ghana the theater group of the Workers Brigade launched into themes from Gā mythology. Saka Acquaye's *Obadzeng,* a folk opera based on the Gā legend of creation, received tremendous acclaim in 1961 both in Africa and in Eastern Europe. Music, mime, and dancing were the basic ingredients of the drama. In Nigeria Kola Ogunmola's *Love Is Money* attempted, within the scope of a social satire, to come to grips with the problem of using Yoruba mythology and contemporary history. His adaptation of Tutuola's *The Palm-Wine Drinkard* for stage had a successful tour of Ghana in 1965.

Perhaps the most exciting experiments in indigenous drama using mythology, rites, historical narratives, and legend can be seen in the work of the Yoruba dramatist Duro Ladipo. Ladipo obviously inherits his art from the Yoruba tradition. Like Tutuola, he has had very little formal education and still writes only in Yoruba. But his work may be described as an attempt to fuse two theatrical traditions—Yoruba and Western. He uses a wide range of Yoruba music and the *dundun* talking drums, the *okiti* drums, and flutes to provide an essential feature of his dramatic art—an authentic mood and atmosphere. His best-known play, *Oba Koso,* has a rich musical arrangement, combining singing, chanting, and dancing. He goes back to Yoruba history and legend and to Yoruba music and oral poetry.

Oba Koso is an eight-scene play, dramatizing the legend of Shango's life as a man and of how he became the god of thunder. Shango worship, as stated earlier, is still active in Yorubaland, extending as far as to the Ewe of the west. His celebration and rites constitute a religious drama of the utmost importance to his worshipers. The plot of *Oba Koso* is a simple one. Shango, in the predivine state of a man, was the King of Oyo, ruling over a town known for its two obstreperous generals, Timi and Gbonka. But Shango establishes peace. These two generals intend to continue the wars and thus plunge Oyo into more turmoil. The townspeople approach Shango begging him to end the war and restore peace. He dispatches Timi to Ede, to defend the frontiers of his kingdom there, a move calculated to remove him from the scene. Timi is received and made king by the people of Ede. Shango sends Gbonka to fight against Timi in the hope that the two will perish in the bloody conflict. Gbonka overcomes Timi through his magic, captures and brings him back to Oyo. Shango and the people, shocked by the return of the men, ask them for a rematch in the market place. Gbonka again conquers Timi, but this time cuts off his head. Gbonka, growing fierce and reckless in his victory and suspecting Shango's ulterior motives, declares open rebellion against the king. Shango, in his ultimate anger, kills his own people and is therefore banished into the forest. Here, deserted by all his slaves and his wives, he hangs himself. He becomes a god, as thunder is heard through the skies. Thus, there is enshrined the legend and the rituals of Shango, which are still part of the Yoruba mythic system. Ladipo, writing in Yoruba, goes to the very sources of the *oriki*, or praise poem, for the language of the play. Song, dance, ritual prostration are part of the atmosphere of the drama. The play opens with Iwarefa, the court poet, and the Oloris, Shango's wives, making elaborate salutations to their king to the accompaniment of Yoruba *bata* drums:

IWAREFA
We greet you
Father of mankind
Of divine power
Second only to God
OLORIS
Kabiyesi, we prostrate before you.
IWAREFA
Mighty one!

You control the most stubborn!
You bring trouble to your disobedient children!
   OLORIS
Born to be king!
   IWAREFA
You are a huge sacrifice, too heavy for
the vulture,
He staggers under your weight.[1]

Iwarefa and the king's wives proceed through elaborate praise names which are set by tradition; this whole scene is marked by drumming and dancing:

   IWAREFA
You wake up in a gentle mood
But anybody who looks down on you
will be swept away[2]

(*Bata drums and dance.*)

Shango's attributes are taken directly from his known *orikis* or sacred praise salutations, "too heavy for the vulture," a reference to the legend of the vulture carrying the sacrifice to heaven and getting a bald pate as a result. He is also the "masquerader spitting fire" and the "banana planted near the river." These images greatly enhance the drama of the story of Shango's movement from a king to a deity. The character of Shango achieves a roundness that suggests his majesty and subsequent deification. But Ladipo also suggests that Shango was a man first, weak in the face of evil, who achieves his deital status only after succumbing to the evil impulse of anger and destruction, crimes for which he was justly punished. The other characters that achieve a direct and simple fullness in the unfolding of the plot are Timi and Gbonka. Timi bounces upon the stage announcing his evil nature with a nonchalance that recalls the villains of Shakespearean drama:

I am small but I am evil
No fight has ever seen me hesitate
I am small but I defy the elders
I defy the elders who are forging weapons.[3]

In this tone, he calls Shango by name and asks him not to be offended:

> For we have known your name from times
> before you were king.[4]

When he arrives at the outskirts of Ede, with poetry replete with boasts which achieves a cumulative effect through the repetitions of magic attributes, he invites the citizens of Ede to approach him:

> I come gently like the rain in the evening
> I come swiftly like rain in the morning,
> I come suddenly like rain in bright sunlight.
> Spirits of the place:
> Asarewa, Arintona, Atuyanya
> Let the people move quickly to meet me
>
> Let the wind blow all towards me.[5]

Gbonka as a character is also fully realized. As the one whose fate is closely intertwined with Shango's, he is very much aware of his importance; he is given some ornate poetry which emphasizes this sense of self-importance. He enters proclaiming:

> The termites eat away the house slowly
> If I shall not die a natural death these twenty years
> None of you shall see me buried!
> Can you behead a snail with a sword?
> Whose father can kill a tortoise with a club?
> Can anybody behead a fly?[6]

But he is also a man who respects Shango whose praise names he sings and whose enemy he is not:

> But the oracle will reveal
> That I am not their enemy
> And I shall go in peace.

> (*Gbonka dances and sings to the agogo bell.*)

> Don't be wicked in this world.
> Remember heaven
> When you reach the gate of heaven
> You will do much
> To justify yourself.[7]

Against Timi's "flaming arrow," he is the "poisonous yam" who

> Looks harmless enough,
> Yet it kills another man's child.[8]

In Scene IV, anticipating the fight between himself and Timi, Gbonka enters after the *bata* drums and the chorus that sings his praise names, he, "the hand that leads the food to the mouth and returns safely" proclaiming:

> Some people look at things
> Without understanding the cause:
> They see two birds on top of a tree,
> But they do not know
> That the woodcock alighted on the banyan
> tree from the air,
> While the coockall climbed the baobab
> from the ground.[9]

In the short scene depicting the confrontation between the two men, to the background of *bata* drums and the chants of the chorus, Gbonka overcomes Timi and ties him up for the return journey to Oyo. When Shango orders a new fight between the generals, Gbonka consults witches for help:

> You my mothers, you with small knives
> I am bringing you a viper's head,
> A dog's tail and freshly plucked cotton
> Here are all the things you wanted
> Just let me conquer![10]

The play moves very briskly, employing very little dialogue, depending upon set speech pieces for the movement of the plot toward the climax which comes at the end. Scene VIII is set in an open field; Shango stands abandoned by all his people, attended by Oya, his faithful wife, who is soon to desert him. She sings to him a farewell song which intensifies Shango's predicament:

> My Lord, my husband, the one I trust,
> The one I adore, the one whose tongue commands,
> Small bird, whose song carries far in the forest,
> Though small, he is still the husband of all the queens.
> Ajala Iji,

I have tried too much for you—but I will
follow you no further.[11]

Overwhelmed by this final betrayal, Shango, holding her, chants:

What can I think, what can I say.
All my friends have deserted me.
All my wives have run away.
All my slaves have dispersed.
You alone remain

Farewell—now only death is sweet.
I will hang—I will hang from the ayan tree.[12]

Against Oya's remonstration, Shango tears loose and hangs himself. The people of Oyo enter, announcing the confusion that has overtaken their town, and, prostrating themselves before their hanging king, they ask him when he will return. Shango's friends, the Magbas, following the townspeople, chastise them for driving their king to suicide, announce his immortality and deification:

Shango is not dead—he has just gone to look for food.
What has caused the vulture to become bald?
What has caused the hornbill to go in rags?
They were deserted by their friends.
You deserted Shango when he was fighting for you!
He hangs from the ayan tree
But when the bata drum will sound—he will speak to you
When the Dundun drum trembles—he will dance for you.[13]

Fire, Shango's element and epiphany, has been raging through the town since the king died. The Magbas announce that the king is like the self-generating bat:

Ever renewing itself!
The King does not hang!
When the kite flies high in the sky,
People think he is lost,
Yet he returns to his nest.[14]

Suddenly thunder is heard from above, and the voice of Shango bursts through, proclaiming his divinity as the people fall prostrate:

E E E E E ! ! !
Two hundred glowing embers
Must bow down to the fire
One thousand warriors
Cannot fight death.
Two hundred stars
Must pay homage to the sun.[15]

The play ends with the people making proclamation to Shango, asserting their debt to him, and promising to worship him always. His offer of peace and happiness is in return for their eternal homage.

Oba Koso, though a thoroughly modern play that utilizes the conventional stage, is essentially the dramatization of a piece of folk legend, utilizing material from the rites and worship of Shango as they are still observed among the Yoruba. The ingredients of drum, song, and dance are essential aspects of the ancestral and cultic rites. Their use on stage in relationship to the theme of *Oba Koso* appropriately highlights the role of these features of the traditional art. Besides, Ladipo, working in Yoruba, achieves an authenticity in language made possible by the adherence to oral poetic diction, imagery, and style, which do not suffer much even in the translation done by Ulli Beier. The play's integrity is achieved through brief and well-executed scenes marked by the rustle and bustle of the processions, the chorus of chanters, wives, and the typically colorful atmosphere of a Yoruba *oba*'s court.

Ladipo's other play which shows a close reliance on traditional drama form for effect is *Oba Waja.* The theme of this play, unlike that of *Oba Koso,* is derived from recent history, even though its thematic development is treated in the manner which is suggestive of its traditional orientation. The story is taken from an event that took place in 1946. At the death of the Alafin of Oyo, his commander of the horse, according to tradition, must commit suicide in order to join his master in the other world. As he goes through the ritual preparations, the English district officer in the area, at the insistence of the d.o.'s frightened wife, arrests the man and places him in protective custody. Confusion breaks out, for the spell of the ritual has been broken and disaster will befall the people. The commander's son returns from the Gold Coast in order

to preside at his father's funeral, only to see the poor man alive,
half-relieved by his escape but terrified of the imminent anger of
his departed king, still sitting among his people who were hurling
insults at him. Driven by a deep sense of shame and fear of the
wrath of the gods, his son commits suicide.

The play is divided into five short scenes. The first scene opens
in the household of the dead Alafin whose funeral rites are in
progress. Again, as in *Oba Koso,* the emphasis is on dancers and
drummers, who provide atmosphere for the funeral and for the
whole play:

> ELDERS
> We must not see it.
> It is forbidden
> The King is dead
> And never shall we see him
> Leaving the palace in procession.
>   CHORUS and AGOGO
> We must not see it
> It is forbidden.
>   ELDERS
> The coconut is lost
> Under the huge silk cotton tree.
>   CHORUS
> Yeeee!
> The coconut has failed
> To bear another fruit
> The iron gongs resound
> The funeral gongs
> Make us tremble with fear.[16]

The poetry of the play, drawn from the vernacular, is replete with
imagery from nature, and enhances the speech of the play. When
Dawudu, son of the commander of the horse, commits suicide,
the lament raised is drawn from the *ege,* the Yoruba dirge:

> O pain, O pain! O cruel death
> Death breaks the honeycomb
> And spills its sweetness.[17]

In the chorus chants at the Alafin's death:

Our father returned home
He entered into a deep forest.[18]

In the elders' lament:

The king is dead
He has crossed the river of life.[19]

And when Dawudu's wife sings, saying her husband will join his ancestors whose eyes are

. . . gleaming in the darkness
Their backs are glittering in the shadows
Alafin has become a spirit
Hot like a burning sun
Shining like a red hot iron.[20]

The central theme is one of disintegration and confusion brought upon the people by the white man's interference with tradition. For the belief is that the Alafin cannot cross the river alone; he cannot confront the gatekeeper of the spirit world unaccompanied. It is the commander of the horse who must row him across the river and share in the Alafin's glory and shine like a burning sun. Olori, at the height of his preparation, chants: "Who can obstruct the elephant?" His fate is sealed, and he is happy and ready for his role as the sacrifice. As the magic spells intensify and he bids farewell to his people, the district officer enters with policemen and Olori is arrested. The people of Oyo, amazed by what had happened, burst into a song whose theme is reiterated later by the district officer, Alafin's spirit, Olori himself, and Dawudu:

The world is spoilt in the white man's time
Shall the commander of the horse
Remain behind to eat earthworms and centipedes
And who will give food to the king
On his way to heaven?
Alafin, owner of the palace
The white man's rule has spoiled our world
Vengeance is in your hands.[21]

When Olori reappears on stage lamenting the abomination, the voices of the people of Oyo are heard backstage, proclaiming the lament:

> Commander of the king's horse
> The world has spoilt in your time.
> We must leave you to your fate.[22]

He himself, aware of the ruination, seeks frantically to repair the damage. But it is too late. The judgment of the people is that he must die of the machete:

> like a cow
> Slaughtered in the market place.[23]

His anguish mounts as he witnesses the death of his son, Dawudu:

> Save me, save me my people!
> I must witness the ruin of my life
> O my child, my child.[24]

Like the dove, he must leave the house, the scene of his shame, proclaiming the final doom:

> Oyo people—the world is spoilt in my time
> The world has broken over my head.[25]

Taunted by everyone, including Dawudu's wife, he kills himself. The district officer, overwhelmed by events, is taunted by the people who finally place the responsibility for the turn of events at his door, asks:

> What mockery is this?
> Can good intentions turn to evil?[26]

Ọba Waja attempts to dramatize a theme that is similar to that of Achebe's *Things Fall Apart:* the collapse of the traditional world brought on through contact with European ways. But the play's concern is to heighten the tragic consequences of this contact, even at the most minimal level. Ladipo uses the district officer only in order to create the dramatic tensions of the play and is not concerned with the total impact of this clash on the protagonists. He brings the story back into the Yoruba world, exonerating the white man from every responsibility. In the last chant by the people of Oyo, Eshu, the Yoruba trickster-god, is blamed for the confusion:

White man, bringer of new times.
Your work was confounded by Eshu
Confuser of men.
Nobody can succeed against the will of Eshu.[27]

Thus we are brought back to the principle of conflict, divinely sanctioned in Eshu-Elegba whose work is to confuse in order to complete the task of harmonizing all the forces, to put men to the test and try their will and spirit in their effort to achieve rapport with the gods. At the end of the play, Olori is freed from the divine retribution that the district officer's intervention would have imposed. The women's chorus chants him on his way beyond the grave:

Cross now the river in peace
Today you shall see the king of the river.
Today you shall face the king of the sun.[28]

These two plays can best be appreciated when seen in performance. Their impact is not in the dialogue, which in dramatic terms is minimal, but in the music-drumming and the ceremonial dances. The *bata* drums and *agogo* bells are not only significant as background sounds, but assume their own importance in the denouement of the story. The language of the plays is loaded with proverbs, allusions, and imagery drawn from the world of animals, men, and gods. Finally, the themes themselves, concerned with serious aspects of Yoruba history and legend, carry their own austere dignity and tragic tone within the context of the life of the people.

The most prolific contemporary African dramatist writing in English is Wole Soyinka whose plays have played to packed houses in Africa and have also invaded the stages of Britain, France, and the United States. Soyinka's freshness as a dramatist does not lie in the fact that he has acquired the Western dramatic technique and mastered it completely. Rather it is because he has been able to create a new dramatic material which is based in the techniques of ritual drama, with its ubiquitous accompanying drums and dances.

Educated at the University of Leeds, Soyinka served a brief

period of apprenticeship at the Royal Court Theater in London. He was one of the initiators of the program of the School of Drama at the University of Ibadan, Nigeria. He is perhaps the most conscious African dramatist writing for the stage. Very aware of his Yoruba traditions, he attempts to synthesize them into the mold of a sophisticated theater form that shows a remarkable grasp of its possibilities as a vehicle for literary and artistic statements.

For the purposes of this discussion, I will limit myself to the way in which he exploits themes and ideas from Yoruba philosophy for his art and also illustrate his debt to Yoruba speech in specific plays.

A Dance of the Forest, his most ambitious play, attempts a fantastic unification of both the living and the dead and of men and gods, a theme which derives from the West African mythic system in which gods, men, the dead, and the living exist in a unified world. This world of the play is established, as in Tutuola's work, within the forest, the primeval landscape inhabited by all the combined forces of the universe. This forest is also a mirror of the real world, even though it also serves as the world of countless spirits. The town dwellers mingle freely with the forest dwellers who are the elemental spirits representing universal attributes. The action of the play enables a long intercourse between the town dwellers and the forest dwellers.

The effectiveness of *A Dance of the Forest* lies in its elaborate use of a significant segment of the Yoruba pantheon for the purpose of seeking a unity between men and gods and between the living and the dead. The dead, represented by the ancestors, are returned to the Gathering of the Tribes to be present at the feast. When Aroni the Lame One is asked to send illustrious ancestors, he approaches Forest Head whose attributes are those of Olodumare, or Olorun, himself. Forest Head sends two spirits of the restless dead. The first dead was in a former life a warrior at the court of Mata Kharibu, a mythical emperor over an African kingdom during the Middle Ages, who was put to death by torture for refusing to go to war to regain the trousseau of the capricious queen, Madame Tortoise. The second dead is the warrior's wife, a pregnant woman put to death for her husband's rebellion. The reason why they are returned instead of an illustrious array of ancestors, is, Aroni reveals, that in "their previous life they were linked in violence and blood with four of the living generation." This is an attempt to link the dead and the living through blood with the cycle of violence and upheaval which is at the center of Yoruba thought. The dead woman, as is expected, is the inevitable mother of the Abiku half-child, who is born, dies, is born again and again. This emphasizes the pain and suffering of mankind. She also emphasizes what becomes the continuous and relentless process of suffering and regeneration. She recalls the sorrow of the world during Obatala's, the god of creation and peace, imprisonment, the era of Ogun's ascendance, the period of stagnation and decay which anticipates the rebirth. Her cry as she appeals for help—

> I who yet await a mother
> Feel this dread
> Feel this dread
> I who flee from the womb
> To branded womb, cry it now
> I'll be born dead
> I'll be born dead.[29]

—will go unheeded.

Underlying and playing the most significant part in the thematic structure of the play is the contest between the gods themselves. Forest Head is the representative essence of the great god, Olodumare, bearing also in his patience and benevolence a close resemblance to Obatala. It is his wish that provides the world its determining principles. Chastising Eshuoro, an archetypal resemblance of Eshu-Elegba, he cries:

> Enough. Do not deny that all goes as you
> planned it. But only because it is my wish.[30]

Forest Head's effort to liberate the carver Demoke's soul is supplemented by Ogun's attempt to protect the artist from the consequences of his unwillful crime against Eshuoro whose head he cut off in preparing the oyo tree, sacred to the god for the carving of the totem. At the center of the whole confusion, supervising and deepening it, is Eshuoro who obviously is Eshu-Elegba, the trickster-god. Pitted against Eshuoro is Ogun, the god of iron and war, whose role paradoxically seems to be one of a placating spirit rather than of the vengeful god of orgies and blood. The quarrel seethes between the two of them after the court scene when the warrior is sentenced to castration and death:

OGUN

Face to face at last Eshuoro. So you come here
with your loud words and empty boasts? Soulless
one, Demoke is no empty nut that fell, motherless
from the sky. In all that he did he followed my
bidding. I will speak for him.

ESHUORO

I have suffered this too long. Perhaps the master
must first be taught and then he can teach his minion
to be humble.

OGUN

Minion? This minion of mine—is it not rumored that
he has done you service lately as a barber?

ESHUORO

(*Between his teeth*) I have borne too much already
to take your taunts lightly. Ogun, I warn you beware . . .[31]

Ogun's non-aggressive aspect is shown here projecting his protection of carvers and artists, those who use iron to fashion objects of worship and veneration. Eshuoro's nature in this play is emphasized by his capriciousness and petulance. Annoyed and pledging revenge, he launches a series of pranks calculated to annoy his enemies. He is also the master of disguise, whose vengeance can be relentless. The dramatic use of the confrontation between two gods, as Ogun searches for his servant, Demoke, to protect him against Eshuoro's anger, provides a deeper level of meaning to the play. As Aroni, in his prologue, proclaims:

It was not as dignified a dance as it should be.
Eshuoro had come howling for vengeance and full
of machinations. His professed wrongs are part
of the story.[32]

Eshuoro, we are told, is the wayward flesh of Oro—Oro whose agency "serves much of the bestial human."

The play's main purpose is perhaps to assay a reunion between men and gods, between the dead and the living. The symbol of this will be Demoke's carving. The link must be found. Demoke explains to Rola, the reincarnation of Madame Tortoise, believing that she is the link:

DEMOKE
. . . I needed a link and you provided it—you do see
why, don't you? I take it you do know of the
legendary Madame Tortoise.
ROLA
(*Subdued*) No. What was she?
DEMOKE
A woman.[33]

Demoke's role as the artist coincides with that of the seeker and the carrier, the celebrant, and the priest who acknowledges the gods' divinity. In a long speech retelling the story of his carving of the totem, he reveals how lonely the priest-carver is in his confrontation with the divine essence:

Alone,
Alone I cut the strands that mocked me till head
and boastful slave lay side by side, and I,
Demoke, sat on the shoulders of the tree,
My spirit set free and singing, my hands,
My father's hands possessed by demons of blood
And I carved three days and nights till tools
were blunted, and these hands, my father's hands
Swelled as big as the tree trunk. Down I came
But Ogun touched me at the forge and I slept
weary at his feet.[34]

With him, operating within the same religious world, is Agboreko who is a priest of Ifa, a seeker after the truth in the spirit world. An old man, Demoke's father, goes to him to divine the whereabouts of his son, who, confused by Eshuoro, is lost in the forest. Agboreko, as if in possession of the information and yet unaware of the gods' contest, proclaims:

The eye that looks downwards will certainly see
the nose. The hand that clips to the bottom of
the pot will eat the biggest snail. The sky grows
no grass but if the earth called her barren, it

will drink no more milk. The foot of the snake is
not split in two like a man's or in hundreds like
the centipede's, but if Agere could dance patiently
like the snake, he will uncoil the chain that leads
into the dead.[35]

These are a series of oracular proverbs of Ifa, each with a specified
meaning that will be made manifest through sacrifices. "Agere,"
here, refers to the old man; the meaning is clear that Demoke is
in the spirit world, but beyond that information Agboreko cannot
venture because he does not have the knowledge.

The theme of release of spirits in order that they may achieve
fulfillment also plays an important part in the realization of the
unity between the world of the living and the dead. Borrowed from
West African religious thought, it also reiterates the cycle principle. The drama highlights the breaking of the cycle for the dead
man and the dead woman, both of whom, by the manner of their
deaths, were condemned to wander on the outskirts of the spirit
world, tormented and without peace. Seeking a place of rest, the
dead man, Mulieru, confronts Forest Head and Questioner:

    DEAD MAN
    Three lives I led since first I went away
    But still my first possesses me.
    The pattern is unchanged.
        QUESTIONER
    You who enter sleek and well fed
    Have you, at least, a tale of
    Pleasure and content?
        DEAD MAN
    My father said, and his great father
    Before him, if you find no rest, go home
    And they will know you.
    Kind friends, take me to Forest Head.
        FOREST HEAD
    I knew you, Mulieru.
        DEAD MAN
    Then you are Forest Head. When I died
    and still they would not let my body rest;
    When I lived and they would not let me be
    The man I felt, cutting my manhood first

With a knife, next with words and the dark
Spit of contempt, the voice at my shoulder said
Go seek out Forest Head. If I am home, then
I have come to sleep.[36]

When he pays his debt for earlier misdeeds in the service of Mata Kharibu, he will be allowed in from the rain and storms to a place of rest. Forest Head, after the dance of the passive masks, relieves the dead woman of her child and announces the "moment for the welcome of the dead." But the half-child's essence continues the cycle as she searches for her soul in the earth: "I found an egg, smooth as a sea pebble," she announces. But, as she stops her spinning, her destiny is announced:

Still I fear the fated bearing
Still I circle yawning wombs.[37]

Eshuoro is at the heart of her distraction. She is the expressive object and instrument of his function in the cosmic order of things.

Soyinka's language borrows directly from Yoruba speech, especially in portions of the play where he uses oracular language, loaded with proverbs and allusions. Agboreko is the bearer of words as he is the *babalawo,* a man who grasps and unfolds the secret magic of words, yet taking umbrage in silence as his escape from the burden of the Word:

Have you seen a woman throw away her pestle when
she really means to pound yam? When Iredade took
her case to Orunmila, he said, If the worm doesn't
jig near the roost, the fowl may still want to peck,
but at least it can't say the worm was throwing
dust in his face. Go home, therefore, go home.
Iredade turned sadly away as Orunmila called her back.
He said, They say the forest is more cunning anytime
of the year, but who ever lay back in his house
and watched the creepers grow over him? Oracle
to the living and silent.[38]

The other play in which Soyinka makes an extended use of a Yoruba concept as the thematic center and the main dramatic principle is *The Strong Breed*. The theme of the carrier is prevalent in most West African religious systems. The carrier represents the principle of evil and also its expiation. When the year comes to a close, most African societies enjoin a ritual cleansing that will signify the removal of all the sins and ill-will of the old year in preparation for the new year. This, most of the time, coincides with the festivals of first fruits, mainly yam in most parts of eastern West Africa. But the underlying principle is one of public cleansing. In olden times a man had to be found to carry the sacrifice to the gods; some groups used a stranger believed to be sent by the gods, some the favorite son of ruling clans. In the former case, the crippled and the handicapped were readily believed to be chosen by the gods by the very nature of their deformities to serve as carriers. Among many groups, the ritual itself is only symbolic, for the priest himself serves as the carrier who receives the people's sins and pleads before the gods on their behalf; it is in this state that he achieves a spirituality. More generally, however, animals, especially the ram, are slaughtered to serve as the messenger who bears the sacrifices to the gods. But this is probably a later development when most groups abandoned ritual sacrifices of human beings.

Soyinka's use of this theme in one of his clearest and most simple plays, *The Strong Breed,* emphasizes its dramatic dimensions without making any effort to pass judgment. The story is straightforward. Eman, a young wanderer, had fled from home on the eve of his circumcision rites. After many years he returns, lives briefly with his betrothed, Omae, who later dies in childbirth. He wanders into another village where he takes up semiresidence and establishes a relationship with Sunma, a schoolteacher, and Ifada, an idiot boy, who is homeless. The annual ceremony of cleansing is near. Ifada is marked as the carrier. He seeks refuge in Eman's house after escaping his captors. In a confrontation with Jaguna, Sunma's father, and the people who come to recover the boy, Eman taunts them but releases the boy as they threaten to burn down the house. When they in turn accuse him of cowardice, he offers himself as the carrier in place of the boy. But after going through the preliminary tortures, he escapes and thus breaks the fulfillment of the ritual intentions.

Soyinka, through a series of very subtle subplots, leads the audience into the workings of the main theme. A little girl, ill with an unmentioned disease, appears at the house of Eman at the opening of the first scene dragging an effigy:

> EMAN
> So you are all ready for the new year.
>> GIRL
> I am not going to the festival.
>> EMAN
> Then why have you got that?
>> GIRL
> Do you mean my carrier? I am unwell you know. My mother says it will take away my sickness with the old year.[39]

The child invites Ifada to take part in the beating of the effigy, but insists that he cannot be cured. Sunma, who loves Eman and fears for his safety as a stranger during the festivities, attempts to keep him at home after he had refused to leave town with her:

> SUNMA
> It is the time for making changes in one's life, Eman. Let's breathe in the new year away from here.
>> EMAN
> You are hurting yourself.
>> SUNMA
> Tonight. Only tonight. . . . Let us go away this one night.[40]

But Eman rejects her plea, in the knowledge that being the stranger his destiny is total. He is driven by a desire to offer himself as sacrifice in place of others:

> EMAN
> Let me continue a stranger—especially to you. Those who have much to give fulfill themselves only in total loneliness.
>> SUNMA
> Then there is no love in what you do.
>> EMAN
> There is. Love comes to me more easily with strangers.[41]

He has cut loose from all ties of blood, seeking a place of spiritual peace, an abode of escape from the memory of his tormented youth. But he is marked. In a series of flashbacks, Soyinka re-creates scenes out of his past, depicting his father whose role is also that of the ceremonial carrier of the dwarf boat on a river, a traditional function performed by his family from generation to generation. This role recalls the ferryman on the river between the living and the dead. The function is spiritual, thus the carrier must possess the knowledge and the strength for it. When Eman plans to go away after Omae's death, the old man says to him:

> Ours is a strong breed, my son. It is only a strong breed that can take this boat to the river year after year and wax stronger on it. I have taken down each year's evil for over twenty years. I hoped you would follow me.[42]

The suggestion is explicit that Eman cannot escape his destiny; his role as the bearer of others' burdens must be fulfilled. Beneath his rebellion in leaving home is a dumb acceptance of his fate. As Oroge, one of his captors, explains:

> He is the kind who would let himself be beaten from night till dawn and not utter a sound. He would let himself be stoned until he dropped dead.[43]

Eman, like Ifada, came from nowhere. Jaguna asks:

> Why do you think we give refuge to idiots like him? We don't know where he came from. One morning he is simply there, just like that. From nowhere at all. You see, there is a purpose in that.[44]

After Eman has fled his tormentors, he is pursued throughout the night, running what is the symbolic race of his carrierhood, a mission he had refused to undergo. The old man also runs the race to the beating of drums as he carries the boat, and "as soon as it touches his head, he holds it down with both hands and runs off, the men give him a start, then follow at a trot." Eman, in the second flashback scene between him and Omae, his betrothed, on the eve of his initiation, states his own obligation to life, and defines his role:

> A man must go on his own, go where no one can help him, and test his strength.[45]

He enters into manhood alone; it is this knowledge that enables him, when the agony of Omae's death overwhelms him, to reject all ties of blood and home and to wander from place to place, refusing peace and rest. He runs the race into the past where he meets his father, carrying the dwarf boat on his head. Driven by thirst, he pleads to partake in the rites, but his father turns him away as he himself proceeds to the self-sacrifice:

> EMAN
>
> But, father, I am your son.
>
> OLD MAN
>
> Then go back. We cannot give the two of us.
>
> EMAN
>
> Tell me first where you are going.
>
> OLD MAN
>
> Do you ask that? Where else but to the river.
>
> EMAN
>
> I only wanted to be sure. My throat is burning. I have been looking for the stream all night.
>
> OLD MAN
>
> It is the other way.
>
> EMAN
>
> But you said . . .
>
> OLD MAN
>
> I take the longer way, you know how I must do this. It is quicker if you take the other way. Go now.
>
> EMAN
>
> No. I will only get lost again. I shall go with you.
>
> OLD MAN
>
> Go back, my son. Go back.
>
> EMAN
>
> Why? Won't you even look at me?
>
> OLD MAN
>
> Listen to your father. Go back.
>
> EMAN
>
> But father . . . (*He makes to hold him. Instantly the old man breaks into a trot. Eman hesitates, then follows, his strength nearly gone.*) Wait, father. I am coming . . .[46]

His role is finally fulfilled; inevitably, he returns to his destiny as the carrier.

But Soyinka is perhaps the most eclectic of the African writers writing in English today. His absorption of the Western idiom is complete, and at times takes over entirely his artistic direction. His freshness is in his return to his Yoruba sources, to its poetry and ideas for language and themes that dramatize his concern for fusion for the new African.

17

Contemporary art forms

Colonialism brought Western drama into Africa. To the folkloric drama in which animals raised families, quarreled, and sat on thrones and to the ritual drama of worship, history, and rebirth was added the dramatic forms of the European stage. Shakespeare came to Africa with the European (British) educator. Most African schools have Shakespeare on their syllabuses. The tragedies are most popular. *Macbeth* has been a roaring success because, for the European teachers and the African pupils, it dramatizes the story of a bloody struggle for a throne (Africa has its fair share of fierce dynastic quarrels and feuds). *King Lear* is the story of wicked daughters—many a patriarch in Africa has very wicked and ungrateful daughters. Shakespeare still has a formidable hold on African schools and colleges simply because for years it has been part of the examination system, with a persistence that defies even bloody revolutions. Before Shakespeare (the Bard, remember, can be "wicked" and "sinful" at times) were plays that were adapted from religious texts by missionaries who ran most of the schools in colonial Africa. Bible stories like David the shepherd boy, the Nativity, Saul, the Crucifixion, Nebuchadnezzar, the Garden of Eden, the Prodigal Son were some of the most popular subjects for plays.

An important development in African theater is the emergence of professional actors' groups. One of the most important of these is the Union Artists group based in Johannesburg in South Africa. This group also runs a school of drama and has given birth to such talented writers as Athol Fugard (*Blood Knot*), Ben Masinga (*Back in Your Own Backyard*), and Gibson Kente (*Manana the Jazz Prophet*). Its experimental theater is a training ground for producers, actors, and other technicians of the stage. A similar experiment was carried out in Ghana with the founding of the Ghana Drama Studio under Efua Sutherland and Joe de Graft. This provided opportunity for training amateur and later professional drama groups and was the forerunner of the School of Drama at the University of Ghana, Legon. The Mbari Writers and Artists Club at Ibadan in Nigeria served the same function in the birth of what is a prolific theater in that country today. Wole Soyinka, who once headed the School of Drama at Ibadan, has been responsible for a fantastic upsurge in the theater movement. In Uganda a national theater exists, though its building seems to have been planned without reference to the humble needs of an indigenous theater. The work of Robert Serumaga in recent years has enlarged the scope of the theater there. But a traveling theater company started by a Mapereri group in 1966 has taken the initiative in carrying theater to the rural areas. One of its leading lights is Mrs. Jo Bevin, who was connected with the theater group at the University of Ghana. This Uganda company produces plays in Swahili, Bunyoro, and Rutoro, apart from English. It plays to schools, colleges, institutions—it played to a leprosarium in the summer of 1966—and plays in the daytime in open spaces for nothing.

Today in Ghana, Nigeria, Kenya, Uganda, and the Ivory Coast numerous professional theater groups are active. The Institut des Arts of Abidjan, Ivory Coast, for example, produced and toured nine French-speaking African countries with Bernade Dadie's *Monsieur Thogo Gnini* in 1970. The Ghana Playhouse continues to extend its earlier experiment into African drama when it abandoned Shaw and Thornton Wilder for Soyinka and De Graft. The Tausi Dramatic Club of Nairobi presented sketches written by Bob Leshoai, the South African-born head of Dar es Salaam University's Theatre Arts Department. In Uganda, the Kampala City Players put on Kawadaw's play *Saint Lavanga,* on the occasion of

Pope Paul XI's visit to that country. The production was by David Rubadiri, the Malawian poet and actor, who also later directed Serumaga's *The Elephants*. The Theatre Association of Zambia produced an adaptation of Oyono's *Boy* in 1970. The various government-sponsored institutions such as the Arts Centre of Ghana and the National Theatre in Kampala seem to have had a new lease of life. But lack of foresight and imagination sometimes retards the progress of some of these institutions. An example is the frightful civil service mentality that runs the Arts Centre of Ghana, to the excruciating pain and annoyance of any artist who comes in touch with it. The professional groups seem to have come into their own in Nigeria where the School of Drama at Ibadan continues to produce a good corps of actors. These groups function efficiently, in spite of initial financial problems, because of their stubborn dedication to a growing and exhilarating experiment.

What of the future? First the play itself, for the play is the thing. A good number of African writers see the experiment in synthesis as the most legitimate pattern of growth for the theater in Africa. This means that the dramatists and playwrights will use elements from traditional ritual drama and folklore as the basic technical ingredient of their stagecraft. Difficulties imposed by the conventional European stage will be eliminated by a balanced use of forms which come naturally to older dramatic structures, e.g., theater in the round has been used very successfully in the Drama Studio in Accra—it promotes audience participation which is an important feature of traditional African drama. Boldness and imagination are needed on the part of planners of the theater buildings—copying European and American models can be ruinous to the development of African drama. The theater building in Kampala is an example of this lack of imagination and enthusiastic imitation. A theater's primary function is *not* to beautify the city center. Aesthetic considerations are important, but less so than considerations of function and utility. In an age in which Africa is starting to build, to reproduce an English theater in the tropics is plain stupidity. An eye must be kept, if aesthetic reasons need also be served, on the architectural demands of the African landscape and on the content of the drama itself.

In the recent years, classical European plays have been pro-

duced using African theatrical conventions—costume, audience
participation, chorus movement, drumming, dancing, etc. This has
been a wonderful success. Joe de Graft's production of *Hamlet* in
Ghana led to a film version. The nature of De Graft's adaptation
lies in the use of a northern Ghanaian Frafra courtyard, with its
minareted walls.

The experiments of dramatists like Duro Ladipo, it seems, will
peter out, simply because they demand an accumulation of many
talents by one-man musician, actor, etc., since he is composer,
stage manager, and playwright. Besides, the technique seems to
lend itself to one-dimensional treatment; the music—unless the orchestra possesses a fantastic expertise and creativity—will bore
easily, especially if a wide variety does not exist or gets invented
to suit the themes of the plays. The demands of the technique are
rather forbidding; in the hands of a less talented person it will become a woeful drag.

The most fruitful direction that the theater movement can take
in Africa would seem to be toward more literary drama. By this I
mean the type of work Soyinka is doing. Some of his plays, like *A
Dance of the Forest, Kongi's Harvest,* and *The Lion and the Jewel,*
lend themselves readily to the use of music—drumming, dancing,
and singing. An enterprising producer can make much of them.
Others, like Clark and Nkosi, seem to be concerned with the ring
of their poetic and "literary" voices and therefore write plays that
remain unproducible. But to try to force traditional African material into a pseudo-classical mold is to miss the relevance of the
theater in modern Africa.

Other new art forms can be found in the dance and in popular
ballet based on African dances. The most widely known of these is
Guinea's *Ballet Africaine,* which has achieved international fame.
Traditional African dances are difficult to present on stage, but
with the application of choreography, they are appearing on sophisticated stages in Africa and overseas. The Sierra Leone Dance
Troupe, the Ghana Dance Ensemble, and other dance groups are
made up of young men and women drawn from various ethnic
backgrounds who are taught the various dances of their nations
as choreographed by African experts, some of whom have studied
abroad. Purists may object to the methods adopted, to the styliza-

tion and elaborate costuming, but this does not diminish the impact of the experiment. Nor does it destroy the integrity of the dances themselves.

The twentieth century is, in more than one sense, Africa's century. Having lost herself in the nineteenth century, abused and exploited in all other centuries, she is reassembling the remnants of her shattered personality and building a new identity which does not and cannot deny her historical contacts with Europe and Islam down the ages. The process is, at times, traumatic, but slowly the adjustment is being made, and in time this complex continent will emerge as a unified whole, uniting all her diverse sensibilities.

As has been stressed throughout this book, the art forms of Africa south of the Sahara have been exposed to many influences from historical external contacts. And there is no doubt that indigenous art still flourishes in the vast rural areas. But the artistic thrust of modern-day Africa is for synthesis, acculturation, for the cultural amalgams that will still express her essential nature. Europe and Islam penetrated Africa and left indelible marks upon the personality of the continent. In the case of Islam, absorption, adaptation, and amalgamation took a short time since the religion was a way of life that yielded to change and acclimatization. On this score, it is hard to find pure Islamic features in African art forms. But they are there, albeit finely blended into the aesthetic and social philosophies of the societies that absorbed them. But Judeo-Christian civilization made a more frontal and uncompromising assault, refusing to yield ground in any way. In spite of this, African cultures met the challenge and proceeded to make a slow but aware selection from the new culture; some of the aspects of it Africa could just not escape, with the spread of European-type education, economic activities, urbanization, communication networks, mass media, and the building of modern day nation-states to replace erstwhile traditional structures. As a result, we see on the continent a long and continuing process of acculturation and adaptation of European norms to serve African artistic needs.

It must be remembered also that within the urban, modern context, the traditional art forms had ceased to have any meaningful impact. The chiefly spiritual institutions that supported carvers and sculptors lost their pre-eminence in the society. The new

economic activities did not make for long-drawn-out funerals and
week-long festivals. Where these were formerly performed according to the seasons by fishermen and farmers, the onus falls today
on factory and office workers, some of whom do not have the faint-
est knowledge of these matters. What was left for the new urban
communities to do was to begin using the instruments, styles, and
motifs of the received culture and graft them onto the old forms
in order to create a viable cultural continuation and sustenance
for themselves.

Music is one of the areas in which this phenomenon of acculturation was achieved. In the field of popular music, it was the period
during and after the Second World War years that led to the
proliferation of bars and night clubs with dance bands and music.
This period saw the introduction of Western popular music and
the dance rhythms of Victor Sylvester and the American big
bands, particularly Glenn Miller and Benny Goodman. But this
music catered essentially to the urban elite and European sojourners. Later the development of indigenous popular music followed.
In the Congo, this music began with *rumba* from the early 1950s,
retaining features of an earlier music; the *maringa* played in the
local bars using traditional tones, the *likemba* (thumb piano),
with bottle and skin-head drum. This earlier music form shared
much in common with the *beguine, sebene,* and the *ebonga,* all of
which were related to the "highlife" music of Nigeria and the Gold
Coast. Later the guitar replaced the *likemba.* Then began the
growth of professional and semiprofessional groups, orchestras
made up of singers and guitarists whose style was modeled on Afro-
Cuban forms such as the *bolero, chacha, pachanga, merengue,
mambo.* By the early and mid-sixties, electric guitars, trumpets,
saxophones, and other European instruments had taken over
completely. The *boucher,* from Brazzaville, introduced a well-
articulated and smooth style. By this time, brass ensembles were
playing in Kinshasa, where a booming recording industry had been
launched in 1963. The *kara-kara* was a major musical step for
Congolese music, as it was identified with the country's travails
and the martyrdom of Patrice Lumumba. But the underlying music
remained the *rumba,* relying upon African rhythmic patterns, an
antiphonal system, and a jazzy beat. The music of Afro-Latin

musicians such as Pacheco and Machito, of Orchestre Aragon and the Afro-Cubans provided models for African musicians. By the late 1960s "soul music" from black America had entered the scene through the work of James Brown, Aretha Franklin, Otis Redding, and many others. This style was imitated and later incorporated into the *rumba* music and blended into *kara-kara*. The leading Congolese pop group, African Fiesta National, carried out the widest renovations, combining traditional music and jazz, developing new melodies, and singing about subjects that were more philosophic than love or politics. Recordings such as *Salongo Tina* is an example of this amalgam. Twenty years of contact with external musical forms have produced a typically Congolese music style which is rapidly spreading throughout sub-Saharan Africa. This is specifically urban music, relying for its spread on a vigorous recording industry, the availability of cheap battery-operated record players, and a large population of detribalized Africans.

In West Africa the story was no different. Juju music owes its growth to a marriage between Western instruments and an indigenous African musical style. "Highlife," a music whose origin is still obscure, has swept across the whole of West Africa and has received a great boost in the work of musicians such as E. T. Mensah of Ghana and Bobby Benson of Nigeria. The work of I. K. Dairo and other juju musicians represents an unconscious return to more basic African rhythms, even though it relies on European instruments alongside traditional Yoruba ones. There is similarity between this music and the popular Ghanaian guitar music played by E. K. Onyina and Kakaiku, men whose work helped the growth of Ghanaian highlife in the 1950s. The work of the African Brothers, a Ghanaian group, like that of most pop groups in West Africa, dealt with topics such as love, politics, friendship, and death. These groups play to packed dance halls and are beginning to achieve renown outside their own countries thanks to the record industry and radio. They are "mass" urban musicians, largely untrained, composing in their heads, playing by ear, and are very sensitive to all types of shifts in musical tastes.

In the area of so-called "serious music," we come across the same type of synthesis and desire to use the received foreign forms, if perhaps with a greater sense of selectivity and more conscious

artistic deliberation. Colonialism, as said earlier, had attempted
to exclude all African art forms. This was seen especially in the
work of the Christian Church in Africa. African music was ex-
cluded from Christian worship, and, as Laz Ekweme aptly points
out, a number of African instruments had begun to vanish, e.g.,
the Igbo *urbo-*a*kwala* and *une,* now replaced with the guitar.[1]
One significant adaptation of an African instrument was carried
out by E. Amu of Ghana, who re-created the Ashanti flute to form
the main instrument in the Legon School of Music Orchestra.
Gradually, however, African lyrics and choral style began to be
used in church, and today, in the liberated music of the splinter
apostolic churches, drums and gongs are used along with organs
and accordions. The Congolese *Missa Luba* is the most eloquent
piece of evidence in this process of adaptation and change. Among
serious composers there is Ayo Bankole who wrote a cantata,
Jona, in which he utilized Western and Nigerian musical instruments and even an Indian *tambura.* The work of Fela Sowande
and Ephraim Amu represent the most audacious use of European
musical scales to restate African musical themes. Critics consider
the work of these two as borrowing too heavily from Christian and
Western style, but their execution remains essentially African.
Amu's use of a polyphonic system is not unknown in Ewe music,
even though he writes his lyrics in Twi. Emmanuel Agor is an Ewe
musician who utilizes the guitar to re-create songs of lamentation
in a monophonic style. Philip Gbeho, the composer of Ghana's
national anthem, an ace drummer and master Ewe musician, also
heads the Ghana National Orchestra which has performed most
of the European classics. His own compositions, using Ghanaian
highlife and folk tunes, are always featured in any program the
orchestra performs. He is a musician who moves with incredible
ease across the two cultural boundaries, completely at ease in both.
Other musicians whose work continues to expand include Akin
Euba, whose *Olurunbi* is a symphonic study based on a popular
Yoruba legend. In this work, as he says, "The polyrhythmic idiom
of African traditional music is combined with the twelve-tone
technique developed by Arnold Schönberg." Nelson Okoli, Felix
Nwuba, Wilberforce Echezona, and Gideon Okongwu are all musicians trained in the Western idiom, but are returning to Igbo

musical sources without throwing away their Western influences. The growth of specialist music schools attached to training colleges and to universities will continue to produce this community of African musicians whose awareness and mastery of Western musical systems will not deny them a return to their own roots for inspiration.

The position of the African musician today can best be seen within the context of the new economic system in which he lives. While the traditional artist was a member of a larger group, creating anonymously within the conditions set by the group even though retaining his individuality, the new musicians, even those who play pop music, are individuals, professionals, who practice music as an economic necessity. The "serious" musicians are consciously in pursuit of their trade, forging new forms from their intimate knowledge of both worlds. South African music is one of the most eloquent samples of the syncretic direction that African music will take, perhaps at a more conscious and selective rate. South African jazz is already receiving acclaim outside the country in the work of artists such as Dollar Brand. *Kwela* music is an aspect of South African urban life; the quality of choral music in South Africa comes very close to that of Afro-American singing. It is out of this urban and refugee reality of South African black existence that a musical such as Todd Machikiza's *King Kong* emerged. In music, perhaps more than in any other art form in Africa, change will continue to be brisk, new forms, new instruments, and new styles borrowed from other places replacing old ones. Radio, television, and the cinema are the greatest disseminators of music. The arrival of the phonograph and recordings have made overseas music more accessible to Africans now than ever before. This trend will continue. But a true African style and idiom will persist even though the instruments and the manner may be borrowed and expanded upon.

The contemporary art of Africa, contrary to what art historians and critics of art in Africa believe, represents a fantastic renaissance, a rebirth after the darkness of colonial intervention. Some critics have stated that African art was already in a state of decline before the European advent. They draw attention to the

apathy and inaction that characterized life at the Benin court before its sack in 1897 as representing an eloquent testimony to this.
But to accept this view is to deny that from the oldest Nok terracotta heads, some of which go back two thousand years, there had
been fluctuations in the human history of Africa or that the various
representative artistic endeavors enjoyed sustained continuity ir-
respective of the changes in the fortunes of their makers. This view
is a false interpretation and is tantamount to establishing an alibi
for a great deal of the senseless destruction of Africa's art that
took place under colonialism.

The art of Africa, like all other aspects of her cultural life, inevitably came into contact with the two external factors that affected Africa. The influence of Islam in this field remains very
fragmentarily documented. It was a fact that the Moslem faith
discouraged the representation in any form of all human beings.
Thus, human figurines, heads, masks in any material whatsoever
were frowned upon. But Islam encouraged ornamental work in
metals, fabric designing, and calligraphy. The elaborate embroider-
ies on flowing men's robes throughout West Africa and the intricate
patterns woven on joromi, dashiki, agbada, batakari, and other
smocks have their origins in Moslem sources. The elaborate ornamental doors that have become famous in most Moslem areas can
be traced to Islam. Even the court art of modern-day kingdoms
like Ashanti, though not Islamized, have been influenced by
Islamic art in such ornamental and magical objects as talismans,
chairs, embroidered pillows, etc. The famous Ashanti *kuduo,* used
for storing gold dust, is reputed to be a copy of earlier Arab can-
teens. The elaborate architectural forms found in most mosques
in sub-Saharan Africa were copied from the Moslem north and
adapted to suit local conditions. It is obvious that in characteristic
fashion Islamic cultural patterns were absorbed into black African
traditions almost totally, and it is difficult today to document each
single area of influence in the adaptation and change. Islam merged
and blended with what it came upon, leading to new creativity in
many areas; this process took hundreds of years and has been so
thorough that nowhere can one find any clear dichotomy in the
people's art as in the case of Judeo-Christianity. Today the

abundance of ornamental sculpture in East Africa and the art works of the Moslem West Africa bear testimony to this fact.

Christianity came into Africa as a superior cultural institution. It launched a virulent attack on African religious sculpture which it regarded as idolatrous. It denigrated Africa's art as the work of the devil, as instruments of devil worship, grotesque, hideous, and barbarous proof of a decadent way of life. Even today, except in very few instances, the Christian Church in Africa continues to maintain this narrow attitude toward Africa's indigenous art.

Proselytization, however, was carried on with zeal. Gradually Christian or European motifs began to appear even in the old art. The crucifixes and the rock paintings of Mbafu in Zaire and the representation of Portuguese soldiers and envoys on Benin plaques point to this beginning. But this process of adaptation remained sporadic, since the traditional artist's function was defined within a fairly rigid religious and social code pertaining to a life style which the Christians frowned upon.

It is when the colonial era was well established and education introduced that the European cultural style began to be felt in Africa's art. And this is the period of the renaissance we spoke about, beginning with the teaching of art in schools, the training of art teachers overseas, and the encouragement of such activities as sculpture, painting, pottery, arts, and crafts even at the lowest levels of colonial education.

Some of the older artists who emerged during this period reproduced European art, since Western artists were their models in the famous art schools. Ben Enwonwu of Nigeria is said to have worked in two styles—one African, one European. Most of the earlier artists, including the late Kofi Antubam of Ghana, were trained to look at art as their European counterparts did. For them, art is an individualistic preoccupation, to be practiced in "schools." Like their European counterparts, their work reflects where they were trained and what their teachers taught. Some, like Elimo Njau of Kenya, are also fierce Christians who painted great murals depicting Christian themes. Only a few, among them Vincent Kofi of Ghana, are able to achieve an awareness (obviously self-induced) of their own art traditions.

Kofi's sculpture can be described as a fantastic synthesis of

European and African art concepts. His carvings attempt to preserve the organic shape of the trees from which they were hewn, a
principle very fundamental to traditional sculpture. There is a
tremendous spiritual force revealed in such works as *Awakening
Africa* and *Mother and Child,* combining individual awareness of
things and a deep communal sensibility. Even in his *Christ* we are
aware of a great power in the massive and overbearing proportions
of the image, almost like an African deity's. There is a rejection of
Christ's suffering role; in its place there is defiance and a strength
that achieves mastery over his surroundings. Kofi, however, rejects the "coldly scientific limits" of European art for a poetic African statement. He has written that artists must have the courage
to select, reject, and assimilate: "While we accept outside influences
as inevitable . . . no virile tradition will commit cultural suicide
by brainwashing itself and rejecting its past completely."[2]

It is with the same spirit that the Sudanese artist Ibrahim el
Salahi approaches his own work. A product of the Khartoum
Technical Institute and Slade School in London, Salahi turned
away from the Western art traditions to search for his own sources
of inspiration. The only source left for him because of the Islamic
restrictions on art was calligraphy. In a state of withdrawal and
seeking wisdom from the Koran, Salahi began to create a nervous,
tender, and mystical style based on thin moving lines that gradually
assumed haunting shapes—spiritlike, half men, half animals, that
bore a close affinity to a sub-Saharan mythological outlook than to
the ornamented world of Islamic thought. His art expresses, in
Beier's words, "the mystery of African ritual combined with the
other-worldliness of icons, with the introverted dreaming of the
Moslem saint in the desert." Such works as *Death of a Child* and
Revolution represent Salahi's finest achievements.

There are a number of African artists whose works may be regarded as remnants of the great traditions of the pre-Christian
period even though they continue to produce today. The best known
of these is Yemi Bisiri of Yorubaland. He is one of the four brass-
casters for the Ogboni society, a secret society that continues to
enjoy a great deal of prestige among the Yoruba. In their para-
phernalia of membership and ritual there are two figurines—male
and female—which represent the most important objects in the

cultic tradition of the society. Bisiri's father was also a caster, and in traditional style he inherited his father's divine role as an artist, a phenomenon very rare in modern times. His work in the lost-wax method is less severe than that of the older people; it expresses a more personal style, energy, and vitality. This bears testimony to the fact that even within the traditional context, an artist who has only a superficial contact with the forces of change (he never went to school), Bisiri carries on a tradition that, even though it does not enjoy the prestige of former times, continues to receive the respect and reverence of the ordinary Yoruba.

The other traditional artist of our times is Oira Idah, a Benin wood carver. Idah belongs to the same generation as Bisiri and was brought up under similar circumstances. Educated in the traditional way, he was taught how to carve by Oba Eweka. He later joined the palace society of the then-impoverished court whose previous *oba* had been exiled by the British. When things became hard, he left for Lagos where he became a carpenter. Twenty-seven years later he returned to Benin to head the court co-operative of carvers. After years of unimaginative co-op art, he turned to terra cotta. Rejecting Benin conventions, he allowed himself total freedom of invention. Beier compares his work to Brueghel in his very crowded style. He is also known as an eccentric individualist, whose life style is always in opposition to that of those around him.

Lamidi Fakeye, another Yoruba artist, is a much younger man, a descendant of craftsmen, a Moslem trained in the traditional African way. He spent years working for the Catholic Church at Ekiti. His most famous work is *Christ Carrying the Cross,* carved in the traditional style of angles and rounds. He also worked on church doors.

Then there are the young artists, especially in Nigeria, who are products of the modern art schools, whose work is reaching out for a synthesis and seeks to come to terms with history. The Nigeria Art School at Zaria produced a number of these artists. Foremost among them is Demas Nwoko, whose work returns to the Igbo mask in angular sharpness and exaggerated features. He has turned to terra cotta, obviously inspired by ancient Nok and Ife art. He is the most fiercely African of the group and thus inspires

a large number of followers who are striving to capture the purity
and aesthetic dimensions of old traditional art forms. Uche Okeke,
a classmate of Nwoko, whose work searches for an African identity,
contends that it is only in a return to the roots that the authentic
African can be found. He indulges in folkloric fantasies, crowding
his work with Tutuolan figures—scaly creatures, men with feather
hair, and such other characters from West African folklore. It is
no accident that Okeke is also an avid collector of Igbo folk tales.
In Ghana the work of the Akwapim Six, led by Dr. Oku Ompofo,
though not as African in orientation as that of Nwoko and his
group, strives for similar effect. Young artists such as Phoebe
Demasio and Galevo represent this loose community that searches
for African themes and style in the old traditions. But they are not
altogether insulated from their own surroundings. Some of
Demasio's lovely landscapes attempt to capture the somnolent
grace of the little picturesque Fanti villages that dot the western
coast of Ghana.

The greatest influence on the artistic world in Africa has been
exerted by single-minded European missionary artists. These men
and women have been denounced as "cultural imperialists" and
"art vultures" by so-called "nationalist" African intellectuals whose
main claim to an audience is because they are African. But however much these foreign art missionaries are condemned, it must
be remembered that their activities have led to decidedly exciting
revolutions in art and are contributing in no small way to the artistic
renaissance of the continent.

A few of the experiments however were shortsighted. Defosses
founded a studio, Académie Officielle des Beaux Arts, run by
Moonens in the Congo. It produced community art, boring, dull,
bearing the director's stamp. Students were taught to reproduce
the ideas of the teachers. Pierre Lods in Potopoto was obviously
a misguided romantic who was still seeking in Africa that mythical
noble savage, exotic and innocent beyond reason. His students'
art has spread across the whole of West Africa. Highly stylized, it
is painting done on black paper, of gentle moonlit villages perched
on the sides of serene rivers, of African tribesmen dancing some
forgotten steps to elegantly drawn drums, brandishing the ubiquitous spears. Lods' kind of artistic direction is as paternalistic as it

is spurious, denying the African any strongly felt relation to things, to man, or to the world. But some of these new missionaries are more enlightened, for example, Pancho Guedes, the Portuguese architect, in Lorenço Marques, who holds no formal classes but serves as adviser, teacher, and encourager of young African artists. One of his discoveries is Valente Malengatana, who is also a fine poet. Malengatana's work draws upon the everyday world, which he infuses with spirits, demons, and monsters. He is fascinated with the theme of suffering, of fear and horror, a veritable surrealistic world; to him, the real world bears close resemblance to his fantasy world.

Frank McEwen is an English artist who spent more than two decades in Paris, rubbing shoulders with such artists as Picasso and Braque. He was later appointed director of the Rhodesian National Gallery in Salisbury. This gallery was primarily intended to exhibit European art. But McEwen felt that the gallery was in a country whose own great art tradition goes as far back as Zimbabwe, even though there was very little work being done at the time he arrived. He further felt that the gallery had also to serve the African community and that this service could be provided by encouraging African artists to produce exhibitable pieces. As a result he started art schools in Sipollo, Inyanga, and the gallery itself. His would-be artists were all farmers, miners, and drivers. There was even one policeman. About seventy-five of the one thousand or so entrants stayed on. Most of these artists had never worked in wood, stone, or oil before coming to the schools. Their work progressed from a spontaneous, naïve, and almost childlike style to a more mature and conscious one. McEwen's concern was not to teach them style, but to allow each talent to flower in an atmosphere of encouragement. The result has been a tremendously fresh new art in stone and oil. Some of the leading artists are Mukomberanwa, Maringa, Dube, and Manyandure. The best-known sculptor among them is Boira Mteki, who has produced large-scale heads in granite. McEwen's work had been extended into the five-thousand-acre artist colony of Vukutu, where an attempt to forge a link with the ancient art of Zimbabwe has been interrupted by the political developments in Rhodesia. When this writer met McEwen in 1969, he was on the verge of moving back to England.

No clear information exists today on the fate of the artists or their work, or on what became of the great experiment in that embattled enclave.

The other most interesting experiment is that of Ulli and Georgina Beier and Susan Wanger in the Yoruba town of Oshogbo. Of this, Beier has given a fascinating if rather self-congratulatory account in his book *Contemporary Art in Africa*. The whole project started in 1962 with Zukan Bernart's summer art school for practicing art teachers and would-be artists at the Mbari Mbayo Center. In Beier's words, Bernhart designed the program to treat art with a "healthy disrespect. Paint was dribbled, sloshed, and slapped about. Cement, all kinds of scrap, bottle tops, sand, wire—anything that happened to be at hand—would be used." The workshop was later taken over by the West Indian artist Dennis Williams, who provided a more organized and serious direction. Georgina Beier took over from 1964 to 1967. The result has been, according to the organizers, astounding. Most of the young artists who emerged from the experiment had never dabbled in art before they went to the Mbari center. They were ordinary village lads with very little formal education, mostly unemployed or unemployable. Some of them have emerged as the most eloquent artists of the artistic renaissance in Nigeria.

Adebisi Fabunmi, one of the products of the Oshogbo program, is a painter whose incredible imagination is fascinated by the idea of the city or the town. The city he sees as part of a past mythology. His linocuts attempt a realist representation of towns, filled with fantastic animals and birds and a pervasive sense of doom. There is a feeling of tension, a sense of cosmic doom, that haunts his work. Some of his works are *City on the Moon, Flying City,* and *Afro Apollo*. His style has shifted from approach to approach which has given him an eclectic outlook. He has held exhibitions in Ibadan, Lagos, Kaduna, Ife, Berlin, Edinburgh, London, New York, and many other cities. He is now the caretaker of the Oba's palace in Oshogbo and has completed a large mural at the University of Ife's Institute of African Studies.

Another Oshogbo artist is Okemesi, who started as a member of Duro Ladipo's theater group and later became a member of Georgina Beier's painting workshop. He has emerged as a painter and printmaker. His paintings can be loosely described as expressive of the mystery of the animal world. *The Misfigured Toad, The Chameleon, The Wise Lion at the Nigerian Zoo* are some of his representative work. Airplanes, churches, the oracles of Ifa are part of his world, in which animal ogres haunt city landscapes. Paths, rivers, houses, windows are inhabited by these creatures. There are no human beings in his work—which underscores a sense of doom and of human flight. He has also worked in color on tapestries and given expression to a Tutuolan predilection for animal spirits.

Twins Seven-Seven is the Tutuolan Oshogbo artist par excellence. His spontaneous reproduction of Yoruba mythology, legend, and folklore makes him one of the most exciting artists of the Oshogbo group. He has a great sense of humor, especially in the telling of the stories based on Tutuola's *The Palm-Wine Drinkard* and other works where spirits, demons, ghosts, and gods are represented as comic characters. He is no surrealist but a natural mythologist to whom, as to Tutuola, there is no division between the world of waking reality and the world of spirits. Like Fabunmi, he forges a link between the world of mythology and that of contemporary life.

Murama Oyelami, another artist from Oshogbo, is described as a romantic abstractionist, whose interest in technique later moved him to strong imagery. subtlety in handling paint, and a great sense of color. His basic interest is in symbols.

As Beier wrote about the Oshogbo experiment, "no technique was introduced for its own sake." It never formed itself in a "school" or a formal art studio, since each artist expressed his own individuality in such strong terms—color, imagery, symbol, theme—that there was never the fear of it degenerating into a characterless imitation of some other artist. The result has been that these artists, drawn from the ordinary inhabitants of Oshogbo town, have achieved a good measure of recognition from their fellow townspeople and also from more elitist local and overseas connoisseurs of art. Above all, their work represents one of the powerful thrusts of the artistic renaissance of West Africa. As they paint murals for palaces, design and decorate gas stations, cast pendants for market women, they articulate both renewal and continuity in the great art traditions of Yorubaland.

Art continues to be part of traditional religious practice. Thousands of carvers and mask makers are still at work. Their styles may have changed from those of their forefathers, but there is a continuous link with them from the past to the present.

18

The future

Since the emergence of Negritude as a literary and philosophical creed, debates have been raging among intellectual artists' circles both inside and outside Africa as to what will constitute in the final analysis the "true" art or culture of Africa. Some of these debates ignore history and the contact made between Africa and other parts of the world and call for a return to a "pure" African condition. This viewpoint is fashionable among black American political activist and cultural circles where the belief is held that any Europeanism in African culture is tantamount to a betrayal of Africa's fine heritage. Africans heard speaking a European language, wearing European clothes, and confessing to European tastes in food and music are quickly dismissed as not "real" Africans.

This last attitude presupposes that the only authentic Africans are those in the rural countryside, beating their rhythmic drums, and performing long rituals. It denies the importance of cultural contacts with other cultures which have expanded as well as changed the continent's personality. But no nation is an island. Cultural "purity" is a dangerous myth that can arrest a people's growth and impose false ideas of superiority on them. Africa has herself suffered too long from European ethnocentrism to turn around to proclaim her own brand.

It must be remembered that the fascination of sub-Saharan Africa is its immense diversity and complexity, with societies at varying "levels" of development and change. Some are still fruit gatherers, others nomads, while some once had complex political institutions, sophisticated remnants of which still baffle outsiders. By no yardstick can all these various societies be judged primitive, preliterate, pretechnological. These are judgments that come with the narrow-mindedness of Western man's approach, whose language contains a series of calculated insults directed at those who are not members of his ethnic or racial community. It is these attitudes that inculcated a sense of inferiority in Africans, emphasized for them "tribal" divisions, and left certain ugly aftermaths in intergroup relationship in Africa. In the past, undoubtedly, there were wars and rivalries. But there was a great deal of borrowing and interchange in cultural behavior and religious ideas. Gods traveled freely from group to group. Institutions were borrowed from one group and adapted to suit another's own condition. There was growth and expansion of culture in all directions. A typical example can be found in Ashanti court life which, even though it resisted Islamization, borrowed liberally from Islamic religious concepts of talismanic magic. Or the many other groups who borrowed the concept of chiefs from Ashanti and made it their own. Material culture was also in a state of dynamic flux through the proliferation of traditional markets. Styles in dress, carving, weaving, pottery, and music were interchanged across so-called "tribal" boundaries, and local cultures achieved tremendously needed expansion as a result. The artists of Benin and Ife, as pointed out earlier, traveled with their art to other areas and spread it. Other groups were in touch with Islam by way of trade, but when some of them became converted, they did not throw away entirely their important traditions for a totally Moslem outlook. There was adaptation, adoption, and change. Notions of progress and of what was outmoded were prevalent.

The contact with Europe came without Africa's choice; but it released new energies and outlooks. The difficulty was in the fundamental differences in the two world views. These clashed and at times were locked in violent confrontation, sometimes to the frustration and sorrow of one and to the utter dismay and impulsive reaction of the other. Wars of extermination were fought by European powers. Africa did not believe she was superior to Europe, nor that she was inferior. But Europe's penetration into Africa was predicated on a concept of racial superiority, religious bigotry, and greedy commercial and mercantile interest. The traditional mutuality of trade had been destroyed very early when the Portuguese betrayed the trust of the Mani Congo kingdom under Mzinga. What followed was pillage, exploitation, and outright take-over. But Africa refused to yield, to commit cultural suicide as the red man did in America. She accepted European ways, even though with some disastrous consequences, but in many instances she acted in her own interest, retaining her cultural features, albeit utilizing a haphazard sense of selection. Every culture survives in its natural milieu. The survival of African culture in Brazil, Haiti, Surinam, Cuba, Jamaica, Trinidad, and America, for example, is a tribute to its resilience and its dynamic capacity to adapt and change. It is in the same way that the traditional cultures of Africa behaved in their confrontation with European manners and ways on the continent itself. Being the conqueror's way of life, European culture enjoyed a tremendous prestige as the way of life for the ruling class and its allies. It was set up as the most desirable, and the indigenous culture in typical fashion was derided as primitive, backward, and savage. The African was told to escape this way of life to which he had been condemned by geography, climate, and history (and the Christian God). For him salvation lay in accepting European ways *in toto,* and his being a "civilized" man depended on how well he demonstrated his grasp of this way of life. Thus, the first generation of educated Africans, as pointed out earlier, became a sorrowful community of *déraciné* aliens in their own countries, locked into caricature roles of white men; frustrated, yet eloquently persuaded to believe that they have been saved. It was the articulate members of that generation, however, both at home and abroad, that finally protested against the suffocating hold of European culture and clamored for a return to things African. Negritude was and is an aspect of this cultural revolt.

But things European had penetrated too deeply into the African's world to be uprooted now. The growth of urban communities

led to the development of an urban elite that was no longer be-
holding to traditional political and commercial systems. Roads
brought vehicular transport. Harbors and airports created links
with the world. Radio, cinema, and television, the communication
media of the twentieth century, brought Africans international pop
music and the politician's voice. In the cities, night clubs and
dance halls, fashioned after European models, appeared. Africans
flocked to dancing schools to learn the tango and the foxtrot. The
city layabouts picked up the sharp, tough language of American
gangster movies which were rushed to the continent after the
Second World War. A growing community of urban Africans was
being produced, especially in the commercial and mining cities
of Johannesburg, Nairobi, Lagos, Kinshasa, Accra, and Dakar.

In South Africa a section of Africa that made some of the
earliest and the more lasting contacts with Europe from the early
sixteenth-century settlement of the Cape, a more defined Europeanism showed itself, not only in the so-called "colored" population, but also among the blacks driven from their rural homes by
land hunger and economic necessity into city ghettos where they
could sell their labor. An urban culture was bound to result, as
illustrated today by the choral music style, the penny whistle, and
the jazz of the South African black. A purely "tribal" culture
could no longer exist in this context. As Ezekiel Mphahlele suc-
cinctly points out in his book *The African Image,* ethnicity is no
longer possible, for the urban black has brought into the European-
created ghettos that strong artistic sense of his earlier community
and in these veritable graveyards forged a powerful medium of his
new personality. For him, therefore, Negritude will remain so much
nonsense. This is also true of the peripheral communities of all
large African cities, where the so-called "tribal" way of life has
given way to harsh twentieth-century realities.

Even in the rural areas of Africa, the ordinary man's life has
been immensely affected by Europe. Motor roads traverse country
which was once only accessible on foot. Bridges span the great
rivers. Flourishing markets are centers for large-scale trade in food
and local products—salt, meats, baskets, pottery, and dried fish
or imported commodities such as cloth, sugar, and canned goods.
Villages use large amounts of kerosene, lubricating oil, and gaso-

line. The stone corn grinder and the mortar are being replaced by the mechanized corn mill with a piston engine. The village has acquired a post office with telephone communications to the district capital. The police station has come to keep an eye on things and to make sure that no one breaks the law made by the legislature in the capital. The villager can now reach the capital in a matter of hours, covering a distance which he used to dread because it took a week or more in the olden days. Besides, the capital is no longer a "foreign" land where he will be lost. There are many of his brothers and relatives there, seeking to make their fortune in all kinds of ways. Maybe the villager still pursues his father's religion, observes the rituals, and performs the rites, but these do not make as strong a demand on him as they did on his father. He has to respond to newer and harsher economic laws than his father did. He has to send his children to the village school he helped build through communal labor. He still goes when his chief calls him; but he knows that a new power greater than his chief now rules the land. This power is in the capital and has, since colonial times, persuaded him to believe that his chief was essentially its servant; whenever the chief offended this power, his little authority in the village could be taken away. The villager may now and then appear at the village Roman Catholic church where he had been persuaded some years ago to undergo the sacrament of holy baptism. But he is still able to pour libation to his ancestors, perform the ritual of outdooring for his children, marry his daughters properly according to the ancient customs, without feeling any sense of confusion. For him both worlds have harmonized beautifully. There is no dichotomy between the old and the new any longer. The sharp edges of conflict during the earliest days of the confrontation have been smoothed by time and by events. Once, when he resisted, he was beaten on the head and thrown into jail with shackles on his hands. Now he knows his son can enter the highest school in the land and, if even irregularly, drive back into the village in a shiny motor car. Status and achievement are still important in the group code, and desirable today even in European terms. Total mechanization has not occurred in the village yet and is not likely to for a long time. Meanwhile, the villager has time to blend two worlds comfortably, depending on the old for his spiritual sustenance and on the new for his material survival.

The debate on Negritude seems to focus itself on the fundamental question of what Africa will develop into. It must be said once and for all, that Africa cannot remain, however exciting the prospect, in that atavistic world of golden-age virtues dreamed up by the Negritude poets. Too much has happened for this romantic ideal to be kept alive. The frustration of long-exiled Africans overseas at Africa's rapid pace of change and acquisition of European ways is the understandable reaction of cultural zealots and fatherland romantics. The African was never a "noble savage," happy under a mango tree, never just a drum-beating, dancing, and fornicating jackass. He, in his way of life, demonstrated an ability to seek pragmatic solutions to problems of food and survival and to forge a rational system that grasped the basic natural laws governing the group. He above all possessed a metaphysical balancing ideology that assured him survival beyond the grave and placed him in constant touch with spirits, deities, and gods while he was alive. In fact, his perception of the world was anything but simpleminded; it was based on a complex philosophy of survival that ensured harmony and balance for him in both the observable and invisible worlds.

But what of the culture of the new Africa? Theories and concepts of literature, sculpture, and music will change with the changes in life style. The old royal and chiefly courts that provided support for art have lost their powers. African religious systems are daily undergoing change, so the role of the great ritual carvers of masks, figurines, and workers in iron will continue to diminish. With education, young acolytes can no longer be found to enter shrines and go through their training as priests and priestesses. The ancient drummers will not be replaced. But if this picture sounds bleak, there is the consolation that many African governments and bodies are making strenuous efforts to divert the educated African's attention to his real cultural foundation. Today there are London-trained lawyers sitting on ancient stools and university men in shrines and temples. Most of the elite are returning to the drums, the music, and the oral traditions. At the same time, a large community of African artists is returning to these earlier patterns in order to forge, through the newly acquired European instruments, new artistic patterns. Musicians are returning to traditional motifs, for incorporation into their choral compositions. Writers are searching the great subsoil of oral literature for poetic systems of both style and theme to use in new and exciting statements upon the affairs of their own times. Education, Christianity, the growth of nation states, the influence and spread of European languages will continue to exert a large amount of influence on the culture of Africa as a whole.

As much as the present-day rejection of Negritude is based in realistic assessments of contemporary African life, some other theoreticians of art in Africa seem to have fled to the opposite extreme of embracing the entirety of European culture as the most legitimate point of departure for a detribalized Africa. This is as spurious as it is dictated by a sense of cultural inferiority and self-rejection. Europe did not enter a vacuum in Africa. An African who produces a replica of Eliot's poetry or recomposes Debussy or copies Monet is denying himself access to the rich culture of his own people and, like the proverbial antelope, would be dancing himself lame at other people's festivals while he neglects his own. It is like those Africans who meet every week in an African capital to eat roast beef and Yorkshire pudding served by starched stewards on naked feet and then toast the English universities that produced such fine fellows. These gentlemen, to a man, cannot dance one simple step to any of their own traditional drums— those, they have been taught, do not represent "progress."

At the first African writers' conference held at the University College, Makerere, Kampala, in June 1962, it was quite clear that contemporary African writing was still in its tender infancy and debates as to direction were overloaded with rhetoric. Of all the writers who attended, only Chinua Achebe had then published any novels. Ngugi was still an undergraduate. Soyinka had written a few plays, including *A Dance of the Forest*. Many of the writers had only been published in anthologies or magazines. The Makerere meeting brought together writers from all over sub-Saharan Africa, with large contingents from Nigeria, South Africa, Ghana, Cameroon, Senegal, Kenya, Uganda, and many other countries. There were present also delegates from the United States and Jamaica and numerous publishers' representatives. The opportunity to meet and talk about the problems of language, style, and theme was an exciting one for all of us. Most of the young writers gathered at Makerere were products of the new African universities, who were aware of their commitment to an African aesthetics but not clear as to the direction it should take. Of all of us, Achebe was the most self-assured, a rapidly maturing writer who was then working on his third novel. Most of us were full of brilliant ideas, but had only published some indifferent verse, an imitation Greek play, or a couple of not very distinguished short stories. The conference's major achievement was to give these young men and women a firm awareness, though at times in convoluted rhetoric and pompous proclamations, of the cultural problems that face Africa and of their roles as writers. There were no manifestoes or slogans. Writers, or would-be writers, confronted one another with pertinent questions, such as, What do you write about as a twentieth-century African? In what language or style do you write? For whom are you writing? Some of these questions were to emerge again and again at subsequent conferences in Freetown, Dakar, Berlin, and Stockholm, where the issues were examined afresh.

One of the greatest subjects that keep coming up at African writers' conferences is the subject of commitment. In a paper to the conference at Stockholm in February 1967, Wole Soyinka, speaking on the writer in a modern African state, says this, inter alia:

> The writer must for the moment at least postpone that unique reflection on experience and events which is what makes a writer, and constitute himself into a part of that machinery that shapes events.[1]

Soyinka was at the time acutely aware of events in Africa, especially of his own Nigeria of 1967. There followed a confused debate in which the South African journalist Lewis Nkosi held forth for a mystical body of "good" literature. (He did not point out by whose standard literature written in English or French by Africans is to be judged "good" or "bad.") John Nagenda of Uganda, rejecting the role of spokesman for suffering humanity, claimed his right to play football while people die in his country. James Ngugi made a passionate pledge to fight for the peasants and workers of Africa.

Tchicaya U Tam'si denied any revolutionary commitment for the writer whatsoever. As these statements illustrate, there was a tremendous amount of groping.

It took the Nigerian civil war later that year and the example of Christopher Okigbo, who died in that struggle, to show that a writer is primarily a member of his own society and that there is no time when he cannot be committed to ending the sufferings of his people. Soyinka's suggestion that he make this commitment only on a temporary basis is untenable. For where does art and culture stop and the business of life and survival begin? The commitment made by young Igbo writers and artists during the civil war, whether we agree with their positions or not, is an example of the human spirit rising to the occasion and fighting to oppose the forces of death and destruction at all cost. There are no great art theories involved in this. In Africa, where despair deepens in the practice of politics and in the lives of the ordinary people, the writers must represent the vanguard of the armies that will liberate the masses from ignorance and cultural strangulation and restore for them their earlier attachment to life. In this vanguard must be sculptors, musicians, and all those who will bend their talents to forging a link between the past, in all its imperfections, and the future. African culture must represent a continuous growth from the past, through the present, into the future, bearing select gifts from the various contacts it has made with outside forces and maintaining a unique personality in its verve and dynamism.

In literature, by all means, Africans should continue to use the received languages of Europe, namely, French and English, but as Achebe aptly pointed out and amply illustrated in his own work, these languages must achieve adaptation to the African soil, taking on local coloring from the energetic languages with which they come into contact. But this must not push the need for developing literature in indigenous languages into secondary position. Valuable work remains to be done on the languages of Africa to enable a sound literature to have a good soil to grow in. The vernacular literatures of Africa have been left to a few mission-educated people and churchmen, most of whom are dying out. The publication and dissemination of this literature will be giant steps in its nurturing.

Above all, the literature, like the music, art, and sculpture, must return to the traditional sources for inspiration. The traditional forms and styles, which, in themselves, constitute great statements of man, should be forged into the contemporary idioms of our times, enriched by our contact with Europe and Islam but yet remaining eloquently and distinctly African in the truest sense. It is only when this line of continuity is forged that the continent that has been harassed for centuries will recover the personality of her true self and in so doing cease to be a bad caricature and copy of her external mentors. Those who call for a total Europeanization of Africa are calling for cultural suicide. Those who are asking for a pure and pristine cultural journey into the past are dreamers who must wake up. For in the center, somewhere between these two positions, lies the only possibility.

Notes

Chapter 5

1. W. E. Abraham, *The Mind of Africa* (New York, Praeger, 1966), p. 42.

Chapter 6

1. Abraham, *The Mind of Africa,* p. 112.
2. Ibid., p. 112.
3. Florence Fels, ed., "Views on Negro Art," *Action,* April 1920.
4. Ladislas Segy, *Plastic Aspects of African Sculpture* (New York, Dover, 1958).

Chapter 7

1. Ulli Beier, "Yoruba Theater," in Ulli Beier, ed., *Introduction to African Literature* (Evanston, Ill., Northwestern University Press, 1967), p. 243.
2. G. I. Jones, "Masked Plays of Southeastern Nigeria," *Geographical Magazine,* September 5, 1945.
3. R. S. Rattray, *Religion and Art in Ashanti* (London, Oxford University Press, 1965), p. 192.
4. Joan Wescott, "Eshu-Elegba, the Yoruba Trickster," *Africa,* 31 (October 1962), p. 342.
5. Ibid., p. 338.
6. J. G. Frazer, *Folklore in the Old Testament* (London, Macmillan, 1918), Vol. 1, p. 9.
7. Ruth Finnegan, *Oral Literature in Africa* (London, Clarendon Press, 1970), p. 320.
8. R. S. Rattray makes a similar point in his *Akan Ashanti Folktales* (Leiden, Bril, 1954).

9. W. R. Bascom, "Folklore Research in Africa," *Journal of American Folklore,* 77, 1964.

10. Susan Feldman, ed., *African Myths and Tales* (New York, Dell, 1963).

11. The work of the School of Social Anthropology at Oxford is said to be strongly dominated by this approach.

12. T. O. Beidelman, "Hyaena and Rabbit: A Kaguru Representation of Matriarchal Relations," *Africa,* 31, 1961.

13. S. A. Bababola, *The Content and Form of Yoruba Ijala* (London, Clarendon Press, 1966).

14. Ibid., p. 46.

15. Ibid., p. 47.

16. Ibid., p. 48.

17. Ulli Beier, ed., *Yoruba Poetry* (London, Cambridge University Press, 1970), p. 28.

18. Ibid., p. 31.

19. G. Lienhardt, *Divinity and Experience: The Religion of the Dinka* (Oxford, 1961), p. 38.

20. Author's translation of Afa divination song of the Ewe. See my *Guardians of the Sacred Word* (New York, NOK, 1974).

21. W. M. Eiselen, "Art of Divination Among the Bamesola," *Bantu Studies,* 6, 1932, p. 11. Quoted from Finnegan, *Oral Literature in Africa.*

22. F. Laydevant, "The Praises of the Divining Bones Among the Basotho," *Bantu Studies,* 7, 1933, p. 349. Quoted from Finnegan, *Oral Literature in Africa.*

23. This is an Ewe magical spell used in disarming an adversary. Translation by author.

24. Okot pBtek, "Oral Literature and its Social Background Among the Acholi and Lango," B.Litt. thesis, Oxford University, 1963, p. 209.

25. M. Read, "Songs of the Ngoni People," *Bantu Studies,* 11, 1937, p. 14. Quoted from Finnegan, *Oral Literature in Africa.*

26. J. H. Nketia, *Funeral Dirges of the Akan People* (Achimota, Ghana, Achimota, 1955), p. 196.

27. G. Adali-Mortty, "Ewe Poetry," in Beier, ed., *Introduction to African Literature.*

28. S. M. Mofokeng, "Praise Poems in Southern Sotho," honors dissertation, University of Witwatersrand, 1945, p. 128.

29. B. W. Vilakazi, "The Oral and Written Literature in Ngoni," D.Litt. thesis, University of Witwatersrand, 1945, p. 45. Quoted from Finnegan, *Oral Literature in Africa.*

30. Kofi Awoonor, *Guardians of the Sacred Word* (New York, NOK, 1974).

31. Ibid.

32. Jan Knappert, "Swahili Poetry," in Beier, ed., *Introduction to African Literature,* p. 44.

33. Author's translation of popular Ewe love song.

34. G. Moore and Ulli Beier, eds., *Modern Poetry from Africa* (Baltimore, Penguin, 1963), p. 102.

35. J. H. Nketia, *Folk Songs of Ghana* (Legon, 1963), p. 108.

36. Author's translation of Ewe war poems.

37. J. H. Nketia, "Akan Poetry," in Beier, ed., *Introduction to African Literature*, p. 30.

38. Babalola, *The Content and Form of Yoruba Ijala.*

39. Ibid., p. 46.

40. Ibid., p. 66.

41. Beier, ed., *Yoruba Poetry*, pp. 33–35.

42. Ibid., p. 66.

43. Ibid., p. 64.

44. Nketia, *Funeral Dirges of the Akan People*, p. 119.

45. Ibid., pp. 67–68.

46. Ibid.

47. Ibid.

48. Ibid.

49. Ibid., pp. 34–35.

50. Nketia, "Akan Poetry," in Beier, ed., *Introduction to African Literature*, p. 29.

51. Ibid., p. 30.

52. James Stuart and D. Malcolm, *Izibongo: Zulu Praise Poems* (London, Oxford University Press, 1968), p. 41.

53. Ibid.

54. Ibid., p. 54.

55. Ibid., p. 59.

56. Mofokeng, "Praise Poems in Southern Sotho," p. 130.

57. Finnegan, *Oral Literature in Africa*, p. 135.

58. Ibid.

59. Ibid., p. 136.

60. Ibid., p. 137.

61. Stuart and Malcolm, *Izibongo: Zulu Praise Poems,* p. 88.

62. Nandi, Shaka's mother, was fictionalized in Rider Haggard's *Nada the Lily*, 1892.

63. A dirge piece ascribed to Akpalu. Translated by author.

64. G. Adali-Mortty, "Ewe Poetry," in Beier, ed., *Introduction to African Literature.*

65. Author's translation of popular Ewe fishermen's song.

66. Author's translation of an Afa divination song.

67. Author's translation of an Ewe salutation or praise poem.

68. Author's translation of an Afa song.

69. Author's translation of an Afa song.

70. Author's translation of a set of Ewe war poems.

71. Kofi Awoonor, *Guardians of the Sacred Word*, p. 39.

72. Ibid., p. 41.
73. Ibid., p. 40.
74. Ibid., p. 91.
75. Ibid., p. 59.

Chapter 8
1. Don Scharfe and Yahaya Aliyu, "Hausa Poetry," in Ulli Beier, ed., *Introduction to African Literature*, p. 38.
2. Ibid., p. 39.
3. Jan Knappert, "Swahili Poetry," in Beier, ed., *Introduction to African Literature*, p. 42.
4. Ibid., p. 44.
5. Ibid., p. 46.
6. Ibid., p. 47.

Chapter 9
1. Janheinz Jahn, *A History of Neo-African Literature* (London, Faber and Faber, 1966), p. 31.
2. Ibid., p. 32.
3. Ibid., p. 37.
4. Ibid.
5. Lalage Brown, ed., *Two Centuries of African English* (London, Heinemann, 1973), p. 31.
6. Aimé Césaire, *Return to My Native Land* (Paris, Présence Africaine, 1968), p. 101.
7. Quoted in Claude Wauthier, *The Literature and Thought of Modern Africa* (London, Pall Mall, 1966), p. 147.
8. Césaire, *Return to My Native Land*, p. 108.
9. Léopold S. Senghor, "L'Esthétique Negro-Africaine," *Liberté*, 1, 1964.
10. Jean Paul Sartre, "Orphée Noir," preface to Senghor, ed., *Anthologie de la nouvelle poesie négre et malagache* (Paris, Presses Universitaires de France, 1948).
11. Léopold S. Senghor, *Prose and Poetry*, ed. and trans. by John Reed and Clive Wake (London, Oxford University Press, 1965), p. 39.
12. Ibid., p. 157.
13. Moore and Beier, eds., *Modern Poetry from Africa*, p. 65.

Chapter 10
1. Césaire, *Return to My Native Land*, p. 19.
2. Ibid., p. 21.
3. Ibid., p. 23.
4. Ibid.
5. Ibid., p. 27.
6. Ibid., p. 9.
7. Ibid., p. 39.
8. Ibid., p. 49.

9. Ibid., p. 83.
10. Ibid., p. 101.
11. Ibid., p. 125.
12. Ibid., p. 135.
13. Senghor, *Prose and Poetry,* p. 108.
14. Ibid., p. 104.
15. Ibid., p. 105.
16. Ibid., p. 107.
17. Ibid., p. 108.
18. Ibid., p. 109.
19. Ibid., p. 111.
20. Ibid., p. 116.
21. Ibid.
22. Ibid., p. 159.
23. Ibid., p. 166.
24. Moore and Beier, eds., *Modern Poetry from Africa,* pp. 63–64.
25. Ibid., pp. 61–62.
26. Ibid., p. 61.
27. Ibid.
28. Ibid., p. 62.
29. Ibid.
30. Ibid., p. 63.
31. Ibid., pp. 63–64.
32. Ibid., p. 64.
33. Ibid., p. 65.
34. Ibid., p. 66.
35. Ibid., p. 67.
36. Tchicaya U Tam'si, *Selected Poems* (London, Heinemann, 1970), p. 18.
37. Moore and Beier, eds., *Modern Poetry from Africa,* p. 169.
38. Ibid., p. 170.
39. Ibid.
40. Ibid., p. 171.
41. Ibid.
42. Ibid.
43. Ibid., p. 172.
44. Ibid.
45. Ibid., p. 173.
46. Ibid.
47. Ibid.
48. Ibid.
49. Ibid.
50. Ibid., p. 174.
51. Ibid.
52. Ibid.

53. Ibid., p. 175.
54. Ibid.
55. U Tam'si, *Collected Poems,* p. 44.

Chapter 11
1. Donatus Nwoga, *West African Verse* (London, Longmans, 1967), p. 5.
2. Ibid., p. 6.
3. Ibid.
4. Ibid., p. 7.
5. Ibid., p. 9.
6. Ibid., p. 10.
7. Ibid., p. 12.
8. Ibid., p. 13.
9. Ibid., p. 14.
10. Ibid., p. 15.
11. Ibid.
12. Ibid., p. 16.
13. Ibid., p. 17.
14. Ibid., p. 20.
15. Ibid., p. 21.
16. Ibid., p. 22.

Chapter 12
1. Mazisi Kunene, *Zulu Poems* (New York, Africana, 1970), p. 19.
2. Moore and Beier, eds., *Modern Poetry from Africa,* p. 208.
3. Kunene, *Zulu Poems,* p. 11.
4. Ibid., p. 17.
5. Ibid., p. 17.
6. Ibid., p. 23.
7. Ibid., p. 83.
8. Ibid., p. 77.
9. Ibid., p. 35.
10. Ibid., p. 26.
11. Ibid., p. 89.
12. Ibid.
13. Ibid., p. 91.
14. Ibid., p. 94.
15. Ibid.
16. Ibid., p. 95.
17. Ibid., p. 27.
18. Moore and Beier, eds., *Modern Poetry from Africa,* p. 98.
19. Awoonor, *Night of My Blood,* p. 63.
20. Ibid., p. 42.
21. Ibid.
22. Ibid., p. 43.
23. Ibid., p. 44.

24. Ibid., p. 45.
25. Ibid., p. 44.
26. Ibid., pp. 45–46.
27. Ibid., p. 46.
28. Ibid.
29. Ibid., p. 50.
30. Ibid., p. 51.
31. Ibid.
32. Ibid., p. 53.
33. Moore and Beier, eds., *Modern Poetry from Africa,* p. 100.
34. Awoonor, *Night of My Blood,* p. 68.
35. Ibid.
36. Ibid.
37. Ibid.
38. Ibid., p. 69.
39. Ibid.
40. Christopher Okigbo, *Labyrinths* (London, Heinemann, 1971), p. xii.
41. Ibid., p. 3.
42. Ibid., p. xi.
43. Ibid., p. 10.
44. Ibid., p. 12.
45. Ibid., p. 17.
46. Ibid., p. xi.
47. Ibid., p. 23.
48. Ibid., p. 25.
49. Ibid., p. 32.
50. Ibid., p. 65.
51. Ibid., p. 66.
52. Ibid.
53. Ibid., p. 67.
54. Ibid.
55. Ibid., p. 68.
56. Ibid., p. 70.
57. Ibid., p. 72.

Chapter 13
1. Amos Tutuola, *The Palm-Wine Drinkard* (New York, Grove Press, 1953), p. 16.
2. Ibid., p. 11.
3. Ibid.
4. Ibid., p. 16.
5. Ibid., p. 46.
6. Ibid., p. 68.
7. Ibid., p. 31.
8. Ibid., p. 38.

9. Ibid., p. 41.

10. Ibid., p. 25.

11. Ibid.

12. Ibid., p. 101.

13. Ibid., p. 125.

14. Gerald Moore, "Amos Tutuola: A Nigerian Visionary," in Beier, ed., *Introduction to African Literature,* p. 179.

15. Tutuola, *The Palm-Wine Drinkard,* pp. 124–25.

16. Amos Tutuola, *My Life in the Bush of Ghosts* (New York, Grove Press, 1954), p. 21.

17. Ibid., p. 22.

18. Ibid., pp. 112–13.

19. Ibid., p. 121.

20. Ibid., pp. 161–62.

21. Ibid., p. 163.

22. Bernth Lindfors, "Amos Tutuola's Television-handed Ghostess," *Ariel,* 2, I, January, 1971.

23. D. O. Fagunwa, *The Forest of a Thousand Daemons: A Hunter's Saga* (London, Nelson, 1968), p. 94. Translated by Wole Soyinka.

24. Tutuola, *The Palm-Wine Drinkard,* p. 16.

25. Ibid., p. 85.

26. Ibid., p. 7.

27. Ulli Beier, "D. O. Fagunwa: A Yoruba Novelist," in Beier, ed., *Introduction to African Literature.*

28. Lindfors, "Amos Tutuola's Television-handed Ghostess."

29. Beier, "D. O. Fagunwa: A Yoruba Novelist," p. 188.

30. Harold Collins, *Amos Tutuola* (New York, Twayne, 1969).

31. Ibid., p. 39. Italics mine.

32. G. Parrinder, introduction to Tutuola, *My Life in the Bush of Ghosts,* p. 10.

Chapter 14

1. Ezekiel Mphahlele, *The African Image* (New York, Praeger, 1962), p. 161.

2. Chinua Achebe, "English and the African Writer," *Transition,* 18, p. 29.

3. Chinua Achebe, "The Role of the African Writer in a New Nation," *Nigeria Magazine,* 81, June 1964, p. 158.

4. Chinua Achebe, "The Novelist as a Teacher," *Journal of Commonwealth Literature,* 3, 1967, p. 204.

5. Chinua Achebe, *Things Fall Apart* (Greenwich, Conn., Fawcett, 1959), p. 7.

6. Ibid., p. 24.

7. B. I. Chukwukere, "Individualism in an Aspect of Igbo Religion," *The Conch,* III, 2, 1971, p. 112.

8. Donatus Nwoga, "The Chi, Individualism and Igbo Religion," *The Conch,* III, 2, p. 119.

9. Abraham, *The Mind of Africa,* p. 59.

10. Achebe, *Things Fall Apart,* p. 28.

11. Ibid., p. 27.

12. Ibid.

13. Ibid., p. 29.

14. Ibid., p. 28.

15. Ibid., p. 21.

16. Ibid., p. 31.

17. Ibid., p. 32.

18. Ibid., pp. 32–33.

19. Ibid., p. 121.

20. Ibid., p. 158.

21. Ibid., p. 157.

22. Ibid., p. 159.

23. Ibid., p. 167.

24. Ibid., p. 168.

25. Ibid., p. 176.

26. Ibid., p. 188.

27. Chinua Achebe, *No Longer at Ease* (London, Heinemann, 1960), p. 54.

28. Ibid., p. 133.

29. Ibid., pp. 10–11.

30. John S. Mbiti, *Concept of God in Africa* (New York, Praeger, 1970), p. 220.

31. Chinua Achebe, *Arrow of God* (New York, Anchor, 1969), p. 249.

32. Ibid., p. 219.

33. Ibid., p. 150.

34. Ibid., p. 79.

35. Ibid., p. 80.

36. Ibid., p. 82.

37. Ibid., p. 83.

38. Ibid., p. 260.

39. Ibid., p. 157.

40. Ibid., p. 162.

41. Ibid.

Chapter 15

1. James Ngugi, *Weep Not, Child* (London, Heinemann, 1964), p. 7.

2. Ibid., p. 28.

3. Ibid., p. 35.

4. Ibid., pp. 57–58.

5. Ibid., p. 95.

6. James Ngugi, *The River Between* (London, Heinemann, 1965), p. 24.

7. James Ngugi, *A Grain of Wheat* (London, Heinemann, 1967), p. vi.
8. Ferdinand Oyono, *Boy* (New York, Collier, 1970), p. 15.
9. Ibid., p. 10.
10. Ibid., p. 9.
11. Ibid., p. 22.
12. Ibid., p. 19.
13. Ibid., pp. 25–26.
14. Ibid., p. 29.
15. Ibid., p. 55.
16. Ibid., p. 66.
17. Ibid., p. 138.
18. Ibid., p. 142.
19. Ibid., p. 6.
20. Ferdinand Oyono, *The Old Man and the Medal* (New York, Collier, 1971), p. 24.
21. Ibid., p. 55.
22. Ibid., p. 40.
23. Ibid., p. 111.
24. Ibid., p. 158.
25. Ibid., p. 166.
26. Ibid., p. 173.
27. Chinua Achebe, *A Man of the People* (London, Heinemann, 1966), p. 34.

Chapter 16
1. Duro Ladipo, *Three Yoruba Plays* (Ibadan, Mbari, 1964), English adaptation by Ulli Beier, p. 7.
2. Ibid., p. 8.
3. Ibid.
4. Ibid., p. 9.
5. Ibid., p. 15.
6. Ibid., p. 9.
7. Ibid.
8. Ibid., p. 12.
9. Ibid., pp. 17–18.
10. Ibid., pp. 23–24.
11. Ibid., p. 27.
12. Ibid., p. 28.
13. Ibid., pp. 29–30.
14. Ibid., p. 30.
15. Ibid.
16. Ibid., p. 55.
17. Ibid., p. 69.
18. Ibid., p. 55.
19. Ibid.

20. Ibid., p. 71.
21. Ibid., p. 61.
22. Ibid., p. 63.
23. Ibid.
24. Ibid., p. 69.
25. Ibid.
26. Ibid., p. 70.
27. Ibid., p. 72.
28. Ibid.
29. Wole Soyinka, *A Dance of the Forest,* in *Five Plays* (London, Oxford University Press, 1964), p. 74.
30. Ibid., p. 68.
31. Ibid., p. 66.
32. Ibid., p. 2.
33. Ibid., p. 25.
34. Ibid., p. 28.
35. Ibid., p. 38.
36. Ibid., p. 70.
37. Ibid., p. 80.
38. Ibid., p. 40.
39. Wole Soyinka, *The Strong Breed,* in *Five Plays,* p. 241.
40. Ibid., p. 245.
41. Ibid., p. 250.
42. Ibid., p. 259.
43. Ibid., p. 258.
44. Ibid., p. 254.
45. Ibid., p. 266.
46. Ibid., p. 274.

Chapter 17
1. Laz Ekwene, "Igbo Choral Music," Ph.D. dissertation, Yale University, 1972.
2. Vincent Kofi, *Sculpture in Ghana* (Accra, State Publishing, 1963).

Chapter 18
1. Wole Soyinka, in Per Wästberg, ed., *The Writer in Modern Africa,* New York, Africana, 1969.

Bibliography

Abraham, W. E., *The Mind of Africa*, New York, Praeger, 1966.

Achebe, Chinua, *Things Fall Apart*, Greenwich, Conn., Fawcett, 1959.

———, *No Longer at Ease*, London, Heinemann, 1960.

———, *Arrow of God*, Garden City, N.Y., Anchor, 1969.

———, *A Man of the People*, London, Heinemann, 1966.

Armattoe, Raphael, *Between the Forest and the Sea*. Privately published in Londonderry, Northern Ireland, 1950.

———, *Deep Down the Blackman's Mind*. Privately published in Londonderry, Northern Ireland, 1950.

Awoonor, Kofi, *Guardians of the Sacred Word*, New York, NOK, 1974.

———, *Night of My Blood*, Garden City, N.Y., Doubleday, 1970.

———, and G. Adali-Mortty, eds., *Messages*, London, Heinemann, 1970.

Babalola, S. A., *The Content and Form of Yoruba Ijala*, London, Clarendon Press, 1966.

Barker, W. H., and C. Sinclair, *West African Folktales*, London, Harrap, 1927.

Beier, Ulli, ed., *Yoruba Poetry*, London, Cambridge University Press, 1970.

———, *Introduction to African Literature*, Evanston, Ill., Northwestern University Press, 1967.

———, *Contemporary Art in Africa*, New York, Praeger, 1968.

Brown, Lalage, *Two Centuries of African English*, London, Heinemann, 1973.

Césaire, Aimé, *Return to My Native Land*, Paris, Présence Africaine, 1968.

Campbell, Joseph, *The Hero with a Thousand Faces*, New York, Pantheon, 1949.

Clark, J. P., *A Song of a Goat*, Ibadan, Mbari, 1962.

Collins, Harold R., *Amos Tutuola*, New York, Twayne, 1969.

Davidson, Basil, *Old Africa Rediscovered*, London, Gollancz, 1964.

Dayrell, E., *Folk Stories from Southern Nigeria*, London, Longmans, 1910.

Dei-Anang, Michael, *Africa Speaks*, Accra, Guinea Press, 1959.

Diop, David, *Coups de Pilon*, Paris, Présence Africaine, 1956.

Duerden, Dennis, *African Art*, London, Paul Hamlyn, 1968.

Ekweme, Laz, "Igbo Choral Music," Ph.D. dissertation, Yale University, 1972.

Fagunwa, D. O., *The Forest of a Thousand Daemons: A Hunter's Saga*, London, Nelson, 1968. Translated by Wole Soyinka.

Feldman, Susan, ed., *African Myths and Tales*, New York, Dell, 1963.

Finnegan, Ruth, *Oral Literature in Africa*, London, Clarendon Press, 1970.

Frazer, J. G., *Folklore in the Old Testament*, London, Macmillan, 1918.

Frye, Northrop, *Anatomy of Criticism*, Princeton, Princeton University Press, 1962.

Itayemi, Phebean, and P. Gurrey, *Folktales and Fables*, Harmondsworth, Penguin, 1953.

Jablow, Ata, *Yes and No: The Intimate Folklore of Africa*, New York, Horizon, 1961.

Kofi, Vincent, *Sculpture in Ghana*, Accra, State Publishing, 1963.

Kunene, Mazisi, *Zulu Poems*, New York, Africana, 1970.

Ladipo, Duro, *Three Yoruba Plays*, Ibadan, Mbari, 1964.

Lienhardt, G., *Divinity and Experience: The Religion of the Dinka*, London, Clarendon Press, 1961.

Mbiti, John S., *Concept of God in Africa*, New York, Praeger, 1970.

Moore, Gerald, *Seven African Writers*, London, Oxford University Press, 1962.

———, and U. Beier, eds., *Modern Poetry from Africa*, Baltimore, Penguin, 1963.

Mphahlele, Ezekiel, *The African Image*, New York, Praeger, 1962.

Ngugi, James, *Weep Not, Child*, London, Heinemann, 1964.

———, *The River Between*, London, Heinemann, 1965.

———, *A Grain of Wheat*, London, Heinemann, 1967.

Nketia, J. H., *Funeral Dirges of the Akan People*, Achimota, Achimota, 1955.

———, *Folk Songs of Ghana*, Legon, Ghana University Press, 1963.

Nkrumah, Kwame, *Consciencism*, London, Heinemann, 1964.

———, *Toward Colonial Freedom*, London, Heinemann, 1962.

Nwoga, Donatus, *West African Verse*, London, Longmans, 1967.

Ogumefu, M. I., *Yoruba Legends*, London, Sheldon, n.d.

Okigbo, Christopher, *Labyrinths*, London, Heinemann, 1971.

Osadebay, Dennis, *Africa Sings*, Ilfracombe, Devon, Stockwell, 1952.

Oyono, Ferdinand, *Boy*, New York, Collier, 1970.

———, *The Old Man and the Medal*, New York, Collier, 1971.

Parrinder, G., introduction to Tutuola, *The Palm-Wine Drinkard,* New York, Grove Press, 1953.

pBtek, Okot, "Oral Literature and Its Social Background Among the Acholi and Lango," B.Litt. thesis, Oxford University, 1963.

Rattray, R. S., *Religion and Art in Ashanti,* London, Oxford University Press, 1965.

Senghor, Léopold S., *Prose and Poetry,* London, Oxford University Press, 1965.

Segy, Ladislas, *Plastic Aspect of African Sculpture,* New York, Dover, 1958.

Soyinka, Wole, *Five Plays,* London, Oxford University Press, 1964.

——, *Three Plays,* Ibadan, Mbari, 1963.

——, *Interpreters,* London, Deutsch, 1965.

Stuart, James, and D. Malcolm, *Izibongo: Zulu Praise Poems,* London, Oxford University Press, 1968.

Thompson, S., *Motif-Index of Folk Literature,* Bloomington, Indiana University Press, 1955.

Tutuola, Amos, *The Palm-Wine Drinkard,* New York, Grove Press, 1953.

——, *My Life in the Bush of Ghosts,* New York, Grove Press, 1954.

——, *Simbi and the Satyr of the Dark Jungle,* London, Faber and Faber, 1955.

——, *The Brave African Hunters,* London, Faber and Faber, 1958.

——, *Feather Women of the Jungle,* London, Faber and Faber, 1962.

——, *Ajayi and His Inherited Poverty,* London, Faber and Faber, 1967.

U Tam'si, Tchicaya, *Selected Poems,* London, Heinemann, 1970.

Walker, Barbara, and Warren, *Nigerian Tales,* New Brunswick, Rutgers University Press, 1961.

Wästberg, Per, ed., *The Writer in Modern Africa,* New York, Africana, 1969.

JOURNAL ARTICLES AND OTHER SOURCES

Achebe, Chinua, "English and the African Writer," *Transition,* 18, Vol. 4, 1965.

——, "The Role of the African Writer in a New Nation," *Nigeria Magazine,* 81, June 1964.

——, "The Novelist as a Teacher," *Journal of Commonwealth Literature,* 3, 1967.

Bascom, W. R., "Folklore Research in Africa," *Journal of American Folklore,* 77, 1964.

Beidelman, T., "Hyaena and Rabbit: A Kaguru Representation of Matrilineal Relations," *Africa,* 31, 1961.

Dhlomo, H., "Zulu Folk Poetry," *Native Teachers Journal* (Natal), 27, 1947–48.

Echeruo, T. M. C., and E. N. Obiechina, "Igbo Traditional Life Culture and Literature," *Conch Magazine,* 1971.

Fels, Florence, ed., "View on Negro Art," *Action*, April 1920.

Jones, G. I., "Masked Plays of Southern Nigeria," *Geographical Magazine*, Sept. 5, 1945.

Leshori, Robert, "Theatre and the Common Man in Africa," *Transition*, 19, Vol. 4, 1965.

Lindfors, Bernth, "Amos Tutuola's Television-handed Ghostess," *Ariel*, 2, I, January 1971.

Read, M., "Songs of the Ngoni People," *Bantu Studies*, 11, 1937.

Wescott, J., "Eshu-Elegba, The Yoruba Trickster," *Africa*, October 1962.

Index